The Granger Brothers: In Their Own Words

Letters Home from the US Civil War Battlefield

Ray —

Great to meet you! Enjoy the story.

[signature] 2006

ISBN 0-7414-2047-3

Published by:

PUBLISHING.COM

1094 New DeHaven Street, Suite 100
West Conshohocken, PA 19428-2713
Info@buybooksontheweb.com
www.buybooksontheweb.com
Toll-free (877) BUY BOOK
Local Phone (610) 941-9999
Fax (610) 941-9959

Printed in the United States of America
Printed on Recycled Paper
Published September 2004

For my wife, Mary, and our children:

Katie, Julia and Lisa

Acknowledgments

This project begins with the help and generosity of Jeff Shaw. I remember exactly when I met Jeff Shaw. It was a mutual friend, Garry Price, who introduced us. Jeff and I began to talk about history and the US Civil War. After a while Jeff mentioned that he had letters written by his Great Great Great Grandfather, who was a soldier in the Civil War. He wasn't sure just how many there were, or the dates, but he was certain that they were written from the field, right from the battlefield. My curiosity was peaked.

Jeff showed me the box of letters. They were kept in a cardboard box. The same box that had served as their storage container for over 130 years. The last 50 years they were in the attic of Jeff's aunt. When Jeff and I got together to look at the contents of the box I didn't know quite what to expect. What we found amazes me still. A complete set of letters that detailed the wartime adventures of John and Luther Granger. The Granger brothers enlisted together and served together throughout their part in the Civil War.

There were many surprises along the way to completing this project. One pleasant surprise was the encouragement and help I received. I owe an enormous amount of thanks to my editors, Steve Wilke and Nancy Morrison, and to my typist on the project, Annette Dutton. Steve read each letter and provided me with many corrections that often changed the overall meaning of entire letters or key passages from letters. Without his daily review and comment for nearly two years I am sure that this project would not be as complete and accurate. Nancy gave me a new and refreshing look into the short stories that I had written, and provided me with the encouragement to finish the project and get on with putting a cover on it. Her keen eye for style and grammar usage makes the story much more readable than it otherwise would have been. Annette spent months getting the first draft of the handwritten letters into a workable electronic format for me to use in preparing this book.

All of the letters that Jeff owns were written by John W. Granger. Most of them were addressed to his wife Cornelia. The letters, many still in their envelopes, were nearly perfectly preserved and quite readable. They made for fascinating reading. There were letters from Camp Curtain in Pennsylvania where the Granger brothers mustered. There were letters from Washington DC where they reported for their first wartime duty, and there were letters from some of the most famous and notorious battlefields in the Civil War. At Chancellorsville, Fredericksburg and Gettysburg the Granger's saw some serious action. And they wrote home to describe it.

The letters that Jeff lent to the project were the beginning of a research and publication undertaking that was over six years in the making. In pursuit of information I have made trips to Bowdoin College in Maine, the US Army War College in Carlisle, Pennsylvania, the National Archives in Washington, DC, and many battlefields and Civil War sites (Chancellorsville, Fredericksburg, Gettysburg, Manassas, Sharpsburg, Appomattox Courthouse and Cheat Mountain). I visited historic Civil War monuments and conducted research in university and public libraries.

In addition to the letters that Jeff had in his possession, I was able to locate (with the help of the librarian at Bowdoin College) and copy (with the help of the librarian at the US Army War College) dozens of letters written by Luther A. Granger (John's Brother). Luther's letters provide a second and quite different perspective into the events that these brothers shared. The letters were at the US Army War College, and while at Bowdoin College the librarian found the reference and contacted the librarian there to verify that indeed the letters were available for me to review and copy.

This book is a series of short stories arranged as chapters, two separate diaries written by the Granger brothers, and supplemental primary research information that allows the reader to place the subject matter, the events and the emotions into their proper perspective.

Table of Contents

Important Copyright Notice

Preface

I began this project in 1996 when a friend of mine, Garry Price, introduced me to Jeff Shaw. Jeff and I became friends, and finding some common ground in history, started talking about the Civil War. He said that he had some letters written by a soldier that was a distant ancestor of his. By the end of the discussion we had decided that Jeff and I would get together and look at the letters so that I could see them and read a few.

The letters had been well preserved, especially considering that they had been kept in a shoebox in the attic of Jeff's aunt. After reading one letter I was drawn in to the story of Private John Granger. The drama and emotion of the effect that the Civil War had on a citizen volunteer was told in matter-of-fact fashion, and wish-for-a-better-day manner. I knew immediately that I wouldn't settle for merely reading the letters.

I outlined the idea for this project with Jeff. He agreed, and we began the task of scanning each letter, one page at a time in order to make certain that they were not damaged. Hundreds of pages of handwritten letters were scanned into my computer so that I could use the letters as primary reference material. Yes hundreds.

John W. Granger was a prolific writer. He wrote about the weather, his health, his expectations regarding the war, the morale of the troops, his brother Luther who was in the same regiment, and about his desire to be at home. He wrote often.

After the scanning was completed I undertook the task of transcribing the letters into a text file. I began with the intention that John Granger's letters would be presented much as they were written, with limited editing and almost no punctuation. The more I read the more I realized that without any interpretation or editing each reader would be left to decide for themselves the meaning of how John used certain words and phrases. After reading and researching John for several months (which has now turned to years) I felt that I was in a good position to determine how John was attempting to convey certain thoughts and emotions. So I set out to edit the letters into a diary that will provide the reader with a good chronology of the events and experiences of John Granger.

It was in April of 1998, during a research trip to Bowdoin College in Brunswick, Maine that I made a fascinating discovery. I was working in the library of Bowdoin, and the research librarian (I wish I had written down her name) showed me an Internet database maintained by the US Army War College in Carlisle, Pennsylvania. The database was a collection of personal effects and other items that were maintained by the Army War College. I didn't realize how many personal effects, diaries and letters were preserved from the Civil War.

My amazing discovery was there on the screen. A listing identifying letters written by Luther A. Granger. Over a dozen letters written by John's brother. After contacting the custodian of the documents I found that I had access to them. Better than that the librarian at Carlisle provided me with copies of the letters. Now I had side by side writings from brothers. The first person I called with the news was Jeff Shaw.

After scanning and transcribing the letters I realized that I now had source material for what was a fascinating story. Two brothers from the quiet township of Rush, Pennsylvania located in Susquehanna County, volunteer to fight in the Civil War, and through their first hand accounts and descriptions of events, compare their experiences and learn from them what it was like to endure their enlistment.

I began to research in earnest all events and circumstances surrounding their battlefield letters to home. I tracked their movements by the city and state references in the salutation of each letter. I reviewed battlefield reports searching for mention of their participation in the war effort. I found them. The Granger brothers, assigned to Company A of the 57th Pennsylvania Veteran Volunteers, fought in historic battles in the cities of Williamsburg, Fredericksburg, Chancellorsville and Gettysburg. They chased rebels, ran from rebels and cursed just about everyone from politicians to slaves to rebels.

It seemed to me that I needed to relate their story in the context of the battles and the famous engagements they had struggled through. It is amazing how often the 57th Pennsylvania was in the heat of battle. I developed a few short stories to provide some backdrop to the diaries.

With the letters I did take some editorial license. I provided some punctuation and capitalization to make the text more reader friendly. Take for instance the manner in which John ends nearly every letter, "To Cornelia, Edward & Billy Granger." Because of his consistency I found that in the text it was not necessary to use this ending, unless he ended a different way. If the letter was directed specifically to Cornelia, then the content would tend to be somewhat more private, more revealing and telling of John's thoughts and beliefs. John outlined many issues clearly for Cornelia and gave her considerable direction and advice on what she should do in various situations and sought to guide her actions at home from the battlefield.

There were times during his enlistment when John took furlough and returned to Rush, Pennsylvania for a visit. These furloughs lead to a break in the letters and therefore the story. Typically the story picks up with John writing about his furlough as soon as he returns to his unit. While I did not have enough letters to establish a pattern for Luther Granger, his letters add a tremendous amount of depth to the overall story.

Monument to the 57th Pennsylvania Veteran Volunteers near the Sherfy House at the Gettysburg Battlefield.

Introduction

American historians have already documented in great detail the prominent issues facing citizens of the United States of America just prior to 1861 and the Civil War. The issues of slavery and secessionism weighed heavily upon newly-elected President Abraham Lincoln. It was Lincoln's personal belief that if military action was necessary in order to preserve the Union then he was willing to pursue that action. The Union would not dissolve under his Presidency if he could do anything to save it.

President Lincoln and many other pro-Union patriots believed that the seceding bloc of states could be shown the error of their ways with the Union's swift military action. These pro-Union leaders were certain that any rebellion would be short-lived, once the secessionists were brought to order. The Union's call for volunteer soldiers was, thus, intended to swell the military ranks in a show of force that would be aimed at quelling the Confederacy movement and their perceived misbehavior. What had begun as a quick "reminder" stretched into a four-year conflict, with some brothers bearing arms against each other. Conditions were brutal for the men who enlisted "for a short term," and soon food, clothing, shelter, and munitions were exhausted as troops clashed in battle after bloody battle.

This author has been afforded a rare glimpse into the lives of two brothers as they met their personal challenges of battle through their correspondence with their families at home. John W. and Luther A. Granger left behind a legacy of nearly 200 letters penned as the War progressed. Through these letters we are privy to the men's insightful narratives of daily soldiering, as well as the inevitable homesickness and longings that were experienced.

The Civil War claimed its massive casualties from the men and boys that made up the armies of both the Union and the Confederacy. Some of these casualties were due to outright battlefield deaths, others to diseases contracted when infection settled into wounds sustained in battle, and still others due to the various illnesses arising from such squalid living conditions.

What follows is their tale. The Granger brothers' accounts of their War-time trials and tribulations. We are fortunate, indeed, to extend both John and Luther's legacy. As the story unfolds, you will share their hopes, their wishes and their fears. Only one of the brothers returns to his home and family. Their journey is extraordinary, but considering the times and the demands placed on the citizens of this time in our nation's history, it has a familiar and common theme.

While John W. Granger is the primary character in this tale, the fact that his brother Luther was with him from the time of their enlistment to Luther's death on the Battlefield at Gettysburg, creates an opportunity to provide deep insight into the effects that the Civil War had on the family life of so many during that period. The letters that have been discovered and arranged into a daily diary provide a day by day account of John's time in the Union Army. Significantly fewer letters written by Luther have been discovered. They help to fill in some of the gaps and give us the chance to know him far better than by the stories and descriptions afforded us through John's writings.

This project is arranged to give the reader an opportunity to meet the Granger brothers through a series of short stories that include excerpts from their letters and are built on the actual events and battles in which they participated. The letters are arranged into a daily diary for you to read just as they were written by John and Luther. Most of the letters were written to their wives, who you will also meet along the way. Finally, a series of appendices provide further information for those who must have all the details and want a more comprehensive view of the fate of John and Luther.

Chapter One:
Mustering in: "Forgive Me for Enlisting"

When John W. Granger came home to Rush, Pennsylvania, in February, 1864, he was a 1ˢᵗ Sergeant in the Army of the Potomac attached to the 129ᵗʰ Regiment of the 2ⁿᵈ Battalion Invalid Corps. He was 43 years old, and had just left a group of men who had fought side by side in many battles. Together, they had faced the horrors of war for over two years. When John mustered in, in October of 1861, he did so with his brother Luther A. Granger. Together they joined up with Company A, 57ᵗʰ Regiment, 1ˢᵗ Brigade, 1ˢᵗ Division, 3ʳᵈ Corps, Army of the Potomac. Individually, however, they were men who volunteered to make the ultimate sacrifice, if need be, of their life, to ensure the survival of their beloved Union.

That John W. Granger came home at all is an amazing tale in and of itself. That any man could return from serving in the United States Civil War unscathed in some way would be too much to expect. John Granger devoted two years, four months, and twenty-one days to service for his country, performing as a loyal soldier to protect the Union. He was honorably discharged at the end of his term, receiving notice of his discharge while in the middle of writing just one of his many letters home to his wife, Cornelia. On that particular night he was in Camp Cliffburn Barracks in Virginia, and news of his impending discharge overwhelmed him.

John's early letters home originated from his mustering-in at Camp Curtin, PA, in 1861 and Washington, D.C. in 1862. These letters were upbeat and full of hope that the conflict would be resolved as quickly as possible. As time wore on, after the Battles of Fredericksburg, Chancellorsville, and Gettysburg (where his brother Luther was killed), the tone of the letters became increasingly pessimistic. John was dispirited on that cold February night, and he expressed his discouragement in his letter to Cornelia. He had convinced himself that he would never be released from the Army of the Potomac. The letters he wrote in the weeks leading up to February 12, 1864, told of several of his friends who had been discharged, and John was waiting his turn very solemnly. His official tour of duty was to be completed in

1

November, 1864, because he had enlisted for a three-year term. He was convinced he would never live to see the day of his discharge.

The emotional distress that John was under is evident from that February 12th letter:

"Dear wife & children I received a letter from you on the 10th dated 8th. I was glad to hear that you were well but sorry that you feel so downhearted. I hope I shall live to get out of this miserable concern. I have been trying some time to get an examination before the doctor. Well this morning I went before the Board and they thought they could not discharge me so my hopes are gone on that point. I think it is mean for I know they have discharged a good many in my company that is not half as bad off as I am but that is just my luck. Well yesterday there was thirteen in my company got their discharge and in a few days more there will be some ten or twelve more. Well I am glad to seem them get away. I only wish that I might be as lucky. Well enough of this. If they fill this company up and get some scripts here they kiss my arse for all the duty they got out of me. I have done my share."

At this point in the writing, John is apparently summoned away from his tent and to the Captain's office. Back at the tent, he resumes his writing, with a considerably improved mood and state of mind:

"Well I have just been called to the Captain's Office & there found the Board had ordered my discharge. Hip Hip Hurrah. So keep dark. If nothing happens I shall be at home in three weeks or less. Don't say anything about it nor let anyone know one word. I want to take them by surprise. I had felt downhearted all the forenoon and discouraged and when I commenced this letter I did not think I should hear such good news. I am almost afraid to believe it myself for fear there will be some slip about it. I suppose it will take all of this month for my papers to go through quick. My love to you all. Good day. Yours ever."

Consider how happy John and Cornelia must have been to learn of a homecoming so long in the making! What follows tells us about that homecoming, in John's first-person narrative. His story marches through time and territory, of a War from which hundreds of thousands of soldiers, including Luther Granger, did not return to their homes. We can trace the progress of one man, exercising his great patriotic zeal as he enlists to fight in that War, as well as the ebbing of that zeal as he experiences the ravages of that War with its horrors. The initial avid support of his Union gave way to Granger's fervent desire to be discharged. This will be a tale of how men who eagerly enlisted in service were, at first, delusional about the duration of the War. They believed that the term of service would be brief and brilliant. These same soldiers stood witness as their families and friends were killed in bloody battles. They experienced the devastation wrought upon all Americans, and how the War required the families of the soldiers to face head-on their obligations as United States citizens; soldiers and families alike fought to preserve the Union.

This intensely intimate, personal accounting provides the reader with a rare, insightful portrait of John W. Granger, who faithfully penned letters to his wife and children throughout his twenty-seven months of service in the Army of the Potomac. All who read this narrative can vicariously experience the War, described through the eyes of our Infantry Private.

This Civil War story is sad, as it retells the waste, terror, death, and destruction of the Civil War, recounted in nearly every passage. It is sad, too, for that Country, established in unity and with such great potential a mere ninety years prior, was now being threatened with disunity. The Union leaders had decided to face-off with the Secessionists, at the expense of its prime resource—its citizens. Although brothers John and Luther Granger enlisted and served together, the heart-rending story is especially sad on John's personal note, because his brother did not return from the War.

The grotesque Civil War statistics help define and shape what is still the bloodiest time in our Nation's history. Over the four-year course of the War, the Union Army enlisted 2,324,516 soldiers; the Confederate States, over 1,000,000. The Union casualties numbered 360,000 killed; the Confederates, 260,000. These numbers are overwhelming, even by today's standards. Behind each number was a man who may have come from a city, a town, or a farm, all across the Nation. These men were motivated by any of several causes—excitement and glory, God, and Country, to name just a few.

The strong Union support demonstrated by the Granger brothers was evidenced also in their ancestor, who fought to gain independence from England and the British monarchy in the

Revolutionary War. This soldier made his home in New England; it was just a short migration from there to Rush, Pennsylvania, where the Grangers took up their residence. Now, after four generations, the Granger families again prepared to send their sons into war. Brothers John and Luther volunteered; they became attached to the 57th Pennsylvania Regiment upon enlistment. John was the older of the two men, being 41 years old at the time. By contrast, these Granger brothers were going to war to fight for the preservation of the Union; whereas their ancestor risked his life to dissolve a union with England in 1775.

The 57th Regiment was organized in Fall, 1861, at Camp Curtin, Pennsylvania. This camp was named for Pennsylvania Governor Andrew G. Curtin who, because of his swift affirmative response to President Abraham Lincoln's call for men to raise an army, will be remembered as Pennsylvania's "War Governor."

Camp Curtin, which was located in Central Pennsylvania near Harrisburg, was the 57th Pennsylvania Volunteers' center for mustering into the Union Army. The 57th Regiment was divided into ten companies, each of which being designated by letter: A, B, C, D, E, F, G, H, I, and K. Along with several of their friends and neighbors, John and Luther were assigned to Company A; these men were mostly from Susquehanna and Wayne Counties. Details of the formation of the 57th Pennsylvania are preserved for the reader in the book, "History of the Fifty-Seventh Pennsylvania Veteran Volunteers." This book was written by survivors of the 57th just a few years after the Civil War ended, and is an interesting account of the movement and engagements of the 57th throughout the war.

Companies A, D, G, H, and K mustered at Camp Curtin, but Companies B, C, E, F, and I originally gathered at Camp Griffith near Mercer, Pennsylvania, in the Western part of the State. The men in Companies B, C, E, F, and I immediately proceeded to Camp Curtin, where the entire 57th was inducted during an Army mustering ceremony.

The Grangers' hometown was Rush, Pennsylvania. Rush is a small town nestled in the farmlands of Susquehanna County. During the 1800s, the area was a fertile agricultural area within the Susquehanna River valley. Farming and coal mining were the two major means of earning a living for the inhabitants. John Granger was a wagon-maker by trade and profession.

Susquehanna County (1990 Population: 40,380) was created on February 21, 1810, being carved out as a separate section from Luzerne County. The city of Montrose serves as the County Seat. Its name is derived from "mont," which is French for "mountain," and "Rose," for Dr. H. R. Rose, one of its prominent citizens at that time.

Dennis Granger and Nabby Rice, who were John and Luther's parents, had a total of nine children. Two were born in Vermont, and the remaining seven, including John and Luther, were born in Pennsylvania. Dennis Granger was born in Vermont on June 17, 1789 and Nabby on September 9, 1788. They were married in Bennington, Vermont on January 8, 1810. At some point following the birth of their second child in 1812, they migrated from Vermont to Pennsylvania.

Born February 8, 1820 in Northfield, Connecticut, Cornelia Munger moved to Pennsylvania. She met John and in 1840 they were married and established their home and began their family. They were married in Montrose, Pennsylvania on February 20, 1840. Their marriage produced a total of six children, however only two survived. They were their two sons, Edward (January 16, 1845) and Billy (March 24, 1853). Edward was 16 when his father went off to war, and he was old enough to realize and accept that he was expected to stay behind and tend to the family matters. Billy was only 8 in November 1861. Not much is know about their other children, Norman (January 8, 1841), George (January 7, 1843), Julia (January 26, 1847) and Hannah (January 5, 1850).

During the Westward expansion of the United States, like so many others, John Granger lived near many family members, including his brother, Luther A. Granger. Both men volunteered for service in the Army of the Potomac, and both served in Company A.

Luther Granger was married to Sabra, about whom not much is known. We are able to discern that Luther's family endured a great deal of suffering during the two years that Luther was in the military. Sabra probably experienced much pain upon being parted from Luther, as did the other women of that time whose men and husbands were answering the call to serve in the Union army. Sabra and Luther had one daughter, Emily.

5

John Granger had led a good and wholesome life and, up until this time, he had not traveled much. He grew up on the family farm and knew the land well. John Granger was a wagon maker by trade. He appreciated the virtues of hard work and dedication to family, God and country. So, what circumstances would compel such a man, at age 42, with a family and an established position in his hometown, to volunteer for military service? John Granger, himself, through his correspondence and musings, provides fascinating insight into the answer to this very question.

The Granger brothers officially volunteered their services on October 25, 1861. They made the trip from Rush to Harrisburg solely for the purpose of volunteering and answering the call of President Lincoln and Governor Curtin, not to win heroes' honors or medals. The Grangers' families pleaded with them not to go, but both John and Luther felt duty-bound to honor their fervent faith in both God and country, and this faith overrode the families' objections.

John W. Granger, enlisting at age 42, was a religious man. He was a devoted family man, husband, and father to his two boys. He loved his wife, Cornelia, dearly. Luther, born January 25, 1830, was a full 10 years younger than John. Sabra, Luther's wife, was not at all happy with Luther's decision to enter the war. Like so many other thousands of soldiers, it was extremely difficult for John and Luther to leave their families behind and go off to enlist, but they went with the impression that the conflict would end quickly. Just a few skirmishes, and they would return home. Their expectation was that they would be home within a relatively short period of time. Like countless other men, they were very wrong.

Luther left for Camp Curtin with John, not knowing at that time that his fate and destiny were being determined. He saw his wife and daughter only a few times when he was given leave. Sabra lost both husband and daughter in July 1863. Her husband was lost to the brutality that defined the Battle of Gettysburg, and her daughter succumbed to the ravages of disease.

When John and Luther arrived at Camp Curtin, they enlisted as volunteers for a term of three years. Once inducted into the Army as infantrymen, the routine of camp life became the norm. At Camp Curtin the men were molded into soldiers. They learned their drills well and eventually resembled a fighting unit. In

December 1861, the Regiment was ordered to report to Washington, D.C.

John's first letter home suggests that, from the very beginning, the high ideals that prompted both John and Luther to volunteer were far different from the reality of the conditions of war. Preparing for war was much more demanding than the romanticism of fighting for God and country. The idyllic notion that the Civil War would be quick and bloodless was representative of the beliefs among the general public. As time marched on, John's letters display a pattern of increasing disillusionment. Meanwhile, the soldiers were preparing for a much longer and more difficult term of service than either John or Luther had reason to expect at their enlistment.

"Dear wife and children. I take this opportunity to write you a few lines to let you know how I get along. Well when I left home I thought I should come back within one week. But I cannot. Please forgive me for enlisting. Went to camp the same morning. It was very cold. Keep up good courage. Let them know you are a true-hearted woman. Tell the boys to mind you and think of me. We may start for Washington in three or four weeks. We do not know anything about it. If ever I do come back, you nor the children shall not have it to say that I made a ass of myself. I should like to see you and the boys and hope I shall as soon as spring. Do not grieve nor give way to bad feelings. Take care of your health. I shall write to you again as soon as we can get our tent organized and my feelings settled a little. You may think my feeling would not be worked up to this pitch but I have feelings yet. But enough of this. Our camp is large and a good many thousands of soldiers here. I must close for Ad is ready to start. So goodbye. God bless you. From your ever loving husband. J. W. Granger"

Chapter Two:
First Letter from Camp Curtin: A Soldier's First Few Days

John W. Granger, in the first of his many letters written to his wife and children, opens with a greeting typical of his day. It seems somewhat formal in our present time. The letters begin with "Dear wife and children" and proceed to tell of John's health. Next, he inquires about the health and welfare of those at home. Third, he describes his working conditions and soldiering experiences. He discussed the weather in obsessive detail. Last, he often included sound advice for those folks he left behind, mostly for his wife as she manages the homestead in his absence. Occasionally, John will divulge his extreme homesickness and his yearning for his wife. In his first letter, John writes: "Dear wife and children I take this opportunity to write you a few lines to let you know how I get along. Well in the first place I am enjoying tolerable good health."

One of his next letters spoke of a downturn from the "tolerable good health" to "suffering from a particularly hard cold." This letter was written on November 21, 1861, a very blustery winter's day in Central Pennsylvania. Others in Camp Curtin felt the effects of that chill weather, and a hospital was set up to isolate the infirm soldiers. The healthy soldiers were asked to work in the hospital for 40 cents per day, in additional to their military pay. John was one who took advantage of the extra work; he figured he could use the extra pay. "I shall have a chance to work about two weeks, if I do the pay will come good for tobacco & Tea & etc."

November 1861, proved to be an extremely difficult month for all of the newly enlisted soldiers at Camp Curtin. In addition to the horribly cold weather, the recruits had to learn and become accustomed to the routine of military life. The men were packed into tight living quarters, which facilitated the rapid spread of contagious disease among them. A devastating outbreak of measles claimed many men before they even had the opportunity to see a battlefield. Keep in mind that, when we look back into time, these willing volunteers had no advantages of our modern-day antibiotics and other medical treatments. Disease and sickness ravaged the troops, causing nearly as many deaths as the fateful bullets in the midst of battle.

John's letter written home after his first month of service in the Union Army reveals his constant homesickness: "I think of home and the comforts of home. I often wish I was by my own fireside surrounded by wife and children." The optimism with which John enlisted seems to be waning, as he quite obviously has mixed emotions about being so far from home and family. These words are from a man who did not travel much and who would rather plow a field than fight a battle on one.

The December 1, 1861, letter reflects John's doubt that he has done the right thing by enlisting - nearly a "now look what I've gone and done!" attitude. "You know how it has been for sometime past if I wanted to help any of my neighbors their [sic] was a great talk about it. The fact was they all thought it was done for sinister motives. I hope now that I am gone they will have something else to talk about. I do not want you to take any of this to yourself for I have no blame for you. Had it not have been for you I should have left long ago." This passage leads to the determination that John's relationships with his neighbors have been compromised in the recent past, and so have provided him with part of the impetus for his enlistment. Now, from a safe distance, he is able to reflect on his motives, and he is forced to face the realization that his venture into military service was done partly to escape from the neighbors in his hometown. Upon reflection, John feels somewhat regretful about his adversarial relationships with his neighbors. Men throughout time have changed the direction in their lives in order to have a fresh start. It seems that John's term in the military did just such a thing, however reading his letters home, John is not very convincing that he was content with his choice.

"Well in regard to camp life it is a dogs life to live. To stand in the mud up to your ankles and eat your bread and stinking meat with a pint cup of something they call coffee (but do not know what it is) and shiver with the cold until you are in danger of biting your tongue off is no great fun I tell you. But we will stand it somehow or other at any rate for a while. Do not let anyone know but we fare first rate. We can tell each other our little affairs without letting the rest know it." John seems to feel that sharing the true living conditions in a letter to his wife is allowed, but he concludes with a caveat to her to maintain best appearances. She is directed to tell others at home that the soldiers are enjoying "first-rate" food and living conditions. John's serious tone demonstrates his somewhat awkward adjustment to his new circumstances. We can only speculate on how difficult it was for him to put pen to paper and, how difficult it would be for Cornelia to read such news.

Several aspects of John's situation made him doubt his reasons for enlisting. The living conditions notwithstanding, there were issues of long hours of hard work for little pay, plus the interpersonal relationships among associates who weren't as pleasant as John envisioned when he joined the Army. From our vantage point, it would appear that John may have re-enacted the strained relationships in camp that he experienced with his neighbors back home. "Now I will tell you about my enlisting. I enlisted as a teamster but cannot get that situation until I get into regular service. I have to drill as a private while in Camp Curtin for they have no teamsters here." What this meant to John was that he would be restricted to a private's privileges, instead of enjoying the relative freedoms of the teamster. As recruits of the 57th Pennsylvania Volunteers, Company A, both John and his brother, Luther, were most likely to serve as infantrymen.

The prevalent belief that the term of service would end quickly boosted the men's morale. "I think we shall be sent home in the spring, hope we shall. If we stay in Camp Curtin this winter I shall be at home about the 1st of June if nothing happens and maybe before so wait with patience." This belief was held not only by the infantry soldiers, but also by men ranking all the way up to the Generals. All hoped that the Civil War's outcome would be determined within months.

The orders finally came on December 14, 1861, for the 57th Pennsylvania to report to Washington, D.C. Troops were transported in railroad boxcars, which meant overcrowding, bouncing, jostling, and general unpleasantness. The travel-weary men suffered either from motion sickness or from the harsh cold December air. This first trip away from Camp Curtin resulted in widespread illness among the 57th. Despite these deplorable conditions, John and Luther made the trip with relative ease. They had survived their indoctrination into the Army of the Potomac, the measles epidemic of Camp Curtin, and the train ride to Washington, DC. Near Washington, they disembarked from the train and hiked on foot to their new campsite along Bladensburg

Road. This would be their camp until February 1862, at which time the regiment broke camp and, crossing the Potomac River, took its place in the left wing of the Army, near Fort Lyon outside of Alexandria, VA. While at the Fort, the 57th PA was assigned to Jameson's Brigade of Heintzelman's Division. Later, when the Army Corps was organized, this Division constituted the First Brigade, First Division, Third Corps. [History of the Fifty-Seventh Pennsylvania Veteran Volunteers, page 16] The Brigade comprised the 57th, 63rd, and 105th PA Regiments and the 87th NY. Now the full and proper title of the fighting troop of which John Granger was a member became, "Company A of the 57th Regiment, First Brigade, First Division, Third Corps of the Army of the Potomac."

Brothers John and Luther Granger readily established a habit of writing home nearly as often as every other day - a practice maintained from their very first days of their enlistment at Camp Curtin until the final days of the War. John's letters reassured his wife, Cornelia, that he was alive and well, or alive and not-so-well, but overall surviving in the Army of the Potomac.

Chapter Three:
The Battle of Fredericksburg

The Army of the Potomac had assembled near Washington, DC, and their numbers included our 57th Pennsylvania. John and Luther Granger were among those called to participate in one of their first major offensives as Union soldiers, in the Battle of Fredericksburg, Virginia. As was told by Luther in a letter home, both the Union and the Confederate ranks were reduced substantially by wounds and death. During the battle, the carnage strewn about the battlefield became so disturbing to the commanding generals that a temporary truce was called, in which both sides were permitted, during the course of a single hour, to gather their dead and wounded from behind the enemy lines and carry their men back to their own soil. The hour's time did not allow for retrieval of all casualties on either side, and there were many men who remained where and as they had fallen in the battle. Those who were rescued were carried on the run by their fellow soldiers, because the sixty minutes were passing so quickly.

The Confederate stronghold on the high-ground around Fredericksburg repelled the Union's attacks to the point where the Union was forced to retreat. Following the Fredericksburg battle, disturbed at the failure of General Ambrose Burnside, President Lincoln appointed Joseph Hooker to lead the Union forces. This was a common theme developing for President Lincoln during the war, to replace his general following a military defeat, then appoint another who became responsible for taking command to pursue the war effort.

Luther's letters home describe his first battle experiences. Observe through Luther's writing how the impressions left by this battle impact him - mentally, emotionally, and physically.

"Dec. 17th 1862, Near Falmouth VA, Through the mercies of God I am spared to write to you again although I must confess that the thing of writing has looked rather scaly since I wrote before. I thought it very doubtful case of my hardly living to tell the tale but they say some are spared and so was in our case. But few comparative to the number that was engaged in the fight. John & myself came off without a scratch but still enough others were hurt to make it all up. Why we were spared God above knows. I hope for some good end. Wm. B. Hinds was mortally wounded. Henry Hinds came out safe without a scratch. No one else from our company was hurt that you are acquainted with. There was but thirty-five or six was all that was engaged in the fight from our company. Two was killed dead, four wounded. We know of six missing either killed wounded or prisoners. We hope they are not hurt but will yet turn up as some of our men have since the fight safe and sound. Last Saturday the fight was and Monday evening we returned back across the river. I guess that the generals thought the place was to hot for them or at least I thought so for my part and I hope that I may never see so hot a place again. I received a letter from you Monday. On the battlefield the enemy drawed up in line of battle not more than forty rods just in good shooting distance. I read it in a hurry tore it in pieces thinking that I was shot no rebel should get the letter. I must confess that I could not tell now much you wrote for my mind was on anything else but letters. I believe there was nothing very secret if they were I have forgot. You stated in your letter that you did not know whether I had received those likenesses. I have certainly wrote about it in three letters before this. I know of a certainty that you do not receive over half the letters I write for I have averaged two letters most of the time a week ever since I have been in this place and when we were on the march I wrote one once a week all but one time and that time you remember when that was and I wrote not having the time over ten days betwixt times. But enough of this for I must end for this time but will write again this week if my life is spared. I am yet fat as a bear eat like hog and can have my whiskey twice a day if I wished but do not drink much. I have drinken one drink that is all as yet. I will send this letter inside of Johns for I do not think it long enough to pay the postage on it. John has wrote midling short letter. Also next time I write I will give you a full detail of things in reality. This from your husband and friend. L. A. Granger"

Luther holds true to his promise to write at greater length, in his letter home two days later.

"Near Falmouth VA Dec 19th 62, Dear wife, As I told you in my other that I would write you a letter of some length I though I would commence this morning. Although there has nothing of much importance happened since I last wrote but as the other was nothing but a substitute I will fulfill my promise by writing long enough letter this time. Although I may take two days to accomplish it because to day is washing day and I have plenty dirty cloths to wash. I wish you were here to help. I guess we would get through sooner but enough of this. I told you in my other letter that I would give you as near a correct account of the battle of Fredericksburg as I could and I will do so although I may differ from the paper correspondent whether I do nor not I believe I saw as much of the scene as any one paper correspondent or not. So I will commence my tale. Last week Tuesday evening we received orders to be ready to march with one hours notice after Wednesday six o'clock. So we held ourselves in readiness for the march but did not start till Thursday morning eight o'clock. That was the commencement of the bombardment of that noted place Fredericksburg. Most of the day was occupied in artillery firing long just at night our troops crossed the river or at least a portion of them. Our division did not cross that night but stayed this side. The next afternoon we received orders to cross the river three miles below but did not accomplish it until the next day at noon. Then we were pushed forward to the front where the enemy were in force. The Pennsylvania reserves were drawn up in line of battle. They went into the engagement first. How long they were in is not more than I can say but not long. I assure you our brigade was ordered in double quick to check the enemy before they farther advanced the rest of our division being back in the rear or at least they had not arrived on the spot in time to go in with us. The enemy seeing the weakness of that point concentrate their forces on that point. The scene became terrific. Our brigade determined not to yield but we were overpowered by numbers. We had to fall back a short distance and just at that critical moment one brigade from our division happened to arrive to our assistance. Then we made the rebels fall back to the woods. We held the field the rest part of the day. That night our reg. (what was left) was put out in front to watch the progress of the enemy and were relieved in the morning before light and went back to the rear of the division for guard to prevent any from falling back. We remained there all that day it being Sunday. Monday morning we were again ordered to the front, not a very desirable place I assure you. It looked as the old saying is rather bilious to see the enemy drawed up in the line of battle about forty rods off. It was anything but a pleasant sight to lay on your arms expecting every moment that the battle would open but fortunate for us they did not commence

14

the fray. About three o'clock a flag of truce went in for the purpose of removing the dead and wounded inside of our lines and the rebels inside of theirs. It was the greatest sight I ever saw, two hostile armies meet shake hands in the most friendly terms and then at their work they went they carrying our dead and wounded to a certain fence that being the division line and we carrying theirs. As there was but one hour given for the removal it had to be accomplished under a run. It was the greatest sight I ever saw when the hour was up. Each one had to return to his own lines whether their work was done or not. I guess ours were mostly removed but not so with the rebels. They had many left yet but that night we fell back over the river so they had a chance the next morning to get their men. Why we fell back is best known to the one who ordered us over the river. I have my opinion but will not express it because I cannot turn one hair white or black. Therefore I will keep my mouth shut thinking that a silent tongue makes no enemies if not any friends. But enough of this for the present which will be the next move I know not nor do I much care for. I am contented with my lot let come what will or at least I try to be and am willing to endure most any hardships to crush this rebellion. Could peace be once more restored to this once happy republic? I think for once I could enjoy peace and freedom once more if it could be obtained and I hope that may soon be the case. We are now in our old camp trying to enjoy our lives if we had a few luxuries from home. I think we could make camp life sweet. I guess you will think I am an old beggar. I must confess that I have a great liking for luxuries home or abroad it makes but little difference where it comes from. I could eat it if it came from you. I guess I will say no more about for I have begged enough and I do not fear but what the friends from old Rush will send us something if they have a chance. I want to come home this winter if there is half a site for me but cannot tell you now how that will be till we get settled down. Some say we are going back to Washington this winter. I hope we may if we do I will be pretty sure to come home.

"I have seen Steve since the fight. He came out all safe. Their Regt was not in the fight. They came out safe and sound. His health is good so is Johns & mine. I have no reason to complain but to thank God for his goodness and guess I will close for I think I have kept my promise good on length if not very sensible excuse all mistakes and write soon. This from your husband and friend. Luther Granger."

Luther's details give us insight into what must have been a most confusing time of service - crossing the river, then retreating, and always being "at the ready" for the next marching or fighting orders. His second letter mentions his longing for some good home-cooked meals and for some of the "luxuries" of home. He yearns to return home just for a visit during that 1862 winter, but he is not overly optimistic about having a furlough so soon. However, given the prevailing impression that the conflict will be over by summertime, perhaps Luther's dreams of home were within the realm of possibility.

We have an additional glimpse into Luther's inner turmoil and torment, in part of an undated letter to his wife, Sabra:

"You said in your letter that you freely forgive me for all the wrongs that I have committed to you and you asked me to forgive you. All that I can say is this. All that is past I do forgive and may you long and happy live and peace and plenty be your lot. I do not want you to suffer because I do but perhaps I do not have as much ask ought to for I have done a great many wrongs and all the way that a person can atone for the past by living well in the future that is all the atonement we can make. I guess I will say no more about that for we both have done wrong and need much reformation. If you could see me now you would hardly know me for my face is all covered with hair. You must pay mother that two dollars that I borrowed of her and the interest and the rest of it you may keep till you receive another letter from me for I may want some of it and if I do I will let you know next time. For Cornelia you need not worry for when John pays me than I can talk about paying that but John says that he is willing to return it to me. Write as soon as you receive this. L. A. Granger."

Chapter Four:
Burnside's Mud March: A Long and Curious March

General Ambrose Burnside put his men into camp along the Rappahannock River, following the disastrous loss at Fredericksburg, Virginia, in mid-December, 1862. Just five weeks after the Battle of Fredericksburg and still during the winter season, Burnside, intent upon taking the fight to the Confederates, attempted yet another crossing of the River, this time using pontoon bridges.

Mother Nature, however, had different ideas for the General and the Union Army. After a 15-mile march up the Rappahannock the Army neared Bank's Ford. With the plan of crossing there the Army camped for the night. Around midnight the rains began, and lasted for three days. The rain left a trail of devastation and wash-outs severe enough to prevent the Army including the 57th Pennsylvania Veteran Volunteers from successfully crossing at that time. What the men faced was three days of torrential downpours, unlike any that they had ever before seen. The River swelled past flood level, swamping roads and passages. Burnside ended his attempt at crossing the river and was lucky to have been able to make it back to the camp.

John Granger and the other soldiers often gave descriptions of the weather conditions in their letters to families back home. On January 11, John reported, "It rained all day. Cleared off cold in the night. I think it will not stay fair long. The weather has been favorable but we must expect some bad weather soon." His words were prophetic, and that night, the weather did take a turn for the worse, the cold hard rains resumed.

John's letter of January 19, 1863, reflects: "We still remain in our camp. We expected to have marched Saturday (17th) morning but we did not. Then we were to start Sunday at one o'clock and then we were ordered to wait until today at one o'clock. But now they say that we will not go today so we do not know when we shall move. So I guess we do not know one minute what we shall do the next but have to take it as it comes." Their delay was weather-dependent, in addition to having logistical obstacles.

Another popular topic in John's letters to Cornelia were the rumors among the camp soldiers: "There is a report in camp that our men undertook to cross the river above here about 12 miles yesterday & had to back out. That may be the reason that we do not move. But I think when we move we shall have a fight." The weather continued to deteriorate, and the threatening skies once more brought heavy rains.

The failed attempt to mobilize the army under these unrelenting and harsh weather conditions, eventually became known as "Burnside's Mud March," certainly unflattering to the General. Tales of horses and wagons being completely buried in the deep mud were standard offering in soldiers' letters home. The artillery was too heavy to transport through the muck, and often the guns had to be abandoned after they were disabled by the mud. More than 150 mules and horses died from exertion while trying to pull their loads through the mud. Not only were these stories to be found in the soldiers' letters—they also were published in various newspapers, both North and South.

Confederate troops, who could see the Northern Army flail hopelessly as they tried to move, carried signs on the south bank of the River that read, "Burnside Stuck in the Mud." Given the conditions faced by the Union troops, with their artillery and livestock hopelessly mired in the mud on the north bank of the River, it soon became apparent to the military leaders that the Army could not go forward, and neither could they retreat. The Army spent nearly an entire week's worth of precious time attempting to salvage anything that the mud would relinquish. The men were exhausted and soaked to their bones, so this work was extremely strenuous for them to perform. When any munitions were recovered, the men dragged them slowly back to the camp. This would have been difficult at the least, in good weather; in these conditions, this work was nearly impossible.

On January 20, 1863, just as General Ambrose Burnside had made the decision to move the army to initiate a winter campaign, the rains returned with a vengeance. On January 21st the rains continued, unimpeded by prayer or curse, and the army once again was bogged down in the mud. By Thursday, January 22nd, the rains still hadn't lessened, so yet another attempted crossing of the Rappahannock River was officially called off by the officers. Returning to camp became the primary item on the agenda. The retreat from Fredericksburg continued on Friday, January 23rd. General Burnside's "Mud March" was an unmitigated failure.

By Saturday, January 24th, most of the troops were returned to their camp near Fredericksburg. President Lincoln had entertained high hopes for a successful Union winter campaign but, upon hearing of the "Mud March" fiasco, he was again disappointed by the lack of leadership demonstrated by his commanders. He had solemnly watched as the Union's military advantage in the winter campaign lost momentum due to lack of vision, perseverance, and initiative. Believing that a change in his commanding general was the only way to remedy these issues, Lincoln replaced Ambrose Burnside with "Fighting Joe" Hooker on January 25th, 1863. Hooker immediately assumed control as General in charge of the Army of the Potomac. Lincoln neither wanted nor could tolerate a leader so inept that he could not win a battle or organize successful troop movement. The President was deeply disappointed in Burnside, who proved to be a complete disaster as a General. Not one significant military gain was made under his direction.

Press coverage of the military actions in the 1860s relied on "inside" sources, just as it is today. Of particular interest is an excerpt from the <u>Valley Spirit</u>, in the issue printed on February 4, 1863. [February 4, 1863, page 2, column 3] A grand time was to be had at Burnside's expense, following the failed "Mud March." This particular story was submitted by the regular columnist of the "Spirit and Times," although he received the story from an unknown author from the camp of "Tyler's Brigade, 3rd Division, 5th Army Corps," near Fredericksburg, VA.

"The weather was decidedly unfavorable. The air was raw and close, and the dull black clouds were to reach a certain point that evening and cross the river of Pontoons early next morning. However, we were brought to a halt and ordered to bivouack [sic] for the night before we had accomplished two miles. All night long the wind howled and the rain poured, and our condition when the morning broke, can better be imagined than described. We were in mud nearly up to our necks and very considerable in the fix of a certain fisherman. At 8 o'clock the bugle sounded 'forward,' and we waded in. That day, (Wednesday) we succeeded in getting four miles in about eight hours and encamped in a woods. It was an exhausting and laborious march. Rain fell all day and the mud as we progressed seemed to be attaining an almost unfathomable depth. The ambulance and ammunition trains were the only ones that had left the old camps. The ambulances got along comparatively well, but all along the road hundreds of am[m]unition wagons were tight in the mud, and all efforts to extricate them seemed impossible. The artillery suffered in this respect likewise. A gun that four horses could haul with comparative ease on a good road required the united strength of sixteen mules to move it a short distance at a time. Mule and horse flesh you may know were tortured no little and the drivers seemed to give up their work in dispair [sic]. Such swearing and cursing, pulling and tugging, was never heard or witnessed before. There were many ludicrous scenes, but in the main we could not help pitying the distress and suffering of the poor animals and their impatient and irritated drivers.

"Literally stuck in the mud, and unable to move forward, it became evident that the plans of our commanders for crossing the river and attacking the enemy must be abandoned. It was found impossible for our supply trains to come to us and arrangements were made for a return to our old camps. On Thursday the whole force was taken out to corduroy the roads. This they did with pine boughs and rails. It was a very unpleasant and laborious job, but as Col. Gregory remarked, our getting fresh rations depended on its complete execution. Friday morning by order of Gen. Hooker the command received the first whisky rations yet issued to them. It was done by the advice of the Surgeons, and to those gentlemen was entrusted the business of distributing it. Two ounces were allowed each man. Some, in mistake perhaps, got more, but still managed to keep their 'pins' and their propriety.

"Saturday morning early we started for our old camp and owing to the improved condition of the roads moved along with less exertion and somewhat faster than on our outward trip. We came into camp about 2 o'clock and as I write the boys are in their old quarters as contented and merry as ever. I am told that the Rebel pickets for miles along the river have put up large boards with charcoal representations of "Burnside and his army stuck in the mud"—a good joke for them but a very costly one to our Government, as it will require thousands of dollars to replace the horses, mules, wagons, &c., lost by the movement."

John and Luther Granger, along with the remainder of their Company A of the 57th Pennsylvania Veteran Volunteers, had a direct role in the infamous failed "Mud March," they were very much part of the drama. Company A was "at the ready," waiting to march when the order came. The retreating troops brought news of the various losses, the false starts, and the final postponement of the River crossing. This failed military strategy, flawed from its outset, signaled the termination of General Ambrose Burnside's career as the head of the Army of the Potomac. Another example of alternating excitement and disappointment for the troops who were called to execute against an ill conceived and poorly executed plan. The stage has now been set for a spring campaign.

The Union Army commanders, waiting for the bad weather to improve, made plans for an early spring campaign. The restless Army finally moved from their winter quarters in April, and they traversed familiar roads near Fredericksburg. Richmond, Virginia, remained the target city, but the Union troops had failed even to approach it for the past two years. This time, however, the outcome promised to be different. After all, General "Fighting Joe" Hooker was in command of a superior army, in terms of sheer numbers, supplies, and training. They would march to Richmond and bring an end to the Civil War. Such was the prevailing mood as the winter chill warmed to a welcome spring in the Union Army camp.

Chapter Five:
"Always Be Prepared"
April Fool's Day, 1863

The winter quarters for Pennsylvania's 57th Veteran Volunteers found our troops encamped in Falmouth, Virginia. Following both the disastrous December 1862, defeat at Fredericksburg, and the demoralizing, humiliating Burnside Mud March in January 1863, it was time for the Union Army to settle in and prepare for the next round of battles. The men truly needed rest.

Responsibility falls upon the shoulders of the military officers for maintaining the readiness of their troops, for the unsuspecting troops are those routed and killed in battle. Unprepared officers are either taken captive by the enemy or demoted by their own side. During the long months between campaigns, it was the officers' duty to keep their troops both prepared and ready for battle. The best troops were those who could, on a moment's notice, assemble into battle lines, break camp, and prepare for long marches. Officers depended on their troops' quick response to orders to assemble and march. Forced marches were mandated to move the troops over long distances on foot. Frequently, at the end of the forced march, the exhausted men were plunged head-first into a raging battle.

They knew that they would be required to act immediately when the order came to move. They soon learned the art of packing gear efficiently and quickly, gathering food and drink, and enduring the strain of marching hard. Despite growing proficient with these chores, the troops still did not enjoy the vagabond's lifestyle. The prospect of breaking camp and marching several miles to a new location was never really welcomed by the men. Hampered by the primitive modes of communication and the extremely fierce battle conditions, the men were constantly challenged by their situations. Even on the best of days, the unknown was a constant companion of the Civil War soldiers. Rumors were rampant throughout the camp, each day increasing in ferocity and intensity. Replete with reports of imminent battle, forced marches, attacks, troop deployments, and Confederate troop movements, the rumors easily commanded the troops' utmost attention.

In April 1863, the Union Army troops were preparing for the upcoming spring campaign. The fighting season was certain to be both fierce and bloody. President Lincoln, disillusioned by General Burnside's failures, had replaced him with General Hooker. "Fighting Joe" Hooker exhibited qualities Lincoln had hoped to find in Burnside: discipline of the troops and a sense of order to the Army of the Potomac. Under the new General, the Army prepared well, practiced a wide variety of maneuvers, and renewed their self-confidence. The men realized that their drills and training would give them a decided advantage for the battles yet to be fought. News reached the camps that there was anti-draft rioting in New York City—this could become troublesome, as the Union needed to conscript new men to replace those lost in battle or to disease. The soldiers had no way of predicting that in less than five weeks they would be involved in fighting at Chancellorsville—one of the most costly battles of the War. Or, that in little more than three months, the entire fate of the Union would forever be decided on the Gettysburg battlefield. For now, the men of the 3rd Corps, 1st Division, Company A, 57th Brigade, lived through another day in camp, and another day away from home, family, friends, and loved ones.

The hardships of battle evoke both the best and the worst in men. An untried man never really knows how he will react to a situation, unless and until he faces it head-on. "Expecting the unexpected" becomes a mantra and part of the very fiber of those men facing extreme conditions like those endured by the soldiers in the Civil War. All this leads to men taking themselves very seriously. It is a tribute to the excellence of an officer, when his troops have internalized this skill of being ever-vigilant. However, living under the constant threat of attack was enough to test the extreme limits of a man's very sanity.

The officers would sometimes take advantage of their position and the stress of camp conditions to have some humor at the expense of the men. One such opportunity arose on April 1, 1863. The officers collectively concocted a ruse to occur on April 1, 1863 - April Fool's Day. Long an American tradition, April Fool's Day has represented an annual occasion when rules for "normal" behavior can be suspended, at least temporarily. Folks can poke fun at one another or indulge in otherwise frowned-upon mischief and pranks. Such harmless fun might include replacing the sugar in the sugar bowl with salt, the ends when the perpetrator gives a gleeful shout, upon this discovery, "April Fool."

True to mischievous form, the officers' plan proceeded. On April 1, 1863, at 3 o'clock in the morning, the camp officers roused their troops from sleep. There had been rumor of moving from camp to engage the enemy. With a great sense of urgency, the officers had the men draw three days' rations. Now, drawing rations was a sure sign that a hard march was to ensue. The men had drilled and marched hard and were not eagerly anticipating another spell of discomfort and heavy labor. However, things are not always as they appear!

John Granger's letter to Cornelia expresses the April surprise: "Some of the officers played a great April fool on us this morning. At 3 o'clock they got us up and had us draw three days rations and be ready to march at a moment warning for the Rebs were advancing in force. I could not believe it but did not know but it might be so. But it was a sell to come April Fool on us. Well I had rather be fooled then have to march. Such going as this…"

It must be a complex, bizarre set of circumstances when officers can conceive of such an April Fool's prank. John's letter home demonstrates his relief that he did not have to march - by the time he penned the letter, he had ceased being upset by the early morning awakening. He actually thinks this has been a good trick.

Chapter Six:
The Chancellorsville Campaign:
April – June, 1863

Following the embarrassing and horrible losses that the Union troops incurred in Fredericksburg in December, 1862 and the infamous "Mud March" in January, 1863, President Lincoln sought to replace General Ambrose Burnside with a candidate more suitable to the post of Union General. Lincoln needed someone with qualities that included strong leadership, who could command, attack, and win battles. Burnside's replacement was General "Fighting Joe" Hooker. The change did affect John Granger and his brigade and General Daniel Sickles was placed in charge of the 3rd Corps, which included the 57th Pennsylvania Veteran Volunteers.

President Lincoln, in naming Hooker to take change of the Union Army, penned a famous, insightful letter to the new General. In Lincoln's words, "You have confidence in yourself, which is a valuable, if not indispensable quality. You are ambitious which, within bounds does good rather than harm. I have heard, in such as way as to believe it, of your recently saying that both the Army and the Government needed a dictator. Of course it was not for this, but in spite of it, that I have given you the command. Only those generals who gain successes can set up dictators. What I now ask of you is military success, and I will risk the dictatorship. Beware of rashness, but with energy and sleepless vigilance go forward, and give us victories." Lincoln's dry sense of humor is evident in this letter. We can only shake our heads in perplexed disbelief when we tally the constantly changing leadership for the troops.

With these new men in charge, and as the war progressed into April 1863, the troop morale and expectations surged upward for the 57th PA. John W. Granger continues to provide his wife, Cornelia, with an accounting of his excitement that the War will soon end so that he can return to his family. "I think there is more signs of this rebellion being crushed out now than any other time, for when you see them writing at the North & leaving political matters alone until our country is safe & all unite to put down this rebellion, it will soon be done. I am glad to see such a feeling prevail." This renewed optimism represented quite a turn-around from the news media's constant negative coverage of the prior months. "Fighting Joe" Hooker's upbeat bravado, though, provided much more favorable material for the newspaper coverage. We must continue to keep in mind that newspapers were readily available for the troops; the papers furnished the full stories of troop movements and battles, with a much wider perspective than that available to the Granger brothers and their fellow soldiers.

Hooker's agenda demanded that he organize and strengthen his troops. He accomplished these objectives by ordering ammunition and provisions, along with food, liquor, and other supplies. Preparedness for victory in battle required Hooker's troops to be in a state of top-notch readiness. Morale improved as living conditions improved, and soon the men were rejuvenated and ready to fight once more.

At some point in time prior to Hooker's appointment, deserting troops accounted for nearly 30 percent of those soldiers gone missing after battles. Desertion presented itself as the grand tempter to those men on furlough. Consider how easy it would have been for them just not to return to duty! General Hooker immediately established a stern policy that would deal harshly with the tempted ones. Letters from the soldiers to their families serve as testimony to this strictness, as evident in John Granger's letter home: "I think more of home & I know that I have warm friends there & a respectable family & if I ever came home to stay I do not want those friends ashamed to meet me. I should be as glad as you if I were out of the service but it must be in an honorable way or I shall stay until the war is over if I live that length of time." John's prevailing attitude that the he would only return if he were honorably discharged, if the war ended, or if he died. He was truly an honorable man. General Hooker's attention to the problem of desertion injected some much-needed boundaries for the men. The policy engendered respect and relief among the troops; it was important enough to John Granger that he told Cornelia, "I hope every deserter will be brought back & every loyal man will use their best endeavors to crush out this rebellion."

John's lack of patience with the mind-set of the deserter is demonstrated in his April 1863 letter to his wife. He has heard the story of one deserter who happened to be from John's hometown -

Rush, Pennsylvania. "Luther got a letter from Sabra [his wife] stating that she had just received a letter saying that J. Kinyon deserted while they were in Louisville, Ky. But he did not want her to tell of it so you must keep still, for if he should come back & refuse to pay that debt you can use the information to some advantage." We can only believe that this same J. Kinyon owed John Granger some debt. If Kinyon was one of John and Cornelia's neighbors, we have already learned of the strained relationships between them. However, there is no further indication that either John or Cornelia needed to use the threat of exposure to coerce J. Kinyon to repay his outstanding debt.

Daily routines for the troops included drilling, both to keep the skills sharp and to stave boredom from being idle. President Lincoln, eager to track the progress of his new appointee, paid an inspection visit with his wife on April 10th. The Army of the Potomac was on parade for the President and Mrs. Lincoln, and the men were proud to show off their newly honed skills. Afterward, John wrote, "Yesterday we had to be reviewed by the President & his wife. That took so much time that I could not write yesterday & we had to be mustered besides. So you see it took all of the day. Well this is excuses enough." "Just" having the President and Mrs. Lincoln visit camp to review the troops could be quite an excuse for any of us not to write home!

General Hooker instilled a sense of pride and competition in his troops by introducing the system of corps badges into his Army. The soldiers in the 57th PA Volunteers were assigned a red diamond as their field badge. The field officers could readily identify which troops belonged where during battles. Hooker had trained and drilled his men efficiently. They could now be easily recognized for placement on the field, and they had been reviewed by their Commander-in-Chief. Hooker was anxiously waiting to test his men in an actual battle; he didn't realize that he, himself, would also be put to the test.

The Chancellorsville Campaign was getting under way, and Hooker was planning to move his troops into Virginia so as to take the fight to the Rebels. John Granger continued to offer his support to his wife, albeit long-distance support: "I know it is hard for you to be left there along with but little prospect of ever meeting again but we must not give up to despair. So far we have passed through some trying times & our lives have been spared thus far. It may be the will of Him that rules the Universe to spare our lives to see the end of this accursed rebellion. Let us hope on. Let us hope ever." These lines reveal some of John's contradictory attitude toward his prolonged military service—he wanted both to fight and to return home. However, his spirits are high now, and he reminds both himself and Cornelia that they will depend on God to remain in ultimate control of the universe. Private Granger would need to summon every bit of faith and strength to survive the new several months.

General Hooker's strategic plan in late April was to send a large force up the Rappahannock River, where they would cross the River and then repel the Rebels. Simultaneously, Hooker would send a force to a point below Fredericksburg to feign a crossing there. By April 9, 1863, John Granger and the others knew they were heading back toward Fredericksburg. "It is evident that we will have a hard fight at Fredericksburg & no doubt but a great many of us will fall." This new endeavor began just a few short months after the Battle of Fredericksburg, during which the Union sustained horrible losses—it was still fresh in John's mind, so he didn't look forward to a repeat performance of the brutal slaughter of thousands of his fellow men. This time, however, the fighting would be in an area just outside Fredericksburg, a place that was known as Chancellorsville.

Chancellorsville was neither a town nor a village. Rather, it derived its name from the Chancellor House, of course named after the owner. Located eleven miles west of Fredericksburg, the House served as an inn for travelers seeking lodging mid-journey. A group of several smaller buildings surrounded the grand house on the same property, where five roads met in a centralized crossing. Similar to real estate developers of our current age, Chancellor envisioned that an imposing village would grow up to surround his buildings and property. Though this vision never materialized due to the wasteland location, the Chancellor property did serve as an important Union foothold for the Battle of Chancellorsville. General Hooker utilized the Chancellor House as his command post until May 3rd, at which time the Confederate artillery shells ignited a grand fire that rendered useless Hooker's base of operations. "Chancellorsville" was in the middle of a wasteland, was appropriately known as "the Wilderness," in the midst of which great battles were later to be fought.

The gift of hindsight, in our examination of history, allows us to sense that, at some level, John Granger knew what he and his fellow soldiers would face in the upcoming campaign. John's April 23, 1863, letter mentions: "Our move does not take place yet. I suppose it is on account of the weather. Today it has rained all day." The Chancellorsville Campaign was encumbered with deplorable weather conditions and legendary mud. John's anxiety reflects his prior experience with the "Mud March" fiasco. Or perhaps it can be attributed to this soldier's need to feel a degree of control over some aspect of his existence. When presented with unpredictable and rapidly changing conditions, man searches for meaning and answers. Men in the direst circumstances with only limited influence on their condition, seek even more desperately to explain their lot. Regardless, John's writing accurately describes the foul and deteriorating weather. "It hailed & rained almost all day. I tell you it was tedious. I think it is a very backward spring. The oldest inhabitants say they never saw the like. The mud is deep…"

Battle preparations proceeded and, on Wednesday, April 29, 1863, the men who had been waiting for the orders to move found themselves between one and three miles south of Fredericksburg. Hooker's left flank crossed the Rappahannock River, and from there they would march on, to Chancellorsville. General Hooker was pleased with the progress his Army had made: the troops were moving efficiently and quickly into the strategic positions that he had mapped out for them. He spoke with characteristic boldness as he addressed his men on April 30, 1863, in a speech that would become famous and oft-quoted. "The operations of the last three days have determined that our enemy must either fly, or come out from behind his defenses and give us battle on our own ground, where certain destruction awaits him." The next military move was for Confederate General Robert E. Lee to determine: to fight, or to flee? Lee, not being one to retreat, chose to fight, and the battle was on. Perplexing to the Union leadership, Lee would frequently choose to fight, even when he was totally overwhelmed by sheer numbers and strategically challenging circumstances. He proved to be a supreme military genius, however, and armed with stubborn determination, Lee was able to succeed where others would have failed miserably. Lee, acknowledging these unlikely victories, attributed his genius and good fortune to the Grace of God.

Also on April 30, 1863, Lee issued Special Order Number 121. Exercising his talent for strategy mixed with an element of surprise, Lee, in a highly controversial move, split his numerically inferior army into two, and he sent Stonewall Jackson and his foot cavalry west on what was to become Jackson's most famous—and final—flanking march. As General Lee proceeded to implement his plan, the Union forces, led by General George Mead of the 1st Corps, were closing to within one mile of Chancellorsville. Mead was the first Union General to reach this point, entering the field from the north. John Sedgewick, Union General of the 11th Corps, commanded the left wing of the Union Army south of Fredericksburg.

Dan Sickles and his 3rd Corps followed Hooker's orders to proceed from their vantage point overlooking the crossings below Fredericksburg. Under cover of darkness, they made their way to Chancellorsville via U.S. Ford. The 57th PA Veteran Volunteers served under Sickles 3rd Corps, so they found themselves crossing the Rappahannock River on April 30th at the United States Ford, which was located a few miles below the confluence of the Rappahannock and Rapidan Rivers. By Midnight on April 30th, these soldiers were halfway to the Ford; they completed the crossing early on May 1st. The 3rd Corps moved steadily toward nearby Chancellorsville, where they fell into their ranks. The ensuing Battle of Chancellorsville began at 11:20 a.m. on May 1, 1863. The 57th PA regiment was held in reserve for the initial, inconclusive skirmishes during that first day of May. They stayed "at the ready" awaiting their battle orders. Soon, the 57th would be involved in heated action.

Unbeknownst to the Union Army, Confederate General Thomas "Stonewall" Jackson's troops stealthily closed in on the Army's right flank. David Birney's 1st Division of Sickle's 3rd Corps, which included the 57th PA, was ordered to mobilize. They assumed their position on ground between Slocum's 6th Corps and Howard's 11th Corps. Birney's men were spread along a section of the battlefield called Hazel Grove. We can imagine an aerial view here: Slocum's 6th Corps to our left; O. O. Howard's 11th Corps, representing the Union Army's extreme right flank, to our right and stretching past Wilderness Church and Dowdell's Tavern. Jackson and his men crept toward the Tavern, where he would launch his first attack.

General Birney received orders to send one brigade to reinforce General Howard's line. We must keep in mind that this line is on the extreme right and, as such, is relatively vulnerable. Our 57th PA men were sent to Dowdell's Tavern, far removed from the rest of their Division. Howard, though, deeming himself more than able to hold his line, returned the 57th to General Birney, along with his compliments. Fortunate for the 57th was this trip back to the main force. Jackson's troops were now moving to the exact site from which the 57th had just been returned! Howard and his men were caught by surprise, and so were ill prepared to face this impending challenge.

First sighted by Birney's Division, from their vantage point at Hazel Grove, Jackson's troops were moving west across the front of the Union Army. However, when Birney reported the situation, General Hooker's staff of Union Generals mistakenly believed this to be the incipient retreat by Lee—the inglorious flight predicted by Hooker's earlier speech. At this time, Sickles asked Hooker to let him attack the Rebels moving across his front, because they were in plain view. At Noon, the permission was granted, and Sickles sent Birney's Division south from Hazel Grove to attack Lee.

Birney's push south opened a gap in the Federal lines between Generals Howard and Slocum. Birney's men encountered heavy fusillade from the Confederate 12-pound napoleons. When Birney's troops eventually reached the road and fired on Stonewall Jackson's troops, harassing the so-called "retreating" Confederate soldiers, they inflicted little damage on the Rebels and stopped their pursuit after just a short distance. Had they pursued Jackson, instead, they would have been privy to his ordering troops to begin a northward march to gain access to the Union's exposed right flank.

Jackson began his initiative to confront the right flank of the Union Army at 6 o'clock am on May 2, 1863. Lee's gamble that of dividing his troops in half paid off. The crux of his plan was to attack this exposed right flank. Jackson, avoiding both suspicion and detection, marched his troops nearly twelve miles just to gain a position that was roughly six miles west-northwest from their starting point that morning. This march was not a record-breaking one, in either its speed or its distance covered, but the suspenseful element was afoot, as prologue to the 6 p.m. attack by Jackson.

31

Jackson's storm on the unsuspecting 11th Corps sent them streaming in defeat and retreating to their rear. The Battle of Chancellorsville should have been notched as a Federal victory, for the Union had both positional and numerical advantages. However, O. O. Howard had neglected to anticipate a rear attack, and so he didn't take proper precautions. This attack by Stonewall Jackson dashed all hopes of a Union victory. After the routing of the 11th Corps, the Union Army did successfully establish some defensible lines near Chancellor's House. Amazingly enough, the Yanks even attempted to re-group and launch an offensive. As Hooker determined that the chances for a Union victory here were steadily dimming, and as darkness fell, he doubted his men's abilities to retaliate, and his "inglorious flight" seemed more appropriate as the Union troops retreated from the field.

Joe Hooker, after reassessing his situation, ordered Sickles to make a night attack from Hazel Grove against the right flank of Jackson's command. So, at 11:30 p.m., Sickles launched the night attack. Once more, Birney's Division got the call to charge. The attacking forces, beleaguered by darkness, soon lost their way and became so disoriented that they skirmished with their own Union troops before they returned to Hazel Grove. Despite all of this, the Union charged a few Rebel-held positions, and they inflicted some minor damage. We must remember that night battles were characteristically more dangerous than those fought with benefit of daylight. The cover of darkness made friend and foe indistinguishable. In hand-to-hand combat, front lines tangle, and the advancing and repositioning troops would often have difficulty knowing if troops they encountered were their own.

During that May 2nd night battle, while he returned to his own lines after a scouting expedition, Stonewall Jackson became an accidental target and was shot by his own troops. General Jackson's wounds were more extensive than initially thought, necessitating the amputation of his left arm without benefit of anesthesia or antibiotic. So compromised was his immune system that pneumonia set in, and eventually caused his death on May 10th. Several Union commanders, including Birney and Sickles, were quick to try to claim credit for having shot Jackson, but in fact, the 18th North Carolina had done what the Union could not do. Daniel Sickles even tried to assign credit for the tally to Birney.

With the dawn of May 3rd, Sickles still held the high ground of Hazel Grove; he knew it was worth keeping as a commanding lookout. General Hooker, in perhaps his worst military decision at Chancellorsville, issued orders for Sickles to abandon his position and withdraw. As dawn broke, the Rebels advanced, fully expecting to engage in a fight with Sickles' Corps, but the only Union troops they found were the rear guard who protected the rear of the retreating Union troops. Among this rear guard were Graham's Brigade of Birney's Division, which included the 57th PA Volunteer Regiment. The Confederates were now free to reunite their split forces, using a connecting road so recently vacated by the Union withdrawal. General Lee, once more exercising his superior military genius, then had his army back together again, but this time, he was on the offensive, and pursuing a defeated, retreating Union Army. The Rebels soon gained the high ground of Hazel Grove and promptly set up fifty pieces of artillery that rained death and destruction on the retreating men of both the 3rd Corps and Slocum's 6th Corps.

Amid the volleys and reports of this battle, the woods surrounding the Chancellor House caught fire. The Chancellor House, which was being used as a Union hospital, took a direct hit from Confederate shelling. John Granger could only observe from a distance the devastating destruction. He was deeply affected by the sign of the burning house and wrote home: "…Wounded were burned up. What an awful death. We were drove from all parts of the field and could not take our wounded with us. Only those slightly wounded. In one large brick house used as a hospital was burned by the enemy's shell & I suppose a great many of our men were burned in it."

John Granger's first letter home following the Chancellorsville fight, dated May 7th, expressed in terse sentences his inability to process and then describe all that has occurred. He yields that responsibility to his brother, Luther. John is devastated at the losses suffered by the Union Army. "Well it will not take long to kill what few there is left in our company. Luther is writing today. He will tell who is wounded in our company." Luther's letter was a fascinating revelation of the battle, as told from an infantryman's perspective. "May 7th 1863, Camp near Potomac Creek, Va. Dear Wife, Knowing your anxiety I have taken this morning to drop a few lines to you. We arrived in camp last night after nine days hard marching & fighting. Also never did an army match with greater rapidity or fight with greater desperation than did the Army of the Potomac. We fought them hard driving them some of the time we were driven by them. Such is the fate of war. What we accomplished God knows. As for me I cannot tell only I have my mind relative to it. Although it may differ from the paper correspondence for they will make it out to suit the times. Therefore I will give as near a account or detail of the matter as I can for I was an eyewitness of the scene. Too much for my own good for I saw or heard more balls fly than I wish to hear."

"Our brigade was the first to engage them Sunday morning the day of the hard fighting. Such a fight I never before witnessed as was on that morn. The air was full of bullets and shells. Man's life was in jeopardy in any place whether up to the front or in the rear. Many were wounded running back to the rear. The army was regularly panic stricken at first but with rigid and strict guards was at last quieted and drove the enemy back. Or in others words held them in check. Some of our army run back and crossed the river both officers & men."

"All I can say is such officers as those should be tried by court marshal and shot down for cowardice. If officers are allowed to run what confidence has the men to fight. If their officers will run of course the men will. For my part I think justice should be done should it commence at home. For without order all are confusion. Such things as panic are frequent and when it happens perhaps men and officers are too much blamed for it. Our big officers get out. Generals rush a large force against some weak point in the line causing the line to be broken at that point confusing the men which are stationed to strength or hold that point causing panic amongst others and so it goes. I guess I will not weary your patience by going on with a lengthy detail of matters and things. Suffice it to say we had a hard fight losing a great many men and I think the rebels lost more for they rush on with furious impetuosity right up as it were to the mouth of the cannon."

"They acted more like animals than men but thank God they did not accomplish what they undertook. Although they wounded and killed many of our men but they did not annihilate the whole Potomac Army. They will find there are a few left to fight them yet. I am not quite discouraged yet nor do I mean to get although it seams fate is against us at times. Perhaps all things will work together for good for those that love and serve God. I must acknowledge that we are trusting too much to man."

"I will make a long matter short. I will say Steve came out all safe and sound. John the same. Philand got wounded in the arm & as we were obliged to fall back from that point I think he was taken prisoner by the enemy. He has been taken one before. As for Wesley Devine, I could not say but think perhaps he will turn up in a few days for he is very timid and I think he may turn up in the rear for he ran back toward the rear. He might got wounded or killed for that though for I mind the balls flew over my head like hail stones. Wilson Terry got wounded slightly but not seriously unless some disease sets in. Lieutenant H. H. Hinds was wounded slightly. Captain Lyons was also wounded and quite a number others in our company but none you know."

"I expect we will soon leave this place for I think we will be marching out of this place in a few days. I will close my preamble by saying you must not get discouraged. I expect to see some hardships for a time. Don't get afraid for if God be for us who can be against us. He has protected my life so far and I am willing to trust in him yet. I did get a slight wound on my arm. It keeps me from carrying a gun. You must write often and I will do the same when I can. If we lay around here we can write often. I wish we might lay around for a few days and get rested but as for the rest God knows what and when we march. I cannot tell nor do I wish to know. They say old Abe Lincoln is down on a visit to the Army. How true it is I cannot say. So good bye for this time. This from your husband & friend. L. A. Granger"

John's perspective on what had occurred those first few days in May took on a more personal tone. He needed to tell his family that he had survived the ordeal. "Dear wife and children. I feel thankful that my life is spared to write once more to you. Since I last wrote to you I have passed through scenes of danger and death. Another battle has been fought & thousands of brave men have fallen. Our company lost in all killed, wounded and missing, fifteen. We have been nine days on this tour." Eventually, John was led to work through his distressing feelings, by writing home during those days immediately following the Battle of Chancellorsville. He narrated a story rife with battles, fear, slaughter, terror, and heroic survival. On May 9th John wrote, "Our last fight has caused a gloom to settle over the whole country.

What a sad and terrible thing it was. What a terrible slaughter. I think it the worst I ever saw. The amount of suffering was awful. The ground that we fought over was mostly woods & they caught fire & no doubt that hundreds of wounded were burned up."

"All day Sunday we fought like tigers but of no use. I do not know where the blame will rest now, where is the fault? It is not with the soldiers for they fought until over one half of their numbers had fallen. I know we never felt so discouraged as we do now. Oh where will it end? God only knows. While I was in that fight little did I think that I ever should have a chance of writing to you again."

"Providence has spared my life. How thankful we ought to feel, but how sad & lonely we feel. You hardly see a smile on the countenance of any. We are in the midst of death we see over half our tents vacant. What will our company be after one more fight? The Lord only knows, but I almost despair of ever seeing home again. But if it were not for hope the heart would break."

John Granger had summed up the feelings of the Union supporters. The Union should have won the Battle of Chancellorsville. They were superior in strength, men, and artillery, and they enjoyed a better position. They had actually stolen a march on General Lee's Rebels, to get into position of their choosing. Finally, they had General "Fighting Joe" Hooker in command. However, they were out-maneuvered by a pair of very aggressive and ingenious Confederate Generals—Robert E. Lee and Thomas "Stonewall" Jackson. The men from both North and South contingents fought extremely hard during those days in early May, at Chancellorsville. In the end, the deciding factor was been the confident aggression of the Army of Northern Virginia. They seized the opportunity and carried the day's victory home to the Rebels.

Even in the midst of war, there came a glimmer of man's humane treatment of his enemy. Another of John Granger's letters, dated May 12th, tells his wife: "I understand that General Lee sent a flag of truce to General Hooker requesting him to come over & get his wounded for he had not the means to take care of them. I think it very kind of him for the poor fellows must suffer a great deal. I suppose that General Shermann cut off the rebel supplies so that Lee could not take care of the wounded."

This horrific loss demoralized the Union men. They had been groomed for a victory. Their commanding general had declared that a win would be delivered. He promised one, even before the first shot was fired at the crossroads near the Chancellor homestead. Even the Union itself expected a victory, but it wasn't to be. The Army of the Potomac was devastated.

Another letter of John Granger's details the losses, as follows: "It seems as though our division had it the hardest of any. It lost more men than any other division in the army. Our brigade lost 790 men. The whole division lost 1870. There is three brigades in a division so you can see that our brigade suffered the worst." John's assessment is supported by the official record that carries Birney's Division as suffering the most losses as a percentage of total troops engaged. John's numbers are inaccurate by just a few casualties. Birney's Division sustained a total of 1,605 casualties (72 killed, 490 wounded, 194 missing). The 57th PA Volunteers suffered 10 killed, 43 wounded, and 18 missing.

"There seems to be a gloom on all, it was a terrible sight, so many of our number gone. A few more fights & we are all gone. I hope that we shall not be put in front & exposed so much the next time."

At Chancellorsville the casualty list included men from Rush, PA. John's account echoes Luther's: "Wilson was wounded pretty bad in the side, the two Otis boys were wounded in the arms. Those were all from our neighborhood. Capt. Lyons & Lieut. H. Hinds were wounded. I lost all of my clothes in the last fight except for what I had on."

Among the direst and most brutal events of war, there are battle heroes who are recognized for the efforts. It wasn't chance that determined who received medals in a battle, but, rather, bravery, pride, and a sense of duty. John Granger demonstrated that he was a good soldier who fought for his country. He was especially proud of his brigade and proud to be among the men who were recognized for their valiant deeds enacted at Chancellorsville. "I will send Ed a Philadelphia Enquirer if I can get one. Tell him to look over the names of honor. I need not tell you that such a thing raises our pride a little for we are vain as well as the rest of the folks. What shape these medals are in I do not know, but if I am lucky enough to get one I will let you know.

"Well ma yesterday we had a grand parade & those medals were given to those that their names on the list. For my part I am sorry that it was ever mentioned for it has created a good deal of hard feeling. They are mad at them that got them. Of course all could not get them & for that reason they feel jealous. I will send you mine. It will be something that will give me a good name & at the same time a keepsake for you. I feel proud of the honor but am sorry that it produces such feelings in the company. But it was something I did not ask for nor did I expect to get until I saw my name in the paper."

Private John W. Granger was awarded the Kearny Cross, which was a medal of honor awarded only to those men who perform valiantly under fire. The award was named for the beloved General Kearny of the 57th PA Brigade, who was killed in action.

On June 5, 1863, John sent his medal home to his wife, Cornelia, along with these words: "I hope that you will get that medal. It is not of much value but it will be a keepsake if I never should live to get home. But let us hope that good luck will attend me through."

The envious feeling among those soldiers who did not receive the medals was a topic in John's letters. John receiving a medal was a divisive matter between John and his brother Luther. "Ed wanted to know how Luther like it because he did not get a medal. He did not like it much. I do not want to say much about him. He is queer the best way you can fix him."

The Chancellorsville battle carnage was officially over by May 4th. What truly should have been an outright victory for the North instead had ended in utter defeat. This Rebel success emboldened General Robert E. Lee to pursue an even more aggressive northward thrust. Lee's victory ensured an end to Hooker's command post, and Lincoln counted "Fighting Joe" with those seven generals he had named to confront Lee during the past two years. Hooker, himself, was now a casualty.

What hope there had been for a quick end to the Civil War had long ago been sacrificed; and now, with this most recent Union defeat, the Army of the Potomac realized that there was no end in sight. John Granger reflected the dashing of hope: "The prospect for the continuation of the war is as favorable as it was one year ago. I do wish something would turn up favorable for a speedy close of this horrible butchery & loss of human life. But I suppose it will close when the great ruler of the universe sees fit." His fatalistic mind-set was that God was not ready for the war to end, and that there must be some other purpose yet to be fulfilled.

"A great many more of us will go to our long home before this war will close I fear. I do not see any more prospect of its closing now than I did one year ago, but of course it is one year near its close than is was one year ago." John's reports about soldiers' injuries and deaths caused many tense moments at home. That is one of the reasons John always opened his correspondence with commentary on his health. "I like to have forgot to tell you that Wilson was mistaken about me being hurt. Luther was hurt on the arm a little & excused from duty for a few days, but I have done duty with the exception of about one day. I am well & healthy. There is no one in the company that can do more duty than myself."

John had also received a promotion to Corporal while at Chancellorsville, which enabled him to obtain a better position in the Division. He had entertained aspirations for some time and was glad to be accorded this opportunity. "I have acted as quartermaster from our company since the Chancellor fight."

The Battle of Chancellorsville was significant on several counts. It was the last great victory for General Robert E. Lee, which victory was overshadowed by the loss of Stonewall Jackson at the hands of his own troops. The Confederate troops had completely routed General Howard's 11th Corps, followed then by Lee's improbable decision to split his forces, even in the face of a numerically superior opponent. Finally, Jackson had triumphed with his brilliant flank march. Both Union and Confederacy suffered gross losses of men to death and injury in the fighting that had raged in the wasteland. The battle at the crossroads of the Chancellor House could have been the turning point for an eventual victory for the Confederates, but in actuality it was the beginning of the end. The death of Stonewall Jackson was a brief foretaste of what Lee would encounter as he aggressively led his troops to push northward.

Reflecting the ever-present hope that the war would be brief, John Granger's letter from camp in Virginia dated May 11, 1863 suggested that, while he and the others in the Army of the Potomac were enduring severe hardship, they were not the only ones. "Well affliction & death is amongst those at home as well as in the army. It does seem as though our country is passing through troubles & trials of every kind. Let us hope that they will be short but we do not know how long they will be."

John's words provide a summary of events to this point: "There has been too many lives lost everywhere in the cursed rebellion. I wish some way could be fixed upon to settle this question, but if the South are bound to fight it out we must try to meet them. It will be a long & bloody struggle I am afraid. It seems sometimes to me if I were only out of it I should not care, but you know we are selfish beings only looking for our own interest. But I tell you we all feel sad & lonely. It has been the stillest time in camp that I ever saw. Our numbers are small & all feel as though we had narrowly escaped with our lives. There seems to be a gloom on all. It was a terrible sight, so many of our number gone. A few more fights & we are all gone. I hope that we shall not be put in front & exposed so much the next time, but we cannot tell nor can we tell whose turn it will be to fall."

Chapter Seven
The Battle of Gettysburg: "Luther Never Knew What Hurt Him"

The 57th Pennsylvania Veteran Volunteers, including brothers John and Luther Granger, had by mid-1863 participated in a greater number of battles than they ever could have predicted at the time of their enlistment. Following Chancellorsville, where their original enlistment numbers had been reduced by nearly one-third, we may find it difficult to comprehend that just two years had passed since the mustering at Camp Curtin. However, the enormous toll in lost human lives and mental anguish made it seem much longer for the surviving troops. The 57th PA had sacrificed brave soldiers in the Peninsular Campaign, Yorktown, Williamsburg, Fair Oaks, Seven Pines, Fredericksburg, Chancellorsville, and other sites less familiar but just as deadly.

July 1863, found the 57th PA marching into Gettysburg, a small crossroads town in south central Pennsylvania. John and Luther Granger marched with the 57th, under the command of General Daniel Sickles and his 3rd Corps. They would again challenge the enemy, but this time it appeared that the men were to enjoy the home-soil advantage. The Pennsylvania natives of the 57th soon realized that their homecoming would be bittersweet.

Still reeling and demoralized from their ignominious defeat at Chancellorsville in May 1863, the Union Army knew that they had been routed there because of poor leadership, not because they were out-fought. The one-sided defeat at the hands of a Confederate force half their size could be attributed to General Joe Hooker's lack of strong leadership in battle. The Union men were not beaten by soldiers who were better fighters, but by their own Union generals who refused to act. For all his bold talk, bravado, preparation, and strategy, Hooker failed to deliver the promised unconditional victory. At the precise moment in battle when Hooker should have given bold orders to attack, he mistakenly hesitated, doubting his strategy, his plan, and his men. On the opposite side, General Lee could not afford the luxury of doubt, so his troops emerged the victors that day.

The Union troops were still being commanded by General Hooker to shadow the movements of the Confederate Army and to keep themselves positioned between the steadily advancing Confederates and the United States' capitol city, Washington, D.C. This was no small assignment, partially due to the downturn in Union troops' morale following their embarrassing loss at Chancellorsville, and partly due to General Lee's being emboldened after his victory there. Lee, thus, convincingly argued to Confederate States' President Jefferson Davis that he should take the war to the people of the North by leading his Army of Northern Virginia into Pennsylvania. This action would precipitate sufficient bloody battles to show the Northerners just how horrible this was really was. It was Lee's hope that, by his placing cities such as Baltimore, Harrisburg, New York, Philadelphia, Pittsburgh, and Washington, D.C. under the threat of siege, he could coerce the North to negotiate an end to the war.

The march to Gettysburg by Hooker's forces began at a most leisurely pace, much to President Lincoln's dismay. The Army of the Potomac's odyssey soon quickened to the point where the men were in a forced march for several weeks. While the Union men remained unenlightened about their exact destination, they did realize they were heading north, and not just in pursuit of Lee's men. It became apparent that the Union soldiers were competing with the Rebels for topographical and logistical advantage, as well as military superiority. For now, the Confederate master strategist, General Robert E. Lee, had the edge over Hooker. The maneuvering and planning exercise would end finally when one army was in position on ground of their choosing.

During a reflective moment, John Granger wrote home on June 7, 1863: "Let us hope on, let us hope ever. I know that we get discouraged a great many times & we have reasons for being so, for it does seem as though this Army of the Potomac was doomed to disappointment. We have done a great deal of hard fighting & hard work but what has it amounted to? I tell you it is a wonder that the soldiers are in as good spirits as they are. I am satisfied that the soldiers have not the confidence in Hooker that they had in McClellan, nor never will have."

President Lincoln now wrestled with whether to appoint yet another general to lead his Union Army. General Hooker was the seventh in command since 1861, and it was only 1863. The troops anxiously awaited the removal of Hooker as their leader, following Chancellorsville. The prevalent topic of discussion among the men was just how soon Lincoln would make a new appointment. They realized that Lincoln had been blessed with a large portion of impatience, and they knew that he would not postpone his action much longer. Lincoln was convinced that, given the proper leadership, the men in the Union Army could enact a decisive defeat for General Lee and the Rebels. The dilemma remained for the President: which person would be called? He had already been disappointed by his first seven choices.

Lincoln mulled over his decision through the month of May, making no changes or appointments. Lee, being very opportunistic, capitalized on the advantage of the Union's lack of strong leadership to move his troops northward through the Shenandoah Valley of Virginia. Lee's itinerary included passing through Winchester, VA; Martinsburg, WV; Hagerstown, MD; and finally, moving toward Chambersburg, PA. Throughout June, Lee and his men stealthily progressed under cover of the Blue Ridge Mountains. They passed unmolested through the Cumberland Valley, until they came directly into the heart of south central Pennsylvania.

Hooker concluded that Lee had left Richmond unprotected, and sought Lincoln's permission to attack there. Lincoln now was in the habit of providing strategic direction and counsel to his general, and replied tersely, "I think Lee's army, and not Richmond, is your true objective point. If the head of Lee's army is at Martinsburg and the tail of it is on the Plank Road between Fredericksburg and Chancellorsville, the animal must be very slim somewhere. Could you not break him?" Hooker admitted to his Commander-in-Chief that he and his troops were unable to break Lee. Fighting Joe appeared to reposition his men only in reaction to Lee's surge northward. Hooker figured that Lee and his men were planning an attack on Washington, so the Union troops were stationed west of there, in order to defend the nation's Capitol. Lee, however, continued to march north.

President Lincoln's frustration with Hooker grew, as he realized that Hooker's army was always a step behind Lee's. Hooker elected to remain on the eastern side of the Blue Ridge Mountains, thus keeping the mountains between the two armies. Hooker's actions served only to delay the eventual inevitable confrontation, not to prevent it. The only remaining issue was the location of that fight.

General Lee directed his troops to cross the Potomac River on June 25th and move toward the Pennsylvania border. Hooker, still intent upon protecting Washington, kept his men between Lee and the Capitol. The Rebels thus moved freely along the Pennsylvania countryside, without any interference from Union troops.

Lincoln watched with great displeasure; his decision must be forthcoming about replacing Hooker. Two days later, on June 27th Hooker asked to be relieved of his command, presumably in response to General-in-Chief Henry Halleck's countermanding his orders to abandon Harper's Ferry. The request was speedily delivered to the President, who sent word from his War Department on June 28th to the Union camp near Frederick, Maryland, that General George Gordon Meade would replace General Hooker. Lincoln's growing list of generals who had failed the Union now included, for the first two years of the War, McDowell, McClellan, Pope, McClellan (for another term), Burnside, and now Hooker. President Lincoln called on the same General Meade who, at Chancellorsville, was vehemently opposed to, and visibly upset by, Hooker's order to disengage and retreat on May 2nd. This was also the same Meade – a native Pennsylvanian – who had been the first general on the field at Chancellorsville.

The exhausted Union Army had been on the march for nearly three weeks by the end of June. Their objective was to keep pace with Lee's invading Confederate army. By June 30th, Lee had made his approach to Carlisle, Pennsylvania, and he was ready to make another of his critical strategic decisions—which northern city would be the target of his current campaign, and where would be the most advantageous position for his troops. Lee opted not to occupy a city—rather, he would surround it and use it as a stage on which the final desperate act of War could be inflicted upon the Union. If General Lee could manage to break the Union army in the north, he was certain that the public outcry would be sufficient enough to force the North's offer of a conciliatory settlement of the entire War. Barring this, he could still attack Washington, if need be. His first preference, though, would be to engage the Union army and beat them.

Surprisingly, John Granger displayed a cheerful frame of mind in writing home from Maryland on June 30, 1863. John certainly knew battle was due soon, for he recognized the warning signs. However, he was in an especially good humor because he had just received a letter from home. He writes, "Dear wife & children my heart is glading this morning by receive 2 letters from you, one of the 11th one of the 15. The first since we started on this march. Well ma I have not had any chance to write you. We have been on the march almost 3 weeks without any mail, tired & part sore, are now within 4 miles of Pa line. Little did I think when we started that we should get as near Pennsylvania as we are, but the Rebs are in heavy force ahead of us. I suppose & I think that we shall have to do some hard fighting before we get them out of Pa. I received them shirts all right & I tell you they came good for we have had no time to wash anything since we started. I should like to give you a description of our march but cannot now but I will just as soon as I get time if I live. I am glad that my health is good. I have stood the march first rate, although many has died on this march of sunstroke. Well ma I shall have to close for fear that I shall miss my chance to send this. Well ma I hope that I shall have good luck & come out all safe. Well ma good day & good luck to you my best love to you all. Yours ever."

On June 30, 1863, while the 75,000 men of the Army of Northern Virginia were massing near Cashtown, PA, the 95,000-man Army of the Potomac was heading toward Gettysburg, still keeping themselves between the Rebels and Washington, D.C. The Union leaders did not know what Lee had in store for them—they only knew that Lee would be the aggressor once again. The Generals evidenced fear, concern, and much consternation over just where the Confederates would attack them. Given Lee's logistic advantage, he could attack nearly anywhere, but would probably lead a charge into Harrisburg, Baltimore, York, or Philadelphia. Citizens of Pittsburgh were on fearful alert that Lee's forces might attack their city.

Fate played a significant role in the determination of the actual battlefield. At approximately 10 a.m. on July 1, 1863, members of Lee's advance reconnaissance force, sent out toward the city of Gettysburg, encountered a division of dismounted Union cavalry under the command of General John Buford, who was a true fighter. The opposing troops squared off near the ground of

Gettysburg Seminary College, situated just north of Gettysburg. Thus began one of the most spectacular, yet horrible acts of war ever to be seen on the North American continent. The picturesque landscape of this city of 2,400 residents was about to turn blood-red.

General Buford held the Confederate troops at bay until the 1st Corps of Union soldiers arrived on the field, commanded by John Reynolds. On this July 1st engagement, Meade had given Reynolds the option of either holding and fighting, or withdrawing to a defensive position. General Reynolds, another fighter like Buford, chose to stay and fight. He gave orders to his men, "Forward men! Forward! For God's sake, and drive those fellows out of the woods!" As these words were delivered, a sniper's bullet lodged in Reynolds' head, and he died instantly. General Abner Doubleday stepped in to assume command of the Union forces, pro tem.

The battle raged on just north of town on that first day. By 4 p.m., General O. O. Howard, who was directing the main Union Army engaged in the battle, realized that no reinforcements would arrive before dark and in time for him to drive the Rebels from the field. Howard directed his men to withdraw quickly and completely, moving south through town. The Confederates were unable to pursue their positional advantage at this point, because they, too, had sustained heavy losses during the day's battle. At the close of the July 1st battle, the Confederate army had won the day and had driven back the Union troops that were engaged on the field. However, it was not a decisive victory. General Lee was disappointed that the battle had begun without benefit of cavalry reconnaissance from his trusted cavalry commander, General Stewart.

General Meade ordered the 3rd Corps, under General Dan Sickles' command, to support the 1st and 11th Corps, but they arrived too late from Emmitsburg to participate in the July 1st battle. Meade had directed Sickles to move without delay to Gettysburg, but the reinforcements did not arrive until that evening.

General Meade, himself, arrived at 11:30 p.m. and immediately set to the task of arranging his troops in a defensive configuration around Cemetery Ridge. This stance ultimately became known as the "fishhook defense," and it was to become a pivotal alignment in the Union's success at the Battle of Gettysburg. Meade's fishhook-shaped battle line stretched for nearly three miles! From Culp's Hill to Cemetery Hill was an arch formation of troops that formed the barb of the hook; along Cemetery Ridge and extending nearly the entire distance to a rocky hill known as "Little Round Top" was the shank. The Rebel forces occupied Seminary Ridge, which was high ground parallel to Cemetery Ridge, approximately a mile from it. The two armies faced each other across a wide, sloping field that included farms, roads, streams, large boulders, fence lines, and trees. So ended the first day of the Battle.

Next morning (July 2nd) the 3rd Corps was fully deployed along Cemetery Ridge, representing the extreme left flank of the Union army's fishhook defense. General Sickles was dissatisfied with the position he was assigned, because it left him vulnerable to a flank attack on his left side. Taking matters into his own hands, he tried to better his position by pushing forward almost a half-mile toward the northwest; he re-deployed along the Emmitsburg Road. This move left Little Round Top totally unoccupied, even though this had been Sickles' assigned anchor point. Any strategic significance of maintaining a hold on Little Round Top was wasted on Sickles. Instead, he placed Graham's Brigade of Birney's Division, which included the 57th PA Veteran Volunteers, at the furthest point forward on the Emmitsburg Road. Graham's Brigade occupied the extreme right of the 3rd Corps' battle line. This was a site made famous by the brutal fighting that occurred there that day. Today, its name is synonymous with the deadly fighting at Gettysburg, and it is known simply as the "Peach Orchard." The far left of the 3rd Corps was now based at the Devil's Den.

Some historians have chosen to present this movement by Sickles as a huge mistake. Abandoning his position was an error of great consequence; it placed the 57th Regiment in grave peril, not to mention the entire left flank of the Union position. Also, it exposed his men to killing fire from advancing Confederates commanded by General Longstreet, and it prompted General Meade to alter the day's battle plan. On the other hand, had Sickles not moved forward, the Confederate troops would have been able to advance unchallenged all the way to the foothills of Cemetery Ridge. When Meade rode to his left to observe what Sickles had done, he immediately recognized that Sickles had made a critical error. Realizing it was too late to withdraw, Meade sent the 5th Corps to act as reserve and to support the left flank.

The 57th PA brigade was butchered at the Peach Orchard, located at the intersection of Emmitsburg Road and Wheatfield Road. At 6 p.m., the 57th had been routed from the Peach Orchard by McLaws and Barksdales's brigades. The 57th retreated along the Wheatfield Road and proceeded through the Wheatfield, which sustained heavy Rebel fire. The men sacrificed by the 57th PA that day numbered 11 killed, 46 wounded, and 58 captured.

The Confederates had stormed and destroyed Sickles' position, but the remainder of the Union forces had the opportunity to observe the battle in which Sickles was engaged. The 5th Corps was able to react to the dire circumstances, thereby rescuing Little Round Top by using nothing short of heroic measures. The remainder of the fishhook defense withstood assaults from the Confederates through the day.

On July 3rd, the Union's fishhook defense line of Cemetery Ridge was re-established. Only this time, Sickles' 3rd Corp occupied a center position along the Ridge, about half-way up the shank. Their positional advantage enabled them to stand against General Pickett's now-famous charge.

John Granger had survived the assault by Pickett, but in his next letter home, he had devastatingly sad news to report: his brother, Luther, had been killed during Generals McLaws and Barksdales's advance on the Sherfy Farm during the late afternoon battle near the Peach Orchard. John's July 5, 1863 letter provides us both a painful and poignant account of that battle. "Dear wife & children it is by the mercy of God that I am alive to write you a few lines to let you know how I am. Another big battle has been fought & my life & health is spared & so far I am not hurt. But alas a great many have gone to their long homes. Only eight left in our company. How shall I tell the sad news? Brother Luther is among the slain. He was shot through the head & killed instantly. He never knew what hurt him. He was killed on the 2nd of July & we found his body this morning. The Rebels held the part of the field that we fought in until last night. They had took all of his money. Some six or eight dollars. It is reported that they have left last night."

We are afforded a glimpse of the unique kindness and courtesy that not even two years of hard fighting could obliterate in John, as he appends a postscript: "This was wrote in haste so please excuse."

At was typical of the battles in the Civil War, once a soldier was killed, all his worldly possessions were claimed by the troops then in command of that field. Luther's belongings had been picked over by the Confederate troops who held the ground around Sherfy Farmhouse that afternoon. As terrible as was the thought of his brother lying dead on the battlefield and being stripped of his personal effects, John rarely mentions Luther again in any of his subsequent letters home. Once John has recounted the details surrounding Luther's death, he apparently feels no need to re-tell them. What may seem odd or harsh or emotionally cold to us, probably is evidence of the reality of war—John came to understand first-hand that soldiers do not always return home in times of war.

The Union army eventually notified the family of Luther's death by presenting his wife, Sabra, an official report; however, the processed papers required considerable time for preparation and sending. Military rules required that an officer of the regiment must make the official report of a casualty on the battlefield. Following the Battle of Gettysburg, just locating an officer—any officer—was not easy. John wrote Cornelia on July 7th, "Life is uncertain and we cannot tell what will happen, but let us hope that everything will turn out for the best. Sabra will get an official report of Luther's death as soon as some of our commissioned officers come up with us. We have no officer that belongs to our company. Capt. Lyons is at Washington, Lieutenant Hinds is missing the Battle & Lieutenant Green was wounded, so you see we are put into another company."

Delivering the news of his slain brother to the family was an extremely charged emotional event for John. The reality of Luther's having met death in such a violent way caused much internal stress and turmoil for John. He questioned the cause and effect of such events. The war certainly would not end with the slaying of a single soldier; it didn't end with the killing, wounding, and capturing of some 50,000 soldiers during the three days at Gettysburg. How would Luther's death change the outcome of the war? Why Luther? Gone was John's eager anticipation of his trip home. His personal questions, not voiced, had been answered, such as "Would Luther be wounded? Crippled? Would he be right in his mind?" The final answer to "How would Luther return home?" was, "In a wooden box."

Luther Granger's wife, Sabra, no longer wondered whether her husband was cold, hungry, or lonely. She could at least take solace in the fact that the daily anticipation of a letter of news from the battlefront, even a rumor, from Luther was finally over. Perhaps, with the end of the awful unknowns and waiting, Sabra could proceed with her grieving. John's wife, Cornelia, still had her John to be the object of her concerns.

What circumstances put Luther Granger in harm's way on July 2nd? The 3rd Corps filed into Gettysburg late in the evening of July 1st, too late to engage in the fight of the day. Some critics say General Sickles' initial procrastination in moving his corps led to further delays in his ability to provide assistance when needed. Had he arrived earlier on July 1st, he may have been able to save the day. At 9 a.m. on July 2nd, Sickles began to deploy his troops of the 3rd Corps around Big and Little Round Top. The 3rd Corps' position was originally intended to be along the left of the Union position. However, Sickles made a hasty and ill-considered decision in the field that demonstrated his lack of good judgment. He placed his entire command in jeopardy by pushing out into the field, rather than holding his position. From our modern-day vantage point, it is a simple conclusion to place the blame for the devastating losses incurred by the 3rd Corps, directly on Commander Dan Sickles.

Imagine the scene at Gettysburg following that three-day battle: dead, dying, and wounded were strewn about the countryside like the flotsam and jetsam of some unspeakable high tide. Not a view could be had that didn't encompass body parts resting in streams, on hills, in buildings, on boulders, near trees, and out in the open field. The wounded and dying soldiers were everywhere.

John Granger's letter describes the surreal quality of this scene following those awful three days. He writes that the scene was dominated "by large details .... Out on the battlefield burying the dead. The field is covered with dead. For four days we have had hard fighting here & some of the hardest I ever saw." This, from a man who had survived the Battles of Fredericksburg, and

Chancellorsville. "Nearly ¾ of our regiment is gone. Oh how sad & lonely I feel. I shall have to close for now. I hear the cannons road & we shall have to fall in…" John, in all of his references to the Battle of Gettysburg, said it was the hardest fighting he had ever witnessed.

A particularly chilling description of events awaited Cornelia in John's letter of July 18th: "Well ma I will try & give you some description of the battlefield. It presented the awfulest sight you ever saw. The stench was such as I never saw before. Dead bodies lay exposed for five days in the sun. The most of them swollen so that they would burst open & just as black as a hat. Some did not turn black from the fact that they bled the blood out of them. In one small place where the Rebs had their artillery there was 37 horses lay dead. All the horses for that battery. It would be impossible for me to tell the number of horses killed, but it was immense. When we left I could see lots of Rebs that were not buried, no I do not believe they could be very well they were so rotten. When the Rebs left they had rows of their dead laid in for burying, but went off & left them for our men to bury. The ground was all plowed up with shell, houses & barns riddled, orchards cut all to pieces with balls, fences torn down, rails burned to cook our grub & farms cut up with rifle pits. Everything laid waste. Well I cannot tell you half the damage done. If there is any Copperheads that wish to resist the draft & bring war to their doors let them visit the battlefield of Gettysburgh. Let them hear the shot & shell, the sharp hiss of the minie ball as it comes so close as to burn. Let them see the horrors of a battlefield & they will cave. Well ma enough of this. I wrote to Sabra today. I should be very glad if I could come home than I could explain it better, but sometimes I almost give up thinking of ever getting home again. But I have every reason to feel thankful for my life so far."

At Gettysburg both armies were badly mauled. The Federals had lost 23,049 killed, wounded, or missing—approximately one man out of every four. The Confederates reported losses totaling 20,451, but their returns are incomplete; their actual casualties appear to have been nearer 28,000, or one-third of the force. General Daniel Sickles was out of action early in the fight at the Peach Orchard, when he was hit in the leg with a cannonball. Even with the amputation of that leg, he lived to fight another day. Reynolds and Hancock, both aggressive corps commanders for the

Union, were also forced out of action that day. General Lee, though badly beaten, escaped from Gettysburg and with his troops headed for the more friendly territory of Virginia.

Following Luther's death, John Granger became less and less tolerable and charitable toward the Rebel cause, along with their soldiers and their leaders. Often, in those letters written after his first hard encounters, he wished for a quick end to the war and severe punishment for the Rebel leaders. John could be numbered among those who fervently wanted a quick end to the war, but such was not to be.

General Robert E. Lee began a hasty retreat into Virginia on July 5th, immediately after the Battle of Gettysburg. His men were pursued by the Army of the Potomac, which included the remainder of the 57th PA Volunteers. By July 7th, John was able to write Cornelia, "I expect we shall have hard marching to overtake Lee. He has escaped into Va. Again. Well I wish he was under the ground & this rebellion crushed out." John verbalized this wish aloud within the camp, as well as in his letters.

The Union's pursuit of Lee into Virginia was marked by near-battles that never quite materialized. Although the Army of the Potomac was on high alert and expected a fight at any moment of every day, soldier Granger wrote on July 12th, "We have not had a fight since we left Gettysburgh but we expect one any moment. Oh how glad I would be if I were at home to day to spend a Sabbath in peace & quite. But instead of peace & quiet we may be in a hard fight before night. We cannot tell what will happen. So you see it keeps us in a state of excitement all the time. A soldiers life is a hard life to live. Well ma, I hope if I live that I shall get some rest by & by, but when that will be the Lord only knows."

Reflecting on his own situation, John Granger was ever-mindful of the conditions at home. Even when he faced being shot at or worse, he always inquired as to the condition of those at home to whom he wrote. During the Union's pursuit of Lee, John wrote, "We are near the old battle ground of Antietam and expect a hard fight. I do not know if I can get a chance to send this [letter] but will try to get some citizen to take it & put it in the [post] office."

The 57th PA had been so severely diminished by the Battle of Gettysburg that John Granger and the other survivors were re-assigned, to another regiment. John wrote that he was unable to befriend any of these new men. By now, John had passed his 44th birthday. The other soldiers frequently were youngsters aged 18-25. "I do not enjoy myself nor take much comfort for my associates are wicked men & men of mean principles. I cannot bear them nor can I have much to say to them. I never knew how much a man would suffer in such society. It makes one feel as though I were all along, sad & lonely, but I hope for better times. My best companions in the company are all gone. Nate Goodsill was wounded in the ankle at Gettysburgh, & John Harris was wounded too. They belong to the 141 Regt. It was four weeks last Thursday since we broke up camp. Since then we have had no rest night nor day hardly. Some nights we have marched all night through rain & mud. It has been an awful time."

Soldiers in battle situations experience the full spectrum of emotions, from the exhilarating excitement to the depths of despair. Apprehension of the unknown fuels these emotions. In John's words, "Where we shall go from here we cannot tell nor can we tell how soon we shall have to fight but I should not wonder if we run into the Rebs any time. Well let us hope that everything will turn out for the best. Some of the time I feel in pretty good spirits & sometimes I feel discouraged, but everybody has their ups & downs." These extreme emotions are unparalleled by anything a civilian could imagine during peacetime.

By July 14th General Lee was once more south of the Potomac River. On July 17th, General Meade had crossed the Potomac further downstream. The 57th Regiment began a march on July 21st from Upperville, MD to Manassas Gap. Meade approached the Gap on July 22nd, out-pacing Lee. Meade had an opportunity to inflict further damage on the Confederate army. He passed through the Gap with the 3rd Corps leading the way. "We had some hopes of staying behind to do guard duty, but alas for our hopes. Last night we were ordered to cross the Potomac into Va. Once more & here we are in front again. Well I suppose that me must try & stand it. I do hope that we shall succeed in breaking up Lee's army & then I shall think the rebellion about played out." This, from a letter dated July 18th, 1863.

Captain Dan Sickles, alive despite amputation of one leg following a cannon ball hit at Gettysburg, was replaced as commander of the 3rd Corps by General French. The Union troops under French were given orders to attack the left flank of General Lee's retreating army. A hard but short fight in the arena of Manassas Gap left French and his men the losers on July 24th. Lee and his Rebels slipped away toward Culpeper, Virginia. The 3rd Corps received orders not to pursue Lee any further but instead, to report to their new position of duty on the line of the Rappahannock River. John Granger and his regiment were among those who marched toward Wapping Heights, Virginia, on July 25th.

Granger's letters home reflected his extreme pro-Union sentiment, the same fervor that had driven him to enlist, putting aside wife and family to fight for his dear country. A wagon maker by trade, John couldn't help but notice and remark on the various features of the countryside – crops and soil conditions, as he and his fellow men marched southward. "It rained almost every day that we were in Md. & Pa. It must have spoiled a great deal of their wheat. This is a very nice country where we are. Nice crops grow here, but it will the most of it be wasted. I do not pity the inhabitants for they are rank secesh. They ought to suffer."

John Granger also keenly felt the loss of his brother, Luther, in the Battle of Gettysburg, in which Luther had sustained a mortal bullet wound to his head. As fate would have it, Luther had survived through the battles at Fredericksburg, Chancellorsville, and even Burnside's "Mud March." At these other battles, the colossal blunders and ineptitude of leadership caused these men to march directly into harm's way. Luther's life ended quickly, simply, and within 200 miles of his home and on his native soil. John's response to questions about Luther's death was penned in his letter of August 1st to wife, Cornelia: "Well ma you said father wanted to know whether anyone saw Luther after he was killed. That I could depend on their word. There was two of our company saw him. They were well acquainted with him. They say that they know him. His cap had 2 red feathers. One on the right side & one on the top & a piece of oil cloth put in the back of his cap to make it larger. They say that he was badly swollen but they recognized him in a moment. I cannot tell you anything about his burial. The details were made of those that I were not acquainted with & was made before I had found out that Luther was dead. So much for that." And John's letters rarely re-opened the grief-laden subject of his having lost his brother in battle.

If we were to take stock at this point and consider what John Granger had experienced by now, we would be observing a man who had marched great distances, fought terribly hard, lost his brother, and finally, who was grieving, sad, lonely, and overwhelmed that the war had not yet ended. John truly believed that he was fighting for a righteous cause; he was religious and very close to family back home, and would do what it required to preserve the Union and his home. The "rank secesh" were wrong, and he was willingly participating in the military action to justify all the destruction he had witnessed over the past year of the war.

True to military action, the depersonalization of the enemy allows the soldiers to present a united mind-set against the foes. The Union troops' commanders were no exception to this, and the Rebels and general citizenry became the "rank secesh" instead of ordinary folks. John Granger must have felt tremendous animosity toward the Confederates, after engaging in the series of battles and still not having won the decisive battle that would restore the Union. This extended War Between the States had not measured up to the anticipation of a very short-term police action on the part of the North. Weeks and months, and now years had passed, and the Union was still divided. John succumbed to the feelings that the "enemy" was a force to be conquered, in the name of the Union Army. His hope was that the conflict would soon end, and thoughts of home fueled his actions against the Confederates. Surprisingly and despite the strong sentiment against the Rebels, these Union troops fought exclusively against Southern soldiers, not against the civilians.

Chapter Eight
The Last Letter from Camp:
"Hip Hip Hurrah"

Time passed ever so slowly for the Union soldiers when they were in camp. Towards the end of July, 1863 John was reassigned to the 129th Invalid Corps, due to his now-failing health. John Granger's spirits flagged, and he reached the depths of despair as his fellow men were being discharged from military service. The New Year came in 1864, but John was still in camp. He did not see any fighting action after the Battle of Gettysburg, but he did serve, and was promoted to Sergeant. Every soldier alive, no matter what his or her motivation was for enlisting or being drafted into military service, anxiously awaits to hear the news; "You are hereby discharged." They longed to tell their families that they were coming home. In John's case, the news to his family would take the form of a grand letter home, with the words they all hoped to hear from him. "I am coming home!"

"Depot Camp Cliffbourne Barracks Va. Feb 12th 1864

"Dear wife & children I received a letter from you on the 10th dated 8th. I was glad to hear that you were well but sorry that you feel so down hearted. I hope I shall live to get out of this miserable concern. I have been trying some time to get an examination before the doctor. Well this morning I went before the board and they thought they could not discharge me so my hopes are gone on that point. I think it is mean for I know they have discharged a good many in my company that is not half as bad off as I am but that is just my luck. Well yesterday there was thirteen in my company got their discharge and in a few days more there will be some ten or twelve more. Well I am glad to see them get away. I only wish that I might be as lucky. Well enough of this. If they fill this company up and get some scripts here than kiss my arse for all the duty they got out of me. I have done my share. (Well I have just been called to the Capt. Office & there found the board had ordered my discharge.) Hip hip hurrah. So keep dark. If nothing happens I shall be at home in three weeks or less. Don't say anything about it nor let anyone know one word. I want to take them by surprise. I had felt downhearted all the forenoon and discouraged and when I commenced this letter I did not think I should hear such good news. I am almost afraid to believe it myself for fear there will be some slip about it. I suppose it will take all of this month for my papers to get around. Well I shall wait very patiently for them. I guess you may answer this letter and I will write again & let you know how I get along. Well ma I hope my papers will go through quick so I will not write any more now. Give my respects to all inquiring friends. My love to you all. Good day. Yours ever. J. W. Granger.

"N.B. I have not received that letter from Henry that you spoke of & I am very sorry to hear such news from the River. Well they need not get in a family way because I think myself just as good as they. I little thought they would treat any of us cooly. Oh what I mean when I said you might answer this letter was this that I guess I shall have time to get an answer from this before my discharge comes for you know that just as soon as I can get out of this I shall start for home. J. W. Granger"

Many soldiers were still being drafted. John was finally going home. There must have been a tremendous out-pouring of excitement when John W. Granger, battle weary Union soldier, returned home to his family! John's wife, Cornelia, preserved his legacy by keeping all of his letters home. We have been so privileged to share the intimate insight into the thoughts and feelings of one soldier who voluntarily enlisted in the 57th PA Veteran Infantry in 1861. Our gratitude to the Granger family runs deep. Our glimpse of a Union soldier's experiences from John's perspective is intensified by his verbal expression. Rarely has the general historian been blessed with a participant's narrative, as has been the case with the Granger letters. The various battles and skirmishes of the Civil War have been personalized for our benefit, and we feel that we could easily approach John W. Granger to make his acquaintance. "Welcome home, John!"

The Diary of John W Granger
1861 - 1864

In the Fall of 1861 the Civil War was heating up, and most Northern Americans thought that it would be a quick and decisive war. More like a battle than a war. A way of showing the Rebels that the South was a part of the United States of America and not a sovereign nation unto itself. Certainly John and Luther Granger felt this way. At age 41 John was one of the older men in his hometown of Rush, Pennsylvania to volunteer. His brother Luther, a few years his junior, went with him. They expected to be home with a few good stories and a few months of patriotic soldiering under their belts. It was not to be. Here is John's story.

Important Copyright Notice

1861

November 1861

November 19, 1861 - Camp Curtain.

Dear wife and children. I take this opportunity to write you a few lines to let you know how I get along. Well when I left home I thought I should come back within one week. But I cannot. Please forgive me for enlisting. We had a very pleasant time coming to Harrisburg. Got there at 3 o'clock on Sunday morning. Went to camp the same morning. It was very cold. We went to our tents got our own breakfast. In the afternoon Ad and I went to Camp Cameron to see the boys. We found them well and right glad to see us. Came back to our camp the same night. Slept with Luther and the Hinds boys. Lay pretty cold. I thought of our own bed at home but am bound to make the best of it. I hope you will enjoy yourself. Keep up good courage. Let them know you are a truehearted woman. Tell the boys to mind you and think of me. We have enough to eat but it is not such fare as we had at home. Luther has grown fat since he came here. The surgeon thinks camp life will do me good. I could get along first rate if it was not for sleeping cold at night. Please send me a good old comforter and two towels by H W Lung. I may stay here all winter and may not. We may start for Washington in three or four weeks. We do not know anything about it. The company seem to like me first rate. They were determined that I should not come back. It may turn out for the best. Time will tell. It may make a steady man of me, although there is all sorts of vice here, our orders are very strict and I for one shall obey orders. If ever I do come back, you nor the children shall not have it to say that I made a ass of myself. I should like to see you and the boys and hope I shall as soon as spring. I am writing on a board sitting on the floor holding it in my lap. Nerves not very steady and am afraid they will not be when I think of wife and children. Do not grieve nor give way to bad feelings. Take care of your health. I intend this by H W Lung. He intends to start for home this afternoon. I shall write to you again as soon as we can get our tent organized and my feelings settled a little. You may think my feeling would not be worked up to this pitch but I have feelings yet. But enough of this. Our camp is large and a good many thousands of soldiers here. I must close for Ad is ready to start. So good by. God bless you. From your ever loving husband.

Direct Camp Curtain in care of Captain Hunter.

November 28, 1861 - Camp Curtain.
Dear wife and children I take this opportunity to write you a few lines to let you know how I get along. Well in the first place I am enjoying tolerable good health. Have rather a hard cold. Today is pleasant. I am to work in a hospital at 40 cents per day in addition to my soldier pay. I commenced yesterday at noon. Think I shall have a chance to work about two weeks. If I do the pay will come good for tobacco & tea &c. Now in regard to our business affairs you had better have that new cutter finished off and sell it the first good chance you get & take the old cutter, fix and paint that over again. Sell that if you wish for ten or twelve dollars. That new wagon you will see to. See that is finished and painted. Sell it on one years time if you cannot do better. Take tight notes for all you sell. Keep things snug. Take good care of all you have. See that Edward takes care of the things out of doors, and in the shop impress upon his mind the responsibility that he is under while I am absent. Now I will tell you about my enlisting. I enlisted as a teamster but cannot get that situation until I go into regular service. I have to drill as a private while in Camp Curtain for they have no teamsters here. My wages will be when I get out of here $20 per month, so they tell me if we ever go out. But I think we shall be sent home in the spring hope we shall. If we stay in Camp Curtain this winter I shall be at home about the 1st of Jan if nothing happens, and maybe before. So wait with patience. Ad tells me that Jos Gupper and Dunham had a fight. Bully for that. I don't care a darn which whipped. He had ought to have got James revolver and that would have killed him as quick as the rattlesnake got killed when he bit the woman. Today they say is Sunday but you would think of everything else but Sunday. I am to work on that hospital yet and hope to get something to pay a part of my expenses. I want you to take good care of yourself and the boys, should be glad to see you all and hope I shall ere long. I think I have wrote about enough so good by. My love to all inquiring friends. From your Husband

Camp Curtain, Harrisburg

60

December 1861

December 1, 1861 - Camp Curtain, Harrisburgh.

Dear wife and children I take this opportunity to write you a few lines. I began to think you had forgotten me but when Ad came I found you had been mindful of me and wished for me to have things comfortable for which you shall ever have my warmest thanks and the first place in my heart. No other shall share the joys that you and I have. When I think of home and the comforts of home I often wish I was by my own fireside surrounded by wife and children. But you know how it has been for sometime past. If I wanted to help any of my neighbors there was a great talk about it. The fact was they all thought it was done for sinister motives. I hope now that I am gone they will have something else to talk about. I do not want you to take any of this to yourself for I have no blame for you. Had it not have been for you I should have left long ago. You know something what my feelings has been & in regard to Father Henry Warden & Roman. I presume they are sorry that I have left, but do not know but they are glad. If they are I am as well suited as they. I am afraid it will bother you to read this but you must make great allowance I am not at home to write. I am a going to write to father a short letter and you will hand it to him for me. Well now in regard to my going today, I did not go. But should have gone last Monday morning only I had lent all my money and could not get it. For that reason I did not go. The boys made me promise to go with them. Oslo said if I would go with him he would share the last cent with me and Kinyon the same. I am almost sorry I did not go for Oslo felt so bad about it he said to all in the camp I had been his father and he felt safe when I was with him. Jos Kinyon said he had rather I would go with him than his own brother. So much for this. Well in regard to camp life it is a dogs life to live. To stand in the mud up to your ankles and eat your bread and stinking meat with a pint cup of something they call coffee (but do not know what it is) and shiver with the cold until you are in danger of biting your tongue off is no great fun I tell you. But we will stand it somehow or other at any rate for a while. Do not let anyone know but we fare first rate. We can tell each other our little affairs without letting the rest know it.

December 11, 1861 - Camp Curtain.
Dear wife and children. I take this opportunity to write you a few lines to let you know that I arrived here all safe and sound and sound. Found the company here. We shall not start from here until tomorrow. The orders have been changed so that we do not know where we shall go yet after we get to Washington. You need not write until you hear from me again. I found Luther almost sick with cold. He says he is a good deal better now. The rest of the boys are well. I have not much time to write for we have got to go to Harrisburgh to get our guns. We shall have to be very busy until we get started from this place. I think of the pleasant visit at home and never shall forget it nor do I believe you will. You have seen my likeness no doubt. How do you like it? Keep it as long as you live. Afternoon. Have been to Harrisburgh and got our guns and the rest of the lacklins. Our load will be as much as we can carry. I hope to have a chance to write to you soon. Give my best respects to all inquiring friends. Take good care of yourself. Keep up good courage. Your husband and father.

December 13, 1861 - Camp Curtain.
Dear wife, it is with pleasure that I have a chance to write you a few lines. We are in a great hurry at this time as we are about to start from this place to Washington. I wish you would write to me as soon as you can. I am well so is Luther. We did not start before on account of arms. Your certificate you will find enclosed all right. Should be glad to write more but seems a waste of time and confusion. Direct to, Company A, Reg. 57 PV, Washington DC. I can get all letters directed in that way. I feel anxious to hear from you. Hope to see you again soon. Yours fondly.

December 17, 1861 – Washington, DC.
Dear wife and children I take this opportunity to let you know how I get along. Well after packing and unpacking we finally got started from camp on Saturday and got on board on some old freight cars and almost froze until we got to Baltimore. Then we fared better. We got to into Washington at 9 Sunday night, stayed until morning. Went to the Capitol. The greatest thing that I ever saw. I will give you the size of it.

The length is 751 feet long

Width 352

Wings the same, 324 each

Width of wings, 172

Height, 267

I traveled until I was tired. Went on the top. Could see 10 miles and see the camps of over 250,000 soldiers. Such sights I never saw before. We are encamped in sight of the capitol and within three miles of it. Our duty is pretty hard. Traveling and being on guard has at this time has worn me almost out. The weather is fine dry and nice. I am in hopes of getting home again some time but do not know when. Yesterday we heard heavy firing on the Potomac all day. Supposed they have been fighting but cannot hear from there this morning. I was up all night on guard and cannot write but will as soon as I can. Write and let me know how you and the rest get along. While writing this I have probably heard 40 cannon fired. There is camps on every side of us. All is confusion here. You would be crazy in one day here.

Direct to Granger 57th Regt. Company A Washington DC.

How long we shall stay here I do not know but if we go from here our letters will be sent after us. Give my love to all of my friends. Yours ever.

December 19, 1861 - Washington DC
We do not know who to trust here. We dare not buy a pie or cake for fear of poison. We hear of several that has been poisoned in this way. That battle that I wrote to you about I cannot tell anything about for I have not seen a paper since I came into this camp. We do not have the liberty that we had in Camp Curtain. We have not had any snow here. The nights are cold and frosty the days clear and comfortable. Camp life is not as pleasant as it is to stay at home I can tell you but I hope to come out all safe. I think that I shall know how to enjoy home. My health is very good. Have some cold but not as much as should expect for we have slept on the damp ground ever since we have been here. But we hope to have some straw to sleep on shortly. I want you to write to me all about the folks in Rush how they get along & I will write to Maria & Betsy as soon as I can. It is not convenient to write in a small tent where there is 16 noisy men all talking at a time swearing laughing and all confusion and then sit on the ground (all we have for a table is that small chest that I took from home. I do not know what we should do without it). The country is nice around here. We can see from our camp any quantity of camps all

around us. It beats all you can think of but there is not the pleasure in all of this as there would be in the enjoyments of home & the society of wife & children. I hope we shall not be long separated. Keep your courage up and I will mine. Grin and bear it. There is one thing about it I have seen a great deal of the ways of the world that I should not have not seen if it had not been for this war. You will this find this letter full of mistakes. You would not wonder at that if you should see me while writing this. I must lay this by for the present and finish it some other time for the men begin to crawl out of their nest so good morning. December 20th. Well I will try to finish this letter now. Today got hold of a paper. Did not see any account of any great battles. I see by the papers that C. Low brother of G. Low has been taken prisoner by the pickets. I want to send the paper home but it got messed up so that I could not. I filled this sheet full.

December 20, 1861 (morning)
I must write you a little more. I had ought to scold you for not writing to me. Yesterday I saw a negro drummed out of camp for saucing the Col. He had a large stick of wood tied to his back and marched before a file of soldiers with bayonets. My health is very good and Capt. thinks we will not stay here over two weeks, but we do not know anything about it. You can direct your letters to the same place until I tell you. How I should like to be at home and see you and the rest of the folks. I think we have a very healthy place here. Our tent is round and covers 19 feet of ground with 17 men inside. You see we have but little room. Last night we adopted a rule to stop swearing in our tent and every evening read two or three chapters in the testament of first rate plan if they will stick to it. It is so much more pleasant don't you think. So camp life is bad enough at the best but when we all behave our self we can add to such others comfort. Well dear wife I must bid you good by for this morning. Yours truly.

December 22, 1861 – Washington, DC.
Dear wife and children it is with feelings of gratitude that I have the privilege of writing to you again. I received a paper and letter from home yesterday. Was glad to hear from you. I was getting uneasy but the letter done me more good than my food. I always knew your affections were strong for me and mine are the same for you and will always remain the same. I should be so glad to see you and take that kissing as you would be to give it. You know

I always was a great hand for hours but never knew how to prize it before. But I hope to do my country some good if it cost me my life but hope that I may be spared to my family for a long time to enjoy the comforts of home and friends. I anticipate meeting with you all again. Won't that be joyful? I think it will. I must go to dinner. Just eat and feel first rate but it is not home. I have my ups and downs as usual and always expect to. And now about that lying. I never told him any such thing. He accused me of telling Maria about his playing cards. He said to me that she wrote to him all about the Northumberland matter but I turned it off the best that I could. So much for that. You spoke about Lady Jane. What has become of the governor with all his military pride lost. Jim have to chop wood or will he pay in land for I suppose he is short for change. Enough of this. The less I think of them the better I feel. If I had never have seen them we should been better off. But the past we will let go and try to do better in the future. But let this be all forgot. I often feel as though had reasons to dislike me but I know you do not nor never will. I will write a few lines for the rest of my friends. Tell Norman that I feel under great of obligations to him for favors and shall as long as I live. If I live to come back, tell him that I shall bring that revolver back with me and hope I shall bring a good report with me to. Tell Henry and his family that I have a brother's affection for them and never shall I forget them. If you want counsel call on Henry and I presume he will assist you if it lays in his power. Tell father and mother I have not forgotten them. I still have the affections of a son towards a parent and I hope I shall not forget the obligations that I am under to them. Tell the neighbors I should be glad to see them and tell them some stories but do not let them know, as I ever shall have the privilege but hope I shall all alive and sound. If some of them should be here, there eyes would stick out some I reckon. It is something to see. Seventeen thousand horsemen on drill at a time. See artillery training at a times and see them throw shells one mile and a half and burst in the air. Our boys went out of camp yesterday and found some of the shells and balls. They look curious enough. My health is very good. I do not know but I stand it as well as any of them. I think the officers think as much of me as any of the privates. I shall try to behave myself like a gentleman. You know that I always could make friends. Let me go were I would and so will and so will everybody if they believe themselves. Treat everyone with respect if you wish to gain respect. How often I have thought of that short visit at home. I feel like a different person. It done me more good than anything that I ever saw in Rush. But my feelings in regard to my family are such as only a parent can feel but no one can describe it. Seems to me that I never knew how much I thought of you and my two boys. If they should be left without a father what a sad thing. But hundreds have been left in the same way. But I pray this may not be your lot in this cruel war. A war waged by a few of means. Men for political favors and I am afraid those same will try to keep the war agoing while they make a fortune out of it and sacrifice thousands of lifes. I wish they had to take the place of a private and endure the privations that we and others have to endure. They would sure be as sick as I. I sent your certificate. You did not speak of it. Did you receive it? If you did lay in for two months pay. You might well know how I felt when I sat for that picture. I am glad it pleased you. I live in hopes of letting you see the original of that picture between this and spring. But cannot tell but wish I could. My clothes are getting dirty and I shall have to wash them this week. The col. will not let any women come into camp to do our washing. There is just two women in camp. One is a Capt. wife. One is a private's wife. She does some washing but she charges too much. We shall do our own. Our fare is very good better than in Camp Curtain. But the other arrangements are not so good. I do not know as I have any special news to write at this time but will write to you often. Please do the same for me. How I should like to come in and see you and suppose you would. Would you not be tickled? I think you would. Well it is time to quit this for fear of trying your patience.

December 24, 1861 – Washington, DC.

Dear Wife and children I once more have the privilege of writing you a few lines how I get along. I am well and enjoy very good health and I sincerely hope you enjoy the same blessing. I wrote to you on Sunday. Well it commenced raining on Sunday night. It rained all night and Monday the wind blew like fury. Last night I thought it would blow our tent to Halifax. It was as cold as blazes. This morning we were called out on guard. My time came at 11 o'clock. Two hours on. Came off at 1 o'clock. I have to go on at 5 o'clock and then again at 11 and off at 1 o'clock and again at 4 in the morning and stay on until 7 o'clock. Then we should be clear for nearly one week. But we shall have to drill enough to make up for that. We do not have a chance to write only a little at a time and then amid confusion and the talking or laughing of twenty men. I have got so that I can talk and write and get along very well. I shall have to stop until tomorrow then I will try to finish this letter. Wednesday, December 25. Well I am once more at liberty again. It was cold last night to stand on guard. I slept about 1 hour but I felt quite well. Today it is very pleasant. The sun shines and it is quite warm but very slippery. It thaws considerable. I have been about two miles from camp to get cedar trees to ornament our camp for Christmas but it is not much of a Christmas for me. I would give more for me. He wanted I should come to his camp and see him. I think I shall as soon as can. Last night while standing I could see the signals going up in the air in every direction and there was a great deal of firing way over the river. Today we hear heavy cannonading up the Potomac. We think they are fighting somewhere and do not know how soon we shall have to cross the river. But it is not likely we shall have to go into action yet for we are not drilled sufficient yet but will have to say behind for there is a good many thousands here on this side of the river that are drilled pretty good. It will take sometime to get drilled for we drill as skirmishers. That is difficult. We are not examined at all after we left Camp Curtain. We may get were it is warmer than here. If the war will close by spring and let us go home I will be satisfied. Would not you. But we cannot tell anything about it.

December 28, 1861
The mud is about 1 ½ inch deep and is the worst mud that you saw. The day is fine. I want you to write to me all about the folks everyone. How they get along. How do you get along? How does Ed get along? Tell Billy his pa thinks of him every day and hour too and the rest of them. I cannot help but think I shall see you in the spring. Hope I shall. The times passes off very fast. For all it is hard times. Now ma I am not what you would called homesick nor do I mean to be for you know when I make up my mind to do a thing I will stick to it if it takes the hair off. I think if I could get hold of that old jug about this time, it would do some good for I had not had one drop since we came to Washington. Maybe I shall get to be temperate but I will have revenge on some of it one of these days if I live. How I should like to get home and see you and the boys. We expect to get our pay the first of Jan. If we do I will send you some money. I wish you could wash my clothes but it is much to far to carry my washing. Wm. Hinds talks of going home

the last of this week. If he does I will send some of my clothes for I have more than want. I bought one under shirt and gave eighty-seven cents for it brand new at that. If he should come home, send me a vest and them bullet molds that belongs to that revolver or a good lot of bullets. He will not be back here in three or four weeks. I looked for a letter today but did not get any. You must write twice a week and I wish you would three times. I will write three times a week if I can get any chance at all for it does not take me but an hour to write two sheets. Tell me whether Ed got that money for G. Pickett or not. Tell me if he settled with Doc Small and if he got any pay of D. Sely or if Barney Carrol has paid anything on that note. Tell him to be saving as he can but do not scrimp at all. Take all the comfort you can and I hope sometime to share with you. I think if we could live together again, we should take as much comfort as anybody could. We have enjoyed each other's society probably as well as any of our neighbors and maybe better. Try and not refrain at our lot for I think it was ordered all for the best. Hope it will. You know I always get out of a scrape when I get in but this one and hope to get out of this. I feel as though I would and hope it will. I care nothing for myself. I can endure almost anything but when I think of the trouble I have brought upon you I feel as though I ought to suffer a great deal. I know you do not want to censure me. Sometimes I almost wish you would for I know I deserve it. But I believe if I should come home honorable you would be glad to see me and if ever I come home at all I will come in that way. I must close ever more my love to you and the children. My best respects to all. J W Granger

I shall never forget you as long as I shall live. Forgive and forget all that has gone wrong. Happy Christmas to you but not to me.

December 29, 1861
Well I must write you a full letter. I wish you would inquire of Howard where Ferris & Leyman is. If we can find out we will go and see them. I suppose they are in the marine barracks but do not know. Well then let me know where Oslo is whether in Ind. or Ky. You said he was in Jeffersonville and did not know whether in the state of Ky. or Ind. Well you said Ad was at home and had a good supper. I was glad to hear you had something good and should have liked to have been there with you. I think we could enjoyed ourselves first rate. I think I shall know how to enjoy civilian life if ever I have a chance don't you. You spoke of getting up a box of

provisions for us. We have plenty of bread and meat and potatoes once a day. We have rice three times a week. I keep about two loaves of bread on hand. If we had some butter and cheese it would be good. But we could buy it if we had money enough. Butter at 25 & 30 cents per pound. Cheese at 20 cents per pound. But we get along very well without it. Well I must stop and dress for service. It does seem as though the more our officers can bother us the better it suits them. I do feel stiff sometimes I can tell you. Well after standing in the cold for an hour and hearing a dry discourse, I am at liberty to write a little more. If I were to tell you my feelings, it would take a long time. You know enough of them to know I have no feelings of hardness towards you. Although you have reasons to feel hard towards me. I hope you do not. For all of that I think if I live to get home and a free man again, I shall not sell my liberty very soon. I believe that I should know how to enjoy it. I think the war will end by spring. They had a battle in Missouri. Our men took 2500 prisoners and a great deal of munitions. On Thursday they had a battle at Fairfax courthouse in Va. We could hear the firing as plain as day. They fought all day. In the forenoon the rebels got the advantage but our men got reinforced in the afternoon and then they gave it to them. Took 1300 prisoners. Killed 200 of the rebels. Our men lost about 200 killed. Our men are making ready to march on the other side of the river. If the war should last two years we do not know whether we should have to go on or not for they will keep a great many to guard Washington. But for all of that we may have to go. I have not much news to write that will interest you but I will write so as to let you know how I get along. I do not want you to think that I was mad at you for not writing but it did seem so long since I heard from home that I got impatient. This you will please excuse. If I could only see you and the children if only a few hours it would do me a great deal of good. Well my wife I must close and bid you a short goodbye. This you will receive New Years if nothing happens. Tell all the folks that I am well and would be glad to see them. This from your ever loving husband. J. W. Granger.

December 30, 1861 – Washington, DC.
Dear wife and children. I have a chance to write you a few lines. In the first place I received a letter from you the 26. It cheered me up more than anything else in a good while. The same day I sent one to you. The next day we struck our tent, shoulder knapsacks

and all of our stuff and started for another camp. We marched about ¾ of a mile set our tents and fixed our quarters. We have a got a better place to camp than we had before. It was so wet that almost half of our company was sick. My health is better than I could expect. To be sure I have a bad cold but I think my health is better than when it rains. I believe the climate agrees with my condition if we could live as we would at home. Well yesterday three of us got a pass to go to another camp. Well we went through the city and went where Jed Johnson, Curt Dunmore and S. Lothrops boys and I saw John Shove. I did not know him but he knew me. I have seen any quantity of Susq boys since I have been here. John's health is quite poor but he says it is better. Curt Dunmore is in the hospital. I went in and saw him. He said he should be out in a few days. Now dear wife you wished me to give some advice in regard to Maria. I do not know what to tell you. I know that I could not stand it with them children and am sorry for you. If you could get them away home some how or other without making them mad it would be a good thing for you. One of my eyes is very sore but am in hopes it will get along all right. It is painful but I have not even asked from anything yet. But I think I could if I should ask it. You know I do not mope around nor do not mean to. What I have to do that I will do cheerful. That does not make half as hard but enough of this. Last night when I came home I found a letter from you. Now you do not know how much good it does me when I get a letter from you. It made me feel bad to with all the rest you spoke of your troubles and you thought there was not anything but trouble for you. I feel for you and would gladly do anything that was in my power to comfort you and favor you but I am now placed in a situation that I cannot do as I would but I hope to be at liberty again but do not know when. If it where not for hope the heart would break. You spoke of a testament each of the soldiers where presented with one. So I shall not need another one. We have not got our pay yet but we expect it the first of this week.

December 31, 1861 – Washington, DC.

Dear wife and children. I take this opportunity to write you a few lines. I have just received a letter from you dated Dec 27. I tell you it does me as much good to get a letter from home as it does to hear of a battle. I tell you I am uneasy about you all the time for fear you or some of the children will get sick or something happen to you but when I get a letter from home and you say you are all well then I feel better. I have received three letters from you since I got to Washington and feel thankful for them. My feelings have not changed towards you nor ever will. Let people say what they will. That Ad Lung I begin to think as little of him as anybody for I plainly see he intended to make believe that there is something wrong in me when the fault is in himself. As for me saying anything about you of the kind that he told Maria I say it is the most willful falsehood that was ever told. He nor any other person ever heard me speak of you in that manner and furthermore no person ever heard me speak disrespectful of you so much for that. Well now about the Northumberland scrape. I do not know what he means unless it is to make believe that I done something wrong but I am not aware of any act of mine that I am ashamed of and anyone need be either. Now the times that I came back from home he accused me of telling Maria of his playing cards and losing by it at Northumberland. But I turned it off the best I could. He told me that he promised Maria that he would not play when he left home. But he did play and supposed the reason he told such stuff about me so as to shelter himself. But there is one thing about it I am willing for any decent person to follow me where I go and see if they can find anything unbecoming or ungentlemen. If they can then I will give it up and not until then. But enough of this. You spoke in your letter about being in pain when you wrote that letter and wished for me to be there with you. If I could have that privilege it seems to me it would be as happy an hour as I ever saw. The thought of that visit that we had in that place will never be forgot by me as long as I live nor the hurting that took place on the morning that I left for Camp Curtain. Let a few of them mean ones howl as much as they please. They have prayed upon my family all they ever will. I hope if ever I come back I shall know enough to take care of myself and family and look to my own reputation. You spoke of Mrs. Kinyon and the old lady. Tell them when I see them that I have not forgotten them nor the little ones neither. Should be very glad to see them and hope to. I am of the opinion that we shall all get home in the spring if we live. But it is a hard case to live in a camp. We catch cold so easy while standing on guard around the camp you a continual coughing and sneezing and snoring enough to scare anyone.

1862

In 1862 the Civil War entered a new phase. The South had won the first battle. The North was still convinced that the end would be quick and certain.

The Granger Brothers were sent to defend the Northern capital city of Washington, DC.

1862 brought the Granger Brothers to places like Williamsburg and Fredericksburg. 1862 brought them face to face with the death and misery of war. 1862 made it all seem very real indeed.

1862

January 1862

January 4, 1862 – Washington, DC

Dear wife and children, I take this opportunity to write you a few lines to let you know how I get along. Well in the first place I am in comfortable good health and spirits for me. I sent you a letter on the 2nd or the 3rd. The weather was rather cold but it did not storm today it snowed enough to make the ground white and it is pretty cold. It looks rather lonesome but I think it will get warmer in a few days. Hope it will for it will seem more comfortable. Our tents are pretty cold but we manage to get along. We do not know how long we shall stay in this place. We may stay all winter and we may not stay one week. We may not move from here until the war is over. The soldiers do not know anymore where we shall go than you do at home. There is all sorts of talk where we shall go. Some say to Beaufort. Some say to one place and some to another. But when we move I will let you know. I do not believe we shall go far this winter and I do not care if we do not for I think the war will be over by spring. Hope it will so that we can all get home. Well ma it is Saturday night and three of us are sitting around that little chest and writing at the same time. Cold on one side and not very warm on the other. When the weather is very cold some of us sit up and keep fire. That is when we can get wood. What little straw we had is all gone and we have to take the bare ground and that is damp and cold and hard at that. I have been vaccinated in my arm and it is quite sore but I have kept around and intend to for if a person gets sick here it is not like home. I can think just how much comfort I could take if I were at home in that snug parlor with you and a good cheerful fire, but when that time will come the Lord only knows whether it will be or not. But rest assured of one thing my thoughts are of home and those I think are friends. I looked for letter tonight but did not get any, but think I shall on Monday. Yesterday there was a great deal of firing across the river. About ten miles from us they had quite a battle. They sent over on this side of the river after one or two batteries of flying artillery they went out and drove the rebels back. It was a continual war for half a day here. Much they done I have not learned. They have a little brush with the rebels two or three times a week but do not seem to do much. I should not wonder if they had a large battle at Bull

Run. It is the opinion of almost everybody that if we gain that place we are all safe for that is their strong hold. I hope we shall do better this time than we did when we attacked it before. Well you may know more about the war news than we do here. Well I should like to just come in and see how you get along. And if you could just peep in and see us and not let anyone know it, I should like it just to see how we soldiers file in together. I tell you it is a caution to cripples. We suffer great many inconveniences but the officers think anything is good enough for a private but I think quite different. And I feel myself just as good as any of them. Well ma I must close for a night and will try to finish my letter tomorrow, if I live. Here is hoping you will rest good and hope I shall to. I know I should if I were at home with you and a good by.

January 5 - Sunday morning 10 o'clock.

Washington, DC. So they say it is Sunday but you would not know it by their actions for there is no Sunday here. It is cold this morning and disagreeable weather. I find myself quite comfortable this morning. How is it with you? Could I step in this morning and see how you get along and spend the day with you I think it would be a great pleasure. Indeed it would do me good to see familiar faces again and enjoy their society once more and hope it may be so again soon. But do not know as it will be granted to us to enjoy such others society again in this world, but we must hope for the best. It will not do to give up to despair but we must keep up good courage. You was speaking about Ad and Maria and her children that they were a going to leave. I am glad to hear it for I am sure you will take a great deal more comfort. I do not see how you stand it as long as you did for they are such a pest. I had as live in camp as with them noisy brats. I do not feel very well towards Ad either for I believe he is just as mean as mean ought to be. You cannot believe anything he says. I did not think he would be so ungrateful as much I as I have done for him (I think it is just what we must expect of such whelps). But enough of this. I have not got my pay yet and am a getting short for money, have got just eight cents left. If you should lend me one dollar just as well as not it would come very acceptable just now. I may get my pay this week and may not. If you cannot send it just as well or not, do not put yourself to any trouble for I can get along. It is to bad to have to bother you I know but we have to pay the highest price for everything we get it takes the money off pretty fast. They owe me over three dollars in Camp Curtain yet and guess they will owe me when I left. They agreed to get the money and send it to you but I guess they will forget it. I have lent a little money in this camp but am sure of getting that as soon as they draw their pay. Our tobacco cost us more than twice as much as it did at home. Mine cost me eight cents per day, that is about fifty-six cents per week but I guess we will get along some how or other. We have some first rate fellows in our tent and some rather mean ones. Well I wish I had something to write that would interest you but cannot think of anything that will please you. Well I will stop now and wait a little. Well I have been down and seen Simon Myres he says he has just sent a letter to Clarinda so she will hear from him before you get this. Well ma give my love to all the friends. Write as often as you can tell me all the news. Tell me if Huntsman has sent his clothes back or not. Yesterday Judge Reed's son came to our camp. He is with Harris in the barracks. We expect to see Harris in a few days. Tell me tell me if Mrs. J. Kinyon hears from James often. Tell her where I am so that maybe James or Orlo will write to me. Well ma I must close. Wishing you and the children all the good luck in the world. Yours Truly and ever.

No.2 1862

Well Cornelia I will try to finish this letter. Well what do you think? I received a letter from you tonight dated Dec. 30 and was glad to hear from you and glad to hear that you were all well. I have been looking over my letters that I have received five letters from you. I guess your letters come all strait. I overlook one of them. Luther got a letter from Henry tonight. I have received two newspapers from home today. I received two papers from Montrose, one Democrat and one Republican and I received a letter from Wesley Faurot of Montrose. I got acquainted with him going from Montrose to Scranton. When I left home he made me promise to write to him and he would send me the papers so I can. So I have wrote to Betsy and Maria since I have been here but have not yet an answer got. Tell the folks I should like to have any of them write to me but do not know as I could get time to write to them for when I get time to write I must and will write to my family for I think it will be received with more pleasure. Tonight H. Hinds and me are sitting up to keep fire for the rest to sleep so that they will not take cold. It is pretty cold tonight although there is not any snow nor have we seen any since we have been here. It makes me feel a little home sick when I think of a good woodshop to work in and stay at night to think of that good warm old kitchen. Say nothing of the parlour and then a good warm bed. Say nothing of bedfellow (but of course I have to think of that too) and it is enough to make a child strike his father and then not do your country any good in the end but just eat up their captures. That I don't care anything about for we get punished enough I should think to pay for all our sins that we were committed against our government (well I guess you will think I am getting off some of my old notes there is some of the old John in me yet.) We have not got but three men in our camp that is older than myself. But I act about as young as any of them. I will bet you if we should all come home safe and sound we would have our gay old time, don't you think to? I was glad to hear that you was a going to get rid of them noisy children. I am sure you can enjoy yourself a great deal better than you do now. Well Cornelia you must not let any of the folks know that I grumble. Tell them that I get along first rate for I do, but I tell you everything just as I feel for I think you are entitled to all of my confidences, and I write to you just as I feel but should not like to have everyone know. There is a great many in our company that are homesick and some are sick otherwise. There is one boy that I think will die. His name is Potter his father lives on the North Branch and a reckon if he should die some of the Hinds will come home with his body. We have not drawn our pay yet. We were mustered for pay on Tuesday but we have not received our pay nor do we know when we shall. Now ma I must close by sending my love to you and the boys tell them pa would like to see them and hopes he will before a great while. Keep your courage up I will try to see (illegible name) as soon as I can and write in my next. My cold is a little better tonight. Hope I should get along without any trouble. Good night. Yours till death does us separate.

No.3 1862.

Well old lady it is about ten o'clock and I do not want to go to bed and I thought I would scribble a few more lines. Yesterday while I was in the Michigan Barracks I saw the man that took old John Brown at Harpers Ferry. He is a big stout fellow. Geo. Goodwin was here to see us yesterday morning. We had quite a visit before we went to the city. If we had some butter here (illegible) reckon of it but is so much trouble to you at and them so many in our tent that I do not know as it would pay but I know it would taste good. I have not tasted butter but once since I left Camp Curtain. Well now this is the titest time I have had to endure since I left home.

The boys are all laying on their blankets while Fred and I are writing to our wives. I read your letters over about a dozen times. I was sorry to hear Father was lamer than when I left home. I am afraid he will not stand it a great while but I hope he will live so that I can see him again and I hope all the neighbors and enjoy there friendship. You must excuse me for not mentioning receiving your letters for there is so much confusion here that a person cannot think of anything hardly. Well I am afraid you will get tired before you get this far so I think I will stop until about Sunday. Write as often as you can. Yours ever till death.

I must give you some description of the place around here. Well the hills are different here from what they are with you. The ground is rolling not steep. We can look from hill to hill for miles and in almost every direction can see the tents of the soldiers. The soil is of a reddish color, sandy and some of it stony. That is small round sandstone. It does not look as thought it would produce very good crops. Their fences are nothing at all. They do not build their houses by the road as we do but se them out in the lots. Well they do not have any roads but turnpikes in a good many places. They do not have any fence by the side of the road at all. We would think it a poor chance for farming but we saw some nice farms above Baltimore when we were coming down here and nice buildings. They looked like living. And the City of Baltimore is a nice place. Almost every building is made of brick and it looked very nice. It is a very large city. The bay comes up to the city. The route from Baltimore to Washington is not as pleasant as it is from Youk in Pa. to Baltimore. But the city of Washington is a great place. Take Pennsylvania Avenue is just as nice as it is pictured out. I should like to have a chance to go all through the city and see it and hope I shall. How long is Ad a going to stay around, and do you know whether he has joined another company? Them Hunters tell me how Jos Gruppers folks get along. See whether Mrs. G is jealous of him. We had a visit from Messers. I. L. Post and Chas Neal of Montrose on Sunday. They stayed some time and appeared to be glad to see us. I have not seen Herres since New Years. We expect him to visit us in our camp soon. We have not got our pay yet nor have we drawn any clothes since we have been in Washington, but we expect to draw our dress coats this week and we may get our money this week but do not know. I am sorry that I wrote to you for money for I am afraid you do not get as much as you need at home but when I draw my pay will try to send you some to help you along. Well I have wrote about all that I can think of. Write as soon as you can. Let me know how all the folks get along. I do not think it best to say much that will provoke them Jerseyites of Huntsmans for fear they will do some damage. Let everything remain as it is until I get back. That is if I should get back in the Spring, which I hope I shall. Have nothing to do with them about settling and I will tend to it. Now about the place of ours. I wish you would talk with Norman about it and see if it can be done with safety. If it can get him to draw up the deed and you can send it to me and I will sign it. You can tell him it is nothing more than right for you to hold it on account of your mother. This you need not let anyone know anything about, but him and our folks. Well it is almost 12 o'clock and I must close hoping that we may soon meet and see each other face to face. Good night. Hoping you will rest good. Should like to be with you. From you dear husband. Edward & Billy you must not forget your pa he would be glad to see you.

January 10, 1862 – Washington, DC
Dear wife & children I take this opportunity to write you a few lines to let you know how I get along. Well in the first place I am as well as could be expected. I have a bad cold and a hard cough but otherwise I am well. The weather is rainy the mud is 2 or 3 inch deep it has rained 2 days. We cannot stir out of our tent without getting in the mud. This is enough to make a fellow think of home. I can tell you but there is hundreds in the same fix. There is no saying a word you know I have nothing to do to day but write and cannot think of anything to write at that nor I do not believe you would either if you was in a small tent and chock full of noisy fellows talking laughing some swearing some playing cards. Our arrangements for reform I guess have gone up the glow hole. They are a wild lot in camp and it seems to me that a soldier has enough to provoke a saint but as for me I am a going to behave just as well as I can. I will not use profane language nor join in card playing but it is hard finding ways to amuse one self but for all that time passes very very fast. I do not feel homesick at all but for all of that I feel as though I had ought to be at home. I never had ought to have enlisted although my life is no better than anybody else but my business was such that I ought not have left but I may live to come home and straiten things up. Then we shall take comfort enough to make up loss time. It is the opinion of most of learned men that the war will close by spring if I live until

spring I shall try to come home if only on a furlough if I can get one. We have not got our pay yet nor is there any more prospect than there was ten days ago. I shall be glad when that box arrives. I think that a little butter will taste pretty good for we have not tasted of any since we left Harrisburgh. But after all we have not suffered much nor do we want too. Well ma I am afraid this letter will be dry for you but I hope you and the children are well. I hope D. Sely has had you some wheat and that beef he promised if he does not pay up I will write a letter to him. Tell Harry Johnson he must put in and work in that shop or he will never be worth anything. I am sorry Leon is a going to leave the shop but it may be all for the best if I should get home in the spring. Suppose it will take me some time to straiten things if I should live to get home. But I guess if I should get home we would put up with almost anything and feel happy at that don't you. Well ma you must think of me one in a while and presume you do. I often think of you and the boys and wish I was there to share your joys and sorrows but the bet we can do now is to write as often as we can and comfort each other. I need not say to you to be true to me for the thought never entered my head that you would be otherwise. That is one good thing to comfort me. Well I must close by sending my best love to you Ed and Billy. Give my best respects to all inquiring friends if any. Let me know as often as Mrs. Kinyon gets a letter from Jos or Sally Ann. I should like to hear from all of them boys. Good day write often. Yours ever until death. Be good boys and mind your ma.

January 14, 1862 – Washington, DC

Dear wife I take this opportunity to write in answer to your letter which I just received tonight. It came to hand all safe. The contents one dollar came very acceptable for I was out of money and that was bad. The worst of it is there is no money in camp. Sylvester Edsell was here yesterday and he let me have 50 cents so that I could buy me some tobacco, and it came very good for I got some tobacco and a good drink besides. Edsell is camped within 1/2 mile of here. He is a good hearted fellow as ever lived. He has been here a good many times to see us. (Illegible Name) was here on Sunday and made our camp a visit. You spoke in your last letter about Ed and Huntsman had settled. I am sorry he settled in the way he did for he allowed them so much for their butter. For they appeared to settle with me and take my 14 cents per lb. and I would not do that for 14 cents was a plenty enough and that was all they could have got. And you will see by what I wrote before I wanted that to apply on rent on that lot you spoke about. That other lot now I want them to know that I shall not be forced to let them have it. You may tell them I will tend to that part of the matter myself if I live to get home. They have beaten me out of enough already. If she wishes to make money she must get it off those that ran her breaking, for I am done with them. Let them by this learn of (illegible) or (illegible) or (illegible) or of just who they dam please. Let them howl about that piece of land. Tell them to show their deed if they can. If they have a deed I know nothing about it. You can tell them a verbal contract is good for nothing for land and if it was and ever there was a verbal contract they violated it in the first place and cannot claim under it. I do not want you to think that I blame you at all about settling but I do not want you to do anything about that other piece of land. Only to get the rent on it. I should like to have turned it on rent so as to get something, for they intend to cheat us out of everything they can. Well ma I am sitting by the fire in our cloth tent and it is hailing like fury and it is very cold. It is rather cheerless tonight but we should not mind it if we had a good house and fire and a good bed and all of those things. It would not be so bad to be a soldier but we have to take things as they come and there is no use of grumbling for that will not do any good. I inquired about that box and could not hear anything about it. I should like to get home and see you again and hope I shall. Sometime I think we shall get home in the spring and then again I get almost discouraged about it. But I mean to come home in the spring if I can get a furlough. Anyhow but we do not know where we shall be in the spring nor do we know as we shall live until spring. If we do I think we shall be pretty tough. Well ma I must close this by wishing you all the goodness in the world. Hoping all you wishes will be fulfilled in a short time. Good night. Hoping you have a more comfortable place than I have. Yours ever till death.

January 15, 1862 – Washington, DC
Dear wife and children I take this opportunity to write you a few lines to let you know that I am well and hope you are enjoying the same blessing. I have a chance to send this by Fred Hinds and have not a chance to write but a few lines. The weather is cold and it is snowing like fury. That box I have not found nor can I hear from it. You have better send me the receipt of shipping so that I shall know when to look for it. This you should have sent that

receipt at the same time you sent the box. Henry ought to have tended to it. But it may come out all right yet. Yesterday I went to Georgetown got pretty tired but rested good last night and feel very well this morning. I wish you would send by Fred Hinds me ten lbs. fine cut tobacco. That is when he comes back he will call on you and get it. I intend to send a pair of shoes & some shirts by him but do not know for all is hurry and blurry. You would think bedlam had broke loose if you should hear the noise while I am writing this. I will write to you in a few days and maybe you will have a chance to send a box by him and then you can send a gallon of whiskey. I will speak to him about it and if he can bring it I will have (illegible). I must close. I tell you this looks like winter in earnest. We drawed our new dress coats and pants and shoes yesterday. We shall not get our pay until next week and do not know as we shall then. If you send a box by him put in some writing paper and envelopes. Tell Ed to make the box for him and he will call and get it. I hope you are comfortable this cold winter. It was warm here for three or four days but it is cold enough now to make it up. I expect we shall suffer with the cold but I guess we can stand it. Well ma I must say good day for this time. Hoping these lines will find you well. From Your ever loving husband.

January 15, 1862

Well this morning it was sleet and ice. It looks like sure to storm, and the worst I have to go on guard. My turn comes at 11 o'clock and off at 1 o'clock, then on at 4 and off at 7 then on 11 and off at 1 and on again at 5 in morning. And then I shall not have to come on again in two or three weeks. So much for that. Well ma I am well this morning as common and mean to feel well as I can anyhow so long as I have to stay here. You know I always did get along without any fuss and mean to but I wish we were at liberty to come home. I think we should improve it but we must live in hopes. I want you to write as often as you can. We will try to communicate with each other often if we cannot see each other we can think of one another and that is some comfort. Well ma maybe you will get sick of this stuff but you must put up with it for a little while. Well ma I must close this. I tell you this a dreary day. Well good day. It would seem good to be in the shop such a day as this, but so be it. This from your ever loving husband.

January 16, 1862 – Washington, DC

Dear wife and children I take this opportunity to write you a few lines to let you know how I get along. Well ma I am well, as a sack now but I was sick all day until tonight. Standing on guard yesterday in the storm I caught cold. The ice covered me all over just standing 2 hours and I think it was the worst storm that I have seen since I have been here. But that is got along with now. Well last night I got a letter from the express office that there was a box there for me. Today I sent to town and had it brought to me and just as that came I received a letter from you dated 13 & 14 of this month and a letter from (illegible name). He wrote that they were all well but he little thought when we were there that I was in earnest about the war. So much for this. Well ma I received a Republican paper dated Jan 15 from (Illegible name) more. Ma above everything else the letter from you and the contents of that box done more good than all the medicine could have done. I cannot express my feelings in regard to it such a variety. That vest was admired by all and the contents of that box took every thing down. I could hardly repair from shedding tears and should enjoyed a good burst of tears if I had been where I could to think of those little luxuries. Ma I can never forget and for me to think I have friends that are so mindful of me. That bundle of cigars, that popped corn the cake, the candy, cloves, pie, sausages, cheese, butter. That is the first that I have tasted that was like butter. I tell you the boys looked at those nicknacks with wonder. I gave all of the boys in our tent some butter and a cake tonight and they seemed to enjoy it first rate. That kerchief looked good to me to see clean linen again. I want you to thank all the friends for there contributions to me and I will always remember them as long as I live. Tell Anson I have not forgotten him nor his mother nor father. Hope I shall live to see them and all the rest of the folks in Rush and enjoy their society for many years and I hope this Rebellion will be crushed out and we enjoy peace and prosperity again. I was very glad to have to hear you was well and hope you may enjoy good health. For if there is anything I wish it is for your welfare. It seems to me sometimes that I could endure almost anything to make you comfortable but after all I am not making you comfortable, for I know you nor I cannot enjoy ourselves apart. But it is a great comfort for me to think of home in my solitary moments, and I think if I should live to get home we neither of us would regret that I enlisted. So it is something that we owe our country. If we could have such officers as we could like we would not think so much of it but they have considerable to put up with for some of the men will not behave and that makes it hard for them that will behave. Well ma I must go to bed for we have for put out our lights at the tap of the drum. To obey the orders is strict. Well ma how I should like to sleep with you tonight.

January 17, 1862 – Friday Morning

Well ma I feel pretty well my cold is better this morning. I have just had a first rate breakfast out of that box with Lute. I tell you it seemed like home. Anything that comes from home seems good to us here. Yesterday there was a lot of men in our Regt. Went to town and got pretty drunk and the result is they this morning have doubled the guard and we will be kept pretty strict. Well it will not make much difference with me. Well you know I wrote about another box to be sent by Fred Hinds. He will bring it through with him you can take some old blanket that is not worth much to wind around the things. Send them bullets and molds if you can. I shall send a box of shoes home in a short time that is H. Hinds and myself we can buy very good shoes from 12 cents up to one dollar and I think we can make something on them. The shoes that we pay one dollar for are new. Second hand shoes from 10 cent to 50, and some of them are hardly soiled. They cost the government $2 per pair but the soldiers want a little money and they hate to carry them, so they sell them for what they can get. Well ma I must close this letter by wishing you all the good luck that anybody could have and I know what you would wish that would be my safe return and I hope that will be in a short time. Write as often as you can. This from you ever loving husband. Tell the boys to be good to you and I can tell them some good stories when I get home if ever I live to get there. It is pleasant today but pretty cold. Well good day ma.

January 19, 1862 – Sunday Morning. Washington, DC

Dear wife and children I take this opportunity to write you a few lines to let you know how I get along. Well in the first place I am well and hope these lines will find you the same. We have the worst weather you ever saw. The mud is shoe deep. You cannot get a dry place anywhere I tell you. Now while I am a writing it rains like all fury, our tent leaks some and you cannot step out without getting all mud. This is enough to make a fellow think of

83

home but it is strange I am not homesick at all. The time passes up very fast. It does not seem to me that I have been here the length of time that I have. I do believe that box of provisions done me more good than you could possibly think. I tell you we have had our blankets spread out all over the floor our shoes off and some of them with their pants and coats off then they will commence to sit back and carry on laugh and eat up all the shines you ever saw. Well that does us some good and whiles away the time. We have not drilled any for some days on account the mud. Well ma you may think by what I have wrote above that I do not feel as anxious to get home as I did last but ma I am just as anxious as ever to get home and to have this war closed but I do not expect to get home until the war is over for if we have to cross the river there will be no chance to get a furlough very soon. I find time passes up faster when I am content. For that reason I shall try to be content but for all that I feel very anxious about you. If it were not for that I should be as content as a fool. Well so much for that. Well I wish it would stop raining and clear off once more. I think it will be very unhealthy if we have such changeable weather. I should not wonder if one half of would be sick. Well enough of this we will wait and see. Well ma I should not wonder if there was something done in a short time about this war. Everything will be kept a secret from everybody but the war department but we can see by the moves that something will be done and I think it will be shortly. Hope it will. The sooner the better so that we can get home. I think that will be the most joyful news that ever sounded in the land. Well ma I should like to be at home today so that I could get along without waiting in this place for I get discouraged trying to write here and I guess you would to if you was here. Well ma I guess I will finish this letter tomorrow and have a chance to think of something else to write good day.

January 20, 1862 – Monday Morning. Washington, DC
This morning the mud is as deep as ever. It is foggy. It is so thick you cannot see twenty rods and it will wet a person almost like rain. I hope we can get around without getting mired. Well ma what kind of weather do you have in Rush. Do you have snow or is it a Jan thaw. How do all the widows get along for wood this winter? How do you get along for wood? Have you got any drawed from over in the woods? Has there been snow enough to haul it or not. Has Clarinda froze to death this winter. I suppose Sally Ann gets some wood by Ads folks being there. Has Mrs.

Kinyon had a wood bee this winter? Does she come to see you after you said she did not get a letter very often from James? Tell her I have not forgotten her and family. Tell old Mrs. Kinyon I remember her and them little children and hope their pa will come home and see them. How does Mr. Low get along in the shop? He of course works if he is able I suppose. Henry is driving business but more in the house than in the shop. I read a letter from father to Luther he seemed to entertain some fears or gave us some caution not to dishonor our name or our country. He need not have any fears on that subject for it is the last thing that I shall do is to desert and furthermore I intend to behave like a gentleman let me be where I am. Well ma you may get tired of this trash. I wish I could write you some of the best news you ever heard but I cannot. But one thing I can tell you I think just as much about home as ever I did and should be just as glad to get home as you would be to have me but will try to come home so that I shall not have to send my clothes back. We have not got our pay yet. It comes slow. We may get it this week but I can get along. You need not send me any more for I guess I shall get my pay before you could send it. Well ma I shall have to say good day by wishing you all the good luck in the world. From your husband ever. J W Granger

Well ma I just received a letter from Mr. Low and I will write him on this sheet and you can hand it to him. I do not know as I have any more news to write and shall have to close. I saw one whole Regt. go out this morning on picket duty. Some eight or ten miles they have to go. They say that is considerable from sometimes but I should think it would not be very pleasant in such weather as this. Well ma I must close hoping the time is not for distant when we shall be restored to each other's embrace. This from your ever loving husband to his wife and children.

January 23, 1862 – Washington, DC
Dear wife & children I take this opportunity to write you a few lines to let you know that I am well and hope you are the same. My health is very good at present for all the weather is very bad. The mud is knee deep and still it is cold and sour. Our camp looks like a hog pen we cannot find a dry place to put our feet. Our tent floor is covered with mud for we cannot step out without getting in the mud but enough of this. I send by Wm. Hines 10 pairs of shoes. I want Ed to clean them off and sell them the best he can. I will tell you what they all cost $4.53 cents. Those new shoes had

ought to sell for $2 per pair but do not expect to get much more than $1.50 or $1.75. The old shoes some of them have not been worn enough to hurt them and some of them ain't quite so good but make the best of them you can. Them shoes are first rate leather they cost the government $2 by the quantity they being good shoes. I hope you will be lucky enough to make something on them. We have not been paid off yet and I do not see anymore prospect of it than I did three weeks ago. Well ma if you should see the place we are in you would think we would catch our death of cold. It is just like taking up quarters in the middle of the road when the ground is breaking up in the spring. I never saw it so muddy at home but that I could find some dry place to put my feet but here you cannot find your foot on a dry place. How long this weather will last I do not know but hope it will not last long. You said in your last letter that Henry said he could not see any prospect of the war coming to a close than when it first began but I think they are getting along pretty well. You see they are surrounding the Rebels on all sides as fast as they can. They are cutting them off every chance they can but I suppose the folks think because they do not rush on and have a Bull Run disaster they are not doing any thing. I am perfectly willing to have them careful for I do not want to sacrifice my life for nothing and furthermore I am willing to stay on this side of the river. It is the opinion of most of the folks that the war will be at an end between this and next May at the outside. Well ma I received a letter from you on Tuesday night dated 18 and was very glad to hear from you and was glad to hear you were well. It does me a great deal of good to hear from you for I feel a great anxiety on your account and I would be very glad if I could be there with you and I hope the time will shortly come when I can come home to stay with you. I think we should know how to prize home and the comforts of home but these things will happen. Some of the best of folks will miss it. Well I hope it will all turn out for the best. I do not feel half as discouraged as I did I think my health improves and I am getting tougher and I think if I do not die (illegible) it will be strange but enough of this. We can put up with almost anything. Well ma I must close by wishing you the good luck to see me at home to stay by the first of May and sooner would suit me better. Write as often as you can. I suppose Kinyon will not come home with (illegible). How does (illegible name) like it. Yours truly from your ever loving husband.

January 24, 1862 – Washington, DC

Dear wife and children I will try to write you a few lines to let you know how I get along. Well H. H. Hinds, Luther & myself got a pass to go to the city yesterday. Well we started and traveled about 3 miles and stopped and got a dish of oysters and one drink of brandy that was the best treatment that I have had since I have been here. Well then we took an (illegible) and rode about two miles. For 6 cents we went to the (illegible) then we went to the Marine Barracks & there we saw Harris Shoemaker and had a first rate visit and ate some cake and cheese that Granger sent them. (Illegible name) had gone to see so that we did not see him. Harris is about 2 miles from us he enjoys first rate health. He says he likes it and I think I should if our place was as good as theirs. They have a nice room warm and nice. A good dining room. They are dressed first rate. So much for that. Well we had quite a New Years but not like I could have had if I had been at home. Last night I caught a very bad cold the worst that I have had since I have been in camp. I told the Capt. this morning unless we had some straw we should all be sick for sleeping on the ground. With only one blanket under you the damp comes up through so that every one will catch cold. My legs feel pretty sore this morning but for all of that I have been drilling this morning nor will I give up if I can help it. I am in hopes of getting over my cold so that I shall feel first rate if we could sleep good at night we would feel like somebody. But enough of this you will get sick of this complaining nor do I wish to complain without a cause. Our provisions are very good and we have enough such as it is but not any nicknacks. I want you to let me know what kind of times you had New Years. Let me know what kind of times Jaz had and Snyder too. Whether they had a great crowd or not. It seems to me they could not had a great time. It seems to me the folks have all gone to the war. There is some things to comfort a person that is there is a prospect of this war coming to a close within three months. If it should and I live there could be one glad fellow and I guess more than one family would rejoice. There would be the most glad hearts than was ever known at one time since this nation gained it independence. I was glad that Edward took hold and helped you. I hope he will be a great help to you and himself. He has got the ability and judgement to make a smart man and I hope he will for he has got a good chance better than his father ever had. Tell Billy his pa has not forgotten him. Tell him I have got his little papers in my pocket book and have kept them well. I cannot write anymore today but will try to finish this tomorrow.

January 24, 1862 – No. 2
Well ma Fred brought me a bill of another box directed to me. I sent downtown today to get it but I guess I will get it tomorrow, hope I shall. I had just wrote a letter to you the same day and I thought I had ought to write you another. It gives me pleasure to hear from you and hope it gives you pleasure to hear from me. You say it does. Well ma you may think because I write on those fancy sheets I delight in it but we cannot get any others. We pay a penny a sheet and a penny for a envelope you see. Any way to cheat a soldier of his money. You said in your letter you sent back that undershirt. I wanted you to keep all the clothing that I sent home for Ed. I have four shirts here now. I was to blame for not telling you of it. Everything that I send home I want you to use. I can get them for a small price. The Capt. tells us we shall have our pay the first of next week. If we do I will send some money to you. Ma I feel sometimes as though I was all alone in the world but I know that they think of me at home and they think a great deal of me here. The Capt. often says that Granger is a live man. He is kind to me and so is the rest of them. Ma you know I always had warm friends and bitter enemies, that is the way the world goes. I do not know as you can read this. I guess it will keep you busy for a while. In the morning If I live I will finish this letter. You must excuse this poor writing and all mistakes. Tomorrow I expect to go on guard. Hope it will not storm as it did the last time I was on, but one good thing I have got me a good rubber blanket to keep the wet out. Tonight if I could be at home I would not want to sleep. It seems to me I should not want to sleep for one week. Ma you must excuse me for all the trouble that I have made you and I will ever remain yours truly. In the morning I will try to finish this letter. Am afraid it will bother you to read it.

Saturday morning January 25, 1862.

Well ma I am well this morning and on guard. Have stood two hours and just got off and have time only to write a few lines for the mail will leave soon. The snow and ice that fell last night, it is cold and chilly here and sloshy. We shall get our pay on Monday I expect. Well ma you must write as often as you can and I will as often as I can. Hope you are all well. I must close in order to get this in the mail. So good day. This from yours truly. J. W. Granger

PS. Harris Shoemaker was here a few days ago and made us a visit. He was well. He looks hearty and well. So much for this.

January 27, 1862 – Washington, DC

Dear wife and children I take this opportunity to write you a few lines. I received a letter from you dated 22 & 23 was glad to hear from you and very glad to hear you were all well. It does me good to hear from you. I get lonesome and feel a little sad once in a while but I get over it. You spoke in your letter about that had I owed Mr. Snyder. Well I owe him 75 cents and I told him that Ed would pay him after a while. I paid it without having him to wait a little for it is honest and he should have it but you know that we cannot pay all of our debts at once. But enough of this. Well ma I find myself well this morning I suppose it is washing day with you today. How do times go with you? I suppose you have your regular days for washing and making a meal. Your work goes on just the same war or no war but it is not so with my work. I often think about it and think what could be done and what ought to be done and often think I should like to be there to see to it but I do not think that I shall, but after all I would not give up the hope of getting home for a good deal. You often say in your letters that you hardly ever expect to see me again but after all I do not believe you would last half as well as you now do if you had no hopes at all. Well ma I know that we have seen a great deal of trouble and do not know but we shall see more but hope we shall not. I hope that we shall see each other in the Spring and I hope to the war will be at an end and peace and quiet will be restored to our once happy land again. If the war should close and we get safe home I think there will be more joy in the land than was ever known since we gained independence. You are afraid but I will get out of patience reading your letters I do not want you to think that I think so little of you or your letters for I am very anxious to hear from you and it does me good to read your letters over and over again would I get another, so you see that your letters are interesting to me. Anyhow I do not hear anything particular about moving now a days. I want you to let me know whether Jas is in Rush. I heard that he had deserted but I did not believe it. The story came from (illegible) and (illegible). They said they got a letter from home so stating. Well ma they say that we shall get our pay today.

February 1862

February 1, 1862 – Washington, DC

Dear wife and children I take this opportunity to write you a few lines to let you know how I get along. Well in the first place I received one letter from you on Wednesday in the afternoon the same day that I wrote you. You see that our mail goes out at noon and the mail comes in at 4 o'clock in the afternoon so you see that I often get a letter from home the same day that I write. I received a letter from you last night dated Jan 27 & 28 and I was very glad to hear from you. In your other letter you spoke about getting discouraged. Now ma you must not feel in this way. We must hope for the best. We cannot tell how it will turn out. If I should give up I should be most miserable and I must say that I have kept my courage up better than I thought it possible under the circumstances. It is the most discouraging weather you ever saw. The mud has been as you ever saw it in the spring of the year and no prospect of its getting any better. Last night it snowed about 3 inches and this morning it rains laid fury so that we have to stay in our tents. Well it is not agreeable I can tell you I often think of the place that I used to have to work in but it does no good to cry for spilled milk. There is one thing about it I hope I never shall be left to bring a disgrace upon you or the friends that have been so kind to us since we enlisted. I had much rather die an honorable death than to show myself at home a deserter. You shall never blush for an act of mine of that kind and I know that you never once thought of such a thing of me. Ma you may think strange that I did not thank you more kindly for that last box but ma I did feel very thankful for it. I can tell you it done me a great deal of good. The paper was not hurt hardly and the rest of the things were all safe with the one exception. Ma I hope I shall live to thank you personally then I can tell you something of my feelings. I should be as happy as any one to see home but I had rather never see home than to desert. I came here for a soldier to fight for the liberties of my country and if needs be I hope I shall have courage to perform all duties that devolves upon me with credit to myself and friends so that when I come home you nor any of my friends will be ashamed of me. Well enough of this. Well ma I drawed my pay or a part of it the day. I wrote to you last by a mistake in the pay roll I did not get as much as I ought to but the Capt. says he will have it all right the next pay day. I was very sorry about it for

I wanted to send you some money but I cannot spare you only five dollars this time. You see that I had to pay for them shoes and I must buy me a pair of boots. Those boots that I brot from home were to small and I had to trade them off. Now I shall have to pay $5 for a pair and I only drawed $15 so you see I shall not have much left but hope it will answer all purposes. Luther drawed $36.40 they made a mistake of over one month in my pay but if I get it next pay day it will be all right. Now this money that I send you is just as good as the gold and I want you to use it for your comfort. I hope I shall have some to send next pay day to pay on some of my debts. Ma my health is very good. If any one had told me that I could have stood what I have since I have been here I could have believed it but strange as it is I stand it as well as any of them and hope I shall for I want to live to see you all again.

February 1, 1862 – No. 2

Well ma this is lonesome times how I wish we were all honorably discharged and safe at home but we must be patient and wait the fortunes of war. I am sorry that Cummins has made an ass of himself. I hope Orlo and Kinyon will prove themselves men. I should like to hear from them. If I knew the number of their company I would write to them. If you see Mrs. Kinyon give her my best respects tell her that I have not forgotten her and should be glad to see her with all the rest of the friends. Well ma I had much rather be at home to day and talk the mater over with you than be here in this awful hole. I can tell you and I do not doubt but you had to you spoke about that letter of Dan's. You done right in giving it up. I do not care anything about it only just to let them know that we knew here they had lied so that they may be ashamed of themselves. But enough of this. Well in regard to the war news well they are making a great stir here. They are cleaning out all of the hospitals here in Washington and sending the sick home and to Philadelphia. We think they are fixing for a great battle and want the hospitals to put the wounded in. I think as soon as the going is such that we can move I think that this move will decide the matter. Well if it must come let it come sooner the better. You know we soldiers know nothing of course but you know when we see clouds we can judge something of the weather and this is the way we tell anything about the affairs. Well ma I must close by wishing you all the good luck in the world. Well ma take good care of your self. Good day write often yours ever To Cornelia Granger Ed & Billy be good boys.

February 2, 1862 – Washington, DC

Dear wife & children I take this opportunity to write you a few lines in answer your letter of the 30 which came to hand last night. I was very glad to hear from you. I can tell you I received one letter from you Friday night ma. All of those letters do me good you may depend upon it. It makes me feel sad to think you feel so sad for me. I had rather you would not think so much of me but after all it gives me pleasure to think you remember me at home. Ma it is the greatest pleasure to me to think of friends that I have left at home and I hope to meet them once more. Oh ma when I get to thinking about the times that we would have if I were at home I do not feel as though I could stay away from home three years nor do I believe I shall have to. I am in hopes yet that I shall be at home if I live by the first of May. Ma it is Sunday night today it has not stormed any today nor has the snow all gone yet today. Me and one of the men went out of camp where I had my washing done and we had a good time. I tell you we get some good whiskey and a first rate dish of oysters. We found that the man belonged to the oddfellows and he was a first rate fellow and it done me good to see one of my fellow men that I could associate with. Ma you may think that I am getting unsteady but it is not so. You need not be alarmed about me I will never do anything to make you blush again if I can help it. My feelings are such towards you that I feel under obligations towards you. I would give a good deal if I could be at home with you tonight and talk of matters and enjoy the comforts of home. It would give me the greatest pleasure in the world. I hope some day to enjoy that privilege and if I do I shall know how to prize it but ma I do not know but I reckon to much of it. Sometimes I almost get discouraged myself and think my time may be short here on earth but I still hope that I may be prepared for all that is laid up in store for me. It would be hard ma to think that I should never see you again but we cannot tell anything about it. If we should go into battle I might fall the first fire and I might go through safe which I hope might be the case. Ma I think that if ever I should see you I could tell you some queer things but enough of this you may think I am gasing. But it is not so I wrote to you on Saturday and enclosed five dollars which I hope you will receive safe and sound and I hope it will do you a great deal of good and am very sorry that I could not send you any more, but I hope I can send you more when the next pay day comes. Ma you must keep cheerful and wait with patience until I come home. It would do me good to get back to old Rush again. I hope Ed will try to do as well as he can and try to earn something. I have some lonesome times here when I get to thinking about home but I will try to stand it. I had rather die than desert. If I must stay then stay it is but ma I must close this by hoping that I shall soon see you safe and sound. Ma good night from yours ever my love to all.

February 3, 1862 – Monday morning
Well ma I am well this morning and hope you are the same. Well it is snowing and looks like a stormy day. I am going to the city today to get me a pair of boots. Hope I shall have good luck. My health remains good strange as it may seem through it is so muddy. Well ma I must close this by wishing you a good day. My love to you all.

February 4, 1862 – Washington, DC
Dear wife and children I take this opportunity to write you a few lines. Well ma I just received a letter from you and a deed. To that deed I will attend to as soon as I can get a chance.

February 5, 1862.
Well ma I thought to write you a few lines last night but could not get a chance. Well I will try to write you a few lines this morning. Well I have just off guard and it is a very fine morning. It froze pretty hard last night and it looks spring of the year. I was very glad to hear from you and to hear that you are all well. I hope your health will be spared you and hope mine will be too. You spoke of that box in your letter. Well ma I was very much pleased with it. I can tell you it pleased me. To get such favours never will be forgot by me. We have good living now. The folks at Rushville made up a large box and sent it to us so we get along first rate. You spoke about sending me another box. Well ma I must thank you for it, but do not think it best to send any more at present for we do not know how long we shall stay here nor do we know where we shall go. I am in hopes the ground will get settled before long. As soon as it does I suppose we shall move. I will send Billy a paper today. Tell him he must be a good boy. My health is first rate I weigh 151 lbs. So you see I have not fell away much. I went to the city on Monday. It snowed most all day but for all that three of us eat three pecks of oysters they cost us only 25 cents. Pretty cheap. I bot me a pair of boots very good ones. I wish you would write me something about Jos Cumins. I should like to know something

about his coming home in that way. Well ma as soon as I can get a chance I will have that Deed fixed and send it to you. I do not know as there is any news to write that would interest you. I should be very glad if I could write you some news that we were a coming home but we cannot tell. Sometimes I think it will be over in a short time and then I do not know. Well there is one thing about it I shall not desert if I have to stay three years but still I hope that I shall not have to three months. Well ma you must do the best you can and I hope to be with you soon hope I shall. This war I think will be remembered for a long time ma. I must close by wishing you all the good luck in the world. This from your ever loving husband. Write as often as you can good day Cornelia.

February. 6, 1862 – Washington, DC

Dear wife and children have just received a letter from you dated Feb 4 stating that you were all well and I was glad to hear from you and hear that you are all well. I have more anxiety about you at home than I have for myself. I am afraid all the time that you will get sick or something will happen to you while I am far away from home. Well ma Philo Sherwood stayed in the tents with us last night. When he goes home he will take Nathan his son home with him for he is sick and I am afraid he never will be any better. I am sure he never would if he stayed here for it is not any place for a sick person I can tell you. Ma you spoke about the Montrose papers being sent to me. I will tell you through the kindness of Mr. W. Faurot I get both of the Monitors papers every week. I had ought to have told you before but I forgot it so you must excuse me for that. Well did you get a lot of shoes and what do you think of them. I think you and Ed can dispose of them so as to make something on them. Well ma I sent you five dollars all I could spare in a letter Feb 1. Hope you will receive it and hope I shall have some more to send you next pay day. Ma my health is good and I think it will be a benefit to me to stay in this climate that is if some of them rebels do not send a bullet through my bread basket. That sort of fun I do not think I should relish. I suppose we shall go some where as soon as the ground gets dry but I do not know as that will ever be. Yesterday was the first fair day we have had in a good while. Well today it has rained all day the roads are almost impassable on account of the mud. Well ma and Sherwood and Mr. John Hinds from Brad Co. stayed together here. We had a good visit with them. Hinds said if he had to stay here he would not have his wife see such a place as this and him in it for all the world. Well I think myself if you should see this place you would say that no man could live here in this mud hole. Friday morning 7. Well ma I am well this morning and hope you are the same. Well this morning looks like fair weather hope it will be. Well ma sometimes it looks rather dark about this war but still I hope it will soon end. If I can get a chance to get home this spring I shall come and see you once more. Hope we shall get discharged so that we can come home to stay. I think that I shall know how to enjoy civilized society for we had so much of the vulgar that I am disgusted with it for we hear nothing but cursing and swearing all the time. I tell you it is sickening to hear and then if you wish to have anything to yourself you cannot for there is so many around. Well ma enough of this. Well ma about that deed I will attend to it as soon as I can. It may be some time before I can get a chance but hope it will not be. I will do it cheerful. You need not be alarmed about it. Well ma I should like to see you but do not know when that chance will be. Tell me about Maria. I heard she had moved to Monitors. She has had luck I am sure she does not stay long in a place. Well ma I shall have to close this letter. I will write to you again soon. Be of good cheer. Write as soon as you can. Well ma good day. Tell the boys to behave themselves and be good boys think of their pa for he thinks of them. Yours ever. To Cornelia Granger. Ed & Billy be good boys mind your ma.

Ma I guess it will bother you to read some of this letter. Well ma I wrote the first of it between daylight and dark and could not see the lines so you must excuse the blunders. Well ma the devil is to pay here all of the time. In the first place they get to playing cards. Well it was all confusion all the time. Well the Capt. stopped that. Well then some of them got a dice box. Well then it was play all day spit and track mud all over the floor. Well yesterday the Capt. put a stop to that. Well then I thought we should have some peace but what do you think comes next? Well I can tell you some of the boys went some where and got an old fiddle. Well I expect we shall tormented for awhile with tom cat squalling and dying pigs. Well ma I guess you will laugh when you read this. I guess you think I have more trouble than a day with a sore head. Well I keep just as good natured as I can. Well ma I had to stop writing to you and get some water to cook with. Well ma I must stop thought I should stop when I finished the other sheet but keep scribbling. I remain yours truly and ever shall to Cornelia Ed & Billy.

February12, 1862 – Washington, DC

Dear wife and children I received a letter from you last night dated Feb.8 and was very glad to hear that you were well. I had not heard from you since last Thursday night. It seemed quite a long time but I was glad to hear that you got that money all safe for I know you must need it. I should liked to have sent you more but I could not at this time but hope I can the next pay day and still more I wish it might be our good luck to get discharged early this spring. I think as soon as the ground gets settled they will move rapidly to the south. You can see by the papers that the enemy is in a tight place and I hope they will tighten the rope still tighter until they will submit to the laws and embrace the constitution. If they will submit it would be the best move they could make but when Northern abolitionist and Southern fire eaters will mind their own business then we may look for peace and quiet in our land. Well ma T Sherwood stayed with us night before last and yesterday. I got a pass and went to the city with him and got that deed fixed for you and will send it to you by him and in the envelope will send you those pieces of brass that came off the Goddess of Liberty for you to keep. Sherwood stayed with us last night. It seems good to have some of our old friends come to see us once in a while. Well we live in hopes all the time of getting home at an early day hope we shall. The firing we heard on Sunday night we have not found out yet what it meant. We see the Burnsides expedition has done first rate and all the moves that we make tells on the Rebels. Well I am glad of it. Well ma you must try and get along the best you can until I get back. You have my best wishes and all of my sympathy. You said that Ed wished he could take my place in the army. Well he could do nothing at all. He could not stand one drill just once think of to carry a heavy gun and drill for three hours at a time and some of the time at double quick at that and then the fare is not such as he would get at home. Well then when we have to march we have to carry on our backs. At the least calculation 60 lbs. He would make poor head way. The fact is we have too many boys and babies in the army. when I say baby I mean those that should be men. A good many of the small boys in the army are sick. You can see Nate Sherwood that will convince you of the folly of letting such boys enlist. To make a good soldier it wants a stout able bodied man and one that is willing to take hold and not flinch from any duty. To obey orders is the first duty of a soldier. Since I have been in the service I have not been excused from a single duty. So you see my health has been pretty good and I never have complained in camp about any of my duties yet so much for that. Ma I will try to finish this in the morning good night

February 13, 1862 – Thursday morning
Well ma I am well this morning and hope you ad yours are the same. By this morning papers we see that the Burnsides expedition has done the fine thing with the rebels and we expect the Army of the Potomac will move shortly. I am in hopes now there will something be done. I think we have been inactive long enough but it may be sorrowful times for us but we must put up with it let what will come. Well ma it looks some like spring this morning. It is quite muddy. It did not freeze any last night but for all the mud we have got to go out and drill our officers are bound to put us through. Well let them rip that is what I say. Well ma I shall have to close for want of news to write and for want of time for the call to fall into line will be sounded in a few minutes and I must put this in the mail before going out to drill. Well ma I must say good day. Give my best respects to all inquiring friends. My love to you and yours. Yours ever.

February 15, 1862 – Washington, DC
Dear wife and children I take this opportunity to write you a few lines to let you know how I get along. Well ma I am well as usual although somewhat tired for I have just come off guard. That kind of business tires me considerable but it only comes once in about ten days and that is often enough to suit me but enough of this. Well ma I got a letter from you the same day that I wrote you last and I was very glad to hear from you and to hear that you were well. It does me a great deal of good to hear from home and I think it would do me more good to get home again which I hope I shall. The prospect of the war coming to an end I think. The rebels are a getting fits in some places and I hope they will throw down their arms and submit to the Laws and Constitution well enough of this. Well ma Sherwood has not gone home yet. He has not got Nate's papers made out yet but he thinks he will start to day. Well to day it snows and it is very cold looks rather lonesome here. Our accommodations are not very comfortable for cold weather. Well we are in hopes that we shall not have much more cold weather while we stay here. How long we shall stay in this place we do not know. Well ma I think if I were not very fond of writing to you I could have a good excuse for it is nothing but jogle and jam all the

time. It makes my writing look like all pauses but for all of this I write from two to four letters every week and should write more if I could have a half chance. Well ma I hope that my health will continue good while I stay here for if I should get sick here I know that I should be homesick as a dog, but we do not know how long our health will continue good. We have got the small pox in our camp. One case only. How many more we shall have we do not know but hope we shall all escape. You know that my vaccination worked good the last time.

February 15, 1862 – Washington, DC. No. 2
Well ma enclosed you will find some trinkets for the boys. They are those gift concerns not worth much. They were good for nothing to me and they will make nice little presents for the boys. They must think something of them for my sake if nothing more I should like to give them something of more value but they must wait until I get home if ever I do. I often think of home while walking my lonely beat while on guard as I do any where for then my thoughts are of home and friends and not any one to curse and swear in my ears all the while.

February 17, 1862 – Washington, DC
Dear wife and children I take another opportunity to write you a few lines to let you know how I get along. Well ma I received a letter from you on Saturday night dated Feb.13th and was glad to hear that you were all well and hope you may be blest with good health until my return home (if that time ever comes) which I hope is not far distant but we cannot tell. The future may look dark to us when day is about to dawn. I hope this may be the case now but it looks dark enough now to me although our armys are victorious in almost every case. Within the past week our country has gained several important places. There is several more yet to be gained and a good many lives to be lost and who they are we do not know. And it is well that we do not. If we did they would be more deserters then there is now but enough of this. Well ma we have at last got our marching orders to leave this place and it looks like anything but firm to me I can not tell you how for we shall go. We do not know but it is somewhere in Virginia. W ell if it was good weather I should not mind it but to think of pulling up stakes and moving in such going as this looks discouraging. The mud is froze up some now and about 2 inch of snow on the ground and to day it rains a cold rain. Ice and sleet. And tomorrow morning at six

o'clock we must have everything packed and slung on our backs and in line to march. But I think if it storms like this we shall not go tomorrow for we could not stand it. But we shall go as soon as it is fair. I suppose we shall go somewhere near Bulls Run but do not know how near. Well ma I suppose we shall be in more danger over there than here but for all of that I may live through it all and return to you safe and sound which I hope may be the case but most likely that a good many of them that cross over the river this time or the last but. I suppose that everyone thinks as I do that my chance is as good as any ones well if we do have to put up with a good deal we must not complain but must bear up under our troubles with all the fortitude that we possible can. Oh if we could hear the joyful sound of peace once more in our land it would brighten the countenances of thousands in this country. This war does desolate the land to such an extent that it will take years of hard toil to make it up and years to heal the grief that it has occasioned. Well ma you spoke about Maria and Betsy being up there on a visit. Well I should liked to have been there and seen them but that was impossible for me although my thoughts are of home and friends but I cannot see them at present but their society will be all the more pleasant when I get home if I live to get there. My health is good and it seems a wonder that it is. So much exposure as we have here a person would think we would all die but I believe that a man will stand almost anything without dying and then they will die for almost nothing. That is the way of the world. Well ma you may direct your letters just the same as ever until you hear from me again for they will follow our Regt let us go where we will. When we get in among Sesesh we may have some warm times and it may not be so funny as some think for it is not a very nice thing to stand up for a mark to be shot at. Well I don't care how much they shoot at me if they don't hit but after all it would make me mad to have them shoot at me anyhow but enough of this. I will let you know where we are. Write as often as you can and I will do the same. I shall ever remain Yours Truly, to Cornelia Ed & Billy Granger. excuse all mistakes. Remember me. Wish I was with you. Good day.

Since I have been sitting here writing P Sherwood just came in. He has not started for home yet. He has not got Nathan's papers made out yet. When he gets home you will get that deed. It storms like all possess yet I think we shall not start tomorrow for we could not stand it but we expect to go as soon as it gets done storming. Well good day. Again I tell you I could take more comfort at home in such a storm than here.

February 20, 1862 – Alexandria, Va.

Dear wife and children I have a few moments of leisure and I will improve them in writing to you. Well ma in my last letter I told you that we were under marching orders. Well on Tuesday at 2 o'clock in the morning we were called up and had to get ready to start on our march. At six o'clock we started with our knapsacks on our backs and two days provisions in our knapsacks. Well the mud was very deep. We marched through the city and down to the Potomac and crossed the Long Bridge then we came into Virginia. We passed through the city of Alexandria. By the way this last place was a regular sesh hole. Well the place is not much now to them for it is strongly guarded by our troops. Well we halted a few moments to rest and then took up our line of march for about 2 miles where we encamped where we are now. Well now ma if I should tell you that I felt homesick that night it would not do the subject justice. I think of all the hard days work that ever I done this was the hardest. My legs were mud clear above my knees. My feet wet and so tired that I could hardly stand up. Well we had to pitch our tents and no floor the ground full of water and mud 6 or 8 inch deep. You had better believe it looked rather squally. Well we got some brush and laid in the mud, spread our gun blankets down and the rest of our clothes and down we went for the night. I tell you I would not have you seen me as we were that night for nothing. I tell you that soldering is rather hard sometimes. Well we lay in the mud and water until morning got up and felt lame and sore. Well we took a cold lunch then set about to make our tents more comfortable. We had the good luck to get boards by backing them 1/2 mile and glad we were to get them at that. Well it rained like all possess all day but for all that we got a floor laid down and our stove set up and a good cheerful fire that began to seem like home. Well ma last night I rested first rate it cleared off last night. This morning the sun arose fine ad I felt thankful for it I have got over being homesick this morning and am contented as ever but still I feel anxious to get home but do not want to come until sesh is at an end. The accounts are very favorable now and it is the opinion of almost every body that the back bone is broken. I hope it is and I hope the war will soon be at an end so that we can return home. I suppose that we shall take a ride on the Potomac in about ten days and with some of us it may be our last. We expect to have to help take some rebels batteries but we do not know for certain. We passed by the House that Col. Ellsworth was killed in at Alexandria and saw some strange things on our route.

No.2. Well ma you may direct your letters to Alexandria Va. and the rest of directions the same as ever. I received a letter from you last night and it cheered me up a good deal. I was very glad to hear that you were well and hear you had plenty of provisions. All such things gives me comfort. I hope that I shall live to get home and see you and the rest of my friends. I think my chance is just as good as any of them and my chance is just as good to get killed, but there is no use to fret nor worry. I hope if we have to go into a battle my courage will not fail nor I do not mean it shall but enough of this. I hope we shall not have to go into a battle at all. I think Luther stood it first rate considering the chance he had on the march for he wore shoes. When he got into camp his feet was wet and his clothes up to his knees. I had a dry pair of shoes and socks and had him change as soon as we got our tent up and then he took a good dose of pain killer and he lay down with me. In the morning he said he felt smart as ever. Well ma I cannot send this letter today and will have to wait until tomorrow. Well ma I thought I had better finish this letter tonight and not wait for fear I should not have time. Well the more I see of this place the better I like it. The sun has shone nice today. The wind and sun has dried the mud up fine wonderful. Well ma I have seen two rebel prisoners today brot past our camp. They were caught by our picket, not of this Regt but next week our whole Regt has got to go on picket duty and expect to be gone 4 days. Well ma that seems to me I shall like but do not know. Our camp is on the borders of sesesh. Our pickets extend clear to the enemy's pickets. I have seen some that have been on picket and they like it. They say there is some danger but think it is fun. Sometimes they would not see a rebel and then again they would see several hundred. Sometimes they would fire away at each other. Well enough of this, we can see any quantity of camps here. The hills as far as we can see from North to east is dotted with tents. In the morning at reveille we can hear the music in every direction. Well ma I must bid you good night. Hoping that it may be my good luck to meet you face to face where we can enjoy each others society and have it to say the war is ending. We have the most cheering news from every quarter and it seems to me they will submit and lay down their arms so might it be. Yours ever and truly. Alexandria Va. 57th Regt Company A in care of Capt. P Sides

Friday 21.

Well ma I am well this morning and hope you are the same. It looks like a storm. The more I see of this place the better I like it. I have got over being tired and feel quite good natured. Well ma good day I hope to see you again.

February 27 1862 – Alexandria, Va.

Dear wife and children I take this opportunity to write you a few lines. I received a letter from you dated 18 on Monday and another one on yesterday. Well ma I was glad to hear from you and to hear that you were well. I am in pretty good health not withstanding the weather. It rained all day yesterday and last night and the worst of it all I was on guard I did not get any sleep last night and this morning have had to clean up my gun and equipment and pack up my clothes for a march. We are under marching orders again. How far we shall go I do not know nor any of us either. Nor do we know whether we are a going into a battle. We are provided with two days rations. We are not going to take our tents with us now. I rather expect we are going in the direction of Manassas but cannot tell. We may find a good camping place and send back for our tents. We shall leave some men to guard our camp while we are gone. We expected to have started early this morning. Wish they had for if they had gone this morning Luther and myself would have stayed to guard our camp, but they put it off until the afternoon so he and I will have to go with them. Well ma go or stay you shall not blush for my behavior. I had rather die than desert. For all the service is so hard. I have wished myself out of it a good many times on your account but I have pride enough about me to behave well and respect for my family if nothing else. Well ma just as soon as we get settled again I will write to you and let you know how I get along. I mean to write to Orlo just as soon as I can get time. I was glad you sent me his address. Well ma we may go into a battle before I write to you again. If we do I hope that kind providence will protect me and spare my life to my family and I be the means of assisting in enforcing our laws and crushing out this rebellion. But to tell you the truth I wish they would lay down their arms and return to their allegiance but I suppose they will stand out just as long as they can. Well ma I am in a great hurry and cannot write one half that I want to but hope my life will be spared so that I can write many times to you yet. And hope that my life will be spared to you and our children for many years but we cannot tell that is hid from us. You may direct your letters just as I told you last until you hear from me. Our duties are harder here than when we were at Washington. If we make a move there will be over one hundred thousand move about the same time the whole line on the Potomac you may expect to hear of some big fighting before a great while. We belong to General Hintzelman's Division Brig. Jameson's Brigade. How many thousands belong to this division I do not know. Well ma it is noon and we are looking every moment to be ordered out for our march but for all of that we may not go under three or four days. It is nothing strange for the generals to issue such orders and keep the men in suspense for a whole week. Well ma I must stop and get my dinner. Wishing you all the good luck in the world. I remain the same to you and always shall, and our children tell them to love their pa for he thinks a great deal of them. So good by for the present. I had got my letter finished when the mail came in but it brot a letter from you dated 13. I was glad to get news from you & glad to hear that you were well. I received 3 stamps for which you will have to accept my thanks for it is all that I have got to pay with now until we get our pay that I hope we shall get. I am well ma the trouble that I allude to was not altogether what we talked of when I last saw you, but in looking over my life since we moved on the creek to live some hard feelings would arise in my thoughts if we could see each other we could talk these things over. I do not want you to think that I blame you or hold any hardness against you. Far be it from me I still remain your loving husband and hope to embrace you all yet. May all this be so. Hope it will. Well good day. My love to all inquiring friends. Excuse me this time for I am in such a hurry.

February 28, 1862 – Alexandria, Va.

Dear wife I wrote you a few lines yesterday stating that we are under marching orders and expected to march every moment. Well we have everything ready and expect to be called before 24 hours. There cannot be any doubt about the matter. There is all the preparation made for an attack on Bulls Run. Artillery is a passing here all the time almost. The men are out by the thousands repairing the roads. Our officers say that we must leave everything. Only what we can carry on our back. Tents and such like we are to leave we shall have to sleep on the ground after this without any thing over as well. We must stand it. What the consequence will be time will tell but no doubt a great many of us will never see our homes again. Some of us must get killed and I think a great many of us will. I suppose you will look with a great deal of anxiety for another letter from me. Well ma if I live through it I will write to you but you need not be alarmed if you should not get another letter in some time for I suppose that we shall not have a chance. It comes rather tough ma for us to leave our little chest that we have kept so long with us for convenience, but we must obey orders. Well ma I commenced on a part of a sheet so I will write a little on this sheet. You must excuse me for not writing much this time ma I feel as though we were placed in a critical condition. But ma I hope that I may be prepared for all that is prepared for me. If I am all will be right. If my life is spared I think I shall feel thankful to that divine providence that has always watched over us and cared for us, but ma I cannot write near all that I want to. We shall be mustered in for pay this afternoon but we shall not get any pay until the first of April and may not then. Well it may be a good thing that we are a going to be mustered for pay before we go into battle because it will be less trouble for their friends to get their pay but enough of this ma. If I do not survive you must get along the best you can but I hope that my life will be spared to you these many years. Yet I mean to be cheerful and do the best that I can and leave the rest to providence. So ma I must bid you good day hoping that I may have good news to write you the next time. My love to all. Please write as often as you can and I will do the same my warmest love to you and the children. Good day. It is quite cold here today and windy.

March 1862

March 3, 1862 – Near Alexandria, Va.
Dear wife and children I take another opportunity to write you a few lines to let you know that I am yet in the land of the living and well and in good spirits. For all those I feel thankful. Ma I have received a letter on Friday from you directed to Alexandria. It came through safe and in good time. I was very glad to hear from you and to hear that you were all well. We did not march when we expected to nor do we know what moment we shall for we have two days rations on hand all the time cooked and in our haversacks. We have to hold ourselves in readiness at a moments

warning to march, but I hope we shall not have to start until the weather gets better. It snowed yesterday Sunday almost all day. The snow is 2 in and thawing now and it will be very muddy and bad to sleep on the ground. We expect to see some hard times yet before we get home but if our lives are spared to get back safe and sound I never shall be sorry that I came. It is the opinion of the most of the folks that the war will be over before long. Hope it will. We still have good luck so far. Last week Wilson Ferry and some others arrived in our camp in good health. I suppose that Mr. Low is as glad that Ferry is in the army as Huntsman was when I enlisted, but enough of this. I have wrote to O W Palmer and Kinyon to find out about the Cummins scrape. I think that Huntsman & Cummins have showed out just what they are that is they are both thieves and liars and are not of any use in the neighborhood and I do not believe anybody wants them there. Well ma you may tell Edward that I have not shaved my face since I left home nor do I intend to until I get home. Tell him that I have a very nice moustache I have trimmed my whiskers and keep them about the same length that I did at home. Well ma I suppose you would like to see them just to see how I would look in this new style. Well now to tell you the truth I think it would give me the greatest pleasure in the world to show you the same. Well just dog my cat if I would not like to do that same thing. Well ma I have some pleasant dreams of home. I have several times dreamt of it but there was always something wrong about it. Sometimes I would not be dressed and at others I would forget some thing. Well I hope some of them dreams will come to pass but ma we must wait and time will tell the story but I hope for the best. I know I get discouraged sometimes and no wonder that I do for we have it pretty hard sometimes but we shall know how to enjoy ourselves when we do get home if ever we do. Well ma I have packed up my spare clothes in that chest and they will be stored in Alexandria until the war is over. So if I should not survive you will know where to send for my things. They are all marked. There is a coat for Luther and a bundle for H. H. Hinds all marked. We expect when we leave this place to see some hard times but I hope we shall be able to stand it and live it through. Well ma in regard to that other matter I have not the least hardness against you in the world nor do I blame you for feeling bad about it. I felt bad for I was in hopes they would let me alone. I think that I have suffered enough from them. They have ruined themselves & they are the ones that ought to suffer. It is one comfort to you that others have got into the muss & we have got pretty much out of it. Well in regard to the watch it is a great deal of company for me but I could trade it for a revolver but I could not send it home for a soldier is not allowed to send any box home any more. So you see there would not be any chance for Edward to get it. Well ma I feel so thankful for that shirt I cannot express myself. Suffice it that it just suits me. I sent that other envelope to you but am afraid you will not get it. My anxiety to see you is all that keeps me up. Oh will the time ever come that we can meet again? I hope it will. I want you to write just as often as you can & I will do the same but I do not have the chance that you do. Ma if you will send me a cheap kerchief just roll it in a newspaper & it will come through for a penny. If I were not so tired I should like to write a good deal more but I must close & wait until another time. My love to you & the children grows stronger every day. My anxiety to see you is great. I hope the time will soon come that we can meet again. My best respects to all inquiring friends. My love to you all. Yours Truly. You had better direct to Washington DC. Good day.

March 5 1862 – Alexandria, Va.

Dear wife and children I take another opportunity to write you a few lines. I received a letter from you yesterday dated March 1. I was very glad to hear from you and to hear that you were well. Ma my health is good and I am glad it is for I have it pretty hard. We have to drill rain or shine mud or no mud. We expected to have moved before this but the weather is so bad I suppose is the reason, but we are in readiness to move at a moments warning but I mean to write you just as often as I can. Ma I have just seen a hard sight. Well the 63 Regt PV are encamped just by our side. They started out on picket Monday morning in good health and spirits. Well today they sent in three of their men that was shot by the rebels this morning. I tell you it looks hard. All of them young men in the prime of life. One of them was Capt. one was quartermaster and one a private, and one Lieut. was wounded. In war a man holds his life in his hand and he does not know what moment that it will be taken from him but I hope that my life will be spared me until my return home. But by what I hear some of them things that live near you that they hope I never will return but for all their threats I feel very anxious to get home. I will just enclose one that I received tonight. I think I know who wrote it but I want you to keep still and say nothing about it. This writing may be of some service to you. You can ask Jesse if he mailed a letter of that stamp. You will see that it is not post marked and it must have been neglected by request and he will be likely to remember it. But keep still. I will tell you what I think best to do. Say nothing about that lower lot at present. You know that they have not a scrap of writing for it and you know they cannot hold it. But let them work until their wrath cools off a little. The use of that lot is not much and they <missing the rest of this letter>

No. 2. Ma we may have to move tonight and may not but I hope they will wait until the weather gets better for I tell you it most awful muddy and it is cold sour weather. I tell you it would give us a hard one to sleep on the ground without any cover over us. I should think that that woman might let my family alone as long as I kept away. I presume if I were at home she would be as good as pie but she could not come any of her games over me. I have helped them all I ever shall of my own free will. Well ma enough of this. Please write as soon as you can. Let me know all you know about the matter. Well ma I must say good night. I shall ever remain your husband and yours only. Be good boys.

Ma my clothes are all packed up and will be stored in the military storehouse in Alexandria so if I should get killed they would be sent to you.

March 9, 1862 - Sunday. Alexandria, Va.
Well ma I must write you a few lines this afternoon. I received a letter from you yesterday and was glad to hear that you were well. I am in comfortable health although I was quite sick last night but feel better this morning. I have been out to day to work on the road. There is hundreds at work on the roads to make them passable for the artillery to pass. We are in hopes that the weather will be such that the artillery can move this week. I suppose the reason that we have not moved is because the roads were so bad. It its the opinion here that we shall advance on the enemy the fore part of this week. We are in readiness to march at a moments warning and have been for sometime. We have sent all of our things to Alexandria where I expect they will stay for sometime. Well we shall not be bothered with them that will make us less load to carry on our backs. Well ma the weather is fine here. It freezes pretty hard nights but it thaws in the daytime so you see it keeps muddy. But I think the roads will get settled soon. Ma I have not much news to write this time but I wish I could tell you

the war was over and we were ready to start home but that time has not come yet if it ever comes to us. But we must live in hopes. If it were not for that we should give up to despair but we must not give up. I think the war that is the hardest of the fighting will be over in two weeks. Ma you spoke in your letter about having W Granger settle up my books. I think it would be the best thing that you could do for if I should get back it would not do any hurt and if I should not get back it would have to be done by some one. I wish I could have a good chance to send my watch home. I would do it although it is a great deal of company for me but I would do without it. The war news is cheering all around us but here I think they will make a bold stand here at Manassas. We are about half way from Washington and to Manassas. That is their strong hold but I hope they, that is the rebels, will get scared and run. But I am afraid that place will cost us a great many lives but hope it will not. Well ma I guess you was surprised when you got that last letter from me and especially that one that was inside. Well ma perhaps you can tell who wrote it. I think I could guess but the lest said the quickest minded. I am almost afraid that they may do you some sly injury. They have no principle and are of a bad disposition and we do not know what they might do while I am away. But if I live to get home I will tend to their case and they had better be careful or they will get their foot in. Well enough of this. You must tell Mrs. Grupper to keep Jim away or he may get shot with that mine revolver. Oh if she only had her revolver here in the army she could find plenty of use for it for I believe we have the worst lot of fellows to talk that I ever saw. I get sick of such trash and shall be glad when I get where the society is more refined and sensible. Well ma I would give a good deal if I could spend such a day as this with you and the children. I think I should know how to prize it. Ma you would laugh if you could see me sitting on the floor with a knapsack in my lap writing this letter. Well ma to tell you the truth I am entirely out of money to pay postage but I hope to get some. Money goes fast when a fellow has it. I have not had one drop of liquor since I came from Washington for it is so high and money is so scarce that I cannot get it. Well I do not know but I am just as well off. Well ma I must close for want of news. Write as often as you can and I will do the same. We do not expect to get our pay until some time in April but we were mustered in for pay the last day of Feb. Government is slow to pay. Well ma good day. I hope I shall live to write to you a good many times yet and see you to. Good day.

March 10.

Well ma I am well this morning and have just heard that we have got to send to Alexandria and get our clothes and carry them with us. It will make a heavy load but we must carry them. Where we shall stop I cannot tell but our letters will follow us. Yours Truly. You had better direct to JW Granger 57 Regt., Company A Heintzelman's Division Va. Well ma it rains this morning but it is like April warm and nice. Good day ma.

Alexandria Va. March 13

Dear wife and children it is with pleasure that I write you a few lines to let you know that I am well and hope you and yours are the same. Today I received two letters from you dated 8 & 11. I was very glad to hear from you and hear that you were well. I suppose the reason that I did not get them sooner was the mails were stopped for a few days on the account of the forward movements of the army of the Potomac. Well ma after all we did not have any battle at Manassas. After all we were expecting to have a hard time of it but you will see by the papers that the rebels run as usual. Where they have gone we do not know and where we shall go we do not know yet. Some think we shall stay here until the war is over and then be mustered out of service and some think we shall go down the Potomac on a fleet. But after all their talk they do not know anything about it. For my part I should be very glad to have the rebels lay down their arms and submit to the laws and obey the constitution and let us all go home to our families. And I think a great many thinks the same. Well ma the weather has been fine for three or four days. The roads are getting quite good. The ground settles and it looks like spring in earnest. Well I am glad of it. It seems good to have nice weather once more. There is a great deal of news but you will get it in the papers more correct than I can write it. I think the news will cheer many a heart and bring hope to a great many families. I am in hopes that we shall get home this spring. Maybe in one month and it may be some time we cannot tell. Well ma we had to send to Alexandria and get our clothes. We have them now safe and sound. I hope they will send us out a scouting for I would like to see some more of the country before we leave this place. But if they will let us go home I shall not stop to look around a great while but shall start for old Rush. I was sorry to hear that Mother was sick. I hope she will get along and was sorry to hear that Aunt Parmelia was sick to. Tell her that I hope she will get along and I should be very glad to see her and hope that I shall. Tell little Lotty she will get a good hugging when Uncle John gets home and the rest of the little girls. Well ma I often think of the walks that we used to take on the banks of the creek and often think of the other comforts that we used to enjoy and still hope to enjoy the same again. We shall know better how to prize them if we are ever permitted to meet again which I hope we shall. There was quite a serious accident happened in a camp joining us on last Sunday night. They had a bomb shell in their tent and was fooling with it when it exploded mangling one man most shockingly. It tore one of his arms to pieces and one leg so that they will have to be amputated and strange to say there was four other men in the tent at the time and escaped without injury. It tore the tent all to pieces almost. Well ma so far I have got along without any accident and hope that I shall. Well ma you said that you wanted me to forgive you. I will tell you I have nothing to forgive. We all of us have our imperfections and it stands us in hand to do as well as we can and then we shall do bad enough at that. Well ma I hope that we shall all get safe home this spring but we cannot tell. There is many a slip between cup and lip. Well ma our drill is pretty hard but I hope it will not last long. Well ma I must close. It is about as much as I can do to get enough to pay postage. I do not know as it would be best to send me any for fear I should not get it. But we may not move from here in some time. If we should not I suppose it would come through safe. You may do as you think best. Well good night. This from yours ever.

One o'clock Friday morning 14
Well ma we have just been called up and prepare three days rations. The camp is all alive getting ready to start. For what place we do not know or where. It looks like rain. I think we shall have a bad time for our march. When we know where we shall go I will write and let you know where we are. Well I suppose we shall know when we get there. No more at present I remain as ever.

Fortress Monroe March 20, 1862
Dear wife and children I take this opportunity to write you a few lines to let you know that I am live and well. Ma I am about 200 miles farther from you than when I last wrote you. Well ma after a

long delay we started from our camp on Monday at noon. We got on board of steam boats just at night and lay on board that night and started on Tuesday morning for Fortress Monroe. We arrived there on Wednesday night. It set in raining. We marched about one mile from the fort and halted for the night. I tell you the prospect was anything but favorable. Just think thousands of men lying on the bare ground without any tents or anything over them but their blankets. But thanks to a company of Cavalry that was camped close by they came to us and offered us the use of their shed lofts which we gladly accepted. I can tell you we kept dry and nice and slept soundly. They furnished us with warm coffee and this morning they fed us out of their rations. And I can tell you warm vittles never tasted better to me. Today is rainy and it looks gloomy enough but when it clears off I think it will be a nice place. Ma the fleet that we came down the river on was one of grandest things that I ever saw. Just think of 75,000 men can well ma. Where we shall go from here we cannot tell. We are quartered in a large shed loft. It is not likely that we shall stay here any longer than they all get landed. It takes a good while to unload so many men and horses. This place is alive with soldiers and I expect we shall have hot work before long. I hope they will put down this rebellion and let us go home. If we live (which I hope we shall). I tell you this will try the courage of every man. When we know we must face the cannons mouth once, perhaps lose our lives. But now is the time that we must stand firm and never blink. But enough of this. I hope we shall see each other again. While we stay here the boys that are here say they fare first rate. I could have got along a good deal better if had only had a little money but I was out of that stuff. I tell you a person wants a little money let him go where he will. Well we are in hopes pay day will come after a while. I want to save all I can, but once in a while I want to get a few things for comfort. I should have wrote to you for some but thought it would be to bad for I know it is hard for you to get money. And another thing I thought we should get our pay before we left our camp but we did not. Well ma sometimes things look dark to me but you know I was always lucky to get out of a scrape when I got into one and hope I shall be lucky enough to come out of this one safe and sound. It seems strange that time passes so swiftly and I do not get homesick at all. Although I feel a great anxiety to get home and to see my family and friends again. W Ferry is sick with the measles we left him in Alexandria at the

111

Hospital with four or five others of our company. Well ma I must close this by wishing you all the good luck in the world. Write and tell me how you and Huntsmans get along. Let me know all about them. Luther is well and in good spirits. Give my love to all inquiring friends. My love to you.

Ma I guess it will bother you to read this but I could not get any ink to write this. Well ma tell Ed & Billy to be good boys and not forget their pa. Give this little trinket to one of the boys. It is not of much value but they may prize it. My love to them all.

March 21.
Ma I am well this morning. It is rainy yet, rather cold very muddy. I rested good last night. I am in good spirits. Hope my health will remain good. Yours Ever.

March 28, 1862. Hampden near Fortress Monroe
Dear wife and children I take this opportunity to write you a few lines to let you know how I get along. Well ma I am well as usual and hope you and the children are the same. I received a letter from you on the 26 dated March 20. The first I had received in two weeks but I was glad to hear from you but was sorry to hear that you was almost down sick but I hope you are better. I think that I am as tough as any of them. Our fare is rather hard but we are getting used to it. When we shall start from here I do not know nor do I care. I have just this moment received a letter from Orlo Palmer. He was well he did not write anything about Jim Cummins, only that he said that his Capt. said he would have him dead or alive. But I guess he is glad to get rid of him. Well enough of this well ma. Orlo says there is a prospect of his Regt being disbanded. Well I hope they will and I wish ours would be too. Well at any rate I wish the war was over and we were ready to start home for I am sick of this dogs life. One thing I feel thankful that my health and life is spared me. For if I were taken sick here I do not know what I should do. Well ma I must stop writing now for the sound to fall in for drill. How tired I get of that sound and hope soon that it will be over and be my own nigger again. Well ma I have been out and drilled about four hours and just came in and got my supper. Well I am tired enough. I hear heavy firing towards Newport News. Should not wonder if they were having a skirmish for we have a heavy force that has marched by us. I rather think our division will be kept in reserve. That is what I hear. Well I am glad of it if it is so for we shall be more out of

danger. I am in hopes the rebels will retreat as we advance. We have in this army that came down the Potomac about 80,000 men. The fields are covered with soldiers and they still come and pass by us and advance towards the enemy. Well I hope we shall hear of something being done. It looks hard to see so much property destroyed. Our teams go out every day and haul loads of rails to burn in our camps. The farms are being stripped of everything. The Secesh have fled and left their buildings and in a good many cases they have burned their own buildings rather than have them fall into our hands. Well ma I will leave this until morning and then finish it so good night. Saturday morning 29. Well ma I am well this morning and hope you are. It was cold & windy last night. I slept cold & little at that. I tell you we miss our tents. We thought it were tough with them but if we only had them now I should be content. Well I hope it will be warmer at nights before long. Well ma I hope the war will be over before long. I have seen Peter Roe several times. He is well and as fat as a bear. He was glad to see me I tell you. Well we see a good many that we are acquainted with. We lost one man. He died at Alexandria with measles. He was only with us two or three weeks. He was a nice young man. We feel his loss. Well ma I must close. Good day. Give my love to all. I remain yours ever.

April 1862

April 1, 1862 – Hampden Near Fortress Monroe, Va.
Dear wife and children I take this opportunity to write you a few lines. Well ma I am well and hope you and the children are the same. I received a letter from you on Wednesday and one on Monday one dated 20 and one dated 25. I was very glad to hear from you and to hear that you were all well. I had become quite anxious about you. Well ma I have not seen many of them rebels yet for all we are close by them but it seems as though they are afraid of us. Well I hope they will get scared and give up. It would give me the greatest pleasure in the world to hear that news. Well ma you spoke in one of your letters about that woodwork for that wagon. Well sell it if you can but I think Norman charges too much for that revolver for it was a poor poor thing. I could not keep it in order and there was no dependence to be put on it so I sold it for $12 dollars and am to have my pay when payday comes. You know that such revolvers can be bought here new from 10 to

14 dollars but I will not complain. If you can get 4 dollars and the revolver for that wagon let it slide. You was speaking about your good living. Well ma I am glad to think that you have a plenty. It gives me great pleasure to think you do not have to fare as I do. But I get enough to keep me alive if it is rather hard. I have eat just 2 eggs since I left home. eggs are worth 30 cents per doz. and everything else in proportion. Well ma we had a pretty hard time on Saturday and Sunday. It rained like fury and it was cold. The wind blew and you would laugh if you could see our houses that we live in. Well we take 4 oil cloth blankets and fasten them together. Stick some crotches in the ground and spread them over. It makes a little play house like. Well we cannot sit up strait in it and five of us crawl into this hole to sleep and get out of the rain. Well it leaked like fury at that. Well I thought it would kill hush. Well Sunday morning we went to work in the rain and carried brick and built a fireplace in one end of our hut and well yesterday it cleared off and was warm and nice well. Ma it looks pleasant this morning and I hope it will be pleasant for I dread a storm. Well ma I got a letter yesterday from Aunt Permelia and Nett I. will try to answer them just as soon as I can. You must tell them that I appreciate their kindness and it gave me the greatest pleasure to hear from them and to know that I was not forgotten by them. They said they thought of me when they had any rarities and would be glad to share with me for which I thank them very much. They spoke of the sugar bush. Well ma I should like to be at home and get some warm sugar but I guess my warm sugar has gone up the blow hole for this spring. Well if I live to get home I will make it up some other way. Tell Nett that Uncle John remembers her with pleasure and if he lives to get home she may expect a good hugging from Uncle John. Tell her to write as often as she can. I tell you it cheers a person up when they know they have warm friends at home wishing them well. You spoke about them jerseyites. I have not heard from them yet. Well ma when the time will come that I can come home I do not know but hope it will not be a great while. We still stay near Fortress Monroe. That is within four miles of it so we have all of our letters directed to Fortress Monroe. Well ma I do not know as I have any news to write that will be interesting to you but if we could see each other we could talk for hours and find it interesting. But I must close for want of time but will write as often as I can and want you to do the same. Well ma I must say good day. Give my best respects to all

inquiring friends my best love to you and yours. Tell Ed & Billy to be good boys. Ed had better stay with you until I get home. I think it would not be proper for him to leave now.

April 7, 1862 – Yorktown, Va.

Dear wife and children I have no more privilege to write to you after so long a time. Well ma I am yet in the land of the living and well and hope you are the same. Well ma I have just received a letter from you this morning dated April 1 was very glad to hear from you and am glad that my life is spared to receive it. Well ma we started the 4 of April the day was fine but our march was hard our loads was heavy and we got very tired. Well we camped on the ground that night and started at six o'clock in the morning and camped at night within a short distance of the enemy's batteries. Well I was tired enough but I was dictated to stand guard. Well it was tough but I stood it first rate. The enemy threw a ball into our camp but it did not happen to do any damage but knock one man down but did not hurt him. Our men had been fighting them almost all day. Oh I forgot to tell you our first days march the roads was good but the next morning we had a heavy thunder storm that made the road very muddy and it was hard traveling. But we had hard fare nothing but that hard bread to eat and had water to drink. For three days we lived in this way. I tell you it made me think of home. At last our wagon has arrived and we have a little meat and now we have but little bread but I guess we shall get along somehow if we do not get killed in battle. I have not had any rest since I came here. One night on guard and as soon as I got off our whole company had to get out on Pickett and stay in the woods all night and watch the rebels. I have just come in and got a little shelter over us and am determined to write you a few lines for it may be the last time that I ever have a chance for I expect we shall have a hard fight. The cannon balls whistle over our heads and Saturday and Sunday there was a constant firing in every direction. This morning while on Pickett I saw the rebels batteries and could see the men in large quantities. This is one of their strong places. Last night I could hear the rebels talk & laugh and hear them sing and ride through their camp while we were skulking in the woods. All the time while I am writing this the cannon are booming sending their missiles of death and destruction. How many of our men (that is on our side) is killed I do not know but have heard of several and a good many wounded. The most of the fighting done so far is done by the artillery but we are expecting every moment to be called out. I tell you ma it is hard but I am determined to do the best I can. I do not fear but it gives us rather unpleasant feelings to hear the balls whistle around our heads. But if they do not hit us they will not hurt us. Well ma I hope my life will be spared till we meet again. So far providence has been on my side and I hope it will bring me safe through. Ma that money and letter I never received at all. The letter this morning had three postage stamps in it for which I thank you very much. I think you had better not send any money for there is no telling about our mails any more for there must have been three or four letters that I ought to have had which I have not got. But let them go we are in amongst the Secesh in earnest. Well ma it rains and it is rather cold. The nights are cold as fury but the days are warm. When it is fair we marched through the nicest country that I ever saw. Oh what a pity that so nice a country should be laid waste but so it is. In the whole distance about 24 miles we did not see many but blacks left. The white men had fled. We moved slow but our army threw away more clothing blankets shoes & boots than twenty wagon loads. What a pity. I had to leave one pair pants and one good shirt and then my load was as heavy as I could carry. Well I hope I shall get out of this scrape some time safe and sound. I suppose you will feel anxious about me until you hear from me again. But ma you must not worry for it may be some time before I can write if I should live. Do no be alarmed if you should not hear from me in two weeks but I will write to you the first chance that I can get. Well ma about the hay I guess you had better keep enough for another winter. I should like to see you and talk with you and the rest of my friends. It is almost four months since we parted but I hope it will not be four weeks longer before we can meet again. I think I shall be content to stay at home when this rebellion is crushed out. I want to see the end of it for our cause is just and conquer we must the sooner the better. How I wish they would submit and save their lives and property. You will see that I have wrote this letter in a dirty sheet of paper but it is the only one that I had. Well ma I wish I had some good tobacco but all that we can get here is poor stuff and scarce at that but you know that I would get along somehow or other. How I should like to be at home today then I could have a good shelter and a good fire and a place that I could sit up strait in. But this place I have to sit bent over and it leaks at that. Well while I have been writing this the cannons roar so you may think that I do not have much chance to think. Our forces here are about 80,000 men and 300 pieces of artillery. I tell you the rebels has got to give up or they will get rubbed out. It is foolish for them to resist but they may bother us in this place for a week for the place is well fortified and they have some good fighting men as well as we. When we shall but I hope we shall pretty quick for I want to hear from home. Well ma everything remained quiet in our camp until Friday about three o'clock in the afternoon when we were alarmed by the long roll. We flew to arms double quick I tell you and had our Regt into line in less than five minutes and on the march out of the woods double quick (by the way I had forgot to tell you our camp is in the woods and the whole division is the same) into a large field and formed into line of battle. Well two Regt was sent in one direction and we were sent in another to support one of our Regt that was on picket. And it happened to be this same Regt 63 PV that the enemy were driving in. Well we ran just as hard as we could. Our officers and men shouting. The balls flying like hail. We were in the road until we got pretty close and found ourselves in range of the enemy's canon then we deployed into the woods and came to the edge of the woods to a fence where we poured our fire into them. There we found the 63 PV firing with all their weight at the rebels. Well the way the rebels ran was a caution to cripples. Our Regt did not loose a man and only had three wounded. Our company did not get hurt at all. The 63 lost 4 or 5 men killed and several wounded. We did not follow the enemy because they would have led us in range of their fort where they would have blown us sky high. Well ma it made me think of a nest of bumble bees around my ears. There was no use of dodging for they would come on every side of you just to accommodate. Well for my part I had no fears at all. I kept as cool as though I were hunting deer. I hope my presence of mind never will forsake me in times of danger. Well ma it is something of a dread to face danger like this but our general said he never saw a better charge made than the 57 made on that occasion. Well we have got our name up and I hope they will not place us in more danger on that account but I suppose they will. For they will place men that they can depend upon.

Well ma I have just had the good luck to get 2 letters from you. One dated April 5 and one the 8. The first containing one dollar for which you have my warmest thanks. Ma I could not help shedding tears I was so overjoyed to hear from you and I never wanted money so bad in my life. I think this will stand me if I can get tobacco enough. As for sending provisions to me now, you cannot know how but I thank you for your kindness to think of me. You must excuse me for I have got my dinner over cooking and the men act like a parcel of wolves. While writing I hear the boom of cannon and like. As any way we shall be called out in a few moments we cannot tell anything about it. We are not permitted to leave camp for a moment. So you see we have no liberty at all. My time is all filled up with cooking. I have almost 100 men to cook for. You may judge that it keeps me busy as bee. Well ma accept my warmest love for your kindness and a good kiss for you all. Yours truly. Ma you will see this was wrote after the rest. My hands are a little greasy and I am in a great hurry. A good kiss ma and hope for a speedy reunion. Again good day.

April 13, 1862 – Near Yorktown, Va.
Sunday morning. Dear wife and children another week has passed by and I am still alive and well and I hope you are. Well since I wrote last to you I have seen considerable hardship. It commenced raining and kept it up for three days and nights. Cold and mud. It was the hardest time I have yet seen. Our cook was taken sick and I took his place and consequently had to be exposed to the weather more on that account, but thanks to kind providence my health is good. Well on Wednesday we moved our camp back about one and half miles out of range of the enemy's guns. The roads are so bad that we cannot get our big guns through. I suppose this is the strongest place that the rebels has got anywhere. No doubt it will cost us great many lives to take it but I hope and pray that it may not be as bloody a battle as they had in Tenn. I presume you have seen the account of it. We have not received any mail since last Monday nor do we know…..<missing the rest of this letter>

April 18, 1862 – Friday Morning Near Yorktown, Va.
Dear wife & children. I take another opportunity to write you a few lines to let you know that I am alive & well for which I feel thankful. Well ma I have not heard from you since last Sunday but I hope you are well. I think I shall get a letter today when the mail comes in, hope I shall. Well ma I wrote to you last Sunday. I have not had time since we had to go out on picket duty on Sunday night and came off on Monday night all safe & sound, but I tell you some of us came near getting killed or taken prisoners and I was in the muss. I lost my gum blanket in the scrape and was glad

to get off as easy. You see that 4 of us were posted about 30 rods in advance of the rest of the company and a lot rebel cavalry came upon us and we had to run like whelps. We skulked in the brush until we got to our company then we fired upon them. They returned the fire but did not hit any of us but we found plenty of blood where they were the next morning. Well we got along very well and I was glad to get back to camp safe and sound. Well ma this is not a very pleasant life to live to have to skulk around and hurt your fellow being and pick them off every chance you can get, but they do the same to us. Well ma we had to go on picket again on Monday night and just came off last night. The enemy kept popping away at us all day. The balls would whistle by us like fury. Well they fired their shells at us and killed two men and wounded one but not of our company. Our cannon were playing into them all the time and have been for sometime. How long the rebels will hold out we do not know but we shall give them fits when we get all ready. We have not got all of our heavy guns mounted yet and may be it will take a week or more but this is a strong place. We, that is on our side, have men killed every day and we of course kill a good many of them. I tell you I am sick of this fun for we have to hold ourselves in readiness at a moments warning. Last night we were called up twice and formed in line ready to march. The night before I did not sleep a wink and you can guess how much I slept last night after being out in line twice all harnessed for battle. There was heavy firing along our picket lines last night and we supposed our picket would be drove in but they were not. I have not heard this morning what it amounted to. We cannot tell what moment we shall be called out. It may be in a minute and it may not but I shall be glad when this war is over if I live to get out of it and I hope it will not be long either. Well ma you had better have what manure there is hauled on that piece of ground and planted just the same as it was last year. I was in hopes I should get home in time to do it but I am afraid it would be late planting, but I think the fighting in Va. will be done up in two weeks at any rate and it seems to me they will have to give up. I wish they would today. I tell you it would please me. Well ma I must close for I shall have to get dinner. It keeps me busy but as long as my health remains good I do not care. How I should like to see the folks in old Rush and hope I shall sometime and that before a great while. Luther is not very well but is getting better. He stayed in camp when we were out the last time. Well ma remember me. My love to you all. Give my respects to all. A good kiss for you and the children. Yours ever. Write as often as you can. Good day. The weather is fine and warm.

April 22, 1862 – Near Yorktown, Va.

Dear wife and children. I take another opportunity to write you a few lines to let you know that I am well and hope you are the same. Well ma I wrote to you on Friday and kept looking for a letter from you but did not get any until last night. Wm. Hinds came here and brot a letter and some tobacco, sugar and postage stamps. Well ma we had just got into camp wet to the skin. I felt discouraged. The mail had come in and no letter from you, but in a few minutes Hinds came and I felt like a new man. You cannot think how it cheers me up. You will not wonder when I tell you how we fare. Well ma Saturday morning we were called up at three o'clock and formed in line with arms and stood till day light but did not have to go out of camp. But we had camp duties to do through the day and at night we had to go out and dig in the entrenchments. Almost all night the rain pouring down in torrents. Well we were wet to the skin came home and crawled into out holes and slept with our wet clothes on. Well Sunday it rained all day and we went to work to fix up our cabin a little, but at night we were wet as rats. Well we rolled up in our blankets and slept as sound as you please. Well Monday it looked as though it would clear off and we had to go and work on the road. It did not rain until just at night. Then came a heavy thunder shower. Oh it poured down. It wet us through so you can see what made me feel so discouraged. Last night we slept in our wet clothes and this morning we had to get up at 3 o'clock all wet and mud, harness up and stand in line till daylight. This is now just at sunrise. It is clear and nice, looks fair. Hope we can get our clothes dry today. I tell you this is pretty hard fare. We do not get rations enough to make us comfortable. We have not seen any bread but hard crackers since we left Hampden and I have got tired of them. But we do not get enough of them at that. But when we get the roads fixed we shall get enough. Well it is strange that we do not get sick but we enjoy pretty good health. We are in hopes that we shall get things fixed here so that the enemy will give up and not fight at all. Hope they will give up for they have got to be whipped at any rate and I hope they will spare their own lives and ours too. I should not wonder if we were here three or four weeks before we attack them for I believe McClellen meant to have had the war ended here and

I hope it will. It is the opinion of the most of the folks that this siege will end the war. Well I suppose that keeps our courage up so that we can stand almost anything. I have quit cooking. It was to hard for me. I had to go on picket just the same and do other duties and I quit. I do hope it will remain fair weather. It will be so much more pleasant. While I am writing this I am wet to the skin. I tell you ma this is not like home for then I could have dry clothes to put on and a good shelter and dry bed and a good bedfellow. I shall know how to prize such things if I live to enjoy them again.

April 28, 1862 – Va.

Dear wife & children. I will try & write you a few lines for I do not know when I shall get another chance. We just came of picket. We got into camp 9 o' clock at night very tired I tell you & this morning we are to have inspection so I shall not have more than fifteen minutes to write in. Well ma I am well but tired. I expect that we shall move today. The army has been moving for two days. We have our eight days rations to carry with us. They make a heavy load but I guess that we can stand it. We must try any way. Well ma the pay rolls has just come in & I think that we shall get our pay today. If I do I shall send some money home. Well I must get ready for inspection. If we do not move right away I will finish this letter. Well inspection is over & it has commenced raining so I think if we move we shall have a nasty time. Well we shall have to take it as it comes. You wanted to know if I had enough to eat. We get along very well. We buy considerable stuff such as butter fish & sometimes fresh beef also apples. But when we get on a march we shall have to live on hard tack. It will come tough but I guess that we can stand it. We have & can again. But how I do wish this thing was settled so that we could live at home once more. It would seem so good but it may be a long time before this is settled. But if they at the north will only unite & put shoulder to the wheel & help put down this rebellion I think it would be crushed out in a short time. But you know that they always have to have politicks mixed up with patriotism so as to spoil it all. I am afraid sometimes that they will get to fighting among themselves. If they should I would like to have our Regt up there we would give the cowards fits. But enough of this. I am in hopes that we shall be successful in this move & drive the rebs so far that they will never get back. But then they may drive us we cannot tell. Well ma the peach trees are in blossom & it looks like spring. I am glad to see it. When we were on picket we could see the rebs just across the river. They appeared harmless. We could not talk with them for the noise the river made. They would sit on the bank on one side & our men on the other without arms. I think that they do not want to fight & if it were not or their leaders it would soon be settled. Well ma I have wrote all the news that I can think of & shall have to close. Give my best respects to all inquiring friends. My love to you all so good day. Yours ever. It rains yet. One o'clock in after noon.

You will see paper is scarce here as well as money and everything is scarce except rebels and I wish it was just the reverse, don't you? I never received that letter that you sent me with money in nor have we got our pay yet and I hope we shall not til after the great battle for it might get stole from us, but I wish I had a dollar or two by buy tobacco with in case I could find some. Well there has always been a way provided and I guess there will be in this case. Well ma keep your courage up. Do not worry about me any more than you can help. Tell the boys to help you all they can for they do not know anything about what a soldier has to suffer to secure to them the liberty they enjoy but ma I must bid you good day hoping to see you yet in life and health with all the rest of my friends at home. Give my best respects to all inquiring friends. My best love to you and the children. Yours ever.

May 1862

May 1, 1862 – Near Yorktown, Va.
Dear wife & children I take another opportunity to write you a few lines to let you know that I am still alive and middling well. I do not feel as well this morning as I could wish but think when I get some rest I shall feel better. I received some paper & envelopes on Sunday night and on Monday I received a letter from you dated April 24. Was very glad to hear from home and was glad to hear that you were well. I had got quite anxious to hear from you for fear that you were sick. I told you in my last letter that I thought we should get our pay this week but I guess that we shall not. Today we are a going to be mustered in for pay that is for March & April. That of course we shall not be paid probably in two months to come. They will manage to keep back 2 months pay or more until the war is over. On Sunday night we had to go out and guard in the rifle pits and stayed all night did not sleep any. Well on Monday night we rested all night. Well I had forgot we did not

for we had to get up Tuesday morning at 2 1/2 o'clock and keep under arms till day light. Well Tuesday we moved our camp 1/2 mile to get a little dryer place. It is awful muddy & rainy here. It does seem as though it would rain all of the time and the storms are very cold indeed. If it were as cold up with you I am sure it would be snow instead of rain. Well we had just got to bed on Tuesday night when we were told that we would have to get up at 2 o'clock and start off on duty for 24 hours with our rations. Well it was dark and stormy but away we went to guard the batteries. No more sleep. We stayed till this morning after daylight when we were relieved and we came back to camp tired enough. Well we did not meet with any accident but close to us there was a sharp engagement this morning at 3 o'clock. Very sharp firing so close to us that some of the bullets came close to us. But it not being in our division I have not heard how they made out. We were placed at the extreme right of our division and this skirmish took place on the left of the other division. That is the reason that I do not know how they came out. Well ma we spread out our blankets this morning after we got into camp and thought we would sleep. We all lay down. I tried to sleep but my bones ached so that I could not sleep. So I got up and here I sit with a little piece of board in my lap sitting on the ground scribbling a few lines to you. The rest of the boys in our dog hole asleep well. Let them rest. I get very tired a great many times. So tired that I can put my blanket on, sit down in the wet and cold and sleep as sweet as in bed. It seems strange but we get used to it. We can even sleep when the cannon was within a short distance and while on Pickett. I have seen some of them sleep sound when the balls were flying around our heads and an enemy in sight of us. It seems strange but it is true. It does not seem that we could stand it but I do not know but we enjoy as good health as the people do at home. I shall be glad when this great struggle is over if we live to see it. I think this will be the greatest battle ever known. You can see in the Herald a map of the enemy's works that we shall have to take if we conquer them. Well ma I was glad to hear that the work was going on in the shop hope it will continue. You spoke about that woman being sick. She may sacrifice her life yet but that is her last out and not mine. I guess they will find out they will not get along as well when they are sick as they used to. Well they must look out for themselves. I shall have to close for want of time but I will try to write some more and put in with this for the mail will not go out till tomorrow morning. So good day Cornelia.

Well ma we have just been mustered in for pay for the past 2 months. When we shall get it I cannot tell. Well if we get the other 2 months pay pretty quick, if we should I shall send some home as soon as possible for I do not want to keep much by me for we do not know what will happen. If I should fall on the field my pockets might get robbed but I hope that I shall come out all right. Today it is quite still on the lines but very little firing today. It may be a calm such as is before a storm. More like than any way that we shall be called up tonight, such is the life that a soldier has to live. I shall never forget some of the scenes that we have passed through. Well enough of this. Well ma I am glad you do not get discouraged. I hope you will not. I shall try to keep up good courage just as long as I can. I want you to write to me as often as you can. I am in hopes that I shall get a letter from you tonight hope I shall. I feel better than I did this morning when I was writing but I feel lame. If I could rest a few days it would be all right but there is no rest here. The greatest activity prevails amongst the soldiers for all our fare is hard. Well ma I must close this letter for want of news that would be interesting. Ma I should like to be at home but I want to see this war to close and that as soon as possible. I often think of home while on Pickett duty in the lonely night. Think of it to sit all night by the side of a tree or stump watching for a deadly foe. Well it makes me feel sad to think that mankind will be so foolish and wicked to meet their judge without being prepared. Ma I must bid you good day not forgetting to thank you for your kindness to me. My love to you all. Be good boys. Good day.

May 4, 1862 – Near Yorktown, Va.
Dear wife and children I received a letter from you last night. Enclosed I found one dollar. I feel very much obliged to you but I could have got along without it. I got some of Wm. Hinds but I thank you just as much as though I were out of money. Well ma I had looked for a letter 2 or 3 days before I got it but I did not blame you at all. I was very glad to hear that you were well. It is my greatest trouble that some of my family will get sick or something happen to you. But I know that you are amongst friends and I am in the face of an enemy ready to take our lives any moment. Well ma I was surprised in reading your letter to think

that my name as Capt. This is the first I ever heard of Capt. JW Granger. As for myself I am nothing but a private yet nor do I know as I want to be. Although I should like the pay of an officer but that is not my luck. But if the war will close and let me out safe and sound is all that I will ask of them. But enough of this we have not been in any fight since I wrote you last. Our duty is just about the same. There is heavy firing everyday and we expect the great hell will open soon. Maybe tomorrow morning. And it may not. But it is the opinion of almost everyone that it will open within 2 or 3 days at the farthest. I expect it will be one of the greatest sights ever seen almost. Only think of 500 pieces of artillery on each side opening fire at one time on a space of ground only 8 or 9 miles in length. The roar will be almost deafening. To say nothing about small arms, but if my life is spared I shall feel very thankful. We have to get up every morning either before 3 o'clock or at 3, harness up, form lines and if we do not have to march out we stack arms and wait until daylight under arms ready for an attack. You can see it is a dogs life to live at any rate. But I hope we shall not have to be here a great while longer. The weather for 2 or 3 days has been very nice and this morning is a pleasant Sabbath morning. The camp is full of life and stir but who knows how many of us will live to see another like this. When I think of the great slaughter at Pittsburgh Landing it makes me shudder to think of this place. But I hope there will not be as many lives lost here as there but we do not know. We have not received our pay yet but we expect it every day well if I should get it I shall send all of it. But just what I want to use for it might get lost. Well ma you spoke of D. Baker ploughing that ground and Gov. Huntsman talk with him. I guess I will write the Gov a few lines and Ed may hand them to him. But let him alone pass him by for he might do him some harm. If I live to get home I think they will haul in their horns. But while I am gone you had not better provoke them any more than you can help but enough of this. I got a letter from H Johnson last night I will write to him today if I can get time. I see he has not forgotten me yet nor the parables that was spoke to that dog. Well ma I shall have to close this for want of news to write that will suit you, and I should like it to come home to tell you it and tell you that the war was over, and I safe at home. Well ma my love to you to all inquiring friends a good kiss for you and the children. Yours Truly.

May 6, 1862 – Williamsburgh, Va.

Dear wife and children I have a moment to spare and I thought I would write you a few lines to let you know that I am alive and well but about worn out with fatigue. Well ma on Sunday we found out that the enemy had left Yorktown. All was confusion in camp. We had orders to march with three days rations. We started 2 1/4 o'clock and marched after the enemy until night and camped (illegible). We had to go on picket all night. It commenced raining and rained all night and the next day. The roads were the worst I ever saw. The mud knee deep. Well as we approached Williamsburgh we heard heavy firing. We have got within 3 miles of there when we were ordered to unsling knapsacks and prepare for action. Well we piled up our things by the side of the road over coats and everything and started double quick through the mud and that was over the tops of my boots in a good many places. We ran about 2 1/2 miles to the scene of action and one of the awful scenes that I ever saw. Men in every direction dead and dying, the roar of cannon. Bursting of shell. The groans of the wounded. Such a sight I never wish to see again. We were formed in line of battle the rain pouring down like fury and we without blankets or overcoats wet the skin. Well after a little the firing ceased but we had to stay in the woods all night without sleep or food until daylight when we were marched out to charge on their fort. But we soon found they had fled in the night leaving all of their dead and wounded on the field. Oh ma it was hard to hear the poor soldiers groan that had to lay on the field in the cold storm. I helped to carry them in until I was tired out. There was a great many killed on both sides. How many I do not know. This morning they were carrying in the wounded as we marched through the battlefield and saw men and horses and men lying in the mud dead and dying. It made me shudder but we passed on and pursued the enemy through the town of Williamsburgh and halted and here we are. Our men are bringing in prisoners all the time. Our company are all safe and I feel thankful. I was anxious to let you know that I were safe. How soon we shall pursue the enemy we do not know. My clothes are mud up to my behind and no sleep for two nights you may know that I am worn out. Luther went back with others after our provisions and has not returned yet. When I shall get a chance to send this I do not know. Well ma I will write to you again. I expect to go on to Richmond. Ma my love to you and all the rest of my friends. Yours truly. I do not know as you can read this but you must make allowances.

May 11, 1862 – Sunday

On the road to Richmond. Dear wife & children I take this opportunity to write you a few lines to let you know that I am alive & well and hope you & yours are the same. Well ma we started from Williamsburgh on Friday and marched until last night. We have passed through some of the nicest country that I ever saw. Large fields of wheat up to our hips. Cattle & horses turned into feed. We camped in one place where they had 192 acres in one field it was almost spoilt. I should think they would get sick of war. The white folks have most of them left. The negroes are as thick as bees. We expect to find the enemy at Richmond. We are within 45 miles of that place. The weather has been fine since last Monday night. I hope it will continue so until we get to Richmond and I hope they will surrender when we get there for I do not want to see another like the last one. Well ma we have not marched any today but the troops are passing all the time. Such a sight I never saw in my life. You write in your letters that everything looks gloomy to you this spring. Well I get somewhat discouraged some of the time and then I feel very cheerful again. It is the opinion of the most of the folks that if we succeed in capturing the army at Richmond and Beaureguard the war will be at an end. No doubt but we shall take Richmond in a very short time. We do not get daily papers very regular now so we cannot tell what they are doing out west but I hope our men will whip them and close this war immediately. Well ma I still think if my life is spared I shall get home this summer. I did think that we could get home this month but I rather think we may get home in June. Well I shall be satisfied if we do. Well ma if you see the papers they will tell something about the fight last Monday. For my part I cannot get a correct account of the number killed & wounded but there must have been a good many. Well ma while I am writing large droves of cattle are passing by for the army. Ma I will send you another letter that fell into my hands accidentally. If I should live to get home I will explain it to you when you get it. You must not tell anyone how you came by it. You will see at once who wrote it and who it was intended for. Well if it is not simple I never saw anything that is. It seems as though she and the Gen. wife were going in partnership. Well I wish Low could get hold of that letter and after you read it if you can place it where he could get it and not mistrust how it came there. I would like it well. I think they have got a nice set in the bag and of the burgh. Please let me know whether Wils Ferry has gone home. I have not heard from him in over a month. I presume he is back by this time. Well ma I should like to be at home and enjoy your company and see my friends again and I hope the time is not far distant when I can. Well ma I must close this for want of news but you have my best wishes and my warmest love. I hope to live to repay you for all your kindness to me. Give my respects to all inquiring friends. So good day ma. Tell the boys their pa thinks of them and wants to see them very much. My love to them. Be good boys and mind their ma. Yours Truly.

No. 2

Well ma inspection is over and I am once more sitting under my little shade. The sun shines very hot and I thought I would talk with you a little while with pen. Well ma since we left Alexandria we have had it pretty hard. We thought that was soldering but since we left that place we have not had good tents, but all the tents we have are oil blankets put those together in this style, a pole across the top and you gave a little shelter. The ends being open. Each one of us have one of those blankets so that two of us have to tent together. Well if we have an extra gun blanket then we have something under us as well. Then we spread our overcoats to lay on and cover up with our woolen blankets. Well this makes our bed. Sometimes our coats and blankets are as wet as they can be but we cover up the best we can and try to sleep. You know I lost my gun blanket at Yorktown and Williamsburg I got a good oil & one good gun blanket so I am provided for. Well ma I will tell you what my load consist of when on a march. Well we carry our cartridge box, cap box, 40 rounds of cartridges & caps, gun and bayonet, one haversack with 3 days provision which consist of coffee, sugar, hard bread, meat & cup, spoon, plate & all things to cook your food, or else eat it raw. Well then a canteen that holds 3 pints of water for your march. Next comes our knapsack with all our clothing, books, paper, tobacco &C, our army blankets, tent blankets, overcoats &C. Well now you would laugh to see a lot of men make pack mules of themselves if there was not any need of it. Well I tell you those loads feel heavy after having them on all day, although we do not travel a great way. The country that we have passed through since we came to Fortress Monroe is as nice as any that I have ever saw. All that it wants is some good

128

enterprising Yankees and it would be as fine a place as need be. The water is first rate, plenty of good springs, plenty of timber. The land level and no stone. What more could anyone ask but peace and submit to the government. I should not want the darn niggers there. I have got so that I almost hate them. Well ma I guess I have wrote enough of this. Well what did you think of that letter that I sent you. Well I think it was rich. Well you may guess that I laughed some just to think she fainted and wrung her hands in despair. Oh 'twas wonderful pity she can not be comforted by someone, maybe she can. Someone had ought to relieve her (poor thing). Well if I ever se that dear husband of hers I shall have some fun. I will bet if we both get home safe it will cost him some treats. Well how does the Gov. take it about that Cat? I expect he will roar but can't help it if I were there I would hold him. Well ma how I should like to be at home with you and I hope the time will shortly come that the soldiers can return to their homes. I think it will be the happiest day that ever I saw if I can return and find my family all safe and well. I must close. I do not know when I can write again but will as often as I can and ant you to do the same. Yours ever. Be good boys and mind your ma. Remember your pa. Good day.

May 16, 1862 – Cumberlands Landing, Va.

Dear wife & children I have another opportunity to write you a few lines to let you know that I am live & well. I received a letter from you dated May 10 and was glad to hear from you. I had been marching in the rain all day and wanted something to cheer me up and it always cheers me to hear from home. We have marched two days since I wrote to you. One day of it was in the rain and mud. We have had a nice spell of pleasant weather until this last rain but thanks to kind providence it looks like fair weather again. Well ma I have sent you $20 dollars and Luther has sent in the same package 25 dollars. When it gets to Montrose you and Edward had better go and get it. You will have to pay the express on it. Also my watch I sent. I have broke the crystal, one hand & lost the ring out of the stem. Ed may get it fixed and carry it until I come home if ever I do. Well ma about the money I want you to pay Jack Chamberlain five dollars if I owe him that much and pay 10 to Mr. Bently. You may keep the rest if you need it but if you have enough without it you may pay Mr. Bently the 15. But be sure and keep the five if you need it. Well ma I told you that I had sold that revolver that I had of Norman. Well I got my pay and bought

129

another one for the same money that is worth 4 of them that I had. I have been offered 15 dollars but I thought I would keep it. I should have been glad to have sent more money home but could not without selling my revolver. I owe Luther some that I borrowed of him the other pay day $5 dollars. Well ma did Sabra pay you half the cost of express on those things you sent me at Washington. Luther paid me and he says that his wife wrote that she had paid so if that is the case I must pay him back. I will enclose the receipt for the express on money & watch. Well ma we are within 23 miles of Richmond but when we shall get there I do not know. I presume that we shall not stay here a great while. We may have to start tonight. We cannot tell what moment we shall be called into battle nor do we know when a bullet will hit us but so far we have every reason to feel thankful that our lives are spared thus far. Well ma you can get the news sooner in the papers about our movements than you could from me but I will write just as often as I can for I know that you feel anxious and would like to hear from me every day. I shall be very glad if the time ever comes that I can write to you that I am coming home but I hope that time will come. I see by the papers that they are fighting out west pretty hard. I hope they will whip them out nice & quick. Well ma I will tell you some clothing prices we have to pay for little luxuries eggs 40 cents per doz., butter 50 cents per lbs., crackers 20 to 25 per pound, cheese 50 per lbs., and everything else as high. Pies, little made things, just about three mouthfuls 25 cts. A piece bread and everything else the same. Just with one cargo of such stuff and a man might make his fortune. The soldiers do not care how much they pay if they can only get it. Some of them will pay $1.00 for enough for one meal. Well for my part I was very hungry when I got here and wet too. I bought 75 cts worth of ginger cake and satisfied my hunger. Well I shall not buy much stuff at them prices. If I had time I would tell you something of the load we have to carry when we march but I will some other time. I shall have to close this. You may direct your letters as usual I hope Secesh will play out & over for I should like to get home. Give my love to all inquiring friends. My love to you all. I will write soon.

May 18, 1862 – Pamunky River. Cumberland Landing, Va.
Dear wife & children I take this opportunity to write you a few lines to let you know that I am well and I hope you are the same. Well ma this is Sunday morning and it is very hot. It is like a

morning in Aug. when the sun shines here it is very hot but thanks to kind providence my health continues good. We feel considerably rested and have plenty to eat again. How soon we shall leave this place I know not. Maybe before night. We cannot tell what a day will bring forth. Well ma this morning before I got up I was thinking of a Sabbath morning at home. How quiet and nice a day of rest a day of quiet but how different here. I have not seen a day of quiet since I have been in the service. The most any day has seemed like Sunday to me was the Tuesday after the Battle of Williamsburgh. That day seemed like Sunday although it was not quiet but it seemed sad and lonely to me. I hope we shall not have to pass through another scene like that but we may a good many of them. We cannot tell what the enemy will do between here and Richmond but I hope they will give up. Well so much for this. Well ma I believe it would seem good to me to be at home and I think I could enjoy a nice stroll around the lots and a good dish of boiled eggs such as we used to have but the question is will that time ever come again. I hope it will. It is hope that keeps my courage up. It is the thought of my family that cheers me in my lonely hours. It is the thoughts of home that nerves me for the onward march. It is the thoughts of peace and quiet being restored to our once happy country that should animate the soldier on to his duty. But for all this ma I sometimes feel sad and almost discouraged to think that the most of the business done by Congress is to fight over the everlasting Nigger question. I sometimes wish that the abolitionists were in the front of the battle. If they were placed there they would shut up for a while I guess but they have no idea of fighting any other way than with their tongues, and they ought to be cut out if they cannot stop talking. Well ma I guess you will get tired of hearing me berate them scoundrels this way but I cannot help it when I think of the misery they have caused. But this will not mend the matter now. Well we must make the best of it we can. Well ma I wrote to you the 16 and sent you 20 dollars and my watch by express and Luther sent 25 dollars in the same package. Write as soon as you get it and let us know. When we get our other pay I will try and send you some more. You see ma I do not forget you. If I could be set down in the old kitchen and spend this day I would not begrudge a good deal but when that time will come the Lord only knows. But I hope the time is not far distant that peace and quiet will be restored to our once happy country. Well ma I must fix for inspection that we have to have every Sunday morning. Everything on ready to march. This is to see if everything is in order our guns all bright, cartridges dry. And I tell you it is no small job to keep our guns bright when we are out in all sorts of weather and our guns lay in the dew at night. We have to scour them about twice a day. Well I get sick of it. I will bet if I live to get out of the service that I will not spend so much time cleaning guns and carrying knapsacks but the sooner I get home the better it will suit me. Well ma I must bid you good day. How I should like to be there with you. Well may love to you all. Tell all of my friends that I have not forgotten them.

May 21, 1862 – Cumberland Landing, Va.
Dear wife & children I take another opportunity to write you a few lines to let you know that I am well. As usual Luther is not very well. I am afraid he is a going to have the plague but hope not. Well ma it has been one week to day since we got here and the most of the time it has been pleasant and very warm. But I have recruited up a good deal. I tell you it seems good to have a chance to rest. There is a good deal of sickness in our camp now but I have stood almost anything and I still hope my health will be spared me until I get home but we cannot tell how it will be. The rest of our brigade left here last Monday. Our Regt was left here to guard some boats and I would not care if they would leave us here until the war was over, but no danger of that for I hear that we shall leave here tomorrow for bottom Bridge and join the rest of our division. I wrote to you that we belonged to Hamilton's Division but it is changed to Kearny's. So you will see in the papers that Kearny Division were not idle at Yorktowne nor Williamsburgh. This place is very pleasant and nice. We are encamped right besides the river. Any quantity of steamboats & ships playing up & down the stream all day. If I were at liberty to get on board and start for home it would please me very much indeed I tell you. Well when that time will come I cannot tell but hope it will before a great while. I think the work is a going on fine. Sescesh must play out the sooner the better for all parties concerned. Well ma you said in your last letter of May 10 that you had just received one from me dated May 1. It must have took a good while for it to go. It has been just a week to day since I received a letter from you. We are bothered to get our mails here but we expect to get them when we catch up with our division. Hope we shall. I have wrote to you as often as twice a week and

will if I can get a chance. I sometimes am afraid that we shall not get home this summer but I hope we shall for I am hearty sick of soldering although stand it first rate. I hope you will get that money that I sent you. I expected we should have got the rest of our pay by this time but we have not, but we are not in want of it yet. Well ma we have got some rebel tents that we are staying in now but when we move we will have to leave them. It seems good to get into comfortable tents again but it will not last long. But enough of this, before sending this I will wait until night and see if I can't get a letter from home. I do not know but the letters will come straight through to direct the same as used to, but I see it recommended to direct all letters to the Army of the Potomac to Washington and the Regt & Company and Division. For instance to me would be Washington DC Company A 57 Regt PV Kearny's Division. But I think they will come through without altering the direction. Well ma I do not know as I have any news to write that will interest you although the news from the army is good. That you can see by the papers. Well I will stop and wait for a while. If I should not get time to any more in this letter I will send you. My best love to you and children and all the rest of my friends. Yours truly.

Well ma I thought I would write you a few more lines but I do not know when you will get it. I have been out fishing a little while but did not have very good luck. But I got very wet. We have had a very hard shower of rain & hail. So much for that. I do not know when we shall get any more mail but I should like to hear from home first rate. Well ma I shall have to move from here tomorrow morning at 4 o'clock. I do not know when you will hear from me again for we do not know what a day may bring forth. Well ma I must bid you good day and will write you as soon as I can. My love to you all. Yours ever.

May 25, 1862 – Sunday. Chickahominy River, Va.

Sunday about noon Dear wife & children I take this opportunity to write you a few lines. Well ma I am well as ever and I hope you are and I hope still farther that you can enjoy your self better than I do. Well ma we started from Cumberland Landing early Friday morning and marched about 8 miles and camped as we supposed for the day but we only stayed a few hours before we had to start again. Well we marched 8 miles farther just to gain 21 miles. Well ten o'clock at night found us in the woods. We halted spread out

133

our blankets and lay down to sleep. The day had been very hot. Well we were tired enough I tell you. Well we got up at break of day and marched 1½ miles where we camped for the day and night. It commenced raining hard but it cleared off this morning. We started at 5 o'clock on our march and we have crossed Bottom Bridge and have got about six miles from where we started and here we are about 12 miles from Richmond. We may stay here until morning and we may not. The roads are very muddy. I feel quite worried about Luther. He was sick and we kept him with several others behind. I feel anxious to hear from him. He is so careless that he will not take care of himself. I am afraid but I hope he will. There is a great deal of sickness in the army. Just one half of company is on the sick list. I hope my life and health will be spared me until I get home. I received a letter from you the same day that I wrote you last dated 17. I was very glad to hear from you and was glad to hear that you were all well. I feel very sorry for Mrs. Kinyon. I pity her very much. I think James ought to write to her but I do not think they have been in a fight for I have not seen any account of it. Tell her to keep up good courage. She has my warmest sympathy. Give my respects to the old lady. Well ma I do not wonder that our friends are anxious to hear from us for a day may make a great change with us. I tell you we are chasing up close on the rebels. A few days will most likely tell the tale. I hope it will come out all right. I have put me op a shade and am lying down on my blanket writing this to you. I am tired enough to go to sleep but I think you would like to hear from me so here I am at it. I begin to think the war will soon be over if we take Richmond. How I should like to be at home with my family & friends today. I should know how to prize such a privilege but I do not know as I ever shall enjoy it again, but still I hope to. Wilson Ferry is with me. He came to us on Friday. He is well and makes good company. We joke and have some fun but you must keep still about matters. Never mind, you know what I mean. Well enough of this. I have stood it as well so far as any one in our company and I feel very thankful that my health continues so good. My face is tanned up black as a negro almost but I do not care for that as long as I feel well.

May 28, 1862 – Va. Somewhere but I do not know hardly where.
Well ma I take this opportunity to write you a few lines to let you know that I am alive and well so far. Well ma on Sunday night I

received 2 letters from you. One of them was dated March 15 and contained one dollar all safe & sound. Well I am glad it was not lost. Well you spoke in the other about Huntsman. Well I guess you will have to reject them off but be sure that have the writ in both of their names so that there will not be any crawl out about the cost. I wish I could be at home and see to things but I do not know when that will be if ever. But still my hopes keep good. Our Regt are on picket and I am with them. This makes the 24 day & we shall have to stay tonight. This is not very hard work here. On Monday I was within 11 miles of Richmond on fatigue duty. I told you in my letter of Sunday that Luther was sick but I thought he would be in camp that night but he did not come. Well I heard from him on Monday night and he was about 8 miles from our camp and was not so well. I wanted to go and see him but could not get leave. It commenced raining and we expected to have to go on that night. We were ordered to send back all our clothes except our blankets and all the sick was to be removed beyond the Chickahominy Creek so I sent a letter to Luther and 2 dollars in money. There is 8 or 9 of our company that will be with him so he will not be alone. I shall try to find him just as soon as I can. Yesterday and today there is heavy firing to the right of us. I think we shall have some hard fighting to do before we get into Richmond. But I hope not for my part I have seen as much as I want to but we must take Richmond in any rate. My health has not been very good for 3 or 4 days past but I am in hopes that I shall not get down sick. I am some better today so that I am well as long as I can keep around. Well ma I should like to be at home the 4 of July and see you. I hope it will be so that I can come. I will if I can you know that. I told you that I bought me a revolver well I traded it for another and got 8 dollars to boot and this one is a great deal better than the one that I had of Norman so that is a little good luck I guess. I will send you three dollars and would send you more but it is all small bills so I won't send but this one bill now. Well ma I am in the weeds writing this & I do not know when I shall get a chance to send it but I have to write just when I can get a chance for I know that you are anxious to hear from me as often as I can get a chance to write and I feel anxious to hear from you. It does me good to hear from you and hear that you are all well. I am in hopes that you have got that money & watch all safe. Let me know. You will wear the war news sooner by the papers and more current than I can write. Well ma I must bid you good day. Oh I must tell you I went to a house today and bought a choc cake such as they make in VA without salt or sederaties and paid 25 cents. Well now our dog would not eat it. If it had been good it would have been about a meal for a man. They told us they would not sell hens short of $1.50 a piece. Well I din't buy, but yesterday while in the woods we found 8 hens & a rooster. That day we shot them with our revolvers. Was nice. I killed 3 and kept one for 3 of us and it made us a first rate dinner. that was the first chicken that I have tasted since I left home. We have to have a little fun once in a while. So ma good day. My love to you & the children. Yours ever.

Wilson is here but do not say anything about that letter nor let it get out if you have not. If you have got it just burn it up. He has just wrote to Mrs. Law and directed it to Mrs. Huntsman but keep still. Say nothing about it.

June 1862

June 13, 1862 – Va. Friday Morning.
Dear wife & children I will try and write you a few lines to let you know that I am alive & well. As common I have not received a letter from you in almost 2 weeks. Well ma what is the reason? Well this morning they have commenced firing in earnest. What it will amount to I do not know but should not wonder if it brot on a general engagement before night and maybe a great many of us will sleep our last sleep in death. I am looking for a hard fight but I hope I may be mistaken. We have moved our camp and we now lay near the place where we fought on the 31 of May. The graves show that our fire told on the enemy at a terrible rate. It is shocking to see in a good many places their legs & arms & heads sticking out above the ground. The smell is horrible. But enough of this. I hope it will close soon. I think that this will close up the war. The sooner the better. only that we get all ready for the attack. Well ma I sent Edward 5 dollars (secesh) and now I will send you & Billy 2 bills. 10 for you & 1 for Billy. They will be good keepsakes. Well ma yesterday & today the weather is dreadful warm but I think it will rain before long. I will wait until the mail comes in before I close this. I may have to seal this without writing more so good by for this time. Yours ever.

Well ma I have waited for the mail to come in but I was disappointed I did not get a letter. I feel discouraged. I have a mind not to write again nor do I know as I will ever have a chance again. I feel out of humor. pray forgive me. I will not write more. Yours Truly. Give my love to all inquiring friends if I have any which I very much doubt that I have got. I feel discouraged & down hearted but I hope I am mistaken. I hope they have not all forgotten me.

June 16, 1862 – Va.
Dear wife & children I take another opportunity to write you a few lines to let you know that I am alive & I might say well, but I do not feel very well. But still I keep around. My health has been poor for about three or four weeks but I am glad that I can keep around. Well ma after fretting a good deal I received a letter from home dated June 5. I received it the 14. It was a good while coming but it done me a great deal of good. I had got so uneasy about home that it almost made me homesick & as for that matter if it would do any good I would be home sick anyhow. any time that we get through with this war I think that I shall be glad to get home. For if ever I was sick of anything it is this awful war. There is no peace night nor day. nor do you know what moment you will be called into action and have to face death in every shape. There is hardly a night but we are called up in line for battle. just as soon as the Pickets commence firing let it be at what time it makes no odds we have to jump for our guns & equipments haversacks canteens & be ready for a start. I suppose this is all right to guard against surprise. But I tell you I shall be glad if the time ever comes that I can be at home & enjoy the comforts of civil life again. You said in your letter that Norman told Edward that our Regt was not in the fight, but this was owing to mistake in the papers. I have seen several papers that put our dead & wounded in other Regts. But it makes not much difference. It was the hardest fight that I ever saw or ever want to see and I tell you it was the greatest wonder in the world that every one of us were not killed or taken prisoners. They must have been 5 to us one and they almost surrounded us at that & we were exposed to a murderous cross fire. I tell you a man did not know which way to dodge (but one thing I think it was whiskey in our officers that placed us in such a perilous situation). If they would drink less & let the soldiers have more it would suit me better. But enough of this I received a letter from Dennis Eaney the 14. He wrote they were all well. his father had been unwell but had got better. It does me good to hear from all the folks while I am here. Well ma last night

I was sergeant of the guard and while standing on my post my thoughts turned towards home. I just thought how it would seem to me to sit down to a table covered with a clean cloth & spread with such food as we used to have. how it would seem to me to have some bread and butter again or even to sit to a table in a chair. It seems strange to think of I have not had a mouthful of soft bread since we left Hampton & that was the 4 of April. I tell you this hard bread is hard stuff. Well we expect every day that the great battle will come off and to tell you the truth I think the rebels will fight hard. They will not give up until they are obliged to. a good many think they will evacuate but I do not think so and I am afraid we shall have the hardest battle ever fought for tis their all at stake here. But ma it may be before you get this you will hear of the fight in the papers. It takes a good while for a letter to come or go. Well ma I shall have to close hoping my life may be spared to see you again. Give my best respects to all inquiring friends. Yours Truly & ever.

June 21, 1862 – Seven Pines, Va.
Dear wife & children I will try & write you a few lines to day to let you know how I get along. Well ma I have not been well since the fight on 31 nor do I know when I shall be again. I have kept around so far but I do not get well. I have not done any fatigue duty nor am I able to. The doctor told me this morning that I had better stay at the hospital a few days but that is no better than the camp for they all have to sleep on the ground just the same. a sick person has to fare pretty hard. I have been taking quinine & feel hard pains under my shoulder blades but I hope to get over it in a few days. We have to move our camp every few days & it almost always rain when we have to move. Sometimes I get almost discouraged & don't care what becomes of me for some cause. I do not get many letters from home the last one that I got was dated June 4 & 5. this I got the 14 & I had not received one from you in almost 2 weeks before. I have kept writing to you often but I had made up my mind not to write any more until you would write to me. But I did not wish to wrong you for the letters might have got miscarried. I feel very anxious to hear from home. You cannot blame me for feeling out of patience but enough of this. We are in daily expectation of a battle but we do not know when it will. almost every day the soldiers are called under arms. We have large forces on fatigue duty day & night. The enemy shell them every day to stop their work but it does no good. Our men will hardly

ever reply to them. today they have fired away at our men but did them no damage. They shot 2 cannon balls right over our camp while I was sitting in my tent (if you would call it such for it only makes a shade). Our Regt is very much reduced by sickness & death. how many will be left when we get to Richmond (if we ever get there) the Lord only knows. Our hard work & exposure at Yorktown and at Williamsburgh will be felt by many of us as long as we live & I fear many of them will not live long at that. more than half of our company are on the sick list & our Regt cannot get over 200 men out on any duty. when we left Alexandria we had in our Regt over 750 effective men. Where are they now? a good many have died some have been killed in battles & a good many are sick. I hope when this great battles comes off if we are not all killed we shall be disbanded & sent home. I am in hopes this will finish up rebellion but it may hang on for years yet. The fourth of July will soon be on hand. how I should like to be at home to spend that day with you. But there is no prospect of that if ever. Luther is getting better & he is out today on fatigue. He ought not to have gone for he may get down again. Well I do not know as I have any news to write that will interest you. one thing I hate that is lice on our bodies. I presume about everyone here has more or less of them nuisances on us. sleeping on the ground and in old camps we cannot avoid them. I tell you they are not pleasant bedfellows. I have to get up 2 or 3 times in the night and hunt them chaps. So you see the enemy on one side with guns & the lice all over you, you do not know which way to dodge. But it is bad enough without laughing but you mought as well laugh as cry. Well ma I must close by asking you if you & yours do they miss me at home & shall I ever be so happy as to see home again. this we cannot tell but I must bid you good day hoping I shall hear from you soon. You would write often if you knew how much it cheers me up to hear from you. Give my best respects to all inquiring friends. My love to you all. good day. Yours ever.

June 24, 1862 – Fair Oaks, Va.

Dear wife & children I take another opportunity to write you a few lines. Well ma I received a letter from you dated June 12 on the 22. I was very glad to hear from you. I had began to think you had forgotten me but then I suppose I was somewhat fretful on account of being unwell. You said you had received one from me dated June 2. Well ma I wrote one dated May 25 & one 29 containing 3 dollars in money & one to Edward with one dollar in it dated 31 the same day that we went into battle. did you receive them? if so let me know since then I have sent you & Ed & Billy some (secesh) money that is of no account of course, only to look at. Well ma you may think that I have scolded you rather hard but I felt bad & discouraged so you must excuse me. I feel a good deal better so that I am able to do duty again although I feel weak but I am in hopes that I shall get along. I tell you this is a hard life to live. We have to keep ourselves ready at a moment's warning to meet the enemy. There is not a day but we have alarms, but I hope the rebels will get discouraged & leave. We are strongly fortified & if they attack us it will cause a terrible slaughter. I think there has been lives enough lost already in this terrible war but where it will end the Lord only knows or who will survive. But I suppose that each one hopes it will be himself but this is not for us to know. There is a great many sick & dying without much care. Preserve Hinds is here now to see if he can get a furlough for his boys to go home. all 3 of them are sick. Henry Hinds is very sick. I guess he will get a furlough, but Fred & (illegible name) I think will have to stay. I tell you they had rather the soldiers would stay & die than let them go home & recruit their health, but then it is a difficult job to do them all justice for there is always so many slinks that play up sick for the sake of getting out of danger that they hardly know what to do. But enough of this you spoke about Maria & Betsy. I wrote to Dennis the 16 giving him a brief sketch of our marching & fight etc. Well ma Mr. Hinds says the fruit is all killed on the creeks but that there is plenty on the hills. Well I am glad if there is a going to be any in reach but I do not know as I shall ever live to enjoy it. But still I have hopes my life will be spared to see you again. So far providence has watched over me & protected my life & I hope still to meet my friends again. I often feel sad when I think of home & wonder if ever I shall enjoy the comforts of home, but cannot answer the question. Well ma the weather has been very warm & I wish I could have cotton shirts to wear & cotton pants or them that is lined with cotton, but our pants are course woolen & they scratch my legs like fury. But anything is good enough for a soldier, but the poor nigger there is nothing good enough for him. So the world goes. But it is impossible for us to get cotton shirts so we must make the best of it that we can. Luther is getting better so that he can do duty. Well ma it takes a great while to get a letter home and as long to get one from home. Well ma since I commenced writing the mail has come in and brot me one letter from you & one from Edward dated June 19. Well you cannot think how glad I was. It done me more good than all the medicine that I have taken. It cheers me up to think & know the kind regards the folks had for me. You said you received 3 dollars well that is safe. Tell Mrs. Kinyon she has my best respects. I wrote to Orlo to see if I could hear from James. I have not got an answer yet but it is all right being she has heard from him. Well ma about Henry's taking my place. That is out of the question. That cannot be done in order to get out of the service a person must be wounded in battle or he must be dead. I tell you it is a hard case to get out but I think after Richmond is taken there will be a good many get their discharge & I am afraid that a good many will go to their long homes but we cannot tell but as for Henry tell him I thank him for his kind offer. But I guess if he were here his knees would tremble a little when he heard them commence firing. He has no idea of the sound nor can he have until he hears it. To hear ten thousand small arms besides cannons at the same time it would make him think the world was coming to an end and then hear them bullets whistle by his ears & fairly burn his cheeks, he would not think it pleasant I tell you, (nor do I either) but all this I have seen & heard & more too. Edward did not say in his letter that he received that one dollar but I presume he did and forgot to mention it. It gave me great pleasure to read Ed's letter & I will try to write to him soon. The fight between the Monitor & Merrimac pleased me much & his opinion about those two women below is about correct. I guess I tell you it would give me the greatest pleasure in the world to come home and even if I should get wounded in battle. I do not know but I should be fortunate at that but after all I hope to escape & see this rebellion crushed out and return to my friends safe and sound. I hope this may be the case. Edward says he has dreamed about my coming home. Well I have dreamed about getting home but there was always something wrong. I could not get my things or was not half dressed or something I had forgot. So dreams go. But I hope it will be a reality that I shall get home safe & sound. Last night we had a tremendous thunder shower. Today it is hot & sultry. Wils Ferry is sick & gone to the hospital today. I guess he is a little scared. You need not say a word nor do I want you to but he is afraid to say not a word. Luther has just got a letter from his wife. He had not heard from her in a good while. He is out of the camp just now so I do not know the news she writes. Well ma I must close by sending

141

my best respects to all inquiring friends. If you see Lorenzo Williams or Maria tell them I should like to hear from them very much. I have thought I would write to him but I cannot get time but think I will soon if I live. Well ma keep up good courage & do the best you can & I will do the same. Hope we shall not be separated a great while longer. My best love to you & the children. Tell Edward to write to me as often as he can. Good day .

I would not care if you would send me half-doz. postage stamps for they are hard to get sometimes and sometimes we can get them plenty.

PS. All is quiet along our lines today so far but we do not know what moment we shall hear firing along our picket line. Such is the life a soldier has to live when his division is in front. This is the case with ours & this is the way we were at Yorktown.

June 29, 1862 – Washington, DC
Dear wife & children last night I received a letter from you dated June 25, was glad to hear from you and to hear that you were well, but was sorry to hear that Ed did not take more interest the affairs at home. Now Edward I want you to be kind to your mother and I want you to work all the time you can get. Make yourself useful. You are at an age to form a character for future life. You have had a good chance which if you live you will regret that you have misspent. Do try Edward to improve on this opportunity to be industrious. I do not know as you will ever see me again. If I should not return there is a great responsibility resting upon you. Think of your mother. think of your little brother. It belongs to you to care for them. Many of younger years than yourself have been left to care for a mother. Remember Edward the care your parents have had on you. Account the feelings they now have towards you. Edward I feel proud of you that is your capability for doing business and I want to feel proud of you for your care and industry. Edward I do not write this to hurt your feelings but for your good. Now I may not ever see you again and I may. Which it will be we do not know. If I should live to get back I should feel proud of you to find my affairs all strait. Do try to be industrious. Be kind to your mother. Be prudent etc. Well ma yesterday it rained most all day so we sat in our tents. We expected to get our pay on Monday but we have not got it yet but we expect it today. Well last night we got that box that started with Hinds well ma one of the bottles was broke all to smash and I guess it spoiled the

paper. But we got two bottles and that done us some good I tell you. It seemed like old times. The tobacco was all safe that under shirt was all wet. I am sorry you sent that back for I had two shirts besides that I have more clothes than I know what to do with. Well ma my health is pretty good considering the chance we have. We got a large box of provisions that was sent from Rushville by Hinds and it comes first rate. It is filled up with almost everything in the shape of eatables for which we all feel very thankful. Ma I tell you there is nothing that makes a soldier feel so tender as such gifts from home. To think they have not forgotten us. Although we are separated we are not forgot. Those favours will never will be forgot by those that are true at heart. Ma there is not any news to write. My feelings are the same and I must own that I am heartily sick of this war and wish it was over. I think when we can return to our homes safe and sound it will be the happiest day this country ever saw and still the opinion is that the war will be over this spring. Hope it will and I guess every buddy else does, but the speculators they would like to see it continue for the sake of making money. Well ma I must close this tell all the folks that I remember them with my best respects and hope to see them again. good day. My best love and wishes to you all. From yours ever. Edward & Billy be good boys from your pa.

July 1862

July 4, 1862 – Va.
Dear wife & children I will try & write you a few lines after so long a time although I do not know when I shall get a chance to send this. The mails have all stopped. Dear wife since I last wrote you I have seen hard times. We have had the hardest fight that I ever saw. Our Regt shot 80 rounds each. I got one scratch on the side of my face and one ball through my knapsack. That is all that I got touched. I cannot give you a description of the battle now but will some other time. We are under arms this moment & in the woods. We expect a battle today. If I should fall perhaps you may get this if Luther should find me. Dear wife my health is poor & so is Luther's. I am almost discouraged but you cannot think how bad I want to see you and the children. Oh ma I would be willing to give all I am worth to get clear of this service but I am afraid I never shall. But do not be discouraged because I am for I told you that I would always write to you, just as I felt (but you need not

tell that I am homesick) those moves that we have made look dark to me but they may turn out all right, hope so. Ma if you should never hear from me again you must not think up you for as long as I live I shall think of you. My feelings I cannot describe but you know that I feel sad to see my comrades fall around me & hear the groans of the wounded that left on the field. It is awful. I cannot bear to think of it. We have been fighting & marching for the last ten days & up 3 nights at a time. You will wonder how we can live & so do I. a great many have died on the road for want of care. when this thing will end the Lord only knows, but I hope in Providence that it will end soon, before every house in the North & South becomes a house of mourning. But enough of this, but ma if I ever live to see you again it will be the happiest moment that I ever saw. I hope God in his mercy will spare our lives until we meet. If not I hope to meet you where parting will be no more nor will one be better than another. May God grant it to be so. Well ma tell Sabra that Luther is with me now but he is not very well. He was not in the fight & I was glad of it for it was hard I tell you. Ma if I can get a chance I will write more & often but I do not know when this will go, but ma you cannot think how bad I feel & I know you feel bad because you do not hear from me but I cannot help it but ma I do want to see you so bad I do not know what to do. But I must wait for I cannot get away. You cannot change of so I shall have to stand it as long as I live I suppose. But enough of this I must close. (Illegible) could see the bright side of picture for I cannot but ma good day my love is yours as long as I live. Give my respects to all inquiring friends. from your husband to his wife.

July 4 afternoon.
Well ma I have just got a letter from you dated June 28. I was glad to hear from you, but about my coming home it is a hard job to get away. You must excuse me now for we are expecting an attack every moment. a good kiss ma. Good day.

Newspaper

> At midnight, while my watch I keep,
>
> When all around are wrapped in sleep,
>
> I think of her I've left behind,
>
> and ask is she still true and kind?
>
> When I was going to march away,

How warm a kiss she gave that day,

around my neck she clasped her arm,

As if to shield from danger's harm.

She loves me well to me is kind;

Therefore no doubts disturb my mind,

In coldest nights my heart glows,

Whene'er my thoughts on her repose.

Oh, if thou weep'st by care distress'd,

To think of me by dangers press'd,

Be calm; God keeps me everywhere,

A faithful soldier in his care.

July 6, 1862 – Va.

Dear wife and children I take another opportunity to write you a few lines to let you know that I am alive & not very well but am some better. I am in hopes to get along if we can have a few days rest. Luther is very poorly and I am afraid will be clear down. Well ma I will tell you something what I have passed through since the 25 of June. On that morning we went out to support our army. Well we stayed all day & night did not sleep any. Well in morning 26 we went on picket it was hard but we had to stand it. Well up all that night and on 27. We had rather hard week of it but got relieved just at dusk & came into camp, but as soon as we got there we had orders to move our camp. Well in five minutes we were ready for a start. We marched about 2 miles & stopped in an open field. I think I slept the best that night I ever did, in the open at that. Well in morning we marched a mile or two then halted, pitched our tents for the day, but before night we got orders to strike tents. Well that night it rained we got wet. at 3 in morning we had our knapsacks slung & ready to start. Then we were ordered in the rear as skirmish. It was very hot we were out until afternoon Sunday. Then we took up our line of march to protect the rear of the army as it was on its retreat. Well we marched some 10 or 12 miles that night & stopped, slept a very little. The next morning we formed in line of battle but nothing happened at the place. at 10 clock we went 2 1/2 miles and stopped and the first thing was to go on picket well about 2 o'clock our advance picket were drove in we fell back to a fence & took our stand then commenced the fight the pa reserves were attacked first we lay where we could see the whole it was an awful sight but the Reserves held them to it then they turned to us the fire became general all along our lines it was terrible well we held them until reinforcements came up just at dark on came the 61st on a charge & drove the rebs & took 250 prisoners we stayed on the field until midnight when we started on our retreat no sleep that night we left all our dead & wounded in the hands of the Rebs well the next day we halted & had another fight but our Regt did not suffer much that day 2 killed & 8 wounded the day before we had 2 killed & 2 wounded in our co & Gen. Earl of Wyoming & JE Lewis of Susq. Co. How many we lost in the Regt. I do not know. We lay on the field all night & started on retreat again. It had been very hot but it commenced raining like all fury. In one hour the mud was knee deep & we were wet to the skin. It has cleared off & looks pleasant again. We are in the woods (said to rest if there is anything like rest for the soldier I should like to see it). We have to get up any time of night & harness double quick when we hear the picket firing. So much for the rest for the weary. Well ma I am almost discouraged about the matter but I hope it will end some time don't you? Homesick ain't any name for what ails me. If I live to get home I shall know how to prize it. I never knew before. It will seem like a paradise. I know it will. So much for that. Well ma Luther got a letter from his wife today all safe. Well ma you must write often as you can & I will do the same. it does me a great deal of good to hear from you well about that Huntsman matter. I guess you had better wait may be that I shall get home sometime and then I can help you. Well ma I must close and if I were at home I would close my arms around you til you were satisfied. So good day ma. Give my love to all. Tell Ed & Billy to remember their pa. This from Yours Ever.

Well ma you may think that I am hard up for paper. Well I have not got but one sheet nor can I buy any so I must be saving. Well ma the 4 I got a letter from you one from Jesse dated 28 and yesterday I got one from you dated 26 & to day I got one from Dennis Hanna & Aunt Maria Enney & I think it has done me a great deal of good. But still I feel sad & worn out. If I could only get home how I should like it. Bt I do not know as that will ever be. But I hope it will. I do want to see you so bad & see the boys again too.

July 8, 1862 – Va.

Dear wife & children I will try & talk with you a little on paper. Well ma I received one letter from you on the 5th & one on the 7. The first dated June 26 & one July 3 and I received one from Dennis & Hanna Enney & one from Jesse Lung. Well it has cheered me up a great deal. I feel a good deal better in health. I am in hopes with a little rest that I shall be well. We do not have the proper rest that we ought to have, but it is enough to discourage any one to see how the sick are used. They are drove around like dogs. The doctor said a man had better be shot than be sick and I think so to. I tell you if our Gov. knew how his Pa troops are used he would have different work and I think he ought to. Our Brigade has been in front at Yorktown & done the hardest work & all the way through then when the retreat commenced we were put in the rear to cover the retreat. We have done some hard work & some hard fighting & some hard marching & we are entitled to good usage gut we do not get it. The field officers of our Regt. are all gone & we come under the command of Col. Hays of the 63 PV. He is the most tyrannical men that I ever saw. If a man is sick he will damn him hill & down & he will get us up every night about 1 1/2 o'clock at night, form line with equipment on stack arms, then we can lay down again providing we lay down with all of our equipment on. Now ma such usage as this for soldiers is outrageous. It is enough to make a soldier hate his country. I tell you the Union will never do us as much good as it does the soldier hurt. Just to tell you the plain truth if I were at home the Abolitionist & the South might fight it out for all of me, for a nigger has more the privilege here that a soldier has. Well ma they have put a stop to the sick going home any more. They make each Regt take care of their own sick but I feel so much better today that I have hopes of yet living to get home, but I am afraid this rebellion will last a good while yet. I am afraid it will not close in a hurry. But we must do the best we can. I tell you I have felt pretty bad along back and I tell you that I was discouraged & no wonder. If you could have seen us in some of our marches & fights & then seen the abuse that we have had to suffer just because we were worn out & sick & you would be mad enough to shoot them & I think they ought to be shot. Well ma enough of this. Now I will ask you how you get along today. How is the old buggy? Have the boys new rimed it & put on new tire has Ed got that other wagon ironed off? Did you sell that wood work to

Norman? Did Ed sell them cutters last winter? How does His Johnson get along with his boy? How I should like to step in the old kitchen (and as for that matter stay there to). Well ma I do not know but you will get sick of this trash but did you sell all of your hay? How does the grass look? That new seeding will it amount to much or not? How does your corn look? Is there any apples on our trees? Dennis says there will be an abundance of fruit there this season so if you do not have fruit you must get some there. Well ma I hope I shall keep on gaining strength until I feel well again. I hope you & the boys are well but I believe I could take comfort being sick at home if I were only there. But that cannot be at present so good day. write as often as you can & I will do the same. My love to you all Yours ever.

July 9, 1862
Dear wife I am about the same this morning. I am in hopes of getting along. Luther is quite poorly. We do not have much chance to gain strength. The trouble is we are completely worn out. I wish the Gov. would recall us & let us recruit our health & that is the wish of every one in the Regt. whether he will do it or not I cannot tell. Well ma it looks like another hot day. I tell you the weather is dreadful hot. Well good day ma. I hope we shall have the luck to meet again. My love to you. Yours Ever.

July 12, 1862 – Va.
Dear wife & children I take another opportunity to write you a few lines and let you know how I get along. Well ma my health is a good deal better and so is Luther's. I feel in better spirits although we have a hard time of it, but for all of this I think it will be the means of crushing the rebellion out the sooner. For I think our Governor will awake and send on reinforcements to our relief so that we can move on and not have to stop and fortify so much. But we have run a narrow chance of being captured or slain. You will see by the papers all about the moves that we have made and understand it better than I can write. So much for that. Well ma we have rested very good for two or three nights and it seemed good I tell you. Although we had nothing but the bare threads over us we have got used to it. We have got so we can stand most everything. Our fare is somewhat better than it was when I last wrote you. Well ma I must talk with you a little about our business matters. I got a letter from you this morning I was glad to hear from you & was glad to hear that you were all well. I was sorry to hear that

you grieved at my absence. I should be the happiest man living if I could only get clear & get home safe & sound. But that we do not know as ever will be, but my hopes are strong. better than they have been for some time that it will all turn out for the best. Hope it will. I know that we are apt to murmur & complain a good deal. The way looks dark to us many times when it is almost dawn. May God grant the morning light to dawn soon & bring us safe to our homes & families. Well ma you spoke in your letter about Low and Gov. Huntsman being in partnership. Well if I were in your place say nothing about it for they will not agree to stay together over 2 months so let them bridle. Give yourself no uneasiness about them. have Edward see to ironing of them wagons & see that he does it good for he must do that work. It had ought to have been done last winter so that Edward could have sold it this last spring. If he does not that is Low. go at them. He will miss it for if a man will not do as he agrees he wont make much out of me in the end. You did not say anything about the boys in your letter. how do they get along? are they good and kind to you? I hope they are for I should feel bad if they were not. You cannot think how I long to be at home with you. I can picture to myself the comfort I would take in lounging in the old kitchen and at the same time not forget the butter, a few boiled eggs & something else that used to be in the buttery. Well the time cannot come to quick for me to get there to suit me nor do I believe it could to suit you. I hope we shall be able to realize some of those anticipations but that we cannot tell. It is the future that we mortals cannot see through but time will tell. Our troubles will come fast enough without borrowing. Our Regt have gone on Pickett today. Our company left me in camp to draw rations. each camp has a quartermaster to draw rations for them. They appointed me to draw for Co A so I do not have to go on Pickett nor on guard. I have to over see the cooking, take care of Co. tools if they have any. We lost all of ours in the general retreat but we expect to have some new cooking utensils in a short time. My wages are the same as they were before and the work is not so hard. So much the better. tell Jesse I will answer his letter as soon as I can get time. should be very glad to hear from him again it is a poor place to write here. We have no conveyances for writing. Maybe a piece of board, an old pen or pencil and most always noise and confusion. no place to sit comfortable nor anything else decent for that reason you will have poor writing poor spelling and poor composing. I could talk with you from morning till night without tiring. I hope we shall have the privilege. It does seem to me that this rebellion must be crushed out within two months at the outside, and I wish it might be today. I think if congress had let the nigger question alone and tendered to this rebellion instead abolishing slavery in the District of Columbia, and all the other nigger questions of the day we might before this been at home with our friends and peace restored to our once happy nation. Oh how many lives it would have saved. how many wives would have rejoiced that now mourn? how many mothers fathers brother sisters would rejoice that now mourn for some slain in battle or died by disease, or are still away from home? but ma why should I bring up such things? we cannot help it but let the blame rest where it ought to. Well ma I guess you will get tired of this long letter of scribbling for I think it will bother you to read it, but I may as well write away awhile longer. how long does it take a letter to get to you now? yours come through quicker than they did. The one I got this morning was dated July 8 it came quick I hope they will come & go regular for I do like to hear from home so well. It does me good for I sometimes get low spirited, feel cast down & discouraged, but I hope my health & life will be spared me so that I can return to my home & family again. Well ma I shall have to close for I am afraid it will not be interesting to you. Maybe you are like me and like a long letter. The more you write the better it suits me. Well ma it rained night before last, all night & all day yesterday. today it is nice weather, just warm enough to be comfortable. So much for that & that is a good deal for our comfort. tell the boys I should like to be there to go fishing with & I should like to be there to work in haying with them but I guess if I live I shall be apt to stay in Va. this summer but it is against my will but that makes no difference with them (that is our bit bugs). Well ma write as often as you can & I will do the same. I suppose you felt concerned about me when you did not get letters regular, but I could not send them nor could I get a chance to write one. I tell you it was the hardest times I ever saw but I have been spared through it all & I feel thankful for it. I hope we never shall have it so hard again. Well ma good day my best love to you all. Give my respects to all inquiring friends. I have just seen Peter Roe he is well. I see him every few days he is a big stout fellow. good day ma. good day Edward. good day Billy. I hope I shall see you all again. Yours Ever.

July 19, 1862 – Va.

Dear wife you will find enclosed $80 dollars, 40 for you & 40 for Sabra. You will of course pay the express between you, whatever it is. We drawed pay for 4 months this time. 52 dollars each. that pays us up to July 14, 1862. Well you know I owed Luther six dollars, then I owed two dollars besides which left me 44 dollars & I will send you 40 of that. I presume I shall want more money before another pay day, but I did not think it best to keep much by me at a time, but will have you send it to me as I want it a dollar at a time, for if any thing should happen to me it would be lost. I want you to pay Bently 10 dollars on that note & pay Sayres 10 on that note that I gave for the stove. The rest you will keep for your comfort you will want some wheat flour, some meat, some groceries etc. to make you comfortable, some clothes maybe for the boys. Well ma if I have time this afternoon I will write you a letter & send by mail. My health is improving & so is Luther's. I got a letter from you last night announcing the death of old Mrs. Kinyon and stating that Billy had the whooping cough. I got a letter from Brother Henry night before last & was very glad to hear from him, but one notion he pretends to have in his head he had better get out, that is coming to this place to serve his country. He had better stay at home with his back broke than come here & get his head & heart broke. If he can not take warning by this he would not believe if one arose from the dead, for I can tell him this is a place of torments. Well ma good day. Yours ever.

July 20, 1862 – Harrisons Bar, Va.

Dear wife & children I take another opportunity to write you a few lines to let you know how I get along. Well ma I am getting along very well. just now I have had considerable rest & it has done me a great deal of good but still I feel lame & sore yet & expect to as long as I stay in the service. The effects of exposure & fatigue a great many of our poor fellows will remember as long as they live the hardships they have endured. But enough of this. Well ma I sent by express yesterday 40 dollars for you & 40 for Sabra from Luther. You will find in the envelope directions for using it. I want you to have things comfortable & good for at the best I expect you feel lonesome & sad but you must try and get along somehow or other. Would be willing to give all that I am worth if I were safe out of the service (all that a man hath will he give for his life) this is a Bible saying & I feel its truth, but still I feel in hopes of living it through and one day seeing you & my family. God grant it may be so & I hope it will be soon the sooner the better it suit me. Ma I would give a great deal if I could spend this pleasant Sabbath day with my family at home in peace & quiet. Oh would it not seem good & talk with each other? I hope the time will soon come that we can enjoy such pleasant scenes but we cannot tell what is laid up in store for us. I hope we shall be prepared for all that is prepared for us. Ma it seems hard for a man that has been brot up to observe the Sabbath & come to this place & see no regard paid for that day, but so it is. duties have to be done on Sunday in the army just the same as any day. But I tell you a great many days seem solemn to me. a person would think that a man's feelings would become hard after a while. It is so with some but not so with mine for I know that every one has friends to mourn for them. Then my thoughts turn to my home & friends. The loss to the army would be small if I should get killed but the loss to you & my family would be great. So it is the world over. You spoke in your letter about old Mrs. Kinyon & told me you would write me the particulars. I am sorry that she could not have seen her son once more but she has gone while he is far away if he is alive. I wrote to Orlo sometime ago but have not got an answer yet. I wrote to Dennis & Hannah a few days ago & I ought to write to Jesse but cannot get time yet so he must excuse me just now. I will write to him in a few days if I can get time. Ma I will tell you the prices we have to pay for some of the things we buy. Well cheese is from 50 cts to 1.00 per lbs. tobacco was for sometime after we got her 10 cts a paper such as we get at home for 3 cts. I see they have a little butter around at 1.00 per lbs. & lots of preserves 1.50 per bottle. about one third of lb. pickles 1.00 pr bottle. one quart small cucumbers. Well everything they sell in the army is about the same price. check shirts, coarse at that, sell for 2.50 to 3.25 for single shirts. You will see that money will not do much good here. from 50 cts to one dollars worth of stuff at a meal if he has a mind & money to buy it. But enough of this. Henry spoke in his letter about Wils Ferry's mother feeling so bad about him but I guess he will keep out of the way of the Rebs if his legs can carry him, for I think he is scarred almost to death. any how you must not say one word so that it will get out for it would make a fuss & I do not want to write anything that will either but you know I write to you just as I think. Wils has not been with us in a long time. I think he is playing sick on purpose to keep out of the fights. Well he is a poor soldier at any rate. I guess he is so beshit after Mrs. Low that he does not know what to do.

No 2. Some of the soldiers play sharp & speculate & make considerable money. They will buy things when they get a chance & sell for larger prices & make money you know. Some will make money if you place them on a rock, but I never was much of a hand for small fish. before we got our pay I was out of money & tobacco. I found a place where I could buy fine cut for 5 cts pr paper by taking 3 doz. at a time. I borrowed the money & went at it & in one day made over 1.50 & had some tobacco left. So much good luck in that small speculation well I was bound to have something good to eat. Well I bought 50 cts worth of cheese & ginger cake, sit down & ate the whole of it up a man can eat. Some of the boys made a good deal of fun about that letter that he had published in the republican and said if they had been in his place they would kept still. But enough of this poor Wils. now I do not like to go into a fight but I hate to be called a coward. There is to much pride in me for that. yet nor will I try to slink from duty as long as I able to get around. Well ma you said Billy had the whooping cough. If he has it hard I would give him some Hyves Syrup. take good care of him that I know you will do. take good care of your self & Ed to. how I should like to be with you. If H Hinds or Fred should come back here & you have a chance to send me 2 good dark colored cotton shirts you may do so. I want them made plain with low collars. dark check would be best. stout & course for we have to do our own washing & wash in cold water at that for we lost all of our camp kettles in our retreat. We have nothing to cook in but our pint cups. We broil our meat, cook our beans rice & coffee all in our cups. Well now it is laughable to be sure every one for himself. I buy some tea once in a while & have a good cup, but then it is black tea. I have not seen any green tea since you sent me that at Washington. But I get along very well. Well ma I have wrote you a long letter this time & could keep on all day if I had time for it seems like talking to you & I get almost lost in thought of home. Ma you may send me 6 postage stamps when you write if you have a mind for they are scarce. paper & envelopes are plenty here now. as fast as I want a little money I will let you know. Well ma I will send you that Certificate of Adams express & all I can do for you now. Give my respects to all our friends. tell Ed never to think of joining the army. good day ma. excuse all mistakes. this from yours ever.

July 23, 1862 – Harrisons Landing

Dear wife & children I take another opportunity to write you a few lines to let you know that I am alive & well (that is smart for me). I feel very thankful that my health is as good as it is. I hope these lines will find you all in good health & spirits but that I cannot tell. Well ma I have not much news to write for we are not doing much at present. We lay around camp part of the time & part of the time on fatigue duty. part of the time on picket. when not employed that way they have to drill. Well this warm weather makes us all feel dull & stupid. We have to rise at 4 every morning & if we get time in the course of the day we cannot sleep for it is so hot. Well ma how do you get along with your work? have you got your haying done? what luck did you have? you of course did not have the one there to help that you would like to have been there, but I hope the time will come that I can be there with you to share your joys & sorrows & pass the rest of our days together. But when that time will come it is hard to tell. I would have Edward work out as much as he is able this summer. He will want some clothes & a good many things & small mites put together will help to get along. I want him to be careful of his health & not work hard for he had better work for small wages than work to hard week. I should like to be there & help you first rate but then it looks sometimes as though it would be a good while before this disturbance will be settled. But I hope some thing will turn up & cause us to settle this difficulty soon for we are losing more lives than the whole south is worth. I cannot tell when we shall leave this place. It will depend on circumstances. But I am sure it would be a bad time for a fight. It is so warm if a man should get wounded it would mortify so quick that it would be almost sure death to get hit. Our Regt. are out on picket & have been since yesterday morn & have not been relieved yet I did not go out with them. I stayed in camp to draw their rations. Luther went out with them. They may not come in until tomorrow morning. It is not so hard work to picket here as it was in front of Richmond. Luther's health is poor yet & I think if he works it right he can get his discharge. I hope he can for he will never be well as long as he stays here & another thing he is so careless & headless. worse than he ever was at home. that you know is needless but I should be glad if he could get his discharge and get home. But what I write about him I do not want you to say one word. You know I always scolded him at home for being so headless but he is ten times more so here. He was sick, lost his knapsack, blankets & clothes overcoat. Well I got 2 extra tents blankets and got him an overcoat. when we started our retreat I threw away my overcoat. I carried my knapsack, one woolen blanket, one gun blanket, 3 shirts, 2 pairs socks, about 4 lbs. smoking tobacco & some other things & Luther started with my 2 tent blankets but lent them on the way & lost them with his overcoat. So it left us without a tent but we have drawed tents but we have not got them up yet but will in the course of a day or so. Well the boys have just come in from picket & I shall have to close for they want their rations & it is all confusion. I have not received a letter from you since the 18th but I shall look for one tonight when the mail comes in. Hope I shall get one with good news in. I wrote to Jesse since I wrote to you. He will of course let you see it. I will try & write to Brother Henry before many days. Well ma I shall have to bid you good day. I received a nice roll of writing paper & feel very thankful for it. although we can get plenty of here now but when I wrote you that time I could not by a sheet for five cts. Well good day ma. Give my respects to all of my friends from Rush. I hope you will get that money all safe, 40 dollars for you & 40 for Sabra. tell Sabra if she wants Luther to write oftener she must write oftener herself, for he says he has wrote 5 or three times since he has heard from her & says he is waiting to hear from her. excuse all mistakes.

July 29, 1862 – Harrisons Landing, Va.

Dear wife & children I take this opportunity to write you a few lines to let you know that I am alive & well. this I think is a great blessing. Well I received a letter from you yesterday & one from Mr. Low & today I received a shirt. You cannot think how proud I feel to get a good clean cotton shirt on again. It seems humane again. I wish it had been colored but never mind I am very thankful for it anyhow. I was glad to hear that you were all well. I was glad that Billy had not got the whooping cough very hard. Hope he will get along without any difficulty. I was sorry to hear that anything had befallen Jos Kinyon for it will cause his wife so much trouble, but he may come in all safe & sound. We had a good many reported dead & taken prisoners missing & all sorts of stories told but after all they would come in for several days after the fights. Some of our men that we supposed were taken prisoners we have heard from in NY & in Philadelphia & in different places in hospitals, so you see it takes a good many days to tell the exact amount of losses. I supposed of course Luther was taken prisoner.

I did not see nor hear of him from the time we left Fair Oaks until we got to the landing three days, yes 4 days from Sunday to Wednesday, but I found him safe but not well. He had nothing but the clothes on his back. He had lost his overcoat & 2 oil blankets. The rain pouring down like fury. I had one rubber blanket & one woolen blanket that made us kindly comfortable. What has become of Wils Ferry I do not know. I heard of him at the Turkey Bar Landing about 8 or 10 miles from this place & we have not heard from him since. I think he must have told a pitiful story & got aboard of a boat & gone to some hospital. (I have not heard from that box yet if you expressed it please send me the express receipt then I can tell where to look for it). If he writes home I wish Ed would find out where he is. I think he wants to crawl out of some small hole to get out of the army. Well I want to get away but if I do it will be in an honorable way or not at all. So far I have conducted myself so that no man can accuse me of cowardice & as long as I stay here & am able to do duty I shall do it. But no man living would be better pleased than myself to have this war closed & have my liberty again & I can say that no person would be better pleased to see their families than myself. But how long oh how long will that glad day be put off? I hope it will hasten roll around the time when we shall see peace restored to our land & see the weary soldiers return to their homes again, when this stripe & contention shall cease & north & south shall meet like brothers again. Well enough of this. The bugle has just sounded fall in so I must stop & into line. Well I get sick of it. no peace. Well that bugle call did not amount to much so I will try & finish. Oh fury how hot it is. To hot for comfort. But we must stand it. Well I have got through with quartermaster business & have gone with the ranks to do duty again. My health is getting pretty good. I have had it quite easy for two or three weeks & might have had it so for a long time if it had not been for (Locket) Lyons. He is one of them small fish & I think as little of him & less than I do of my dog. I do not believe he is honest nor honorable either one. Well ma he is the only officer we have in our company now. Our Capt. & 2nd Lieut. are both off on a sick furlough but they will be back again in a short time. things may go different then. Well I do not know as I have any reason to complain any more than the rest of the soldiers. Well ma Low wrote me about hiring the shop & wanted me to hire it to him so that he could put up another fire light. I will write & let you see the conditions before letting it to him for it belongs to you & if you stay there it is for you to have such as you please around you. I may not live to get home & if I should I may not get home this winter & I may we cannot tell. For that reason I shall leave it to you & Edward, hoping that you will act for the best. You can tell what my mind is after reading what I write & Low. Well ma I wrote more to Low then I intended when I began. For that reason I shall have to be short in what I write to you. I have not heard from Johnny Shove since the retreat. I have not seen his Regt. It is encamped 2 miles from us. I mean to go some day & see them if I can get a pass. tell Ed that I have not time & tell him my opinion of McClellan at this time, but I will tell him I believe the majority have as much confidence in him as over the fuss they made about the White House matter was perfectly simple. Where there is an army of 20 or 30,000 men & all try to get water out of one well you can see that there would be such a rush that no one could do anything without first placing a guard over it. Well then there was some 4 or 5,000 sick & they must have water. For that reason the guard was placed there & the well soldiers had to go somewhere else after water. all perfectly right. I will write again soon. You must not think I am short for paper because I take this small piece. Well good day. My love to you all. Yours ever.

August 1862

August 13, 1862 – Harrisons Landing
Dear wife & children I take this opportunity to write you a few lines we are still here at this Landing although we have been under marching orders for 3 or 4 days & have everything packed up ready for a start any moment, but for what place we do not know. Our knapsacks are sent off on the boats. Our tents are taken away. So I think we shall go soon but we may not go at all. We cannot tell anything what the orders will be. such is the life we have to live. We were on picket on Sunday & Monday came off & packed up everything & here we are yet but we may start at any moment. But one thing certain I think when we do move we shall have to fight & may be a hard one at that but I hope not. Our Regt is attached to General Birney Brigade & the men seem very much pleased with the change. after Jameson got sick & had to leave we had Gen. Robinson over us and he gave us a hard time but I hope we shall have a milder Gen. now. We are in Kearny's Division just

the same as we ever were, so the letters will come just the same as usual. Well ma I have not received a letter since the 9th from you. I received one on the 10th from Dennis & Hannah they were all well. They say Johnny is in a hospital somewhere in NY. My health continues good & I hope yours & the family are good. one does not know how to prize good health until deprived of it. Well ma you did not write anything about Ad Lung. I hear questionable stories about him but do not know whether they are true or not. Well I shall be glad if the time ever comes that I can be my own negro again. I am sick of this war & wish the South had a wall between it & the North so high that nobody could see over the top of it, where they could keep their negroes & cotton forever & then another law in the North to hang every abolitionist & I guess we might have a little peace. Our men & officers are returning to the Regt & it looks more like a Regt than it did, but I expect if we have a hard fight they will skedadle again. I believe they will run sooner than the privates as a general thing but I shall have to close for want of time. Give my best respects to all inquiring friends if I have any. My love to you all & if we are never permitted to meet again believe me true to you until death. good day. Yours ever. To Cornelia Edward & Billy Granger. Luther's health is poor he is excused from duty by the Doctor for the present.

Centerville Va. August 31, 1862
Dear wife I once more try to inform you that I am alive & well. You will wonder why I have not wrote before but I will tell you it is because I could not get a chance to send it. We left Harrisons Landing the 15th & have not had any mail since. I received a letter from you the 14 & one dollar in money which came good. I suppose we shall get some mail after a little. We have been under a march & fight ever since we left the peninsula. We have had another Bull Run you will see in the papers. I have not time to write but a few words for I have a chance to send this to Washington by Rev Emery. He is here today. We expect a heavy fight here tomorrow. If I die it will be Gods will, but I shall remember you & the children as long as I live if I live. write often & I will to you when there is a chance to send them. I wrote to you on the 26 but I am afraid you will not get it. Give my love to all my friends. We had one man killed & one wounded yesterday. We have had it very hard for the last 16 days nor do we expect much rest until this thing is settled. We marched almost all night last

158

night. I have rested a little today. My love to you all. Yours ever. JW Granger. Washington DC Co A 57Regt PV Kearny's Division.

You will see some of this paper is about worn out but I have to take up with such as I can get. Well anyway to get along the news will be just as good if you can only read it. I wish this rebellion was at an end. I ready to go home, that would suit me the best of anything. I suppose it will have to stop sometime or other but when the Lord only knows, but I am afraid a great many will be slain. We had 2 in our company wounded at Bull Run. They have both died of their wounds & one of our Co. died in the hospital at Baltimore all within a few days, so our company goes. Our company is getting rather small. We have lost some first rate fellows. Well ma, I shall have to close for want of something interesting to write. Somehow I do not feel like writing today but will make it up some other time. Give my best respects to all the friends. My love to you all. Yours ever. I should like to see you very much & still hope I shall.

September 1862

Alexandria Va. September 4 1862

Dear wife & children it is with the greatest pleasure that I have a chance to write you a few lines. I feel thankful that I am alive & well after what we have passed through. I cannot give you a full account of all our travels since we left Harrisons Landing but suffice it to say that we have not had a days rest in all of this time. You will wonder how we have stood it & so do I. We have marched night & day fought several battles but kind providence has so far gave me strength to do the duties assigned me. My feet has been blistered & are very sore but I have kept up with the best of them. I have written 2 letters to you since I left Harrisons Landing but I think it is a great chance if you get either of them. yesterday we got back to this place & got our mail, the first that we have received since the 14 of Aug & found 4 letters from you, 12th 14th 18th 21st & one shirt, one dollar in money, 2 postage stamps. now ma you cannot think how much good it done me to hear from home. I was out of money & out of tobacco & out of clean clothes. I had not washed my face or hands for more than a week & have been through dust & mud, waded creeks waist deep, out in all the heavy showers & in fact have not had a good nights rest since we left. You will see by the papers that we have had another Bull Run & on a pretty large scale too. Our loss must have very heavy. We were sure that we should succeed until about the middle of the afternoon of the second day when McDowel gave way on our right flank & let them down upon us like a hurricane. Kearny's Division had drove them the day before and held them until morning when McDowel took his place & we fell back to get a little rest. But the first thing we knew we were almost surrounded and our escape cut off. The soldiers running in all directions to escape the shot & shell but Kearny's Division remained cool although hundreds of solid shot & shell came in to our midst. We marched for about one mile under the range of their guns then formed another line of battle & held the enemy until the rest got away. We then marched to Centerville that night where we stopped for one day, but the enemy were not idle. all this time they had succeeded in getting a heavy force around our right and cut off our train of wagons between Centerville & Fairfax Court House. We then marched on them & drove them back & opened the road for our trains. We were up all night & had a heavy fight. We got through to Fairfax just after sunrise. We got a little coffee & then started on a round-about way for this place & after 2 days hard marching we find ourselves here at Alexandria. We left this place the 22 & got back the 3 in all of this time we have been busy. I am to tired to write much at this time but if we stay here I will write again soon but I think we shall move from here soon. I still have some hopes of living to see you yet, but my hopes were very faint when I was at Bulls Run. I tell you it was a tight place such a one as I never want to get into again.

Alexandria Va. September 5, 1862

Dear Son it may be interesting to you if I should write to you & give you a brief history of my travels since I left Harrisons Landing. The day before I left I received a letter from ma containing one dollar. Well we started the 15th Aug before daylight. We marched for five days through dust & sand over shoe deck in a good many places, but we got safe through to Yorktown where we stayed over night. The next day we got on board of a steam ship and lay at anchor in the stream until the next morning. We then sailed for Aequia Creek but when we got there we were ordered to Alexandria where we arrived the next morning about 10 o'clock. We stayed in Alexandria until sundown. We then got on the cars & started for Warrentown Junction. We got there the next day about noon. We then went on picket where we stayed until the next day when we marched some 6 miles in another direction. We then camped for the night. The next day our company went on picket we were under hopes orders. We helped ourselves to such as we liked best, so we found a nice hog & I shot it & we dressed it in good style & the way we had roast rib was a caution. good fresh pork tasted good after a long & weary march. Well the next day we moved 2 miles towards Fredricksburgh & until the next morning. We then started back toward Manassas we marched hard & long it was very warm. a great many fell out by the way among the rest. Luther gave out but I stuck to it. The second day about noon we arrived at Manassas where we found the cars & buildings still smoking. The Rebs fled at our approach. There was any amount of clothing & provisions destroyed. We halted for dinner then commenced pursuing the retreating foe. We overtook them near Centerville just at night, had a small skirmish with them. They fled for Bulls Run. The next morning we started in pursuit & came up with them in early. They commenced fighting in earnest but we drove them the first day & held them through the night when Kearny's Division was relieved by McDowel. We supposed that all was going well until afternoon when the enemy got our range & the way the shot & shell came into us was a caution. Well we saw that Kearny's Division was surrounded almost. We were ordered to fall back which we did in good order, but I tell you it was the hottest place that I ever saw. The cannon balls came in like hail. It covered me with dirt from end to end. Some of the shell & balls striking within one foot of me. Well we got out of there the best we could & formed in another place & held the enemy until dark when we got away & came as far as Centerville. after wading Bull Run up to our waist I tell you we were tired enough, but there was no rest for us. We stopped for the rest came up & then moved about until night then we stopped & stayed until the next day. Here I came across BB Emery & slept with him that night. It seemed good to find a good old warm friend again. He came out after the wounded. He is clerk in Washington. Well in the afternoon we heard that the Rebs were in our rear. Well we started & came up with them just at night. We had a sharp engagement until 3 o'clock in the morning. Just at night there was a tremendous thunder shower.

No.2 It wet us to the skin. as it then came off cool we suffered bad that night. The groans of the wounded made the night hideous. Oh it is hard to hear the poor fellows beg for water & cry for help when you cannot help them. But in spite of the danger we went in front of the lines & brot in several. Well at 3 o'clock in the morning we were ordered to leave & get to Fairfax Court House which we done in quick time. You will see by this that we were in a tight place but we got out with small loss. Well that same day we started for Alexandria by a roundabout way to protect the rest of the army & after marching 2 days we arrived here on the 3rd tired hungry & worn out. You will see in the papers that the 57 is spoke of highly. We are in Birney's Brigade. You see that is spoken of highly so much for that. We have been beaten badly in the fights & I do not know but they will conquer us yet but hope not. They have come as far as Harpers Ferry so & I hear if they should get into Md. They will give us a hard one. I should like to come home so that I could tell you all about it. We may stay here some time. I hope we shall so that we can get rested. We are in hopes of getting our pay soon. If we do I shall send as much home as I can. I would trade my watch for a revolver if I could get a chance to send it to you, but they will not let a soldier send anything home in a box for fear they will send government property. Some have been catched at it that is the reason. Well Edward when I send my money home I want you to send me five or six lbs. of butter & some 2 or 4 quarts of common good whiskey. box it up so that it cannot spill or break .send it by Express direct to Alexandria just the same as a letter & I think it will come through safe. send me the receipt so I will know when to look for it. Well I shall have to close for want of news & am afraid I shall tire your patience for this is a poor place to write. sitting flat on the ground with a small piece of board in my lap is the position that I am in now. The days are warm & the nights are very cool. So much so that we suffer with the cold for we have not got our woolen blankets yet nor no under clothes but we expect them soon & we expect to get tents soon. as it is we are in the open field exposed to all the storms. You will see the life of a soldier is not very pleasant. They may talk of patriotism much as they please. I think they would simmer down some if they were here. Give my best respects to all inquiring friends. My love to you all. PS Luther has come up & is here. He is not very tough but he has escaped being in the fights so far. He is lucky. This from your affectionate father. To Edward Granger

Alexandria Va. September 10, 1862
Dear wife & children I take this opportunity to write you a few lines to let you know that I am alive & well that is as well as usual.

Well ma I received a letter from you night before last the first that I have got since the 21 of Aug, this was dated Sept 3. I was very glad to hear from you & to hear that you were all well. I have had a great anxiety to hear from you & I suppose that you have felt the same for me. I thought a great many times when on our last march & fight that you would never have the privilege of reading any more letters from me, but thank kind providence I came through safe. a good many times while gone I felt glad you could not see the situation that we were in. If you had you could not have slept until you had have known that we were safe. I hope never to have to pass through another such a scene. those that were in the last years Bull Run fight said it was not half so hard a fight as this one was. this was terrible. You will see by the News papers what Jackson is doing. I think the people will wake up & look about & leave off their political quarreling & try to save their country. after all that has been said about McClellan they will find out that he is the man to put down this rebellion. There is not a man in the world that the soldiers have so much confidence in as him. He has saved Popes army & would have gained a glorious victory had it not been for that traitor McDowel & some others. I understand that President Lincoln sent for McClellan & said to him I want you to take command of the whole army. McClellan said to him (that is the President) that you must arrest such & such ones. So you will see that Sec Stanton, McDowel, Fitz John Porter & some others were arrested & McClellan has command of the whole thing & I hope some of the Newspaper editors will be arrested & make a clean sweep of the thing. while Mr. Emery was with me at Centerville he said he should return with full confidence in McClellan. He was disappointed. He had no idea that the soldiers had so much confidence in McClellan. I understand that the Republicans are down on Mc but they will have to cease their croakings or else see their country go to ruin if it has not already. thousands of lives have been sacrificed already on account of politicks & I wish those same men had to come here & do the fighting. But no, they will keep at a safe distance, poor cowardly whelps. Well ma you said you would like to see me, well not a bit better than I would like to see you. But when the time will come if ever we cannot tell but I do hope it will not be long but am afraid it will be a good while. I think the heft of the fighting will be over this fall. If I live until this winter I shall try to get home if only for a short time. But it is a thing impossible for a person to get a furlough at the present time even if he were wounded or sick. Well in my opinion Wils Ferry will get into a scrape for I think he went home without a furlough. So of course he will be arrested as a deserter. I have seen a lot of the new recruits from Susq. Co. Wm. Magee, John Harris, N Goodsil, H Roberts & S Canfeild & a good many others, all fierce for a fight. But I guess they will see enough before they get through. I got that check, shirt & that money. I feel very grateful to you for your kindness & will try to return it if I live. how I do wish that I could come home & see you, but still I find it the best way to be cheerful & not get discouraged. Well ma I shall have to close for want of room & time. We have not got our pay yet. Give my best respects to all inquiring friends. My best love to you all. this from your husband ever. Edward & Billy you must not forget your pa boys.

September 21 1862, Maryland
Dear wife & children I take another opportunity to write you a few lines to let you know that I am alive & in comfortable health for which I feel very thankful. I should be very glad to hear from home & I suppose I shall when we get our mail again. We have not had any mail in one week. We have been told from one place to another all the time we are now at Stantons Ferry on the Potomac doing picket duty. We hear of some good news but do not know whether to believe it or not. We have not seen a paper for some days so we do not know what is going on, but we hear heavy cannonading almost every day at Harpers Ferry 24 mile distant. Somebody gets hurt no doubt. You told me in your letter of the 12th how bad you wanted to see me. now ma you do not want to see me any more than I want to you, but when that time will ever come we do not know if ever. It does seem to me if ever I get home again I shall know how to enjoy the comforts of home. The times look dark & dreary to me. The prospect of getting home soon are not very flattering. I must confess but still I suppose I am like the rest. am in hopes of living it through I hope I shall. You spoke of Wils Ferrys getting married. I think he must be sick & I guess he will get hunted if he has not already. He will find someone after him with a sharp stick. Well he is no better than the rest of us & had ought to stand it I suppose. If the war is not settled between this & winter we of course will have a winter camp. If we do I shall try to get home & see you but a good many think the war will close up this fall. I hope it may but I doubt it. Well ma I shall have to close. I do not know when I shall get a

chance to send this, but with us now we write when we get time & send when we can get a chance. It is Sunday to day & it seems to me if I were at home I could enjoy a day of rest. how I long for the time to come that we once more can enjoy Sabbaths of rest at home. Give my best respects to all inquiring friends. My best love to you all. hoping to meet you once more. this from your husband ever.

That watch I still keep it is a great deal of company for me, but for all that if I had a good chance to send a revolver home I would trade & get one for Ed. But he must wait a while I want to do every thing I can to please him. Yours ever.

September. 22
Well ma I am midling well this morning. not very smart but am glad & am as well as I be. To tell you the truth I am out of money & tobacco to. You may think that I use money fast, but I tell you that one dollar does not go far where we have to buy such prices, but I will try & be more saving but it is a hard life to live. at best we expect to get our mail today. Oh how glad I shall be when this work plays out. Well ma good day.

Near Poolsville Md. September 26 1862
Ever dear wife & children I take this opportunity to write you a few lines to let you know that I am alive. My health is not first rate although I keep around. I am in hopes that I shall get along without any trouble. We are having quite an easy time just now with the exception of having to drill pretty severe. Our Col. is a very strict man & does not give us much rest. how long we shall stay here I do not know but probably not many days. Where we shall go we do not know. Well ma I received a letter from you the 22 dated 10 & one the 24 dated 17. I was glad to hear from you & to hear that you were all well. It gives me great pleasure to hear from home. We get our mails quite regular now from Washington DC. We have not got our pay yet but we look for it soon. I think if I had money I would have one good meal. at any rate we have enough to eat but we get tired of it & want something else. a little butter a few eggs & a chicken would taste good to me now. I tell you in a good many places we cannot get those things, but where we are now we could if we had money. Well it may be I shall live to get out of this & get home. If I do I shall know how to prize such nicknacks. Well enough of this now. I want Ed to see about those bees at John Hibbards. see what share we have there. You

will recollect that we had one swarm & a half last fall. It may be that there will be a hive to take up. If so you had better take them up soon. I want you to save me some honey so if we go into winter quarters in any place where we can get things I will have a can sent if you please. You spoke of Lows enlisting. I suppose we shall loose the coal & the use of shop & maybe he has spoiled half of the tools well. that is just our luck. If I were only at home I would not care. I could get along some way. You recollect I had a Note against DW Huntsman of $25.00. I suppose there is no chance to get pay on that. If he should sell out you might try & make a turn with them that bought. of them you must hold to the contract & not give any writing until you get all the pay, for I expect they will be just as mean as they know how. Well ma how do you get along with your large family these cold nights? I tell you for my part I sleep rather cold. The middle of the days are warm but the nights are chilly enough. I suppose you have frosts up your way.

September 30 1862, Conrads Ferry Maryland
Dear wife I received a letter yesterday from you dated 22, the only one for some time. I was glad to hear from you, but was sorry that you were left alone. I do not blame you for feeling bad & uneasy about Ed's going away. It makes me feel uneasy for fear that they may get him to enlist in the volunteer service. He has taken one step contrary to our wishes & may be led to take another. I have no objection to his going in the State Militia (for I think they will have nothing to do) but to return home, but after all he had ought to have first got your consent. He knew it was not right to go contrary to our wishes. I hope he will be sufficiently punished by having some snug marches to cure him & I hope he will return home safe & sound, for you need him there to take care of things. I feel sometimes as though some of them abolitionist in that neighborhood had something to do with getting Ed away from you & that makes me feel uneasy for fear they will get him to enlist, but I hope not for I think it is enough that I am here & have to suffer enough for one family. You did not give me any particulars about Ed, when he went or how, whether he took a gun with him or not, or whether he took any clothes. I hope before you get this he will be home. please give me the particulars when you write again. Well ma my health is improving. I begin to feel like myself again. We have it quite easy with the exception of drill that our Col. Gives us fits on. Well I had rather drill than fight if it would

only put down the rebellion, but I am afraid it will not. The weather is dry and nice. The ground is very dry & hard. Well ma I should like to be up in Old Rush roaming over those hills again & at liberty to go & come at pleasure. But will that time ever come? I think of those things often & as often wonder if it will ever be. I hope it will. I feel as though I have been in bondage long enough, don't you? this country where we are now is nice & pretty. If I were only at liberty to enjoy it, but then I had rather be with my friends. I am in hopes if I live until winter that I can get a furlough & come home & see you, but we cannot tell anything about it. Everything has to go according to general orders & we cannot tell what they will be. I do not know but I shall tire you patience with this dry letter but hope not. We have not got our pay yet & we do not know when we shall. as soon as we get it I will send you some money. I presume we shall not stay in this place much longer. Where we shall go we do not know, but I presume we shall cross over into Va. again & perhaps to Bull Run again. For my part I have had enough of Bull Run and don't like the place, but I suppose we shall have to do something before winter sets in. how I do wish this Rebellion was crushed out & we at liberty to return home, but we must be patient and wait for the time to come. write as often as you can. when you write please send a sheet of paper & envelope in the same letter then I can write back without delay. Some of the time it bothers me to get them for we keep moving & when I leave my knapsack behind I have no way of carrying paper only in my pocket. Then it gets wet & mussed up & frequently spoiled. Well ma I shall have to close for want of something to write that will be interesting. Oh tell me how you get along for provision. Do you have enough to be comfortable? What are your prospects for pork & butter this winter? How is your corn & potatoes? Your garden etc.? Give my best respects to all my love to you & family. Yours ever. Billy be a good boy & mind your ma. Would you like to see your pa?

October 1862

Conrads Ferry Md. October 5, 1862
Dear wife & children this is Sunday morning & a very nice morning it is to & I find myself enjoying good health. this I consider a great blessing I hope you are enjoying the same health is of the greatest importance. unless you have that you cannot

enjoy yourself in any place or position. since I last wrote you I have worried considerable & felt anxious to hear from home, but have not heard a word so I am still in doubt as to what has become of Ed. I hope he is at home, but am afraid he is not. I am in hopes that I shall hear from you soon. Our mail does not come regular & that may be the reason that I do not hear from you oftener. Well since I wrote to you last we have had it pretty easy with the exception of one day that day we took a tramp into Va. on a scout. We waded the river twice that day & traveled some 15 or 20 miles. Went to Leesburgh drove the Rebs out of it, took a lot of prisoners paroled them & then we returned the same day. waded the river & stayed on the banks on pickett all night. Well we got some nice peaches & apples & killed 4 hogs. Then we had a nice time roasting fresh pork. We were as hungry as bears so you may depend it tasted good. We sometimes have a little fun in this way but we generally keep sly & not let everyone know it. Well enough of this. I should like to be at home today & see how it would seem to spend a Sunday with civilized people again, but when that time will ever come the Lord only knows if ever. I am in hopes to get a letter from you as soon as the mail comes in so I will leave this a while & see before I close this.

Monday October 6
Well the mail has not come yet so I thought I would finish this letter. Well we got a pass to go out of camp yesterday and we got a nice lot of peaches. I tell you we had a great feast. Peter Roc was with us. He is tough & fat. Well how I should have liked to have the privilege of dropping a bag of peaches in the old kitchen where we could all enjoy them together. when shall we see that time? I wish it might come soon. Well ma after so long a time I have heard from that box. It is at GeoTown DC. We shall be apt to get it in 4 or 5 days if we stay in this place. We may & we may not, we cannot tell what moment we shall have to leave. Well enough of this. My health is good today. I have commenced cooking for the camp today & will have to cook this week so we will have to take turns. The weather is nice everyday, cool nights. I do hope this war will end this fall, but am afraid it will not. I have not seen a newspaper for a long time & cannot tell what our men are doing. We do not get any news. I do not know the reason. Well ma I shall have to close. Give my best respects to all inquiring friends. My best love to you. Yours ever. We have not got our pay yet nor no prospect very soon.

Tuesday October 7

Well ma I feel somewhat disappointed this morning. Our mail came in last night & I thought sure I should hear from home but did not get any letter at all. What is the reason do you write? or is it in the mail? I hope you are not sick. I hope I shall hear from you soon. I am well as usual today. Hope you are the same. Yours ever. To Cornelia.

Conrads Ferry Md. October 9, 1862

Dear wife & children I received two letters from you yesterday that cheered me up a great deal & relieved me from anxiety on account of Ed. I am glad he went seeing it has turned out so well. one of your letters was dated 27 & one 29 containing 12 stamps & one dollar cash. The feelings of gratitude that I feel for such favours I cannot express but hope my life may be spared to repay all your kindness to me. I am sorry to trouble you for money but I hope you will not suffer on account of it. I hope we shall get paid soon so that I can send you back some of this money. Well enough of this. Well ma yesterday morning we got that box that has been so long coming. It was mussed up some. Our tea was all spoiled. The camphor bottle broke. Some ink broke & spilled, etc. was spilled but what there was left will do us a sight of good. I tell you the tobacco came in play cigars & pipes essence pain killer speedy relief & a paper. A part of it is good cheese & cake spoiled, shirt pants & kerchiefs safe thread & needles. Just the thing that I wanted. Everything that was not spoiled was just such as we needed. Little Billy's presents were all moldy & spoiled. I felt bad to think he had taken so much pains for his pa & then have them spoil, but I feel just as thankful to him for remembering his pa. Ma you must except my sincere thanks for that donation & give my best respects to those that aided in getting up that box. I never shall forget their kindness & I hope that my character will be such that they will never regret that they favored us. So far my life as a soldier has been such that I am not ashamed of it. I do say it I think my officers have full confidence in me. If I ask them for a favor it is sure to be granted if in their power. The Capt. always calls me old Silver Grey or Uncle John, so you see the best way to get along is to keep the right side of them. Well enough of this or you will think I am bragging. Well ma you wanted to know how many battles I had been in & when & where. Well in the first I have been in all I ever want to be in & hope I never shall have to be in another. Well the first Battle was at Yorktown this was

169

small. The next was Williamsburgh. The next was at Fair Oaks, May 31. that you will remember was a hard one. The next time we were under fire was in front of Richmond. While on Pickett there they shelled us with grape & canister for a half day. Well then on the retreat from Fair Oaks we skirmished a half day with the enemy then retreated. this was the 29 of June. on Monday June 30 we fought for six hours steady fire. We shot 100 rounds a piece. We looked more like fiends than human beings, our clothes wet as water with sweat, our faces begrimed with powder. We looked like demons. Well the next day at Malvern Hill we were under fire all day. this ended our fights on the Peninsula. Well the next fight was at Bull Run. this was a hard one. If ever shot & shell flew it was there, but strange to say there was not one of our company got hurt with the shell. 2 of our camp were killed with rifle balls. The next fight was at Chantilly Hill between Centerville & Fairfax Court House.

No 2. There we were not in the hottest of the fight but plenty hot enough to suit me. this ends the fights that I have been in & the only ones that our Regt. has been in. You will see that I have been in them all. Luther has only been in two. that was at Yorktown & at Williamsburg. He has been sick or give out & could not keep up with the Regt. If I could only see you I could tell you some hard stories & tell the truth too. Sometimes when I think of the sights that I have seen it makes me shudder. I hope I never will have to pass through such scenes again & if I could have my way about it I would not have any more fighting any how. money cannot purchase lives nor heal the breaches that has been made in families. I feel thankful ma to think so far my life has been spared & I still hope we may be permitted to meet again & live in happiness the rest of our days. Our lives are in the hands of our Creator & to him we owe our thanks for our lives. I was glad to hear that you had apples enough to be comfortable. Your corn you say is good. I hope the time will soon come when this war will close. It would bring joy to many heart & sorrow to many a heart. Well ma my health continues good yet we hear some talk of having to move over to Leesburgh in Va. how soon we shall move we do not know. Well ma I shall have to close. Give my best respects to all. My best love to you. Yours ever. You need not send us a box until we get settled down I will let you know. good day. best wishes to you.

Conrad Ferry Md. October 11, 1862

Dear wife & children I received another letter from you on the 9th dated Oct 6. I was glad to hear that you were well & hope those few lines will find you still enjoying the same blessing. My health is good & hope it will continue the same., the weather has changed some we have some rain & it acts as though we might have cold sour weather. Well it is getting time of the year to look for such. I received a nice lot of paper & envelopes at the same time that I got your letter, for which please accept my thanks. Well ma you spoke of your family matters in your letter & the price that you should or ought to charge them. Well as for that I do not think that I could be a proper judge. My not being there to know how much trouble they make you, but am satisfied that it is a great inconvenience to have them there, therefore I should charge them a good price. You had better get the opinion of some around you that are acquaint with the circumstances. They might come nearer right than I could, but I do not think there is any danger of you getting any to much for they are not that kind of folks. I should be glad to help you to set a price, but I feel myself unable to form any kind of an opinion what it is worth, so ma you must excuse me. You spoke about those bees at Hubbards. Well I think you had better take up what he thinks will not winter & let him keep the rest unless you & Edward had just as leave try your luck in keeping bees. do just as you think best. Sometimes I hope that I shall get home by spring & be with you & then again I think this war may last for years, but I hope & pray it will not for I am sick & tired of it already. Well ma you spoke of going to the river on a visit. I hope you will & have a good visit. how I should like to be there with you. I think you & I could both of us enjoy ourselves better than we do now. We are still in the same camp. Our old Col. has come back & taken the command of this Regt & our Capt. will be promoted to Lieut. Col. of this Regt, so we are all right for field officers again. Well I hope they will do well by us. The talk is that we shall move across the Potomac to Leesburg, Va. For winter, but that we cannot tell whether it will be so or not. Well ma I am in hopes that I shall be permitted to see you this winter if I live, although it will cost me considerable. If I can get a furlough I shall come if it cost me all that I earn this winter. Well I do not know as there is any more news to write that would interest you. Luther is about as common with his pants the arse of them down to his knees worse than when he was at home & more sloven. But enough of this. Give my best respects to all. My best love to you & family.

October 19th 1862, Whites Ferry, Maryland

Dear wife & children I will try & write you a few lines to let you know that I have not forgotten you. I wrote to you on Tuesday 14 & thought I would not write again until I heard from you, but having a few moments to spare thought I would write you a few lines & scold you & Edward for being so careless in not writing to me in so long a time now. It is the 19 & I have not received a scrap from home since the 9 & that was dated the 6, so you see I feel slighted. to be sure I do not know the reason. The next mail we shall get will be next Tuesday, so I shall not hear from you until the 21. anyhow Luther got a letter from his wife stating that you had a first rate visit. Well I am glad of it. I should like the privilege of having a good visit with old acquaintances again, but that is very uncertain whether I ever see any of you or not. We moved from Poolsville yesterday, about five miles to a place called Whites Ferry. It is not likely that we shall stay here any length of time. probably we shall cross over the river into Va., but I have no desire to go there again. Well enough of this. There is some talk of sending this division to Texas this winter. I hope we shall not go for it is too far from home. If we have to go there I shall give up all hopes of seeing home again. It may be all talk & no cider. I hope it is the case. My health is tolerable good. to be sure I feel the effects of the exposures that I have suffered. that & my age together makes me feel like an old man. I find myself lame & stiff after marching, but after all I have stood it as well as anyone in the company. I expect if we stay around here this winter that I shall suffer considerable from lameness & cold. Well I shall try to live through it if I can. The nights are quite cold & we lay pretty cold some nights, but we can get up & stir around when it is too cold to sleep. We cannot have anymore blankets for we have as much as we can carry now. Our loads are very heavy. Well enough of this. this letter is well filled up with grumblings. Well I feel so just now & almost anyone would after going through what I have & no better prospects of faring better. Well I shall have to close or you will think that I find more fault than there is any need of. Well I suppose I do. I hope I shall hear from you soon. today is Sunday. It is a very pleasant day but I do not enjoy it as I could if I were at home. Give my best respects to all inquiring friends if any. My love to you all. good day. Yours ever. I have just heard that we have got to go on Pickett for three days. start tomorrow at 8 o'clock in the morning, so we shall not get any mail until we get back. It is provoking is it not. I hope you will not forget me again so long.

Near Whites Ferry Md. October 26, 1862

Dear wife & children after so long a time I will try & write you a few lines. in the first place on Saturday I received a letter from you dated Oct 16, the first that I had heard from you since the 9 & that one was dated 6th. Well Sunday morning I received 2, one mailed 20 & one 21. The one of the 16 containing 7/1$ which please accept my sincere thanks, you cannot think how much good it did me to hear from home once more. It had been a long time to me. I should have wrote to you yesterday, but it was so cold that I could not. It commenced raining in the morning & it rained all day & night & until 12 today. We got marching orders last night & I had to cook 3 days rations. after dark the rain poured down & the wind blew hard & cold I tell you it was not comfortable. Well to cap all I had just crawled into my little shelter tent, just big enough for 3, when down came the tent & we had to get up & fix it up in the rain & dark. Well we rolled up in our blankets the best we could & went to sleep. when it rained the hardest, down it came again & there we lay until morning. It looked dreary enough I tell you. Well this morning we packed up & got ready for a march in the mud & rain. at last an order came to remain where we are until further orders, so I have gone to cooking for the boys again. It has cleared up pleasant. The wind blows hard but we do not mind that as long as it does not rain. I shall not have time to write much today but will make it up some other time. Well about getting home this winter, I do not know how it will be yet but if there is any chance I shall try, but I do not expect they will let me stay over 30 days. If they do that it will depend on whether we go into winter quarters or not. Some think that we shall make a winter campaign. If we do there will be no chance of getting a furlough, but if any person would like to see home & friends it is this child. But I am afraid sometimes that I never shall have the privilege. But enough of this. We had a good time on Pickett. We got some fresh pork & mutton which was quite a treat & that was not all, I got one or two good drinks of bitters. So much for that. We stayed 3 days & I would not have cared if until this time. You spoke in your letter about your visit. I am glad you went & should like to have been with you, but I am far away. You said if I came home you would hardly know what to get me to eat. Well in the first place anything that you have would be good enough. I guess we could find some chickens & maybe some eggs, some butter bread & potatoes. that part does not trouble me, but the trouble is to get there. Well we must wait with patience & see, just the same as we do for our pay. I think it a chance if we get under a month, yet if we do not they will pay for four months. If I knew that we should stay in one place long enough to get a box from home I would send, but it is not worth while to send until we do. Well ma I must close. I will write again just as soon as I can. You must excuse this poor letter for I have only been 20 minutes writing it. My health is good, I am tough as a bear. It bothers me to get around in the night, I cannot see, my eyesight fails me fast. Well ma I shall have to send this without a stamp for I have let them all go for change & now I cannot get one for this letter. Give my respects to all inquiring friends. My love to you all & best wishes. hoping we may meet again. this from Yours ever.

October 30, 1862 Va. Near the Potomac

Dear wife & children I take another opportunity to write you a few lines to let you know how I get along. Well in the first place I am well as usual & today is pleasant & fine. We have cold frosty nights. They are not very comfortable but we make out to stand it very well so far. Well ma we crossed over the river the 28th & are once more on Va. Soil. We have not got as far as Leesburgh yet, but I expect we shall move from here within a day or two. how far we shall go into Va. this winter will depend on the opposition that we meet with. For my part I wish that they would let us remain for winter quarters somewhere near a railroad so we can get things from home, but I do not know as we will go into winter quarters at all or not. Well ma I see that J. Hubbard is drafted so you will have to get them bees away. I suppose if you have not taken them up that you were again to, I would right away for they will eat up what little honey that they have. I see that HT Johnson is one of the number to come to the war. tell him he had better come & join our Co. I should like his company first rate & the rest of them that is a coming from Rush. I suppose he will leave his wife with her folks while he is gone. Well I think it will come hard on Seth. of course he will grunt a great deal but it is no worse for him than it is for me. He must stand it. Snyder will hire someone to go in Bill's place if he can I presume. Well anyway to fix it up, Levi Guffer will snore because B. Giffin has to go, but I think the draft has hit some of the right ones. I wish they could have got Nels Balles & a few more of them nigger worshipers. They are the very ones that ought to come. Well I guess you will get tired of this so I will change the subject. Well ma you say you get along very well for provisions. Well I am glad of it. I should like to be there with you to share in your mess if it were nothing but a crust, but if I were there I guess we could get something besides crusts. But liberty with a crust would be sweeter than plenty in bondage. as soon as I think it safe to send a box I will let you know. I have made up my mind that I shall not scrimp myself so much as I have for the sake of paying a few debts. They are able to wait & they do not have to suffer the privations that we soldiers do. after this I will send you money enough to live better than you have & I want you to use it for that purpose & I mean to have things more comfortable for myself than I have had. For what is the use of exposing our lives in the way that we do & not have something for comfort? well you may think that I am finding fault with you, but that is not the case. I have not any fault to find with you. only I am afraid you deprive yourself to much & it is a coming cold weather & Ed & Billy will want some clothes & you will want some groceries & other provisions & clothes for yourself, etc. and if I should be lucky enough to get a furlough this winter it will cost me 25 or 30 dollars, but that I do not care about it if I can only get home to see you once more. I have not received any letter from you since I wrote before, but I shall look for one when the mail comes in. Well I do not know as there is anymore news to write that will interest you now, but I will write again soon and hope I shall have something more interesting to write you. There is any quantity of Hickory Nuts here & Black Walnuts. We could gather bushels of them if we could only carry them. If we only had them up home & I could be there & help eat them it would suit me first rate & I guess it would suit you. Well ma I hope this war will end some time or other but I do get discouraged sometimes. But I mean to try & keep my courage up & not give up to despair until I have to. Give my best respects to all inquiring friends. My best love to you & family. Yours ever. good day ma. tell Billy to be a good boy. I am glad that Edward is a going to work for Norman, for he can be at home nights to keep you company. good day.

November 1862

Near the Rappahannock River, November 8 1862

Dear wife & children I take another opportunity to write you a few lines to let you know how I get along. Well in the first place I am well. That is a blessing to me. It has been 9 days since I wrote to you. We have been on the march every day. Some days we have had long marches & some days short. We have been lucky in not having to fight any as yet, but we are looking for one every day, but I hope that the Rebs will keep retreating. We can hear them fighting every day ahead of us. The last time I wrote to you we have just crossed over into Va. Now we are way down on this Rappahannock River near Warrentown. Our march has been through a nice country as ever I saw. We have lived on the best we could find such as sheep, hogs & cattle. Any quantity of fresh meat. We begin to make the people feel the evils of war & I am glad of it. So far as we have been, there is not a chicken, duck or goose or turkey left that could be found. I think that some of the Sescesh will find their horses among the missing. The way they grumble is a caution but they will have to let it such. Well enough of this. The weather is pretty cold. Yesterday it snowed almost all day. The nights are cold & it freezes quite hard, but we manage to live through the nights by burning plenty of rails. The way the fences catch it is not slow. The Reb property has to suffer this time that we pass through Va. & I am glad of it. This is the way we ought to have served them in the first place. Made a clean sweep as we went along. I do not know as we shall go into winter quarters until the war is ended, which I hope will be before a great while for I tell you I am sick of war. I never want to see another fight, but there is no doubt but we shall have one in a short time. We shall not have to go to Texas as we expected. I am glad of that. I received a letter from you Oct 31st, some from father & mother yesterday. Our mails are not very regular. I should have wrote before this but could not get time & today I am writing with my fingers so cold that I can hardly hold my pen, so this will be an excuse for this poor writing. Well ma I wish I could give you some encouragement about my getting home this winter to see you but am afraid I cannot. But still have some hopes that I shall. I am very thankful that my health remains good. Our loads are heavy, all our goods on our backs, 3 days rations in our haversacks & 60 rounds of cartridges, guns etc. which makes a heavy load. Well I do not know as there is much news to write. I received 4 papers from home the 7th. I get the Montrose Republican regular from the office, so you need not send them. I do not get much time to read anyhow. Well I shall have to close. In regard to clothing I am not well clothed. My shoes are all out on the bottom but we shall get new ones shortly I expect. If we were in any place where we could get anything from home I would send for some things, but it is of no use now. Well ma I should like to see you & the boys first rate. Let us hope that that time will soon come. Give my best respects to all inquiring friends. Good day. My best love to you all. Yours ever. Write as often as you can & I will do the same. You have the best chance to write.

Near Waterloo Va. November 12, 1862
Dear wife & children I received a letter from you last night dated Nov 5. I was glad to hear from you & to hear that you were all well. I am in good health yet we keep moving almost every day. We keep in good spirits, so far so good. The nights are pretty cold but we manage to get along very well, but I expect when it comes a long storm that we will catch it hard, but we shall have to stand it well. Sometimes I feel quite encouraged hoping this war will end this winter. I think if we meet with no bad luck in this expedition it will tell the story. I hope it will for I have seen enough of fighting and would be glad to get home to live in peace & quiet. Well ma I shall have to stop for the order is to pack up & move. I will try & finish another time. Well ma I have got my things packed up & I will write until we have to start. The mail has just come in & I have got 2 letters & a lot of papers. On letter from you & one from Br. Henry dated Nov. 3 containing 6 stamps & telling me that Ed had hired to Norman for one year. Well I think Norm does first rate by him & I hope that Ed will do well by him. Tell him to be steady & honest, do the best that he can. As for my wife & children I think of them the last thing at night & the first in the morning & my prayers are for your safety & my safe return home to enjoy your society for many years to come. Well tell Henry I feel thankful to him & his family for their kind regards to us while far away from home. I long to see my parents again. He says father is very lame & often speaks of us. We often speak of him & mother & would like to see them & hope we shall soon. You must excuse this short letter & I will try to make it up another time. We are in such a hurry just now. Give my best respects to Mrs. Kinyon. I feel to pity her from the bottom of my heart. I know her

trials are hard. Give my love to all inquiring friends. Tell Mr. Rae's folks that I see Peter almost every day. He is well. If they want to write to him, direct their letters to Washington DC, Company H, 38 Regt. NY, Kearny's Division. Well it is 11 o'clock & here we are yet expecting every moment, so I shall have to bid you good day. Write as often as you can. You may think that I do not write as often as I might but I do. I do not get a chance very often. My love to you & children. Yours ever. Excuse this poor letter.

Well ma I presume you & the boys are just as anxious to see me. I think of those things at night as well as day. How I could enjoy myself sitting by the stove in the old kitchen, telling you of my travels & fare since I left home. I am sure it would interest you & it would interest Ed & Billy. They would have a great many questions to ask & it would give me great pleasure in answering them. I have for a good many nights dreamed of being at home & seeing different ones but there always was something wrong about it. I was not dressed or had left something on in the wrong place, but I suppose those dreams were caused by my mind being on home when I want to sleep, but I hope so much of them will come to pass that I shall get home & I hope that this war will be settled this winter, but I must confess that there is small grounds to hope upon. Well I guess you will think that I have wrote enough for this time so I thing that I will stop for a while until the mail comes in, if it does today, for I may get a letter from you. This will not go out until tomorrow so I will wait a while. 2 pm. Well the mail has come in but it brought no letter for me so I will finish this, it rains & it hails & it is cold stormy weather. I wish that I could go into some good old farmer's house & drink cider &C but that I can't do. Well ma you ask me if I could be set back in my life one year if you could not persuade me to stay at home. If I knew what I do now it would not be a hard task for I think that I should stay. There is a great many acts of my past life that I am sorry for & they had their bearing on my coming to this place. I hope that I may live & be respected my past follies forgotten. I do not mean that I were not thought enough of by my family but I think my family thought as much of me as they ought. Ma I have a good deal to reflect upon. You & I have talked those things over a great many times & yet no one can tell how much trouble it gives a person thinking over those old slights & the causes that they produce. Many have been ruined this way. Well ma what grieves me most of all is that I am far away from you & cannot provide for you as I want to. I am sorry to cause you trouble but so it is. But ma, whether I live or die, I am determined not to disgrace you nor my family by any act of mine. I mean to act honorable as long as my life is spared. Well I guess you will think that I have wrote you a queer letter but if I were at home with you I could talk more than I can write & with better satisfaction to you & myself. Well our camp is all mud again. I should not wonder if winter set in in earnest. I dread it but may be that we shall live through it, hope we shall & live to se better times. Well ma I must close. Give my respects to all inquiring friends. My best love to you. This from yours ever. It snowed like fury. This is a tedious storm but of course it will end sometime the same as all other storms have done.

Va. November. 20, 1862
Dear wife & children I will try & write you a few lines to let you know how I get along. It has been some time since I wrote to you but I could not get time for we have been on the march every day. I could not tell you the route that we have taken but we are now within 10 miles of Fredericksburgh. We followed the range of the Blue Ridge around to the Rappahannock, thence we have come down the river. My health is good & I have stood it first rate. For 2 days it has been raining but the weather is quite comfortable. Our living has been pretty good. On this march we have had fresh port, mutton, veal & yesterday our boys got 2 ducks & 2 chickens. I cooked them this morning for breakfast with plenty of potatoes. I think it was the best meal that I have had since I have been in the service. So you see I feel quite good-natured this morning. A little good living makes us feel good. Well some of our marches has been hard & some of them quite easy. It came hard on me 2 or 3 days. I marched with my feet out on the ground. It made them sore but I have got me a pair of shoes now & can get along better. Where our destination is we do not know nor do we know when we shall find a place to stop. We have not had any mail for some time. I expect to get 2 or 3 letters from you when the mail comes. This is the second letter that I have wrote since I got one from you but I presume you have wrote & I shall get them soon. I want you to write 2 a week. Tell Ed to write & let me know all the news & what is going on up in that country. He will have a better chance to know about those drafted, and whether they are coming or substitutes in their places, than you & I love to have him write. I like to hear from home as often as I can. There is not much news

to write but I wish I could tell you when this war would end & I wish it would end today. It can't come too soon to suit me for I have had soldiering enough but there is no use of grumbling it will do no good. If the rainy season sets in now we shall have a hard time of it. I wish we could get in some place where we could have good winter quarters. I hope it will be so that I can come home this winter. It seems like a long time since I have seen you & the boys. I shall try hard to get home if I live, but cannot tell yet whether it will be so I can or not. I do not know whether we shall move today or not. The orders may come to march any minute that is the reason I always have to hurry up when I undertake to write. I do not like this way of living but must put up with it. Well ma give my best respects to all inquiring friends. I see someone almost every day that I am acquainted with in different Regt. Our whole Division is long. Well ma I shall have to close by wishing you all the good luck in the world & hope you could get your wish if it was for me to get home safe & sound. My best love to you & children. Yours ever. I wish we could get our pay so that I could send you some money but we do not know when we shall be paid off.

Near Fredericksburgh Va. November. 25, 1862
Dear wife & children I take another opportunity to write you a few lines to let you know how I get along. Well I received a letter from you last night containing one dollar dated 18. I was glad to hear from you. I had not had a letter from you since the date of Nov. 5. I suppose there is some letters back of this one that I got last night. They will come after a while. I am in hopes that we shall get our mails more regular after this. Well ma my health is good & I stand it first rate but I tell you it is pretty cold for comfort. Our winter quarters are played out I am afraid & we shall have to campaign it all winter if we live, but no doubt some of us will go under before spring. I expect we shall have a fight within a few days, maybe before 24 hours passes over us. I have hoped that we could get along without fighting but am afraid that we shall not be of that lucky kind. We shall have to take it as it comes. Today we have had a grand division review. Some of our Regt. looked rather ragged & some of them bare-foot. I hope that we shall get some clothes & shoes soon or our men will suffer for the want of them. Well enough of this, you say your health is first rate & Billy grows like a week & Ed enjoys good health. Well I am glad to hear it & should be very glad to see you all. It would give me the greatest

pleasure in the world. You cannot imagine how much I think of home & how I long for the time to come when I can see home. It seems to me that I should feel perfectly happy but I am afraid sometimes that I shall never see home but still hope for the best. Our living is rather short. We get pretty hungry some of the time. We have got in a place that we cannot forage so you see our regular rations does not suffice. We live like dogs when we have plenty we feast & when scarce we grow poor. So it goes soldering. Well I am tired of it anyhow. I have great reasons to feel thankful for health & strength sufficient to bear up under all our fatigues while so many sink under them. Let us hope that kind Providence will still watch over us & protect us while we live. I wish we were in a place where we could have a box of things sent to us but we are on the move all the time so that we could not really carry anything if we should get them. That money comes good I tell you for I was out of tobacco & money too. Tobacco is very dear here. It is worth 1.25 pr pound & not very good at that. Everything is dear. It is enough to rot a person. I do not see any prospect of our getting our pay. We may have to wait until the middle of Jan. Well ma I shall have to close for the want of something interesting to write. I think I could take comfort if I were at home. Tell me if Low has left or not. What has become of him & family? Has that other man come on or not? If he has where will his family live? Is the cooper shop occupied or not? Tell Edward to pack up the tools in the wood shop so that they will not be lent out & lost. Keep that part of the shop closed up. Give my respects to all. My best love to you & family. Yours ever.

December 1862

Camp Near Falmouth Va. December 8 1862

Dear wife & children I received a letter from you yesterday dates Dec 2. I was glad to hear that you were all well & doing well. It gives me pleasure to hear from home. I am sorry that you feel discouraged but I cannot blame you for I think it looks discouraging. I get the blues every once a while but after all some things looks more favorable than they did. I cannot but think that this trouble will be settled between this & spring. I hope it will. I don't care much how. Any way to save life & release us from this worse than slavery. I suppose some of the abolitionists would call me a traitor for wishing to have it settled without freeing all the slaves but if I could get out of it they might keep their negroes to all eternity for all I would care. Well ma you wished to know what I thought of the President's Emancipation Proclamation. Well it cuts the South hard & I hope it will be the means of making them lay down their arms. If it does not I think they will fight all the harder, but time alone will tell. Since the election there has been more talk of trying to settle this difficulty. Well it may be a good thing for the country to have the Democrats carry the day once more. I hope it will. I am not quite so particular how they settle this matter as some are & I think if they were here & suffered as much & seen as many hard fights as we have they would say settle it as soon as possible. Well enough of this you said in your letter that Clarinda expected Barny home any day. Well I suppose she will be happy. Well I think I should feel happy to get home. Well ma I think if we could have a box of things put up for us & send we could get them. Well I will tell you so far as I am concerned what I most need. One pair of boots, size No. 8. I used to wear 7s but here I have to wear large sized boots so that they will go on & off easy. I do not care for the nicety but want them for service. Thick soles etc. You had better get a tin pale with a cover to put butter in & send us 8 or 10 lbs. (about the same of honey in tin pale) if father's folks has plenty of butter & honey you had better let them send that part. I guess you had not better send much dried fruit. We can get along without. One pair of suspenders. One tine pepper box. If you can, get them send 2 tin plates. Send me 4 lbs. tobacco, 2 lobs plug, 1 find cut for chewing, 1 for smoking. Well I guess you will think this is enough. Well send me one pair of old pants & I will wear them for drawers. I am wearing them that you sent me in the summer for that purpose now. Send some old jayvee ones that are not fit for anything else. A little cheese would be good but you had not better try to get any. We can get along without. Now ma tell Ed to get a tin can like our oyster can that will hold 3 or 4 quarts. Fill it with good whiskey, have it soldered up at the Tinners shop. Label it count oysters, pack it in the box & then if the box should be opened they would not mistrust anything. Label everything that you put in the box. I do not thing they will open the box anyhow but it would be well enough to be sure for I should hate to lose the whiskey, for you know I like it too well for that. This last part tell Ed not to say anything about to anyone, those things will cost you considerable but I am in hopes that we shall get our pay this week. I shall send you money just a soon as I can get it. Please send me one pair of gloves by mail. I do not want leather gloves but woolen or cotton with lining in them. They are warmer than deerskin. I have nothing to wear on my hands & the weather is very cold. It has froze 3 or 4 inches deep in the ground. I think it is as cold as it was last winter. If we should have to leave our quarters we would suffer a great deal with cold. If we should have to lay on the ground. Well ma I will tell you how to direct that box in the first place. Direct to JW & LA Granger, Camp Near Falmouth Va., Company A, 57 Regt. PV, Kearny's Division in care of the Quarter Master of 57 Regt. PV. Well I got them papers that Billy sent me. Tell him that his pa has not forgot him & if he lives to come home that he will bring him some nice present. If I cannot bring him anything else I will give him my watch. He shall have some nice present if he is only a good boy. Well ma this is pretty cold finger work writing but his I will try to get along with. I do not know but you will think that I am asking too much of you but I will send you money enough to make it all right. Well this is a hard way to get along but we have got to stand it I suppose. I hope that we can get that box so that we can have something for Christmas or New Years if we should live that length of time. The snow is 2 or 3 inch deep here so you see it looks wintry here as well as in Pa. Well ma I must close by wishing that I could be at home with you New Years but that I do not expect so. Good day. My best wishes to all my friends. My best love to you & children. Yours ever.

Near Falmouth Va. December 17 1862
Dear wife & children it is with a heart full of thankfulness that I attempt to write you a few lines to let you know that I am still alive & unhurt, but not so with a great many of our brave boys. After an absence of 5 days we returned to our old camp but how deserted it looks. Nearly one half is killed wounded & missing. Our company had 2 killed that we found F. Otis & F. Stevens. 6 missing that we cannot hear from & 4 wounded. Among the number is Wm. Hinds. He is wounded mortally we think. Luther & myself came out safe. I think this one of the hardest fought battles that I ever saw. The slaughter was awful. It was enough to strike terror to the stoutest & bravest men. We were not in but a few moments where we met face to face but them few moments it was hand to hand fight we were in & on the battle field from Saturday noon until Monday night when we retreated back across the river & last night got back to our old quarters. How long we

shall stay here we do not know but I think we may stay some time for our army is badly cut up. What will the people say now? Mc was just no man at all. They must have someone else to command. Some are that would rush on. They have tried it. The people said give us Burnsides. Well they got him but could not let him have his own way but must force him on. Well on he went. The consequences can be seen. The papers will have to tell of another terrible slaughter. Who is to blame? They cannot blame this to Mc. They will hate to censure Burnsides so I do not know how they will turn it but enough of this. My heart sickens when I think of the terrible sufferings of the soldiers on both sides. When will God in his mercy put a stop to this awful war? When will this terrible butchery cease? On Monday our men went over to the enemy with a flag of truce to get some of our wounded. Oh it was a grand sight. The men on both sides shook hands with each other & said they were tired of fighting. If they could have their own way it would all be settled & so our men say & I think that if it is ever settled the people will have to take it in hand & settle it. It seems to me that this is the worst war that ever was & no prospect of its ever closing. Well maybe you will think that I feel evil, well I do. If the leaders could be torn to pieces it would suit me for I think they could not suffer enough. Well ma I feel so thankful that I escaped I cannot express my feelings. I thought when in the battle that we should all of get killed or wounded. They fell like grass. Oh if I could only see you then I could tell you something about it but I cannot give you much of an idea by writing so I will not say any more on this subject. Well ma it was a good thing for us that we did not get our pay before this fight for we might have lost a good deal of it. But I think that we shall get our pay in a short time, hope we shall. We feel pretty much used up. I will write to you in a few days again just as soon as I get rested a little. I hope that I shall get a letter from you today so I will not close this until the mail comes in. Luther will send Sabra a letter in this so I will not write any more at the present. Yours ever in love & truth & memory.

NP. The mail has come in & I did not receive any letter so good night. Hope I shall hear from you soon. The weather is cold & I think we shall have a snowstorm. Oh I dread it. This winter campaign will kill the whole of us I guess. Excuse poor writing & spelling. Good night.

184

Near Falmouth Va. December 23, 1862

Dear wife & children I take another opportunity to write you a few lines & let you know how I get along. Well ma my trip over the river came near using me up. Since then I have been rather lame & stiff. But I think that with good luck to get over it in a few days. I received a letter from you on Saturday dated Dec 16. I was glad to hear that you were all well & had enough to eat. You did not say how you get along for wood. How glad I should be if I could be there to see to things but do not know as that time will ever come. I get clean discouraged sometimes & think that death is the only way that I ever shall be relieved but for all of that I do not know but my chance is as good as the rest of them (& that looks small) but enough of this. I ought not to complain but have every reason to feel thankful that my life & health has been spared as long as it has. You spoke in your letter about being alone this winter & how much comfort we could take there together. I often think of the times that we would have at home. We have taken a great deal of comfort together although we have had troubles & trials as well as other people. But on the whole I think that we enjoyed ourselves as well as the general run of folks. Those times we cannot live over again. If we could I think that we should do different in some respects but let the past dead bury its dead. I often get to thinking about home & it seems to me that if I should get there that I should want to ransack every nook & corner from cellar to garret. I can see in my mind every spot & corner in the house & shop barn & on the place. It seems to me that it is pleasanter than it ever was before. Well enough of this trash. We have just been & buried Wm. H. Hinds. He died yesterday of his wounds. That makes three of our company that got killed in the fight at Fredericksburg. Ma, you know that we used to be in Kearny's Division but you recollect that he got killed at Chantilly. Gen. Birney commands the Division. So you will see that it is Birney's Division the newspapers speaks very highly of this Division. Our Regt. Went into the fight with 288 men & came out with 139. You will see that there was 149 killed wounded & missing. We had of this number 19 killed dead, over 80 wounded (several of those have died since) the balance taken prisoners. Anyhow we have not heard from them since. Well ma since we came back we have had some very cold weather but today it is moderate & thaws some. I think that we shall have rain soon. The prospect of getting a furlough this winter looks slim. I hear some talk of sending this

185

Division back to Washington to rest a while. I hope they will. If they do I presume that I could get a furlough for a short time but I am afraid there will be no such good luck for us. I have not received any letters from Ed yet. Tell him to write & give me all the news about all the neighbors & how Low gets along in the shop. I hear that Agustus Bixby lives in the neighborhood. Does he work for Low or is he in with Nicholas? How do them ites get along? I mean the Myresites? Has Barney got back or not? Keep me some of that cider that you spoke about (I have a great mind sometimes to play off lame & get my discharge but dare not try it yet) (do not open your head about it). For I tell you I am tired of this way of living & wish I was out of it almost any way to get out. But I guess that you will tire of hearing my complain so much. Well before closing this I will wait for the mail & see if I do not get some news. Well ma I guess that I shall not get any news today & I had better close this. Hoping that we may have the good luck to meet on earth once more & enjoy each others society for many years. Give my best respects to all inquiring friends. My love to you & family. Tell the boys not to forget their pa. Yours ever.

Camp Near Falmouth Va. December 26, 1862

Dear wife & children although not any news to write I thought it best to write a few lines & let you know that I am still alive & well & I sincerely hope you are all well. My health continues very good yet although I feel old & stiff & this way of living is hard but so far I have had health & strength sufficient to perform all the duties assigned me. For those blessings I ought to feel truly thankful. Well ma I received a letter from Ed on the 24 dated 14 and mailed the 18. He stated that you were all well & that he was well suited with his place. I hope he will be contented & do well & farther hope it never will be his lot to suffer the hardships that I have since I came soldering. I know that I ought not to complain but such is human nature. We are apt to complain & I do not know as I blame the soldiers for complaining when we see all of our rights trampled under foot. I will give you one small instance that happened yesterday. You know that it was Christmas day, well the General said that the soldiers should have a good ration of whiskey. Well the amount of it was the officers drank the whiskey & got beastly drunk while the poor soldier could not get enough to wet his lips. Not over ¼ rations. While the war is conducted on such principles how can we expect to succeed. The officers spent the day in mirth & glee but not so with the most of the soldiers.

Many of them looked at their broken ranks & saw the places vacant so recently occupied by their fallen comrades. Those things made me feel sad & lonely as well as many others but enough of this. The day is past & gone & so has thousands of our brave soldiers & for what. Let us stop & think to satisfy a few just a few that could not have their own way a few south & a few north. When will they stop & think. I know that some now say in the north, crush them, make them submit but that is easier said than done. Have we not tried it? Have we not lost thousands of men & millions of money & is the thing any nearer done than it was in the first start. I think it does not appear so to me. But I see that the people North howl & yell if anyone says one word about peace but let them come here and be a private soldier one year & see what they will say. I believe that providence favors the South almost the same as it did our forefathers in the Revolutionary War. They claim that they are fighting for the same principals that their forefathers fought for. I do not know but Ed may blow me the same as he did some in Pa. & Ny for wanting the thing settled unless by perfect submission. That thing I contend can never be done. Well what is the next best thing to be done? Well in my opinion it would be to stop this inhuman butchery for this can do no good unless we could kill the ones North & South that got up the fuss. But that we cannot do. Well then let us legislate our difficulties. If we cannot arrange them in that way we might as well give up for this murdering men is all wrong & I believe that it is nothing more nor less than murder in the sight of God. Well ma I guess you will get tired of this letter & burn it up & think that I have turned secesh, but not a bit of it. I am just as loyal as ever & just as willing to fight for my country but when I see so many butchered it makes me sick of this war. Well I shall have to stop & drill so I will close after drill. Well we have had a short drill so I will finish this dry letter by hoping that our people will be guided by a higher power & settle this difficulty but we expect another battle soon & may be before you get this. Perhaps another 20,000 or 30,000 men lost. Oh when will this war cease? The Lord only knows. Well ma give my best respects to all inquiring friends. My love to you & family. Yours ever.

NB. We have not received our pay yet. I think it is a shame to our government to let the soldiers families suffer for the want of their pay. How can they prosper when it will wrong the soldiers of their pay?

Camp Near Falmouth Va. December 29 1862

Dear wife & children not feeling first rate today. I thought that I would write you a few lines although I have nothing in particular to write. The weather is fine but rather frosty at night but we get along quite comfortable. We have quite easy times of it just now but we are daily expecting orders to move, but where we do not know. Some think that the people must have another sacrifice for holiday sport & some think that our move will be in another direction from that last taken. But when & where it will be is yet unknown to us. But I hope that we shall not have any more of Burnsides experiments. It cost too much in human life. The papers will not give the amount of loss that we sustained in that last fight. In my opinion I think our loss near twice as large as stated in the papers. I hope the country are satisfied in turning out a general that has thoroughly tried & one that had the confidence of the whole army & substituting in his place one that has but little experience. Well they have tried it & now can mourn over a great defeat but enough of this. You nor I were to blame for it nor are we to blame for this war, but I wish we could do something to end it. I have for my part done all that lay in my power & do not know but it will cost me my life before I get out of it. But I still hope to live through it & get home, but I tell you that that hope is pretty small sometimes. Especially when the bullets whistle as they did the other day. It seems strange that any of us escaped & then the amount of shot & shell that was thrown in among us. We were in plain sight of their batteries & they threw hundreds of shell into our ranks, but strange they only killed a few in that way. The most were killed with gun shot wounds, but I guess you will get sick of hearing about it so I will quit. I wish the prospects of peace looked as fine as the weather but no, our political horizon is beclouded & looks dark & foreboding. I wish we could see some rays of light breaking through the gloom that overhangs us, but no I cannot see any prospects of peace, but enough of this. I should like to come home this winter & see you but doubt whether I can. Even if I could not be there only for a short time. I think it too bad after we have gone through all that we have & suffered as much as we have, that we cannot have the privilege of seeing our families for a few days. But no, we must stay in the field & campaign it the year around. It is too bad & another fault I find about the matter is that some get great wages & do but little & get their pay when they want it while the private gets small wages & works hard clothed poor & cannot get his pay so that his family can have the benefits of it as they needed. This is too bad. Well I guess you will think that I do nothing but find fault. Well to tell you the truth I am out of all manner of patience & pants out at the knees & seat into the bargain. We are a pretty ragged set anyhow but we have drawn new clothes except our pants & them we shall get within a day or two we expect. Well ma how do you get along about now? What are your prospects for New Years? I hope it is better than mine for enjoyment & pleasure. For mine looks slim. My health is not first rate just now but think that I shall be all right in a few days. I have looked for a letter from home for number of days but it does not come. I suppose it took some time for a letter to go through after the battle so I do not worry as much bout it. Let me know how all the folks get along. There will be a payment due on that contract of Huntsman's the first of Jan. I suppose I would not take anything but the lawful tender. Make them pay up to the mark. Does Ad Lung send his wife any money? What did you do with H. P. Johnson's note? Could he not have paid a part of that when he got his County bounty or did he not get any. I do not know but you will suffer for the want of money before we get our pay but I hope not. Well ma I shall have to close. Give my respects to all inquiring friends if any. Sometimes think they are few & scattering. My love to you & the children. From yours ever.

1863

The Granger Brothers survived 1862 and now optimism was turning to hopeful existence. Soldiers were tired. The country was tiring of the war. The South seemed to win every major battle in the Eastern Theater. Ullyses Grant was making some progress in the West, but the Granger Brothers were fighting in the East, and they were feeling the effects of this war.

1863 led the Granger Brothers through the Virginia battlefield of Chancellorsville and then brought them back to Pennsylvania. Not to return home, but rather to fight General Lee on Pennsylvania soil, at Gettysburg.

1863

January 1863

January 8, 1863 - Near Falmouth, Va.

Dear Wife & children I will try & write you a few lines although I have nothing particular to write except to let you know that I am alive & in comfortable health which is one of the greatest blessings conferred on mankind. But how little we prize it until deprived of it. Well ma the weather is pretty cold here & it is rather hard work to keep warm, but we manage to keep from freezing. I think that we shall get some snow soon. I have not received my letter from you since I wrote last but inclined not to wait but write as often as I can hoping that I shall get a letter the next mail. We remain in our old camp yet. Everything is quiet in front of us so far as we can see. I see by the papers that our army in the southwest are doing great things & I hope it will amount to something but how many families will have to mourn the loss of friends. Oh it is awful to think of. How I do wish this war could be stopped but when the time will come the Lord only knows. But let us hope that it will soon. Well ma in regard to that box. If you have not sent it you need not put in that pair of pants that you spoke about for I have drawers so that I shall not need them & that can that I spoke about Ed's putting, in you may leave it out. It will save you some cost & I can get along without it just as well. I wish you would put in some ground cinnamon to season our apple sauce that is if you send my dried apples. Luther says that Norman is a going to send the box by Capt. Lyons when he comes to the Regt. But he is not coming right away. I would not wait but send by Express to Falmouth Va. Wards Brigade 57 Regt. PV Comp. A. & it will come through almost as quick as a letter. Some boxes have come through in that way sooner than the letters that were mailed the same day. If you cannot get the money to pay the expenses on the box wait a while for I think that we must get our pay or part of it soon. It looks hard that we must wait so long for pay as we do but so it is. Luther went to the 50th Regt. yesterday to see the boys. He found Geo Mitchell, W. Wilcox, Chas Leang & a lot of Jessup & Montrose boys well & hearty & glad to see him. They said that they would come & see us in a few days. I did not go over to see them for I could not travel very well. So I remained in camp. I wrote a letter the other day to Dennis & Hannah to Uncle Richards folks & gave them some hints that if they had more to eat than they know what to do with that I could tell them just send it to us & see how quick we could devour it. Well I guess they will think me a queer fellow but can't help it. They might just as well give us something as not & it would do us a great deal of good if we had money we could buy a few things here but just look at the prices. Butter 60 cents for lbs. apples green 4 for 25 cts. dried we can get at the commissary at 10 cts. pr lbs. that is reasonable. Cheese 40 & 50 cts pr lbs. Tobacco from 1.50 to 2.00 pr lbs. pepper ground 20 cts paper 1/3 lbs. & everything else in relation. You see that money would not go a great way with us if we were to buy much what little sugar that we buy we get cheap. This we get at the commissary by our officers. We pay 4 per lbs. & get the nicest kind white. Nice coffee, sugar that we get at good prices. We sometimes get a little flour to make gravy of & sometimes a few onions we work it every way to get along. I guess you would laugh to see some of our meals. But we have got so that we could almost eat a negro without skinning. I suppose when we get so that we can eat a negro skin & all then we should be fit for soldiers. Well I guess you will think I am getting crazy so I had better close. Well ma I am setting around yet & grunting a little just enough to keep me off duty & when they get so that they do not like my style they may do the other things lump it (say something about this keep dark) things may turn out well yet anyhow so that I can get into some easier place. But enough for the present you will see that I am out of stamps & cannot buy them here so I will have to send this without pay. Well good day ma & my love to you & children. Yours ever.

N.L. I guess you will think that I am not dead if I do stink well I have to get off some notes. If I do not feel well it is best to feel cheerful anyhow to hurry time.

January 11, 1863 - Near Falmouth, Va.
Dear wife & children I take another opportunity to write you a few lines to let you know that I am still alive & well as usual although that is not saying much for my health but I feel thankful that I am not worse off. Well ma I received a letter from you yesterday dates Jan 5th. I was extremely glad to hear from you. It had been some time since I had heard from home. I was glad to hear that you were

all well & in comfortable circumstances but at the same time my anxiety to get home & see you increases but when the time will come the Lord only knows if ever. But let us hope for the best & be prepared to meet with the worst but at the same time it is hard to give up all hopes of ever meeting again on earth. Today is Sunday. Our Regt. has gone on picket. They started this morning & I expect they will be gone three days. I was lame with the rheumatism so the Col. excused me & let me stay in camp & some doz. others. This seems the most like Sunday of any that I have seen in some time. Only now & then a gun fired to disturb our quiet. It seems good to have a little quiet once in a while. Well ma you must not flatter yourself to much on that hint that I gave you for ten to one that it does not fail it will take some time to carry it out if we succeed at all but I hope something will turn up favorable at any rate. I am tired of this way of living. It is a regular dog's life at any rate. But enough of this. I saw Jos Cummins yesterday. Well for all I was glad to see him & I think that I should be glad to see almost anybody from that place. He was fat & hearty said his health was first rate. He is in the 5th Regular's Battery I Sikes' Brigade. He said that he had looked a long time for our Regt. & at last found it yesterday. It rained all day cleared off cold in the night I think it will not stay fair long. The weather has been favorable but we must expect some bad weather soon. I received a letter from Henry with yours. I was glad to hear from him as he would be to see me & if I could have my say about the matter it would not be long before I should see you all. Things look discouraging about this wars closing very soon unless some other nation takes hold of it & I am afraid that would cause more bloodshed but hope that it will be settled with as little loss of life as possible. What a sight of bloodshed already enough to make one shudder to think of. Luther's health is good the best that it has been since he came into the service. Our prospects for pay are slim. We have just heard that we cannot get our pay until sometime in Feb. It is too bad. It is a disgrace to our government to keep the soldiers out of their pay so long while many of their families suffer at home for the want of funds. What heart can a man have to sustain such a government when it will let his wife & little ones starve at home, go naked dependant on the cold charities of the world. Yet our rulers are dressed as you might say in fine linen, pockets full of money, but the soldier is a dog must do their bidding & that without pay. This is what I call grinding the face of the poor with a vengeance. But all this complaining does no good, but it does a person good to free their minds once in a while. I wish we had that box of things but I hate to have you send them until I could have got our pay so that you could have paid down for them, but you see how it is so don't put yourself to any trouble. We can wait until we get our pay. But I do not know what we shall do for tobacco. It is hard times for the weed. In your last letter you did not say anything about them folks selling out nor about the payment on the lot. Well ma I shall have to close you see that I have no way of paying postage but it will make no odds if the letters come through safe. Give my respects to all. Tell Henry I hope that I shall live to pay him for all the trouble on account of my family. He will always have my warmest thanks until better paid. Well ma good day. My best wishes for success in all undertakings. Yours ever.

January 19, 1863 - Near Falmouth, Va.

Dear wife & children. I received two letters from you this morning, one dated 13 & one 15, containing a watch, keys & one package containing one pairs of woolen mittens (just the thing) for which I feel very thankful for. I was glad to hear from you & hear that you were well. I worry a good deal about you this winter for fear that you will suffer for want of fuel or food or clothing. But you say that you get along for such things comfortable well. I am glad of it. We still remain in our camp. We expected to have marched Saturday morning but we did not. Then we were to start Sunday at one o'clock & then we were ordered to wait until today at one o'clock, but now they say that we will not go today so we do not know when we shall move. So I guess we do not know one minute what we shall do the next but have to take it as it comes. You spoke about Mrs. Kinyon. I am glad that she tries to enjoy herself for I think it a waste of time to mourn for such a fellow as he. If he can forget his wife & children so soon he must be a queer fellow. But enough of this. I did not wish for you to think that I thought you would so soon forget me, but that my name as well as hundreds of others would be soon forgot, but I know that I get the blues every once in a while & I suppose that I complain too much. But after all we want our own way sometimes so we have to grumble. That is about the only thing that we can have our own way about. You said in your letter that Ed told you that the box could be sent. Well I hope it can. It would seem so good to have a few things from home & I guess there never was a fellow that thought more of home than I do. But it seems like a long time since I last saw you & the children. I am glad they have not forgotten me. It does me good to hear from home & hear that the children inquire about me. How I do wish that I could come home & see you all but when that time will come if ever the lord only knows. That place that I spoke about as being easier that I wanted to get was in the ambulance train. I should not have to carry any load nor march with the Regt. nor would not be in half the danger but the prospect is small of my getting that situation. I do not know yet how it will be. Wilson Ferry came to us yesterday. He is fat & rugged. He says that he was with Ad Lyons, but Ad did not come to his Regt. he stayed there where he was. My health is pretty good but the weather is cold. I hope we shall not have to march if we do we shall nearly freeze. Well ma I am short for news & not in much of a thinking mood so I shall have a dry letter for you. How I do wish that I could write something encouraging but I cannot see anything encouraging at all. Everything looks dark no prospects of peace that I can see. Jos Cummins was here yesterday well & hearty as a bear. It made me think of home to hear him tell some of his big yarns. He had his wife & children likenesses with him. They looked as natural as life. Peter Ross was here well & hearty. He stays with in 25 rods of our camp & we see him every day. Well ma I shall have to close for want of news. There is a report in camp that our men undertook to cross the river above here about 12 miles yesterday & had to back out. That may be the reason that we do not move but I think when we move we shall have a fight but I hope not I have seen enough of such work. Well ma good day. I wish something would turn up favorable to our wishers. Good luck to you & your family. My love to you all. Tell Billy his pa hopes that he will come out safe & live to see him & have a good many good times with him. To Cornelia, Edward & Billy Granger

Well ma I thought I would write you a few lines this evening. It storms very hard, rain and hail. It is very tedious tonight. It makes me think of home where I could have a dry shelter over me and a good bed and good company. That would seem good to me. If you could see inside our tent and the companions you would not wonder that I do not like it. Two packs of cards playing all the evening. You know some folks think more about playing cards than they think about their families. But there is no pleasure in them cards to me and I wish it was so with some others. Well ma enough of this. I know that I have faults enough of anyone but I try to take care of my things for all of play. Well ma tell the boys to mind you and be good boys. Tell them that I think of them and hope that I can see them before long. I wish this war could come to a close without another life being lost but no doubt we shall have some pretty heavy battles before it is settled. But we cannot tell. Well ma for my part I am not anxious to get into a fight but if it is necessary I shall do the best that I can. Well we do not know anything about it, how we should feel. Well ma I must bid you good night. Wishing you all the good luck in the world. Yours ever.

January 28, 1863 - Near Falmouth, Va.
Dear wife & children I received a letter from you today dated 22. I was glad to hear that you were all well & had enough to make yourself comfortable. Well ma we got our pay up to Nov 1 1862 on the 26 & I should have wrote & sent you some money the next day but I had a chance to go & see the boys in the 50 Regt. Capt. Dimacks Company & I stayed with them all day & night. I saw all the boys that were there & had one of the best visits that I have had since I have been in the army. Well they fare twice as well as we do. We had any quantity of brandy & whiskey & when I came away Capt. Dimack gave me a canteen full of first rate whiskey to take home with me. By the way that Capt. Dimack is just the kind of an officer to have. He does not consider himself any better than his men. Such a man has the good will of all his men. He is quartermaster now & has a good chance to favor his men in regard to provisions. This morning he sent 2 dollars worth of beef stick to the tent where I stayed with Chas Lung, W Wilcox, A. Boldison, Siriel Depew. I saw Geo Mitchell, H. Goodwin, Hugh Mitchell, Tom Smith & a lot of other boys that I was acquainted with. They were in good spirits. Well ma the visit done me good & the good living & whiskey together made me feel better natured than I did when I heard that them God forsaken Hell-bound government officials had confiscated our box. I hope the curse of God will rest upon them. They ought to be damned to all eternity the poor drunken lousy lying dirty pack of thieves. I cannot say anything bad enough about them. When I first heard by Norman that our box had gone up shit hill I felt evil towards our government & I have not got over it yet. But I saw that Norman seemed to lay all the blame on me, but I blame our cursed administration. The whole thing is a robbery & we poor soldiers has got to stand it.

Now ma I do not want you nor Edward to think that I blame you for I do not. I am sorry as you that the box was lost but I will send you money to pay all expenses. Do not let Norm loose anything by the operation then he cannot complain. My faith is not much in our government I can tell you & if I was out of this army they might kiss my arse before they would get me in again unless they had some honest men in government offices. Our whole government has become a mass of corruption, a nest of robbers cut throats & thieves. But enough of this. Unless it is better as there is no express office here we shall have to send our money by mail. So I will send you ten dollars in this letter & then send some in the next unless there is a chance to get furlough. If I can possibly get one I shall. We only got 4 months pay this time. It is snowing like fury & it has snowed all day, mud up to your neck. Our tent looks like anything but being comfortable, but we have lived through hard times & I guess that we can again. You had better not send another box this winter for if you should those thieves would steal it to give to the niggers if they could not use it themselves. Well ma I shall have to close by wishing you all the good luck in the world. My health is first rate. Give my love to all inquiring friends my best love to you & children. Yours ever J W Granger

January 29
Well ma this morning the snow is 8 or 10 inches deep. Things look dreary. We suffer considerable. I wish those that confiscated my boots had to go bare foot & bare arsed in this snow & mud. Well I cannot think of anything bad enough for such scoundrels. Well you spoke about Huntsman's folks building on that lot, but you need not worry about that for they dare not. If they attempt to put any improvements on that lot just forbid them & if they still persist let them go on until they get it fixed to suit themselves & then reject them off it. They will have to lose all they have put on it, but if you should not forbid them they would collect pay for their improvements. So you can see the course for you to pursue. Well I shall have to close for my fingers are cold & feet too so good day.

February 1863

February 21, 1863 - Camp Near Falmouth, Va.
Dear wife & children I arrived here in camp safe & sound last night found the boys all right & glad to see me. That is what were in camp. The most of the Regt. are out on picket & will not be in

until tomorrow in the afternoon. I am the first one that has returned that went home on furlough, so you see that I am all right. I found Luther here. His health is better than when I left. He was quite sick while I was gone but is getting better. My cold is quite bad but I guess camp life will cure it. The visit that I had while at home has done me more good than I can express. How glad I should be if I could come home to stay. Let us hope that the time will soon come that we may all be so lucky as to get home to stay the rest of the days. Tell Willy to keep up good courage for I felt just as bad to leave him as he did to have me leave him. I cannot express the feelings of pleasure that it gave me to visit my friends at home. It will always be remembered with pleasure. It seems like a bright spot in my existence. Oh if I could be there to stay with you what a pleasure but we must wait with patience. Maybe everything will turn out for the best. I have no news to write of importance for that reason I will close & write more some other time. I had 9 dollars left when I got here so you see I have plenty of money. It did not cost me as much to get back as it did to get home. Well ma good day. It is pleasant today but it looks like a storm. Write often give my best respects to all inquiring friends. My best love to you & the children. Yours ever. J W Granger.

I hope something will turn up so that I can get home to stay don't you?

February 25, 1863 - Near Falmouth, Va.
Dear Wife & Children I will take a few moments to write & let you know that we are well & hope you are enjoying the same blessing. We have had the hardest snow storm that I have ever seen in VA. It commenced on Saturday night and lasted all day Sunday. It seemed as though we should perish. The wind blew like fury. Our houses did not prevent the snow from coming in just where it pleased but we lived it through hard as it was. The snow fell about 12 inches deep. It is now about 8 inches deep but it thaws some & will all be gone in a few days. The sooner the better. I think if I had known about this storm I would have stayed at home until it was over but I am here & the boys were all glad to see me except one or two that feel jealous. They were in hopes that I would not come back in time so that they could blow, but as it is they cannot say anything. But enough of this. I saw a letter that Worden's wife wrote Luther while I was at home. The way she blowed me was a caution. She called me secesh & everything else

but a decent man. She thinks I ought to pay Luther for them boots because I was so mean as to have that whiskey put in the box. She guesses that my friends will not be so anxious to serve me whiskey after this if he should make me pay him for what was lost. Well I tell you what I think if she should mind her own business it would be as much as she could do, clear up her own concerns & not meddle with that that is her neighbors, she told Luther that I was just as able to stand it until my time was out as anyone. Well it happens that I shall not ask her what I am to do. But enough of this. I am getting over my cold & begin to feel more like myself. You need not say anything about my seeing that letter that Elisa wrote, but to tell you the truth I think Luther is as deceitful as the Devil. So what matters of privacy I have he will not be none the wiser for. I hope something will turn up right after a while but cannot tell yet. Tell Billy that I will try & do the best that I can. Tell him to keep up good courage. I have not heard from that boy yet but the quartermaster thinks it will come through all right. He says they do not confiscate anything but the liquor & not that if there is an officer there to claim that it was sent for them (that is the officer). So I told him what was in the box & he said he would go to Headquarters when the box came & say that the liquor was for him. So if the box comes it will be all right. There is no news of importance to write for that reason I shall have to close. Give my best respects to all. My love to you & children.

March 1863

March 1, 1863 – Falmouth, Va. Sunday

Dear wife & children I take another opportunity to write you a few lines to let you know that I am well & hope you & yours are enjoying the same blessing. Today it is cold & storming. We have had a good deal of such weather since I got back. I tell you that I think of the comfortable home that I left & the friends that are there & feel sad to think that I am here but I do not regret that I came back in time. Although it would have been pleasant to have stayed at home if I had had the right to have done so but as it was I should not have felt right to have stayed. That visit at home seems like a bright spot in my life. I hope that we may be permitted to enjoy each other's society for many years. I feel proud of the boys and know that they think so much of me. I feel sorry for little Billy. He feels so bad but I hope the time will soon come that I can come home to stay with him. How glad I shall be to see that time if we are permitted to see it. Well ma I have not heard from that box yet but I think we shall before long. I hope we shall. I sold 3 lbs. of that smoking tobacco that I brought with me for $2.00. So I have left 3 lbs. of smoking & one lbs. of chewing so I will send 2 dollars for Ed to pay on the tobacco. Send me 10 or 12 postage stamps. I wish that I could send some little present to Billy. You may give him some of the change for me. Tell him to keep up good courage. I hope Edward got home safe & sound the day he took me to the depot. You see that I have not received any letter from you since I got back. I suppose it is not time yet. I received a letter from Henry Johnson last night. I was glad to hear from him. He says they are all well but I guess that he does not like soldiering very well. He seems to think that they have hard times. Well I suppose that it does come tough on them but they can stand it as well as the rest of us. There is no news of importance to write. Luther is well but I think that he is dreadful homesick since I came back. He says if he could get a ten day furlough he would go home. Well I wish he might. I have just wrote to Jos Kinyon & talked pretty plain to him. I hope it will do some good but I am afraid it will not. Well ma I must close by wishing you all the good luck in the world. Give my respects to all inquiring friends. My love to you & children. Yours ever.

March 6, 1863 - Va.
Dear wife & children I received a letter from you last night dated 28. I was glad to hear from you but was sorry to hear that Edward was not well. I want him to be careful of his health. Do you not think that some such medicine like that Dr. Cornwall fixed for me when we lived in the Town would do him good? I think it was the best for my cough of any that I ever took. I feel very anxious about him. I was very glad to hear that you & Billy were well. I hope that you all will be blessed with good health. I feel anxious to get home to stay with you and somehow it seems to me that I shall get home but cannot tell why. My health is good. The boys all say that I look five years younger than I did before I went home. So much for that. You said it seemed almost like an aggravation so short a visit. I feel out of patience with myself when I think of it that I could not have visited more with you & the children but time flew so swift that it passed like a shadow but it seems sweet to think of that. I have seen you & the children & had the pleasantest visit that I ever had, but I hope my life will be spared to get home to stay a

good many years with you, but we cannot say that we shall meet again on earth. We have moved our camp about three miles towards the Potomac where we have plenty of wood. We have been very busy fixing up our quarters. We got ours fixed up last night. They are a good deal better than we had in our old camp so I rather like the move. I see by the papers that the Rebs are bound to torment us by trying to make raids in our rear but they will not make much that way. I am in hopes that we shall never have to attack them at Fredericksburgh again for they are in strong force there. But enough of this. It seems to me sometimes that there is something about my being here that I cannot help for when I think about getting away on account of poor health my health will improve right away & sometimes I am almost a fatalist in belief for many times we wonder how it happened that we done this & so but it seems that we were drawn in by something beyond our comprehension. Let us hope that everything will work for the best. I am a going to try to get a pass to go & see the boys where Perigas boys are. They are only 5 miles from us & I would like to see them first rate. You spoke about old Leunys young soldier. Now if they turn out like him they will not benefit the government much. So he had better quit for a while. Well how does he get along? I suppose he is not very dangerous anyhow. Well I almost begrudge him his happiness of being at home & wish it could be my good luck to get home to stay. You spoke about that box. I have not heard from it yet but still hope it will come around all safe. You said you had sold the old cow. Well it will just pay for the heifer so far so good. Luther's health is very good. Wilson Ferry tents with us. So we have four in our tent. Since I went home everything about home seems dear to me than it ever did before. Well ma tell Billy & Edward to keep up good courage. I will try to take good care of myself & try to get home as soon as possible & be honorable. Write often give my best respects to all inquiring friends. Yours ever.

March 7, 1863 - Camp Va.

Dear wife & children I have some good news to write to day. Yesterday just after I sent that letter to you that box came in. Well you had better believe I was glad I found everything safe & sound even to that bottle of whiskey. The box had been opened & searched but they left everything just as it was. You can tell Elisa that Johns good friends did not do dear Luther as much damage as she thought, nor did Lute lose as much as she thought he would.

For he has sold his boots for $5 dollars & one lbs. tobacco for $1 dollar & if I am not mistaken that is more than Norm charged him. I sold my boots & one lbs. tobacco for $6.00 & will send you the money to pay Norman. I tell you we had a good time with that whiskey. I treated the Colonel & all of Co A well. We had a jolly time but enough of this. We found the butter, honey, sausage was all right. Everything was in good order even the cakes was fresh & good. You may depend that such things are a luxury with us. How thankful I feel to you & the children for your kindness to me. I hope some day to be able to repay to you & the rest of the neighbors. I want Edward to write & let me know just what was charged to Luther & what articles were for intended for him for you know he is a queer fellow anyhow. Well ma today is warm & spring like rainy & my health is first rate & we have a comfortable place to stay in. If they will only let us stay here until the war is over I would like it but that I do not expect. They have changed our Regt. from Wards Brigade to Robinson's old Brigade. The same Brigade that we first started in. Well I do not know as it will make any difference to us. Well ma I shall have to close for want of something interesting to write. Give my best respects to all inquiring friends. My love to you all.

March 13, 1863 - Camp in Virginia
Dear wife & children I received a letter from you on the 11th dated 5th. I was glad to hear from you & was glad to hear that Edward was getting better for I was very uneasy about him. I hope you will all be blessed with good health while I am gone from you. How I long for the time to come that I can say that I am a free man again. (That is free from the service.) I wish this rebellion could be crushed out at once & we be permitted to return to our homes & families again but things look dark & dreary yet. Only 2 days ago the Rebs made a raid in our rear. Came down to the mouth of Aquia Creek & captured one General & staff & another General's staff & did other damage but I have not learned the amount. Our whole brigade were on picket at the time. We went on Monday & came off on Thursday. So you see that we only got into camp last night making four days that we were gone. We heard that the Rebs had crossed the river & expected they would attack us but they passed around us & hit another place. Well I did not care to have a brush with them but if they had come near us we were prepared for them. The weather was rather bad while we were on picket. It snowed one day & rained one night so you see we did not take

much comfort while we were gone but we lived it through & got back safe & sound. I tell you some of them good things in that box catched it when we got into camp. It done us good. I take comfort eating them things. You may depend such a box is worth its weight in gold to us poor fellows. I hope you got that money I sent you in my last letter. You said that Ezra Devers was dead. I was surprised for I thought he was getting well but so it is. Those that are at home die as well as those that are in the service. Death will overtake us let us be where we will. A great many young as well as old have died within the past year. My health remains good with the exception of being lame by spells, but I manage to get around & keep up with the rest of them very well. I do not know as I have much more news to write this time. I saw Birch here in camp Sunday night & Monday morning. He is fat as a bear. He came here to see John Harris. I guess that he will get him discharged. He is a kind played out. Well ma give my best respects to all inquiring friends. My best love to you & children. Yours ever. Write often & I will do the same. The reason I did not write before was because I was on picket & could not.

March 16, 1863 - Va.
Dear wife & children I received a letter from you on the 14th dated 10. I was glad to hear that you were getting along so well. Those stamps were all right. I was glad to hear that Ed was getting well so that he can attend to the store again. You said that Mrs. Kinyon had got some money from James. Well I suppose she stood in great need of it. I wrote to him concerning that Atwater Note & requested him to send the money to me & I would pay the debt but I expect that he will leave me to pay the debt. That is about the way I get used for doing a person a favor. You spoke in one letter about you & Ed's writing & that bill of express. I forgot to tell you I found them all safe when I got back to the Regt. so that it was all correct. But after all he is a complete shit arse & make the best of him but enough of this. Last night we had a heavy thunderstorm of hail. Today is more mild. For 4 or 5 days past it has been very cold. We had general inspection yesterday & today. Tomorrow I intend to get a pass & go to see Mark Perigo & the rest of the boys in that Regt. You say that you feel lonesome. In fact I enjoy myself a great deal better than I did before I went home. It was a great satisfaction to me to have the privilege of seeing you once more & to find that I had warm friends there. I hope that I shall prove worthy of their friendship. There is a great many things here

to make it unpleasant but still we feel as thought we were fighting for our country. I hope this rebellion will soon be crushed out & we live to get home & enjoy the society of our friends for many years. I send L. Williams a New York Herald. I want Ed to read the editorial. I think his sentiments are democratic & if anyone thinks that I am turning Abolitionist they are mistaken but enough of this. I must hurry or I shall be too late for the mail. I often think of the pleasant visit that I had.

March 20, 1863 - Va.

Dear wife & children I received a letter from you yesterday dated 14 in answer to my letters of the 6 & 7. I was glad to hear that you were well. I received 2 postage stamps. I suppose you received that money six dollars in the letter of the 7 & also $2.50 in a letter before those last. You did not mention it although you received the letters. I presume you forgot it. I am heedless about being particular to mention such things. Well I hope it is all right but enough of this. Well on the 17th I got a pass to go and see the boys in the 148 & 150 Regts. I found the boys well & enjoying themselves first rate. I saw Mark Perigo. Ed was on picket. I saw Seth, W White, Hawes Light, Dack Bissel's son & a good many others that I was acquainted with. I stayed over night with them & had a first rate visit. It does me good to meet old acquaintances & talk with them. I hope this miserable war will close soon so that we can get home to stay with our friends all of the time but when that time will come the Lord only knows. Well ma you say that the small pox rages in the fag end of the villa. Well it may cleanse them out some (perhaps it is a different kind of pox than they are used to) but anyhow if they have got the small pox it is bad enough. To day it snows like fun & the weather looks dreary but it will soon fair off again. I hope we do not have much news of interest with us just now. The best news that I could hear just now would be to see some signs of peace but that we don't see. You speak about being anxious to have me get home. There is nothing that would suit me better than to get home safe & sound for I am sick of this way of living. But as long as I have got to say I should like to have it a little easier. But after all I guess that I can stand as much as any of them. I get discouraged sometimes but shall make the best of it that I can & shall try to take good care of myself. I hope my life will be spared to see you & my family again. How soon we shall move from here we cannot tell for we have orders to be ready at one hours notice. I suppose that is on account of the

Rebs making raids in our rear. We may stay here for some time & we may not. We do not know. I have a mind to have Ed send me my watch if he can. I am lost with out a time piece. It seems lonesome. How does your hay hold out? I suppose you will have enough. Oh that sausage meat was first rate. It only molded a little on the outside. It was tiptop. Everything was first rate. How I wish that I could be at home with you. You said that Ad Lung was all right. I guess so too he played sharp but any way to get out. Well ma I shall have to close for want of something interesting to write. Give my best respects to all inquiring friends. My best love to you & children. Yours ever. Tell Billy I thank him for his token in sending me some of his writing. He gets along very well in writing. You may have Ed send that watch.

March 24, 1863 - Va.

Dear wife & children I take this opportunity to write you a few lines to let you know that I am well & hope you & the boys are the same. I have a good deal of anxiety for fear of the small pox in your neighborhood. I should advise you & the children to be careful of yourselves for it is a most loathsome disease to make the best of it. I hope it will not spread any more but I think that a great many will have it. I understand that Bixbys & Lows families are on the town for support. This is a hard case. They have never been of any benefit to the place nor never will be. Poor shiftless fellows. How many have got the small pox around there. What is their prospects of recovery. Who doctors them? Has the town got anyone to take care of Lows folks yet? I guess she had better sell some of them silk dresses & Low had better sell his broadcloth clothes & dress like poor folks rather than be on the town. But enough of this. The weather is mild. The mud is very deep. I think it will be sometime before the weather will be settled but we are looking for a move soon. I hardly think that they will wait until the going gets good. Anyhow I dread it for there is no knowing how much suffering & lives lost but I suppose it is necessary for us to do something towards putting down this rebellion. I hope it will soon be over although I cannot see any signs of it any more than I could one year ago. Nor as much. But this Conscription Act will fetch us out quite a force. I hope it will cut close on some of the North. I would be glad if those at the North & South that caused this war had to fight it out themselves & would be glad if all of them would get killed. But they will keep out of harms way. I hope that those that have deserted will get brought back for it is mean for them to sneak off & the rest of us to stay. But enough of this. Well ma I get almost discouraged sometimes. For the most of the time since I got back from home I have felt cheerful but I get the blues some lately. But I shall try & make the best of it that I can hoping that I shall come out safe. I long for the time to come when I can be a free man again & be at home with you. I think I should be more contented than ever before. I wish we could see some signs to the war coming to a close but I cannot. I do not see any chance for me to have it easier than before. Well I shall stand it as long as I can & that is as much as the best of them can do. Well ma I do not know as there is any news of importance to write for that reason I will close. Give my respects to all inquiring friends. My best love to you & family. Yours ever.

I have not received any letter from you since I wrote before but I shall look for one tonight or tomorrow night anyhow. If Ed has not sent that watch tell him to put it in a small box when he does send it so that it will not get broke.

March 29, 1863 - Va.
Dear wife & children I guess you will think that I do nothing else but write. Well I know that I write often & but a little news at that. Well this morning it being Sunday my thoughts turn to old Rush & I think that I should like to be there & I am there in thought. It must seem melancholy for I understand that you have had 2 deaths close by & probably before this reaches you there will be several more but I hope not. But when that disease once gets a going there is no telling where it will stop. This disease must spread a general gloom over the place although those that have died ore not of much account in society. Nevertheless they will be missed by their family. It is a serious matter. Death is no respecter of persons. The rich the poor the high as well as the low must submit. Well ma it makes me feel sad when I think of the misery & suffering that there is in our land. Death comes to those out of the army as well as in. Death will overtake us sooner or later let us be where we will, but is seems harder when far away from home & friends. But I hope that our lives will be spared to us so that we can meet again. But we cannot tell how it will be. I may escape the bullets & not escape the disease & then I may pass through safe & some of my family be gone to the land of death. This we cannot tell. But let us always look at the bright side of the picture. Let us try to be cheerful & hope for the best let what will come. I understand that

grain & hay is very scarce with the folks. How is it with you? Will you have enough to get through with? I am in hopes that we shall get our pay before we move from here so that I can send some money home for my creditors. I see by the papers that Sayres foundry is burned down. I suppose they will be a crowding those up that are owing them. But I shall let Mulford have some of the money when I get it & Sayres some too. We are expecting to move from here soon as the mud dries up a little. Our officers yesterday were ordered to send all of their extra baggage to the rear. That indicates a move soon but I should not think they would undertake it until the going gets better. But we cannot tell what they will do. Well I shall try & do the best that I can. My health is first rate & I guess that I can stand as much as any of them. Luther's health is very poor. I hope that he will get his discharge. He is completely broke down. He cannot stand anything. His countenance looks bad. He is excused by the Doctor from all duty but he ought to go to the hospital. If we move soon I think that he will. The weather today is cool but it is clear. Yesterday it rained all day like fury. So you can guess that it is muddy. We had inspection this morning & we shall not have much of anything else to do today but write. So I thought I might as well sit & talk with you a while as not. Well ma I have thought a good many times since I came back about father & myself talking about the Lords being on our side. I do not know but I hurt his feelings but I hope not. If he could see the amount of inequity that is practices in the army he might doubt the Lords being on our side. Our cause if good. There is no doubt. But the way the thing is carried on is a shame. I told you in my last about that steeplechase & horse race at Birney's headquarters. Well just at night the drunken officers began to come staggering reeling while a great many were so drunk that they could not get home & had to be hauled home in the ambulances. It was said that the ambulances were busier that night hauling drunken officers than they were at Fredericksburgh after the battle. What do you think of the Lords blessing such means as that? Well again we see among us for leaders one Sickles who murdered Key in cold blood & many others that were guilty of crimes. Then again look at our Capital. See the amount of corruption there. It is like Babylon of old filled with all manner of idolaters whores & whoremongers & those that love liars. It is enough to discourage anyone. Well I guess you will think it is time for me to stop. Well I guess that I have said enough. Well ma give my best respects to all inquiring

207

friends. My best love to you & family. Write often. Yours ever. I shall look for a letter tonight from home. I am very anxious to hear as often as I can.

April 1863

April 1, 1863 - Va.

Dear wife & children I received a letter from you on the go. I was very glad to hear that you were all well for I had worried a good deal about you. I am afraid that some of you will get the small pox. It is a terrible disease the best way that you can fix it. I had heard of Lows death before you wrote. Wils seemed to feel quite sad to think that he was dead. I do not think that he has any correspondence with her since that other woman left the mail carrier. You know (as near as I can find out she was as much a mistress when he was at home as Mrs. Low was well & guess one was as deep in the mud as the other). But enough of this. I want Edward to look to the tools in the Blacksmith Shop & save all that he can of them for they may be of some benefit to some of us & to me if I live to get home. But then if he & Norman has a chance to let the shops out I think they had better do it. They ought to be earning you something. Every little helps. Well ma how is the weather up in old Rush today? It is real cold here. Night before last we had a snow storm, a hard one at that & yesterday it hailed & rained almost all day. I tell you it was tedious. I think it is a very backward spring. The oldest inhabitants say they never saw the like. The mud is deep but some of the officers played a great April fool on us this morning. At 8 o'clock they got us up & had us draw three days rations & be ready to march at a moment warning for the Rebs were advancing in force. I could not believe it but did not know but it might be so, but it was a sell to come April fool on us. Well I had rather be fooled than have to march. Such going on as this. I see the report in the papers that they were evacuating Richmond & Va. But I do not believe it is so. I believe they are in heavy force at Fredricksburgh yet. Nor do I believe they intend to leave unless they are drove out. I guess they will stand us a hard pull yet. I see by their papers that they think that three months will tell the story. I hope it will for I am tired of this way of living. Not that life is not sweet to me but I wish to have it ended, that is the war, so that I can come home & enjoy the society of my family. This living in dog houses is not so pleasant although I feel thankful that my health keeps good. How long it will remain so we cannot tell. Luther is rather poorly. There is not much news to write. I think of my visit home with pleasure & I feel a good deal more contented than I did before I went home. I hope that my life will be spared to you that we may see each other again. How glad we should be if the matter was settled so that we could come home to stay. I am sorry that you feel so downhearted. You must try and cheer up. Have faith & believe that I shall live to come home. This getting discouraged is a bad feeling but I know I get the blues sometimes & it makes me feel like a fool. I had rather feel in good spirits all the time if I could but this cannot be. Well ma I shall have to close by wishing you all the good luck in the world & I suppose you would think my safe return just the thing. Well it would suit me. Give my best respects to all inquiring friends & my love to you & family. Yours ever.

April 6, 1863 - On Picket Va.

Dear wife and children I received a letter from you on yesterday night & also received my watch. It came through safe & in just the right time for the next morning we had to start on Picket. That is the reason that I did not answer your letter before. We had a pretty hard march yesterday getting here for it snowed all night & in the morning when we started the snow was 6 or 8 inches deep. Last night it froze quite hard & the day is cold & dreary. It beats all what weather we do have. They say here that they never saw such a spring before so backward. It made me very lame coming out here yesterday but my duties are light while here so that I guess by the time we get ready to go in I shall feel better. Well ma I am sorry that you feel so discouraged since I was home. For my part I feel a great deal better not that I think any less of home but on the contrary I think more of home & I know that I have warm friends there & a respectable family & if I ever come home to stay I do not want these friends ashamed to meet me. I should be as glad as you if I were out of the service but it must be in an honorable way or I shall stay until the war is over if I live that length of time. You say that you are poorly calculated to get along alone but I do not think so. I think you manage things first rate considering the chance you have. Well ma I think there is more signs of this rebellion being crushed out now than any other time. For when you see them uniting at the north & leaving political matters alone until our country is safe & all unite to put down this rebellion it will soon be done. I am glad to see such a feeling prevail. I hope

209

every deserter will be brought back & every loyal man will use their best endeavors to crush out this rebellion. I rather think by the appearance of things now that our division will not move from here when the rest of the army moves there is some talk that we shall go between Washington & Baltimore to guard railroad. I hope we shall but I am afraid there is no such good luck for us, but after all we may have some good luck after all. We hear a great many rumors what we are a going to do but enough of this. My health continues good & I feel in pretty good spirits but I am anxious for the time to come when this war will close & we again enjoy peace & prosperity. I feel just as anxious to get home as I ever did & I feel just as anxious to see you as I ever did & I hope the time is not far distant that we can all return to our home in peace & quiet. Well ma give my best respects to all inquiring friends my best love to you & family. I hope Billy is better. He must try and take good care of himself. Yours ever. Write often for I love to hear from home. Tell Ed to write once in a while.

April 11, 1863 – Va.

Dear wife & children I received a letter from you on the 8 dated 2nd while I was on Picket. I was glad to hear from you & to hear that you were all well. The reason that I did not answer it before was because I thought we should be relieved & get into camp that night but we had to stay another day. Well then yesterday we had to be received by the President & his wife. That took so much time that I could not write yesterday & then we had to be mustered besides. So you see it took all of the day. Well this is excuses enough. The weather is getting milder & it acts a little more like spring. I wrote once to you while on Picket telling you that my watch came through safe & I was very glad to get it for it is a great deal of company for me. We had a very good time while on Picket full as easy as we have in camp. Everything was quiet but enough of this. You said in your letter that the small pox was dying out. Well I am glad of it. I hope there will not be any new cases for it is a terrible disease anyhow you can fix it. Wilson had a letter stating that Jos Kinyon was dead. If he is let me know the particulars about it. I cannot hardly believe it is so but I do not know but he would be as likely to die as any one. You said in your last that Jas Hogan was very sick. Well he is an old man & if he gets well this time he has not long to live in this world. I hope that he will get well for I should like to see him if I live to get home. Well ma you say that you are discouraged. I am very sorry for you & I wish that

I were at home with you. But let us be patient. It may all turn out for the best. I saw an order from the war department last night in the Philadelphia Enquirer that gives me considerable hopes that I shall get out of this soon. If there is any prospect I will let you know. It has seemed to me ever since I was at home that some thing would turn up favorable & I hope there will. I think the prospect looks more favorable than it has for some time. My health continues good & I am tough as a bear with the exception of being a little lame after hard marching. I hope that we shall not have much of that to do. It looks now as though we should stay here awhile but we cannot tell. Well ma I have wrote all the news that I can think of & shall have to close. Give my best respects to all inquiring friends. My best love to you all. Hoping the time is not far distant when we shall be reunited. Yours ever.

April 14, 1863 – Va.
Dear wife & children I received one letter from on the 11 & one on the 18. I was glad to hear that you were all well. It does me good to hear from home especially to hear that you are well. I am sorry that you feel so downhearted. I know that it is hard for you to be left there alone with but little prospect of ever meeting again but we must not give up to despair. Let us hope on. Good luck has favored us so far. We have passed through some trying times & our lives have been spared thus far. It may be the will of him that rules the Universe to spare our lives to see the end of this accursed rebellion. Let us hope on. Let us hope ever. I know that we are apt to borrow trouble. It is natural for us. I know that I get discouraged & complain more than I ought. I cannot blame you for feeling sad for I know that you are lonesome but enough of this. All eyes are turned towards Charleston at present. I hope that we shall be successful there. If we are the day will soon dawn. The rebellion will receive such a blow that I think they will soon have to give up for according to their papers they (that is the rebs) are hard up for provisions. It does me good to hear that they are hard up & I hope they will have to submit or starve. I told you in my last that I thought that we should stay here awhile but I guess that our division will move with the rest. We may move any day. I should not be surprised if we should move within a day but we may not move in some time. It will depend on circumstances. In my other letter I told you that Wils got a letter from his folks stating that Jos Kinyon was dead. I guess it was a false report for Lute got a letter from Sabra saying that Orlo had wrote to her to know if Jas had

211

got home. If he had not to keep still. Now there is something wrong about that fellow. I should think by that that he had deserted. I am afraid that we shall have that debt at Atwaters to pay. I do think that Jim is as mean as dirt. If he does come back I want Edward to see him & try to get him to pay that debt. If he will not get him arrested as a deserter if he has not his discharge. Anyhow work it as sharp as you can. Try & save that debt if possible but enough of this. The weather for a few days has been nice although last night we had a heavy frost. But today is fine my health continues good. I am fit & hearty. In my last I spoke of an order from the war department that I saw in the Phil Enquirer that all Regts. that did not number five full companies they should be consolidated and a certain number of non commissioned officers to be mustered out of the service. If that should be the case I would stand a pretty good chance to get out of the service. Hope it will be so but I do not have much faith in it but let us hope that all things will turn out for the best. I have just heard that we have been ordered to have our rations ready & everything in order for a march at any moment. But those camp stories we cannot always believe. We may stay here for some time. We cannot tell. Well ma I shall have to close for want of room & news. How happy I should be if I were at liberty to come home to stay. I think that I could enjoy myself first rate. Well if I live to get home I can prize it all the more. Give my best respects to all inquiring friends. My best love to you all. Yours ever. Please send me a few more postage stamps. I expect we shall get our pay this week. Hope we shall. I will send you some money as soon as I get it.

April 14, 1863 – Short note with letter
Thursday morning. All is well ma. We moved yesterday & I did not get a chance to send this. Well ma I am well this morning & hope you are the same. I had a good visit on Tuesday with Chas. Lunz, W. Wilcox & Geo Mitchell. They were glad to see us. They were in good health. I was sorry that we could not had our visit longer but we had to march & could only see them for ½ hour. Well ma good day. Yours ever.

April 17, 1863 - Camp Near Potomac Creek Va.
Dear wife and children I did not think when I wrote to you last that I should have a chance to write again from this same old camp. But it seems as though Providence was against us moving from here for that same night it commenced raining like fury & it rained

24 hours. So I think it will delay the movement for several days. We sent our blankets & boots & all our extra clothing to the rear but yesterday it came back to us. So I think that they do not intend to move right away. We slept rather cool for two nights with nothing but our overcoats. But we got along. The weather looks bad for a move yet but I suppose that we shall have to start before many days. At the longest where we shall go we cannot tell but I suppose the cry is on to Richmond. I have heard that so much that I am tired of hearing it & I am tired of war. How I do wish that it was over. But when that time will come the Lord only knows & he only knows whose lives will be spared to the end of this war. But it is best for us to trust in him & keep our courage up & not give up to despair. I know that I get discouraged & feel down hearted a great many times when ought not to but I tell you it is a hard place for a fellow to feel first rate all the time but enough of this. I see by the papers that we have not been successful at Charleston. I am sorry for that for I think it will lengthen the war & give the Rebs new courage. I am afraid that we shall get whipped at Vicksburgh. It looks like it now. It seems that just at present we are meeting with reverses on every hand & things look dark. I was in hopes that we could have sunk Charleston & taken Vicksburgh if that had been the case I should have looked for this Rebellion to have been nearly closed up. But now the prospect is good for it to last a long time unless it is true that they are getting hard up for food we may starve them out. I hope we can find a way to whip them. I don't care how. Even if they starve, for I am a getting tired of this fighting. Well ma how do you get along? how are all the folks? I suppose that a good many see hard times up north for I see that provisions are very dear up there & the winter has been hard but they do not have to suffer as much as we do so they may think themselves well off if they are not drafted. I suppose the draft will scare some of them almost to death but it is no worse for them than it is for us. We are looking for our pay everyday. I hope we shall get it before we get on a march so that we can send it home. It is too bad that they do not pay up better than they do, but we are glad to get pay anytime well the boys seem to enjoy themselves pretty well. They are playing ball in the company streets & they are having considerable fun. Wilson has just sprained his ankle very bad we have bandaged it up but it has swelled pretty bad & is quite painful. Probably it will be two or three weeks before he will get over it. So much for fun. We sometimes pay dear for a little

sport. Well ma I do not know but I have wrote about everything that I can think of I hope something will turn up any time to keep us out of a fight don't you? but I suppose that somebody will have to go in but you know that we are selfish mortals & had rather escape ourselves & let others take it. Well ma I shall have to bid you good day. Give my best respects to all inquiring friends. My love to you all. Yours ever.

April 19, 1863 - Camp (Sickles) Va.
Dear wife & children it being Sunday & a nice day & not much to do only on guard today I thought that I would commence a letter to you. Well I have not received a letter from you since Monday night so I feel somewhat disappointed. But may be the fault is not in you. Well we have not moved yet but we expect to every day. I feel lonesome today & for fear that I should not get a chance to write to you very soon if ever I thought it best to write a little today. Well ma my thoughts are of home today & I think of the many happy days spent in roaming along the banks of the creek & noticing the spring buds. When I look back upon those scenes I see that we did not know how to prize them. But will the time ever come that we can live those scenes over again? sometimes I am afraid they are gone forever, that the day of sunshine for us has gone by. But still hope cheers me up & I hope my life may be spared for a long time. It is evident that we will have a hard fight at Fredricksburgh & no doubt but a great many of us will fall, but whose turn it will be the Lord only knows. I often think of the happy hours spent at home & long for the time to come that the weary soldier will be relieved from duty & enjoy the society of friends & home. We are at present having a hard struggle to know whether we shall have a government or not. I hope the right will prevail. Today they have sent all their sick & lame back to the hospital. Wilson has gone with the rest of them & we have just had a review by Generals Sickles, Birney, Berrey & Ward & Graham. It was quite a grand sight but I am sick of such reviews & had rather enjoy the quiet of home if I could be permitted. But when that time will come we cannot tell. There is not any news to write that I know of. I will leave my letter until tomorrow. If we do not move early in the morning for I may get a letter from you tonight. If not I shall feel greatly disappointed. As for pay I guess that we shall have to wait a while. Likely enough a month or two. I think it is too bad but we have got to stand it. Luther got a letter from Sabra stating that she had just received a letter from Orlo that Jos

Kinyon deserted while they were in Louisville KY, but he did not want her to tell of it so you must keep still for if he should come back & refuse to pay that debt you can use the information to some advantage. Well I will leave this letter until morning so good day.

Monday morning 20
well ma I did not get a letter from you last night & I felt quite disappointed about it but I had to put up with it. Well we have not moved yet but we expect orders to march any moment. Give my respect to all inquiring friends. My love to you all. Yours ever.

April 23, 1863 – Thursday Evening
Dear wife & children I received a letter from you on the 20 & one tonight. I was very glad to hear from you. I had got quite uneasy about you but I was glad to hear that you was well. It does me good to hear from you any time. You say that you are a going to try to feel more reconciled. Well I hope you will for we all feel better. I sometimes get discouraged but get over it & feel cheerful most of the time. My health is pretty good. Our move does not take place yet. I suppose it is on account of the weather. Today it has rained all day & I ought to have wrote in the daytime, but I thought that I would wait until tomorrow. But an order has just come in for us to go on picket early in the morning so I concluded to write you a few lines tonight. It seems as though providence was against our going across the river here for every time something turns up to prevent it. For my part I do not want to get over there again. Well ma that butter & honey was gone sometime ago but I tell you it was good as long as it lasted. You spoke about sending another box. Well if I thought that we should stay here any length of time I would have you send some butter & maple sugar, but I am almost afraid to have you send for fear that I should not get it. As for money I am out. But I guess that we shall get our pay before long. You will have to excuse this letter & I will write in a few days again as soon as I get off picket. I should like to be at home to eat warm sugar but it is not my luck to be there this spring but I hope that I shall live to see the time that I can. Give my best respects to all inquiring friends. My love to you all & many thanks for your kisses, but I had rather be there where I could take them warm. Goodnight ma. Yours ever. Write often & I will do the same.

May 1863

May 7, 1863 - Va.
Dear wife & children I feel thankful that my life is spared to write once more to you. Since I last wrote to you I have passed through scenes of danger & death. Another battle has been fought & thousands of brave men have fallen. I cannot give you a description of the scene. You can get an account of it in the papers. Our company lost in all killed wounded & missing fifteen. We find ourselves this morning in our old camp (that is what is left). Well ma we have been nine days on this tour & I tell you it has been a hard one. We have had no chance to write or get any mail but we expect to get it today. I received a letter from you the day we started containing 10 stamps. I was glad to hear that you were all well & that you had had good luck with your heifer. I hope she will make a good cow. How I should like to be there with you but I am pretty well discouraged and completely tired out so you will have to put up with a short letter this time & when I get rested I will try to write you a longer letter. I knew that you would feel anxious to hear from me & I know that you will be glad to hear that I am safe & sound. Well ma good day much love to you all. I will write again soon. Write often. Yours ever.

Afternoon. Well ma I understand that we have got to move so I do not know when I shall get a chance to write again. I feel discouraged & worn out. I shall lay down & try to get some rest. I lost all my clothes in the last fight except what I had on. Where we shall go next I don't know but I think it will be towards Bulls Run up that way somewhere. Well I wish this war was over or I wish myself out of it. Well it will not take long to kill what few there is left in our company. Lute is writing today. He will tell who is wounded in our company.

May 9, 1863 - Va. Saturday
Dear wife & children I received two letters from you yesterday. One containing two dollars. The money was very acceptable for I was out, but it done me the most good to hear that you were all well. You see that we got no mail all through the fight so I felt very anxious to hear from you. Our last fight has caused a gloom to settle all over the country. What a sad & terrible thing it was. What a terrible slaughter. I think it the worst that I ever saw. Our loss is heavy. The amount of suffering was awful. The ground that

we fought over was mostly woods & they caught fire & no doubt that hundreds of wounded were burned up. What an awful death. We were drove from all parts of the field & could not take our wounded with us. Only those slightly wounded. In one large brick house used as a hospital was burned by the enemy's shell & I suppose a great many of our men were burned in it. All day Sunday we fought like tigers but of no use. I never saw men fight better but we were out generaled. They knew too much for us. I do not know where the blame will rest now. Where is the fault? it is not with the soldiers for they fought until over one half of their numbers had fallen. I know we never felt so discouraged as we do now. Oh where will it end? God only knows. While I was in that fight little did I think that I ever should have a chance of writing to you again but Providence has spared my life. How thankful we ought to feel but how sad & lonely we feel. You hardly see a smile on the countenance of any. We are in the midst of death. We see over half our tents vacant. What will our company be after one more fight the Lord only knows. But I almost despair of ever seeing home again. But if it were not for hope the heart would break. It would seem so good if I were only out of this & safe at home. It seems as though I could take all the comfort in the world, but I am afraid that time will never come. Let us hope it will. Well ma I feel tired yet & feel dull so you cannot expect much of a letter from me this time. We have not got our pay yet & we do not know when we shall. We expected to move from here yesterday but did not. But we have to hold ourselves ready to start at a moments warning. I suppose we shall not get much rest. It does seem discouraging but we must put up with it. How I do wish this war could be settled some way or another but enough of this. I shall have to close. Give my best respects to all inquiring friends. My love to you all. Wilson was wounded pretty bad in the side. The two Otis boys were wounded in the arms. Those were all from our neighborhood. Cap. Lyons & Lieut. H. Hinds were wounded & there is four of our company missing. Well ma good day. Much love to you all. Yours ever.

May 11, 1863 – Va.
Dear wife & children I received a letter from you last night dated May 5. I was glad to hear from you & was glad to hear that you were all well. I was sorry to hear that our folk were unwell at the river. I had not heard from them since I came back. I have wrote to them & so had Lute but neither of us had got an answer. Well

affliction & death is amongst those at home as well as in the army. It does seem as though our country is passing through troubles & trials of every kind. Let us hope that they will be short but we do not know how long they will be. Well ma we have just got four months pay this morning so we are paid up to March 1. I shall send home 35 dollars. I am in debt some & want to pay it so I cannot send any more this time. I want you to pay Mulford 20 dollars on that note & pay Sayres 10 on that note. The five keep for yourself. Tell them that I will pay just as fast as I can so they must be patient. If they had to earn their money as hard as I do mine I think they would be willing to give me the debts, but I suppose that they are in a hurry to get their pay. Well I wish I had it for them. I will enclose 20 dollars in this letter & fifteen in the next & run the risk by mail. Well ma we are in our old camp yet but we expect to move everyday. We have got rested up a little but I dread to move. My health is midling good. That is one comfort to me, but I wish this war was at an end so that I could come home. Yesterday was Sunday & a pleasant day it was. It was still in camp & no work going on. It seemed like Sunday with a few exceptions. Some of the officers got some beer & got hearty drunk. But that is nothing for them. Well ma for my part I spent most of the day thinking of home & family. Oh how many pleasant hours we have spent together on such pleasant Sabbaths. It seems as though we could prize it now if we could have a chance again. But I sometimes fear that time will never come again but is pleasant to think & meditate upon such times. Oh that they could come again but only One knows how it will turn out. Let us hope for the best. Well ma I will close this & maybe I will write again today & send the rest of my money. Give my best respects to all inquiring friends. Yours ever.

Well ma I thought I would write you a few lines this evening to let you know how I feel. Well I feel pretty smart. Since writing this morning I have been strolling around and seeing what I could. Well there is a large fort within sight of us. It is a hard looking place. I can tell you they have 90 cannons there besides a good many smaller field pieces. This fort is fort Lyons. It commands Alexandria and the Potomac. They could throw shells into Alexandria all to pieces in a short time. It was built to protect that place against the rebels and to prevent the rebels from coming up the river. I have seen several rebel prisoners brought in today. They were caught by pickets near our lines but you cannot get them to say anything. They are innocent of course. That is about all you can get out of them. Well ma we are not a great way from Mount Vernon and if I live I intend to visit that place before long. Some of our men have been there today. They say it is splendid. They can see the coffins of Washington and his wife. They are made of marble. We have camps all about here. There is three Pa Regts. close to us and how many more I do not know. Well ma I must bid you good night. I should like to be with you tonight but that cannot be yet I long for the time to come that we shall see each other again. You must tell the boys that their pa has not forgotten them. He often thinks of them and hopes they have not forgotten their pa. He would like to see them and he hopes he will and they must try to be good boys. Now ma I must not tire your patience any longer at this time. So goodnight and hope you will have pleasant dreams. I have had some pleasant dreams lately. I have dreamed several times lately that the war was over and I was at home. I hope they will come to pass. Yours ever. My best love to you all. Well ma you must write often as you can for if I should go out on picket it might be five or six days before you get a letter but I think I will write again before I go.

May 12, 1863 - Va.

Dear wife & children I will try & write you a few lines today to let you know that I am still alive & in the enjoyment of midling health. We have not moved yet but we expect to soon. Our ambulances have gone over the river today to get our wounded soldiers. I understand that Gen. Lee sent a flag of truce to Gen. Hooker requesting him to come over & get his wounded for he had not the means to take care of them. I think it very kind in him for the poor fellows must suffer a great deal. It is very hot weather just now. I suppose that Gen. Stoneman cut off the rebel supplies so that Lee could not take care of the wounded, but it will be much pleasanter for them to be among friends where they can have good care taken of them than it would be among strangers. I wrote to you yesterday enclosing twenty dollars & today will send fifteen. I want you to let me know as soon as you get it & apply 20 on the Mulford Note & ten on Sayres Note. The five keep for yourself. I wish that I could send more. I feel anxious to pay my debts but I want some money to buy things with. I suppose I ought to be more saving with my money but what little time we have to live I want to take as much comfort as I can. But at the best this is a poor place to take comfort in. I had rather be at home with nothing but a crust where I could be free than be here. It seems as though our division had it the hardest of any. It lost more men than any other division in the army. Our brigade lost 790 men. The whole division lost 1870. There is three brigades in a division so you see that our brigade suffered the worst. Well ma please send me a few more postage stamps. Write often for it is about all the comfort that I take is in getting letters from home. Well ma I shall have to close hoping that you will have the good luck to get the contents of these two letters safe. Give my best respects to all inquiring friends. My love to you all. Yours ever.

May 14, 1863 - Va. Thursday morning

Dear wife & children I take another opportunity to write you a few lines to let you know that I am alive & well as usual. Well ma I guess you will think that I mean to improve all the time in writing to you. Well we do not know how soon this privilege may be taken away from us so we will improve on it while it lasts. The weather has been very warm for a few days past but today it looks like rain. I hope that we shall get a shower. It will cleanse the air. We are daily expecting to move again. If we go over the river I think if we do there will be a terrible battle fought, this time harder than any that has been fought yet. But I hope not. It does seem as though there had been lives enough lost already on that side of the river & in fact there has been too many lives lost everywhere in this cursed rebellion. I wish some way could be fixed upon to settle this question. But if the South are bound to fight it out we must try to meet them. It will be a long & bloody struggle I am afraid. It seems sometimes to me if I were only out of it I should not care, but you know we are selfish beings only looking for our own interest. But I tell you we all feel sad & lonely. It has been the stillest time in camp that I ever saw. Our numbers are small & all feel as though we had narrowly escaped with our lives. There seems to be a gloom on all. It was a terrible sight so many of our number gone. A few more fights & we are all gone. I hope that we shall not be put in front & exposed so much the next time but we cannot tell nor can we tell whose turn it will be to fall. I suppose it is time for you to begin to make gardens & fix up for summer. Have the meadow cleaned off of all loose stuff such as stones & trash so as to save all of your grass. I would let Ad Lung work the garden on shares. It will save you a good deal of trouble. I should like to be at home with you this summer & should like to have this war close but the Lord only knows when that time will come. Let us still hope on. I try to keep up good courage but I must confess that I get discouraged & downhearted sometimes that we cannot help. I have seen Fred Perigo & Berry Barthopp since the fight. They are well. Their camp is in sight of ours. It is thought that Fred Fargo was killed. He is among the missing. One of our company that was wounded we think will die. Five in our company missing fate unknown. Well ma I shall have to close by wishing you good luck & hoping that my life may be spared to get home & see you again. Let me know all the news. I heard from Wils Ferry last night. He is in Washington. Give my best respects to all inquiring friends. I will send Billy fifty cents so he can have a little money & let him know that his pa has not forgotten him. Tell Edward to be steady & try to please his employer. I feel thankful that you all get along as well as you do. I hope you will get that 35 dollars that I sent you by mail. My love to you all. Yours ever. I have not received any letters from you for 8 or 9 days. I suppose from the fact the nine days that we were out you got no mail from me. But I presume that I shall get answers from my letters as often as you get them so it will be 8 or nine days between this time, but it will come around all right.

May 17, 1863 - Va. Sunday morning
Dear wife & children I will write you a few lines today to let you know how I get along. Well in the first place I am comfortable well & it is a very nice day clear & warm. How I could enjoy the day if I were only at home with my family, but our thoughts can be as one & we have the privilege of writing to each other. That is some comfort, but we could take more comfort if this war was closed & peace restored. Oh it would seem so good to enjoy the society of family & friends & our country at peace. But we often ask ourselves when will that time come? not until a great many more of us return to death. I fear the prospect for the continuation of this war is as favourable as it was one year ago. I do wish something would turn up favourable for a speedy close of this horrible butchery & loss of human life but I suppose it will close when the great Ruler of the Universe sees fit. Let us hope that everything will turn out for the best. Well ma I see in the paper that Maria Williams is married. I hope she has got a husband worthy of her for I think she is a very nice girl. I am not much acquainted with Lambert Picket but hope they will do well. I have not received a letter from you in some time. I suppose it is on the account of you not receiving any from me while on that campaign

of nine days. Well I shall get some after a while. We have had a pretty easy time in camp since we got back. Yesterday I was down to Aquia Creek to load some clothing. Had a good ride on the cars & a very pleasant time. We had six paroled prisoners come to our company yesterday that were taken on the 13 of last December so it makes some addition to our company. We are looking for a move everyday but then we may stay here some time. We cannot tell anything about it. For my part I do not mind moving so much as I do the fighting. That part I don't like. Well ma I told you they thought Fred Fargo was killed but he is only wounded & is a doing well. One of our company that we thought killed has turned up wounded & is doing well. Our chaplain is gone & we cannot hear from him. We think he is killed but hope not. Well ma I have wrote all the news that I can think of & will have to close by wishing you all the good luck in the world. I should like to know how it would seem to be at home on a pleasant Sabbath like this. I think it would seem good don't you? Give my best respects to all inquiring friends. My love to you all. Yours ever.

May 22, 1863 - Near Potomac Creek, Va.
Dear wife & children I received a letter from you last night dated 16. I was very glad to hear from you. It had been a long time since I had heard from home. Well I was glad to hear that you were all well & glad that you had received that 20 dollars. I hope that other 15 will go through safe. I was very sorry to hear that Uncle Richard's folks were so poorly. I am afraid that Maria will see trouble with her breast & am afraid it will kill her if she does not get help soon. It is a good thing for them that Dennis & Hannah is there to help take care of them. Well ma you say that poor old Jimmy Hogan has gone to his long home. That is the way one after another goes. How soon it will be our time we do not know. Sometimes it seems as though it were impossible for us to escape but still we come out safe. I hope that my life will be spared to see the end of this war & return safe home. Well ma the weather is warm & dry. If we could only have a good shower it would cleanse the air & it would be more healthy I think. Well I do not see any prospect of the army moving right away. They are moving camps & putting up bakerys so that we can have soft bread. That will be good. Well ma I am a mind to have you send me a box with some fine cut tobacco & a little maple sugar. I do not know as you could send any butter in it. If you should you would have to put a tin pail & then pack saw dust or salt around it. The tobacco

& sugar would have to be kept apart or the sugar would taste of the tobacco & I should like one of them cotton shirts for woolen scratches me so this warm weather. Send me a little black thread if you please. I do not think of anything else & if it is not convenient you need not send the box. It would come good but maybe we shall not stay here long enough to get it. I think that our moves will depend on the moves of the enemy. There is a good many 2 years & nine months men going home now so I think they will have to reorganize over again. Well so far as I am concerned I had just as soon they would not fight for I have seen so much misery caused by fighting that I dread to hear of a battle. Well ma I will send Ed a Philadelphia Enquirer if I can get one. Tell him to look over the names of honor. I need not tell you that such things raises our pride a little for we are vain as well as the rest of the folks. What shape those medals are in I do not know but if I am lucky enough to get one I will let you know. Well ma I see it in the papers that we are to be paid off again soon up to the first of May. Well I had rather they would pay us as fast as it comes due for you could pay the debts all the faster & stop interest. I do not think of any news to write more so I shall have to close. Give my best respects to all inquiring friends. My love to you all. Yours ever. If you conclude to send that box you had better send it as soon as you can for we cannot tell how long we shall lay here. But at present there is no prospect of a move. I shall have to send this without paying the postage for I am out of stamps.

May 25, 1863 - Camp Near Potomac Creek.
Dear wife & children I received a letter from you last night & was very glad to hear from you & to hear that you were all well. It does me good to know that you are well & have enough to live on. I hope that you will not suffer for the want of the necessarys of life while I am absent. It is bad enough for me to have to be absent & in this place without your having to suffer. Well ma I am glad that you received that money & I wish it had been ten times as much. I wish I had money enough to pay all of my debts but it is a pretty hard way to get it by staying here. But after all if I live & have to stay here we can wear the debts away after a while with good luck. You spoke in your letter about going to the river to see Maria. I hope that you will find her better but I fear that I shall never see her again even if I should live to get home (& the prospect of my living to get home is slim). But let us hope that everything will turn out for the best. Well ma I went to see the boys in the 151

Regt. & 143 & 56 Regts. PV on Saturday & Sunday. I found a good many of them sick & some had gone on picket, but those that were in camp I had a first rate visit with. I saw Seth Shove. He is hearty. Ed Perigo is not very well. Mark was on Picket. A good many of the boys from the middle branch were at the hospital. They was not in the last fight but they had to march & that liked to have killed them. It set them all into the dysentery. New troops cannot stand half as much as the old ones can but enough of this. The weather has been very hot & dry but today it rains a little. Just enough to lay the dust & it is some cooler. I received those postage stamps all safe & thank you very much for them. I hope that we shall not have to move soon. There is a good many troops going home Peter Roe's Regt. will go home this week. How I do wish that this war was over & all of us were going home but a great many more of us will go to our long home before this war will close I fear. I do not see any more prospect of its closing now than I did one year ago, but of course it is one year near its close than it was one year ago. Well ma I do not think of anything interesting to write & will have to close hoping that we both will have good luck & meet again. Give my best respects to all inquiring friends. My best love & wishes to you all. Yours ever. I like to have forgot to tell you that Wilson was mistaken about me being hurt. Luther was hurt on the arm a little & excused from duty for a few days but I have done duty with the exception of about one day. I am well & hearty. There is none in the company that can do more duty than myself.

May 28, 1863 - Va.
Dear wife & children I take this opportunity to write you a few lines to let you know that I am well & hope that you are the same. The weather is dry & very hot through the nights. Well ma we remain here yet. How soon we shall move I do not know. Sometimes I think that we shall move soon & then I think our moves will be governed by the moves of the enemys. But let that be as it will I am not anxious to get into another fight unless we can take the advantage of them in some way. Well ma yesterday we had a grand parade & those medals were given to those that their names were on the list. For my part I am sorry that it was ever mentioned for it has created a good deal of hard feeling. They are mad at them that got them. Of course all could not get them & for that reason they feel jealous. I will send you mine. It will be something that will give me a good name & at the same time a

keepsake for you. I feel proud of the honor but I am sorry that it produces such feelings in the company. But it was something I did not ask for nor did I expect to get until I saw my name in the papers but enough of this. If Ed got that paper I sent him it will explain. If he did not I will send him a copy of the order. Well ma I have not received a letter from you since I wrote before stating that you were going to the river to see Maria. I am anxious to hear from there & hear how they get along. I am afraid that she will not live but hope she may get help soon enough to save her life. Elisha Fargo came to my tent last night. He is down here to see his brother Fred & try to get a furlough for him. He does not know yet whether he will succeed or not. There is not much news to write. According to the papers we are having some good luck in the west. I hope Grant will get Vicksburgh. But for two days the papers have not brought much news from there & I am afraid that he has got drove back. That is the way most of our victorys turn out. But I hope this will be an exception & Grant will take the place. How I do wish this rebellion was crushed out & we safely at home. How often we ask ourselves when it will end but as often ask again. I sometimes think it will not end as long as this present administration lasts but I hope not. Well ma I shall have to close for want of news. Give my best respects to all inquiring friends. My love to you all. Write often. Yours ever.

May 30, 1863 - Near Bell Plains, Va.
Dear wife & children I received a letter from you night before last dated 22. I was glad to hear that you were all well & was glad to hear that the prospect was good for an abundance of fruit. I can think how nice the trees look in full bloom up there & I can think how I would like to be there but instead of being there I am a great way from there with but little prospect of ever getting there. Well I hope this war will play out after awhile but no doubt it will last long enough. Well ma we moved our camp yesterday down towards Bell Plains. We can see the shipping in the river & it is quite a pleasant place. We are in the open field with nothing but little shelter tents. Two in a tent. I tent with a fellow by the name of Wiggins from Wyoming. You may think it strange that I do not tent with Lute but he is a queer fellow. He is so slow at everything but getting mad. Well you need not say anything. The weather is warm & dry today. The wind blows like a storm. I expect that we shall have to go on picket tomorrow. We shall have to go some 8 or 10 miles I suppose. You spoke in your letter about going to the

225

river & about Maria & Emily. I am very sorry to hear of their afflictions. It must seem gloomy to go to Richards & see them in such a way. But ma we have seen grief in our family & we can sympathize with them in their troubles. Although we are separated & may never meet again it makes me feel sad to hear that my friends at home are suffering. I hope that they may get help & recover & I hope that our lives may be spared to meet again but we do not know what is laid up in store for us. We have seen a great deal of trouble & we may see a great deal more but I hope that we shall be permitted to meet again. My health is good I stand it first rate. But what in the world would give more joy than to have this rebellion put down & the soldiers permitted to return to their homes & families. How I long for that time to come. I long for the time to come that I can live like a human being again. But it may never come. We cannot tell but let us hope that everything will turn out for the best. Well ma let me know how Edward gets along in the store. How his health is. I would like to have him write. How does Billy get along? does he go to school? He must try & be a good boy for I know he will be. Tell him that his pa thinks of him & Ed every day & wishes that he could be at home with them & I wish that this rebellion was crushed out so that all of us could come home. Well ma there is nothing new to write. Give my best respects to all inquiring friends. My love to you all. Chas Devers moved down on the creek. Has Eld Gray moved on the Nicolas place? How does Dunham get along? Has Snell got his house finished yet? How do you get along with your farming? Does Ad Lung live in the shop yet? Well I guess you will think that I have asked you questions enough for one time so good day. Yours ever. Oh let me know what you think of the Kearny Cross I sent in my last letter to you. The worth is not much, but the name of the thing is the worth.

June 1863

June 5, 1863 - Va.
Dear wife & children at last I have a few moments leisure & I will improve it. Well the reason that I did not write before was that we were on Picket. Well we have just got back to camp again all safe & sound. Well as soon as we got into camp I had to draw three days rations & divide them out, sign the pay rolls & draw my pay & have been sawing wood to cook our rations with for we have

orders to be ready to march at a moments warning. You will see that I have been busy for the last four hours & am pretty well tired out. We had to march about 10 miles to get into camp. It took us until 12 1/2 o'clock now it is 4 1/2. I expect that we shall march tonight or in the morning & then we may not march for several days. I found a letter in camp from you stating that you were well & I was glad to hear it. You said that you had sent that box. I hope that I shall get it, but if we move there is no knowing. Let it RIP. I dread the thoughts of another fight but I expect that we shall have to stand it. I hope that you will get that medal. It is not of much value but it will be a keepsake if I never should live to get home. But let us hope that good luck will attend me through. Well ma I will send you some money in this letter. I want you to pay Mr. Wilson ten dollars & I guess that you had better keep the rest for your own use. Well ma I shall have to close for at this time there is heavy cannonading going on. I should think in the direction of Fredricksburgh. Well I should not wonder if we had to march tonight yet. My health is good. I have acted as quartermaster for our company since the Chancelor fight. Give my best respects to all inquiring friends. My love to you all. Yours ever. I will write again just as soon as I can get time so good evening

June 7, 1863 - Va.
Dear wife & children I take another opportunity to write you a few lines to let you know that I am alive & well & I hope these few lines will find you well & hearty. I wrote to you on the 5 & supposed that we should move that night but we did not. We are expecting to move tonight or in the morning. I told you in my last that I heard heavy cannonading. Well it was our forces. They had crossed at Fredricksburgh & supposed that the enemy had left but they soon found enough of them & was glad to cross back again. So that fight did not amount to much, but this move that we are to make is a mystery to us all. Some think one thing & some another, but time will tell the story. It is Sunday. Today we have had division inspection this forenoon by Gen. Birney. Such a thing would be a great sight up in our country but here it is not thought much of. We get used to seeing large bodies of soldiers together. But it does not appear much like Sunday nor do we have anything like Sundays here. How I should like to enjoy a Sabbath like we used to at home. We all long for the time to come that we can enjoy the scenes of home. Let us hope on let us hope ever. I know that we get discouraged a great many times & we have reasons for

227

being so for it does seem as though this Army of the Potomac was doomed to disappointment. We have done a great deal of hard fighting & hard work, but what has it amounted to? I tell you it is a wonder that the soldiers are in as good spirits as they are. I am satisfied that the soldiers have not the confidence in Hooker that they had in McClellan, nor never will have. For my part I think the whole concern a mere speculation & money making affair. Unless we can get men in at the head of affairs that will fight for patriotism & not for mere pay & honors our country will be ruined. But enough of this criticism. Well ma I shall have to close for want of something interesting to write. We had a nice shower last night. Today is quite cool. We have sent all of our extra baggage to the rear. I do not know as we shall ever see it again, but it is better so than lugging ourselves to death with such loads. Write often. It may be sometime before I get a chance to write again but I will write as soon as I get a chance. We have not been ordered to carry only three days rations as yet & I hope we shall not have any more to carry for it is load enough. I hope you will get that 15 dollars that I sent in my last. I would have sent more but thought I would keep ten dollars by me to buy some little luxuries with. Give my best respects to all inquiring friends. My love to you all. Yours ever.

June 10, 1863 - Va.
Dear wife & children I received two letters from you yesterday & one shirt I was glad to hear that you were all well. I hope that your health will be spared while I am absent & I hope that my life may be spared to see you again, but that part looks doubtful. It seems as though this war would never end but I suppose it will sometime. Well Edward wrote about the debts & the amount it was more than I expected but I suppose it is all correct. He spoke about getting money of Mother Granger to pay the debts all up. Well I think it would be a good plan you could secure her by giving her a lien on the place & what money I can save while in the service can apply on it without any trouble. You know if I should get killed or die, you would get the one hundred dollar bounty (that is if the government does not alter its laws). I declare I get discouraged sometimes when I think how mean they act. You know when I enlisted the country agreed to pay four dollars per month to soldiers' wives & two dollars for every child under fourteen but they have not done it. If they had it would have been a great help to us, almost half as much as my wages. But enough of this. If you

succeed in getting money to pay them debts at Montrose they ought to throw off considerable. I wish you would try & see how much they will throw off. Plead up poverty pretty hard. I tell you if they had to earn their money as hard as I do mine they would not want to pay half of their debts. But I suppose they will act hogish about it anyway. That debt at Shoemakers I wish that you could get Ad Lung to pay. I presume Shoemaker would take work of him. Any little will help. If they at Montrose would throw off so that it would not be but $200.00 & you get the money of Mother Granger I think we could pay her after a little. I want it fixed up all for the best so that if I should not live to get home you can get along without me. Well enough of this. You spoke about getting some better position. I wish that I could I think that I have earned it but there is no chance here. Our Regt. is so small that it is a hard job to get more officers in & another thing is the Wyoming boys will have the best chance. They are all connected so they have the most favours shown them. If I was only out of the service I could get a Lt. or Captaincy in some new company without trouble. But this is just my luck. I would not care much what if it would only raise my wages. I want to get higher wages so that I can pay any debts faster. I found a pocket book the other day with 33 dollars in it I could have kept it if I had been a mind to. I found the owner's name in it & I returned it to him. He was a Lt. In our Regt. So much for that. It would not have been honest to have kept it. Ed spoke about enlisting for ninety days but I guess that has fell through with. I had rather he would not. I will tell my reasons. They are because it will throw him in the worst society possible & the restrictions of camp life he would not like. The drills would be hard for him to bear nor could he get the privilege of coming to see me if he was a soldier & another reason he has a good place & I do not want him to loose it. I should be glad to have him come & see me & would like to have him see Washington & should like to be there to show him around. It may happen so that chance will be for him yet if I should get wounded or sick & should be at Washington I would send for Ed to come & see me. But I hope that I shall have good luck to get out of this alive. Ed said in his letter that Jas Gupper was playing the agreeable to Widow Lowe. Well it is not surprising at all for she is of that kind. If I were with you I could tell a good deal that I have learned of her & that other one that has left, since I was at home with you last winter. But you must not tell of it nor who told me. It was Wils. He told me of things that I hardly thought possible but I tell you one half of the world does not know what the other half is about. I did not think them so common. I should suppose that Mrs. Gupper would make a fuss. That woman will see a great deal of trouble with Jim yet for I see he is Devil possessed after such characters. Well enough of this. Let them RIP. I expect that Wilson will be at home shortly if he is not now. We have quite cool weather & very windy. We have not moved yet & we may not for several days & we may before night. We cannot tell anything about it. I have heard heavy cannonading this morning way up on our right. What it will amount to I do not know. It may kick up a fight yet. Plague take it. I hate this fighting but shall have to stand it. I do not see any way to get out of it. My health is good & I stand it first rate so far. If you have not sent that other shirt you may wait awhile for I can get along without it at present, but then I can carry it if it comes. Ed wanted to know how Lute liked it because he did not get a medal. He did not like it much. I do not want to say much about him. He is queer the best way you can fix him. That is enough. Well ma I shall have to close for want of something to write & I guess you will think that I have wrote enough useless banter. Well I hope the time will come that we shall be at liberty so that we shall not need to write to each other, but be so that we can communicate by word of mouth. Give my best respects to all inquiring friends. My love to you all. Yours ever. Good day.

June 30, 1863 - Md.
Dear wife & children my heart is glading this morning by receiving 2 letters from you. One of the 11th one of the 15, the first since we started on this march. Well ma I have not had any chance to write you. We have been on the march almost 3 weeks without any mail, tired & part sore, are now within 4 miles of Pa line. Little did I think when we started that we should get as near Pa as we are, but the Rebs are in heavy force ahead of us. I suppose & I think that we shall have to do some hard fighting before we get them out of Pa. I received them shirts all right & I tell you they came good for we have had no time to wash anything since we started. I should like to give you a description of our march but cannot now but I will just as soon as I get time if I live. I am glad that my health is good. I have stood the march first rate, although many has died on this march of sun stroke. Well ma I shall have to close for fear that I shall miss my chance to send this. Well ma I hope that I shall have good luck & come out all safe.

Well ma good day & good luck to you. My best love to you all. Yours ever. Excuse mistakes

July 1863

July 5, 1863 - Near Gettysburgh, Pa. Sunday 12 o'clock

Dear wife & children it is by the mercy of God that I am alive to write you a few lines to let you know how I am. Another big battle has been fought & my life & health is spared & so far I am not hurt. But alas a great many have gone to their long homes. Only eight left in our company. How shall I tell the sad news? Brother Luther is among the slain. He was shot through the head & killed instantly. He never knew what hurt him. He was killed on the 2nd of July & we found his body this morning. The Rebels held the part of the field that we fought in until last night. They had took all of his money, some six or eight dollars. It is reported that they have left last night. Large details are out on the battlefield burying the dead, for the field is covered with dead. For 4 days we have had hard fighting here & some the hardest I ever saw. Nearly 3/4 of our Regt. is gone. Oh how sad & lonely I feel. I shall have to close for now I hear the cannons roar & we shall have to fall in. I suppose I shall be glad if I live until this is over & then I will try to give you some account of this great fight. I guess that the enemy have not gone far for our men are after them. Well ma I must bid you good day hoping my life will be spared to see you again. Give my love to all my best love to you & children. Yours ever. This was wrote in haste so please excuse

July 10, 1863 - Md.

Dear wife & children I will write you a few lines to let you know that I am alive & well but pretty well worn out. We received a mail last night. I got 2 letters from you & it done me a great deal of good. We expect a fight today. We are near the old battle ground of Antietam & expect a hard fight. I do not know as I can get a chance to send this but will try to get some citizen to take it & put it in the office. I have not time to write much but if I live to get out of this I will write you some good long letters. I hope my life will be spared to see you again. I feel sad & lonely & almost discouraged but let us hope on. Oh that wagon I told Ed that Dennis might have it for $25 dollars. I was sorry to hear of Emily's death. It is a sad blow. May God grant us patience to bear up under our trials. I want to get time to write to Sabra but cannot yet. I will just as soon as I can get time & chance. Well ma I must close. My best love to you all. Good day. Yours ever.

July 12, 1863 - Md. Sunday morning.
Dear wife & children I take this opportunity to write you a few lines to let you know that I am alive & well. I feel thankful that it is so. We have not had a fight since we left Gettysburgh but we expect one any moment. So you see it keeps us in a state of excitement all the time. A soldiers life is a hard life to live. Well ma I hope if I live that I shall get some rest by & by but when that will be the Lord only knows. Oh how glad I would be if I were at home today to spend a Sabbath in peace & quiet. But instead of peace & quiet we may be in a hard fight before night. We cannot tell what will happen. For a few nights I have had pleasant dreams of home & I wish that some of them would come to pass. It does seem to me sometimes that I was going home & I hope that I may, but life is uncertain. We cannot tell what will happen. But let us hope that everything will turn out for the best. Sabra will get an official report of Luther's death as soon as some of our commissioned officers come up with us. We have no officer that belongs to our company. Capt. Lyons is at Washington. Lt. Hinds is missing since the Battle & Lt. Green was wounded, so you see we are put into another company. Well enough of this. Well ma I do not enjoy myself nor take much comfort for my associates are wicked men & men of mean principles. I cannot bear them nor can I have much to say to them. I never knew how much a man would suffer in such society. It makes me feel as though I were all alone, sad & lonely, but I hope for better times. My best companions in the company are all gone. Nate Goodsill was wounded in the ankle at Gettysburgh & John Harris was wounded too. They belong to the 141 Regt. Well ma I shall have to close. I shall be glad if we ever get settled down again in camp. I suppose if we do I shall get that box but cannot get it as long as we keep moving around. It was four weeks last Thursday since we broke up camp. Since then we have had no rest night nor day hardly. Some nights we have marched all night through rain & mud. It has been an awful time. Well ma I must close by wishing you all the good luck in the world. My love to you all. Yours ever. You said you did not know but I would be mad because you wanted to settle up my debts but far be it. I am glad to have you get the money to do it. I think it is the best thing you could do. Then we can have it all in one place. I will write again just as soon as I can.

232

Tuesday July 14, 1863 - Near Hagerstown, Md.

Dear wife & children I am still alive & well. So far we have not been in any fight since I last wrote but we are expecting any moment to hear the sound of battle. It keeps us in continued excitement for we do not know what moment we shall have to go in. Well ma I shall be glad when this is over so that we can get some rest. It is my opinion that we shall have the hardest fight here of any place yet for it seems every battle is harder than the other, but I hope not this time. Well ma I cannot write much, only to let you know that I am safe & sound yet. If I live through this & get in a place where I can I will write you some good long letters, but you must excuse these poor letters. Well ma I hope that I shall live to see you & the children again but that we cannot tell. The weather is very warm & rainy. Well ma I must close. My best wishes to all my friends. My best love to you all. Yours ever.

July 16, 1863 - Near Brownsville, Md. Thursday evening

Dear son I will send my watch to you. I have broke the crystal & have carried it in my pocket until I am afraid that it is most spoiled & I do not see as I shall get any chance to get it fixed so you may get it fixed & keep it. I have kept it wrapped up in paper but I have sweat so much that I could not keep it dry & I am afraid that it is rusted inside so you had better get it fixed as soon as you can. Well enough of this. We have been on the march for five weeks today, so you see that we have had a hard time of it & some of the hardest fighting to do that I ever saw. Well I feel very thankful that I have so far came out safe, but I expect we shall have hard marching to overtake Lee. He has escaped into Va. again. Well I wish he was under the ground & this Rebellion crushed out. I have wrote several letters home but I do not know as they got through or not. We do not get our mail very often. I wrote about Luther being killed at Gettysburgh on the 2nd of July & I have not heard from home since then. I do hope that we can get some rest before long for I am about worn out. I hope that you are all well. Write often & I will do the same, every chance I can get. I suppose that we shall cross into Va. tomorrow sometime in the day. Well good night. Keep up good courage. Be kind to your ma & Billy. I hope to see you all again. Yours ever.

July 18, 1863 - London County, Va.

Dear wife & children I have just received a letter from you dated July 11. I tell you I was glad to hear from you. It had been a good while since I had heard from home. I was glad to hear that you were well. My health is good but I wish that we could get some rest. It does seem as though it would wear us all out. We had some hopes of staying behind to do guard duty but alas for our hopes last night we were ordered to cross the Potomac into Va. once more & here we are in front again. Well I suppose that we must try & stand it. I do hope that we shall succeed in breaking up Lee's army & then I shall think the rebellion about played out. Well ma I will try & give you some description of the battlefield. It presented the awfulest sight you ever saw. The stench was such as I never saw before. Dead bodies lay exposed for five days in the sun, the most of them swollen so that they would burst open & just as black as a hat. Some did not turn black from the fact that they bled the blood out of them. In one small place where the rebs had their artillery there was 37 horses lay dead. All the horses for that battery. It would be impossible for me to tell the number of horses killed, but it was immence. When we left I could see lots of rebs that were not buried nor I do not believe they could be very well, they were so rotten. When the Rebs left they had rows of their dead laid in for burying but went off & left them for our men to bury. The ground was all plowed up with shell. Houses & barns riddled. Orchards cut all to pieces with balls. Fences torn down. Rails burned to cook our grub & farms cut up with rifle pitts. Everything laid waste. Well I can not tell you half the damage done. If there is any Copperheads that wish to resist the draft & bring war to their doors let them visit the battle field of Gettysburgh. Let them hear the shot & shell, the sharp hiss of the minie ball as it comes so close as to burn. Let them see the horrors of a battle field & they will cave. Well ma enough of this. I wrote to Sabra today. I should be very glad if I could come home then I could explain it better, but sometimes I almost give up thinking of ever getting home again. But I have every reason to feel thankful for my life so far. I saw some of the nicest country in Md. that I ever have. Thousands acres of wheat & corn. The people were very kind to us & glad to see us drive the rebs out. They did not complain because we destroyed some of their crops but some in Pa grumbled a good deal. I believe they were Copperheads & we had no pity for them. Well ma I must close. I sent my watch to Edward. I hope he will get it. Give my love to all inquiring friends. My best love to you all. Yours ever.

July 21, 1863 – Upperville, Va. Tuesday morning

Dear wife & children I take this opportunity to write you a few lines to let you know that I am alive & well & sincerely hope that you are all well. We are on the march every day. Some days we march hard & some days light, but it is enough to keep us pretty well drilled out. I am not looking for much rest very soon. Well I do hope that it will be the means of putting an end to this cursed rebellion. It is the opinion of some that in the next two months the fighting will be pretty well done up. I hope it will for it seems to me that it will wear us all out yet. For two or three days the weather has been fine. It rained almost everyday that we were in Md. & Pa. It must have spoiled a great deal of their wheat. This is a very nice country where we are. Nice crops growing here, but it will the most of it be wasted. I do not pity the inhabitants for they are rank secesh. They ought to suffer. Well ma enough of this. How do you get along? Are you going to have any fruit this year? Did your gooseberries do well? I hope you have got a good garden this year. There is lots of blackberries here. I have had one or two messes & I had two good messes of cherries. There was any amount of cherries on the road, but we could not stop to get them. I tell you my mouth did water to see whole rows of trees on each side of the road loaded down with ripe cherries but they done us no good. There always is a lot of loafers along that get the best & deserve the least, but so it is in all cases. It is that class of people that bring disgrace on the rest & causes such strict orders to be issued against straggling, but in almost every case the innocent suffer for the guilty. It makes me so mad that I want to shoot some of them slinks. Well I guess that I have complained enough for this time ma. I do wish something would turn up so that I could come home & stay with you & I still hope the time will come that I can get home honorable. We have had 4 in our company desert since we went up into Md., 2 in Pa & 2 in Md. Alonso Bramble & Adam Clink left us in Pa. Jerry Storm & Daniel Carz left in Md. The two last named are from Wyoming Co. Well ma if you do not see me until I desert you will never see me, for I do not intend to disgrace myself nor family in that way although I should like to be at home. Well ma you must write often as you can. I have not received any letter since I wrote before, but I want to hear from you often as I can. My health continues good & I feel thankful to think it does for it would be very hard for me if my health was poor. I shall have to close. Give my best respects to all. My best love & wishes to you & yours. Yours ever. Oh ma send me about one doz. Needles of thread in your next letter I want it to mend my clothes. I have plenty of needles. It may be ever sometime before I get that box in. Oh, I saw H. P. Johnson & James & Henry Nicolas. Their time is out & they expect to go home in a day or so. They have never seen a fight. Well I wish my time was out so that I could go home with them. I saw in the Republican that Seth Sore was wounded. It did not say how bad. Well I guess that I have wrote enough for this time. If you can only read it you will do well. Good day.

July 27, 1863 - Near Warrenton, Va.

Dear wife & children I take this opportunity to write you a few lines. I do not know as you will ever get it for we have had no mail since we came into Va. But I am bound to write just as often as I can, for I know that you are anxious to hear from me. Well ma I am just as anxious to hear from you but I know that you are not to blame for the mail not coming to us. Well enough of this. Well ma I wrote to you on the 21st at Upperville. Since then we went to Manassas Gap where we had quite a sharp fight. We drove the rebs back across the Shanandoah river. We then went to Front Royal then came back through Salem & through Warrenton & camped for the night & here we are this morning 8 o'clock, but we expect that we shall move soon. I tell you we have had some hard marching & I feel about worn out. My health is pretty good & I have stood it as good as any of them so far, but how I long to hear from home. I do hope we shall get a mail soon. Where we shall go to from here we cannot tell nor can we tell how soon we shall have to fight. But I should not wonder if we run into the rebs any time. Well let us hope that everything will turn out for the best. Some of the time I feel in pretty good spirits & sometimes I feel discouraged, but everybody has their ups & downs. I shall be glad if I ever get released from this way of living, that is if I get out safe & sound. I sometimes think that it cannot last a great while longer, but then we cannot tell. It may last for years yet. Well ma I shall have to close by wishing myself & you all the good luck in the world. How I do wish that I could see you & have a good visit with you & as for that I should like to stay at home. Give my best respects to all. My best love to you all. Yours ever.

August 1863

August 1, 1863 - Camp near Sulfur Springs, Va.

Dear wife & children I received a letter from you this morning stating that you were all well. I was glad to read it. We moved camp yesterday about 3 miles so today we are on picket. I have charge of the post that our company occupies so I take it easy & have good company. The boys in our company think a good deal of me & treat me first rate, but we have got some just as mean fellows in our Regt. as ever breathed. But such persons I despise. I never could bear such mean scoundrels but enough of this. Capt. Lyons has come back & takes command of the Regt. Col. Sides had two of his fingers shot off at Gettysburgh & is home on furlough. But we expect him back soon. We expect that our Regt. will be filled with conscripts. There has been three commissioned officers & six privates sent to Pittsburgh after them. How soon they will be back we do not know. I do not think we shall do much for a month or so. The weather is very warm. Today is the hottest day of the season. The sweat rolls off us like rain. I hope we should have a good chance to rest & get recreated up while here. Well ma I must tell you a little more about our travels in Md. I often think of our march through that beautiful state. In every village there was any quantity of flags displayed & every door filled with ladies waving handkerchiefs & cheering us on our way. In some places the ladies proposed three cheers for Pennsylvania & in turn we gave them hearty cheers for the ladies of Md. There we saw nice fields of grain & everything looked promising. That country does not show the effects of war. I think the valley of Middletown to Frederick is as nice as anything that I ever saw. Everything betakens wealth in Md. Now let us look at Va. Said once to be rich and aristocratic her fields laid waste. Farms all destroyed. Buildings burned down & everything laid to waste. The results of their folly for seceding. Here at Sulfur Springs was a nice place sufficient to accommodate some 2,000 people. It has been a great watering place at sometime but is all burned down since this rebellion broke out. So much for their folly. I think it will be a dear lesson for them if peace is declared. If ever that time comes which I hope will & that soon. Well ma you said father wanted to know whether anyone saw Luther after he was killed that I could depend on their word. There was two of our company saw him. There were well acquainted with him. They say that they know him. His cap had 2 red feathers. One on the right side & one on the top & a piece of oil cloth put in the back of his cap to make it larger. They say that he was badly swollen but they recognized him in a moment. I cannot tell you anything about his burial. The details were made of those that I were not acquainted with & was made before I had found out that Luther was dead. So much for that. Well ma you said that you & Edward wanted to publish some of my letters. Well I had rather you would not. I do not want to be brought before the public for you know there will be so much speculating about it that I had rather keep out. I have not seen the democrat paper in a long time. The last one that I saw was last spring down at the 173 Regt. when I was there. Well ma while I am writing this I can hear the boom of cannon & I should not wonder if we had to move. It may not be anything but a cavalry fight in the direction of Culpepper Court House but it may end in something serious we cannot tell. Well ma I will leave this letter until morning & see what the news is if we live till morning. So good night. Well I guess that I might as well finish this up for fear that I shall not get a chance in the morning. So I will send my best respects to all inquiring friends. My best love to you all. Yours ever.

P.S. Write often & tell some of the rest of the folks to write to me for I am lonesome & would be glad to hear from any of them. Sunday morning. Well ma I am well this morning. Some of our boys went out yesterday & brought in 2 fat sheep & the way we eat mutton is a caution. We will learn them to secede. We are living first rate it is very warm this morning. Good day.

August 5, 1863 - Camp Near Sulpher Springs Va.
Dear wife & children I received a letter from you this morning stating that you were all well. The letter contained one hank of thread. You will learn before this that I had received that box so that I did not stand so much in need of it as I did but I feel just as thankful for your kindness to me in sending everything that I want. That is everything that you can. Well ma those dried apples & maple sugar tobacco & suchlike in that box came good I tell you & I feel very thankful to you & Edward for sending them. I hope that I shall live to get home & repay you for all those nice things. Well ma I was glad to hear that you were all well & that you were getting your haying done. I hope you will have good luck & get it in good order. I should like very much to step in and take dinner

with you some day when you had peas, beans or green corn for dinner. I think that I should take a full ration don't you. Well I hope the time will come some day or other but we cannot tell when. We are having pretty easy time just now but I do not expect it will last long. I think that some of our army is going to Charleston SC. It is not likely that our Regt. will have to go for it is so small. Well for my part I do not want to for it is warm enough here for comfort. I hope that we shall soon hear of that hot bed of secession being made to surrender. Rebellion will then be pretty well used up. I want to see it rolled up in a small compass. What a day of rejoicing it will be when the rebellion is crushed out & peace once more restored to our country. May the time soon come is the prayer of every loyal man. Well ma my health continues good. There is no news of importance to write. Yesterday we heard heavy cannonading towards Culpepper. What it amounts to I do not know but I presume somebody got hurt. I have got so that I hate the sound of firearms. If I should live to get home I don't thing that I should be as fond of a gun as I used to be, but I may get over this in times of peace. Well I should like to come home to stay & see how it would seem. Well ma in some of my letters I have cut on the Copperheads pretty hard. Well they deserve it. Any set of men that will set themselves up against the government in such a time as this when their brothers are in the field suffering everything but death & many of them suffering death, I say such men as these are not worthy to be called men. It is hard work to abuse them. Well they may say how comes this? You used to be an antiabolitionist. Have you changed your politics? Well I may have changed a little in some things but not in the main principles. The times demands that every effort that can be made should be made to crush out the rebellion & I believe it is right for the President to use all the means in his power to subdue those states in open rebellion to the United States. I have been opposed to enlisting negros but now I am in favor of it. I begin to think that they ought to be fought with negroes. They are just mean enough. They do not respect their oath of parole. They are destitute of honor. Well now these lickspittles called copperheads want to favor those men. Well I don't. They have had all the chance to come back to the Union. If they would they might have secured their property but no they would not. Why? Because they could not have their own way in everything. Well what is the reason that such & such ones will not support the Administration?

Simply because it does not go by such & such name they think the principle is nothing. Now I will bet anything that more than one half that is opposed to the government would praise the same acts if performed by one of another name. Such is prejudice. I wish they would lay aside all political prejudices. Let party go to the shades until the Union is restored. Then let them talk politics. Until then let them break down all political barriers & political parties. Let us first know if we have a government or not. Well I do not know but it would be best for me to hold my peace. Well I guess I will but if I were at home I suppose that I should quarrel with a good many, but I think now that if I live I shall let politics alone & not bother my head with such affairs. I wrote a letter to Uncle Richard's folks day before yesterday & I hope to get an answer from it for I want to know how they get along. I feel anxious to hear from sister Maria. Poor Norman. She must suffer a great deal. I should like very much to see them all. Well ma I do not know that I can think of enough to fill up this sheet. Well I will make a few inquiries & then close. Well take the salt down the road to father. How are they all getting along? I suppose everything looks about the same as it did when I left. How is it on the ridge? I suppose that Cooley lives on the Crawford place & Dick lives on the Carly place. Who lives on the old Ellis place? I suppose that same awful place is just the same. Well just give him my best respects & tell him to take a good drink for me. Tell him that I should like to hear from him. I suppose the State Militia have been mustered out & have got home. Well they are saved. Probably you have heard for certain whether Seth Shoves is dead or not for I see that Regt. is mustered out of the service. Well ma I will close and I guess that you will think that I have given you a plenty for the time it will be day. But you must excuse all blunders. Give my best respects to all inquiring friends. My best love to you all. Yours ever.

August 9, 1863 - Sulpher Springs, Va.
Dear wife & children I received a letter from you yesterday dated Aug 4. I was very glad to hear that you had got your haying done. If you had as bad weather as we have down here it would be a bad enough for we have showers every day & oh dear how hot it just makes us sweat like rain every time we stir. I do not see how we could stand it if we had to march & I hope that we shall not have to try it. Well I suppose it will come cool weather by & by. We then shall have plenty to do with out a doubt. I see in your last

letter that you feel quite discouraged & seem to think your lot hard. Well I know it is so you have a great deal on your hands that is. When we view it in a right light, you have the cure on your mind that would be on both of us if I were with you & we are deprived of the counsels of each other in a measure. But ma let us try & keep up with it for a while. It may all be for the best. If I should live to get home I never should mind the pain or fatigue that I have suffered in the service. I know that we are apt to look on the dark side of the picture too much. I often get discouraged & often wish that I was out of the service, but I am sure if I was out of the service I should not be content to stay out until this rebellion is crushed out & peace restored again. I think if I live to see that time I shall be content to stay at home & I hope that time will soon come & I still hope the same kind of providence that has watched over me & kept me from harm will still watch over me & protect me until the end of this rebellion. I am glad I am that you & I do not get discouraged at a time. It almost always happens when one is discouraged the other is encouraged. Well I hope everything will turn out for the best. Well enough of this. Today is Sunday. It is very warm. My thoughts are of home. I have been thinking how pleasant we used to spend such Sabbath days. We could keep in the shade until just at night then take a pleasant stroll. How nice it would be. How often I think of the pleasant walks that we used to take & often wonder if the time will ever come that we shall have the chance of doing so again. That we cannot tell. There is no news to write of importance. I forgot to tell Ed that I got them stamps in his letter & am much obliged to him for them & I received that thread that you sent me. I sold some of that tobacco that was in that box & have got some of it yet. I like it first rate. Our sutler has just come up today with a load of goods for the soldiers. You had better believe he will make a pile off his load. I will tell you some of his prices cheese 40 cts per lbs. Raisins 40 cts per lbs. Common wool hats $3 dollars. Tobacco 3 cts papers (such as used to sell for that) he sells three for a quarter. Suspenders one dollar per pair and everything in per portion. Two sheets of paper for 5 cents. Well they run a great risk from the bushwackers. You see by the papers that a great many sutlers with their wagons get captured. Well I shall have to close for I must write one or 2 letters for another fellow to his wife for he cannot write & he is a good clever fellow & I like to accommodate all such. Give my best respects to all inquiring friends. My best love to you all. Yours ever. Write often as you can & I will do the same.

August 11, 1863 - Sulpher Springs, Va.
Dear wife & children I received a letter from you today stating that you were all well. I was glad to hear it. Yesterday I received 2 handkerchiefs & one ink stand & I feel wonderful proud of them I can tell you. They came through safe & are just the sort for this campaigning. Well ma my health is pretty good although I feel old & stiff. Yet my appetite is good. We have plenty of rations. We have drawed since we have been here five days rations of soft bread. That is a great treat for us after living on hard tack so long. It seems good to have a change. We have drawn dried apples several times & we have plenty of fresh beef & salt pork. So you see that our rations are good. We have had a pretty good rest but I expect that it is about over. Today we have received orders to be ready to move at a moments warning so I think there is something in the wind. It is my opinion that Lee intends to attack us. I am afraid if he should he would drive us back towards Washington. I understand that he has been reinforced. If that be so we shall have to fall back but I hope they will keep quiet until we get these conscripts. I suppose our moves will be in accordance with the enemy's moves but after all we may not move from here in some time & we may move before morning. We cannot tell. You said in your letter that Seth Shoves funeral Sermon would be preached on Sunday. Well then it is true poor Seth is dead. Such is the fortunes of war. There is a good many from Rush that has fallen in this terrible war. How many more will fall the Lord only knows. But I hope not any more but no doubt but we shall have some hard fighting to do & I am afraid that the hardest fighting will have to be done in Va. It seems as though they meant to stick to old Va. until the last. Well ma I shall have to close for want of news. You spoke about sending me some money. We did expect to get our pay but by some carelessness in our officers I am afraid that we shall not get paid until after we are mustered again. If we should not I may want a little. I will let you know the next time I write. The paymaster is here paying the other Regts. & we shall know within a day or so whether we get paid or not. Give my best respects to all inquiring friends. My best love to you all. Yours ever. I will write again soon if nothing happens. The weather is very warm. For two days we have not had any showers.

August 18, 1863 - Sulpher Springs, Va.

Dear wife & children I take this opportunity to write you a few lines to let you know how I get along. Well in the first place I am in good health & feel quite comfortable this morning. After all our orders for marching we are still in our camps yet. We have had our things packed up teams all loaded ready for a start at a moments warning. What it all means is more than I can tell. It is the most mysterious move yet. There has been several Regts. In our Division sent off. One the 20th Indiana has gone to Castle Garden NY the 3rd & 5th Mich. Regts. have gone to Alexandria Va. & I understand that several more of the 3rd Corps have gone somewhere. We do not know where. I think that there is some great move on foot somewhere. What it will amount to time alone will tell. The cavalry that was out in front of us have all come in & gone somewhere else. I should not wonder if there was to be a big strike made in another direction but we cannot tell anyhow. I hope that everything will turn out for the best. It seems that we have a great deal to encourage us at the present time. It does seem as though the South would see the folly of standing out & resisting the Federal Government longer for it is only entailing distress & misery on their own heads. It does seem as though they had suffered enough to bring them to their senses (if they have any). Well enough of this. The weather is not quite as warm as it was. We are taking things easy. We have plenty to eat but after all I should like to be where we could get butter eggs & garden sauce & such stuff but we ought not to complain as long as we get enough of other provisions. Ed spoke about going to Scranton when the drafted men went down there. Well that will be a good chance for recreation. I want him to let me know the names of those drafted in Rush as soon as he finds out. In regard to pay we shall not get any this payday & will have to wait until four months pay comes due. It seems hard but we can stand it. I suppose that some families will suffer for the want of the soldiers' pay but they will have to put up with it. There is no news of importance to write. I have not received a letter from you since I wrote before but shall look for one tonight. This rebellion cannot play out too soon to suit me. The sooner the better. How glad I shall be if I live to see this thing settled up & me safe home. Well ma I cannot think of anything more to write so I shall have to close. Give my best respects to all inquiring friends. My love to you all. Yours ever. Write often & I will do the same.

August 21, 1863 - Sulpher Springs, Va.

Dear wife & children I received a letter from you on the 19th dated 15th while we were on picket. I was very glad to hear from you. I am very sorry that Billy is afflicted but I hope that his toe has got well by this time. We are still here & I do not see any signs of moving at present. But for all that we may move any moment. You can see by this the uncertainty of our stay in a place if we could know anything before hand we could know what to do. But as it is we cannot take much comfort. Well enough of this my health is first rate. Our dutys are light so far since we have been here & on the grand whole I cannot see as we ought to find fault nor do I mean to. But for all that I long to have this cursed rebellion crushed out & peace once more restored to our Country. I feel anxious to get home & enjoy peace & happiness again but when I look at the chances for getting home I am almost discouraged. There is so much risk to run. So many chances for a man to loose his life. That a great many of us may have to lay silent in death before this thing is settled is quite certain, but still I believe that this rebellion is on its last legs. That with good luck on our side we shall soon wipe it out. It may cost much blood and many lives. They may make one terrible effort to save themselves & then give up the ghost (I hope they will give up the ghost without the struggle). They must see by this time that their case is hopeless. I hope they will & save bloodshed but enough of this. I hope that Charleston will have to fall & I don't care if it is layed in ashes. It has always been a hotbed of Secession & it ought to be blotted from the face of the earth. Well ma you may think that I am getting crazy. Well I am getting so that I hate to hear anyone preach up treason & hate to hear anyone talk about resisting the laws for this has brought all our troubles. I do not care whether it is from the North or South. I say down with everyone that says resist the laws of his or her country. If it cuts on the party that calls themselves Democrats or Republicans or any other party or sect that preaches up resistance to the laws. Down with them. They should not be permitted to sow their seeds of disunion. There has been too much of that kind of work going on. It has encouraged the South. It has discouraged us in the field. It has led us to believe that our friends at the North had deserted us & would leave us to be overcome by the enemy. But I am glad that they are getting waked up & that we have friends that feel for us. I think that march through Maryland & up to Pa done the soldiers a great deal of good. We were treated like human beings & we found out that a soldier was somebody. We had been so long outside the pales of civilized society that we had almost forgotten that we belonged to the human family. I am sure that it encouraged a great many & I hope that a great many will be better soldiers in future. Well ma I guess you will think this a jumbled up mess so I will close. Give my best respects to all inquiring friends. My love to you all. Yours ever. If Edward can just as well as not he may send me 2 dollars. Probably we shall not get our pay for a month or two yet. The weather is warm. The nights are cool.

August 24, 1863 - Sulpher Springs, Va.

Dear wife & children I received a letter from you last night dated 20th & was glad to hear that you were well. Glad to hear that Billy's toe was almost well for I had considerable uneasiness about him. I hope that you may all have good luck & escape disease & death in my absence. But those things are hidden from us. But so far we have been wonderfully favored. My health remains good & I do not think that I ought to complain although I have to suffer many privations & be deprived the security of family & friends. Those things have to be borne as well as hard marches, numerous nights watchings, suffering heat & cold besides being exposed to the enemy's bullets. All these things. It seems to place a lifetime in a moment. But how soon those things appear to be forgot. We hardly rest one week before all is life & fun in camp. The boys are cutting up all sorts (this is not the case with all of them) but some of them cut up in this way. I have thought many times if I should live to get home that I never could forget the hardships that I have endured. But I find that a few days rest even here obliterates a great many of them. Well I guess you will think I have wrote enough on this subject. You said that H.P. Johnson had moved in with you & you had let him have the shop again. I think it best to try & have the shop bringing in something if you can. Every little will help. I wish you could let out the blacksmith shop to some good blacksmith & have that earning you something. Well in what way did you let the wagon shop to Henry? Just as we had it before or do you rent it to him? I think it would be as well to rent it to him for so much & have him buy the lumber & stock that is there. Let him have the shop & tools & shop fixens etc. Or if he had rather let him have it as I let it to him just as you & he can agree. I am quite sure if I were at home some of them good apples would have to suffer as well as many other

245

good things. You said you did not want me to come home until I could be content to stay. Well I do not see any chance for me to get home very soon. But of one thing I am quite sure that if I can get home I shall be content to stay for it is not likely I shall get home until the war is over or my time is out unless I can get a furlough this winter (which I mean to if I live & can). I think if we are successful at Charleston it will bring the war to a close speedily. I have great hopes that will be the end of the rebellion. I do not want you to think that I would not like to be with you at home but after all my country needs my help & I for one ought to be willing to help enforce her laws & so had everyone that would claim protection under the laws. If it is painful to see so many at the North set the laws at defiance & claim such & such are unconstitutional when all that we are trying to do is to enforce the laws & punish those in open rebellion & in my opinion those same men of the North called copperheads are traitors & deserve to be punished the same as Southerns in arms. Well ma our move has blowed over for the present I guess & everything remains quiet along the lines. There is no news of importance so I will close. Give my respects to all inquiring friends. My best love to you all. Yours ever.

August 27, 1863 - Sulpher Springs, Va.
Dear wife & children I will try & write you a few lines to let you know that I am well & I hope those lines will find you all well. Today we received two months pay which amounted to twenty-six dollars & I will enclose ten dollars in this letter & send some in the next one that I write. I do not like to risk too much at a time. You can use it (that is the money) as you think best. I wish that I could get larger wages so that we could pay our debts faster but patience & perseverance will accomplish it after a while. But what I wish more is that this rebellion was at an end & we ready to start home. If all our news are correct we are in a fair prospect of conquering them today. It is reported that Sumpter has fallen. If that be the case Charleston must soon yield. With that hotbed of secession in our hands we may look for peace in a short time. That is with good luck in the Southwest. I do not doubt but that we shall have a terrible battle in Va. Yet. It will be a hard one or not any at all. I hope the latter will be the case. Since I wrote before I have been on picket. It was on the 25. We had a heavy shower it came off very cool & it was very cool last night. It is warm enough in the daytime. We have no blankets or none but our tent blankets & one

rubber blanket. So you see that sleeping outdoor with nothing of any consequence over you is not comfortable. Cool nights but never mine we shall get toughened to it. Well for my part I do not want to draw any more blankets until we get somewhere to stay for a while. But enough of this. As soon as they draft up with you I want you to let me know who is drafted etc. There is no news to write & somehow I am not in writing humor to day. You know that some days it is hard work to write. You cannot think of anything to write nor can we write or spell as we want to. I shall have to close hoping this will find you all well & enjoying yourselves first rate. Give my best respects to all inquiring friends. My best love to you all. Yours ever. Edward if you should see Nathan Y. Sherwood (Philo's son or Philo), the Capt. wanted you should inquire of him who discharged him. What general & at what time he was discharged, for he the Capt. has never had any notice of his being discharged & he wishes to know so that he can arrange it on his books.

August 30, 1863 - Sulpher Springs, Va.

Dear wife & children I received a letter from you on the 28 dated 25 & was glad to hear that you were all well & in comfortable circumstances. Well your kind letter found me in good health & pretty good spirits. We have plenty to eat & not much work to do & I don't see why we might not to be satisfied. That same night on dress parade the Capt. of our Co. announced that I was promoted to Sergeant to date from the first of July. Well I am glad of it for it will raise my wages to 17 per month. I do not know but I am selfish but I think that I have earned it. I have done sergeant's duty ever since the Chancellorsville fight & so far have only received privates pay. Well enough of this. I received a letter from Dennis & Hannah the same night. They say that sister Maria is failing fast & they would not be surprised if she should drop away at any time. I am sorry it is so. I should be very glad to see her once more. I would give a good deal if I could get a furlough to come home if only for a short time, but that is out of the question. I do not suppose that I could get a furlough under any circumstances so I shall have to wait. The news that we get from Charleston is good & I hope that we shall soon hear of the place being taken or destroyed. With the fall of that place their hopes must begin to fail. Thrash it on. I hope they will have to repent in dust & ashes for the misery they have caused. They can never atone for the one thousandant part of their sins only see the amount of suffering the living have had to endure besides the great amount of slain. It ought to weigh them down forever & these men at home that are advising men to resist the laws & break down our government. What ought to be done with them? I say brand them like Cain & drive them out from among the people. They are bastards. They are not legitimate citizens. No true American would try to break down one of the best governments that the sun ever shone on. It is their business to submit to the decision of the ballot box & because they are in the minority they should not try to overthrow the government. Well enough of this. The weather is fine. Only the nights are a little too cool for comfort. Our Regt. is filling up a little. Some of the sick & wounded are coming back to us. We have not got any conscripts nor do I know when we shall. Everything remains quiet & we do not see any signs of moving. Our Col. has come back to us. Our Major is in Richmond & so is H. H. Hinds our first Lieut. They were taken at Gettysburgh. Our Col. had two fingers shot off but they are about well now. Well I cannot think of anything more to write this time so I will close. I will send you ten dollars in the letter & hope that you have got the other ten that I sent in my last. Give my best respects to all inquiring friends. My love to you all. Yours ever. Send me a few postage stamps if you please. Send about 25 or 30 there is several of the boys that want some.

September 1863

September 8, 1863 - Sulpher Springs, Va.
Dear wife & children I received a letter from you night before last & should have answered yesterday but I had to go on review which took the most of the day. We had to go some six miles. It was a review of the whole third army corps. Such a sight in Susq. Co. would have been worth seeing. In this corps there is three divisions & in each division there is three brigades & in each brigade there is from four to 6 Regts. Each Regt. with its flag. Some Regts. have 2 flags. Then added to this there is some Howitzer batteries with all their equipage. Then comes the Generals & their staffs. All of those things make a grand sight to those that have never seen such military movements. But for my part they were not interesting. I have seen so many of them. In your letter you said that Billy was afflicted with a sore toe. Well I am sorry for him. I hope it is well before this time. You spoke

about sister Maria. I am afraid that I never shall see her again if I should live to get home. I would have been glad to get a furlough so that I could have come home to seen her but I could not. It seems that she suffers a great deal. Poor woman how I pity her but I cannot help her. You said that your health was good & Edwards too. Well I am glad to hear it for I feel uneasy about you at home & long for the time to come that I can be with you. My health continues good with the exception of feeling a little lame occasionally. I don't think that I can stand as much now as I could before we took that tramp through Maryland & Pa. That was a hard one. There is some talk about our going to Texas but I do not believe that we shall go there at all. It is all stuff. But I think that there will be a move with the army soon but in what direction or where is more than I can tell or guess. So we shall have to wait & see. It is very dry here & warm through the day but the nights are cool, but we manage to get along quite comfortable. If we get in a place where I can get a box from home I shall have Edward send me a pair of boots & I do not know but I could get them here providing that we did not have to move soon. He need not send them until you hear from me again. It would be a good plan to have boots for the muddy weather but then I suppose that we shall get along as well as we did last fall & that we lived through. There is not much news to write of consequence here. I should like to know the reason that they do not draft in Susq. Co. I do not see anything about it in the papers. I should think it was time if they intended to have them do us any good. I wish they might get through with the fighting this fall & close the thing up & for my part I wish they would stop now, that is the South. If they would submit the North would not need to fight unless they had to whip the Copperheads & that would not take much for they are cowards anyhow. Well enough of this. Give my best respects to all inquiring friends. My best love to you all. Yours ever.

Oh yes I was obliged for them two stamps for I was just out but I have four or five now. I had lent some to the boys. Tell Norman that I thank him for that paper. There is some good reading in it. We get the daily papers so that we keep posted pretty well. When we do not have much to do we like to read. We must have something to occupy time. Good day.

September 11, 1863 - Sulpher Springs, Va.

Dear son I received a letter from you last night & one from you one night before last. We were on picket so that I could not answer them until today. In your letter you inform me that sister Maria is dead. I have been expecting to hear that for some time. So they drop away one after another. If I should live to get home I should miss a great many friends & acquaintances a good many have fell in battle & a great many by disease. Soon it may come our turn to lay down in death. How important that we should be prepared. This will leave a lonesome house for Uncle Richard. His loss cannot be repaid to him & his family. The neighborhood will miss her. Such a woman as she was will be missed by many. I am very thankful that your health remain good. If your healths were poor I should feel uneasy about you all the time. You said that you applied that money on that note & had sold the old buggy. Well that is good. So far any little helps. I hope with good luck that we shall get it all paid. I did think that I would keep fifteen dollars of my next pay & buy me a good hunting case watch but I guess that I shall not for I want to pay that debt just as fast as I can. You know that you can sell that wagon to Dennis Keeney for 25 dollars. That will help to get stuff to live on for some time & I think that you had better rent the wagon shop & sell the lumber to him & let him pay along as he works it up. (Henry Johnson is the one I meant wants the shop) You can let him have the tools to work with. I had rather you would not sell them. You must manage it the best you can. I hope you will have good luck & I hope that I shall live to get home all safe & sound. I received those stamps all safe and was glad of them. I divided them with the boys. That story that Briggs told will not hurt me so let it go. I may live to give him a thrashing for his poison. I am like to get an easier place. I expect to be sergeant of the ambulance train. If so I shall have a horse to ride & my duty will be light and another good thing I shall not have to go in the fights & shall not have to carry such loads. I do not know when I shall leave the company. Some of them say not until we are about to move. Well let that go. Today we drew our woolen blankets so we shall be comfortable these cool nights, our Texas expedition has played out. I did not believe any of the time we should go there. Well we have all sorts of camp stories but we are used to them. So we believe just as much of them as we have a mind to. Ma said in her letter that Billy's toe was getting better. I am glad of it. I am glad to hear that you have plenty of fruit. I wish I as there. I have not had a good apple or peach this season. I could buy them off the sutlers but I cannot afford it. I have a mind to have you send me a pair of Leisters Kipp boots No 8 & about 4 lbs. of fine cut tobacco & direct it the same as you did the other box. I guess it will come through all right. You need not send a large box. If you had it & could just as well as not send me off a can of honey & butter you know I could carry a little such stuff if we should have to march. But I do not want you to put yourself to any trouble. You said the copperheads were down on me. I cannot see why they should not for I am here to fight for my country & uphold the laws & support the administration that they are opposed to. But every true democrat is for his country & these that are not are copperheads or traitors or rebs or just what you are a mind to call them. I will write you a long letter on this subject as soon as I get time but I have got to fix my clothes today so I shall have to close. Give my best respects to all. My love to you. My health is good. Good day I got 2 stamps in ma's letter.

September 14, 1863 - Sulpher Springs, Va.
Dear wife & children I have not received a letter from you since the one that Ed wrote informing me of Maria's death. He said that you had gone to the funeral. I hope you got back safe. Their house must be lonesome. They will miss her & it will be hard for Uncle Richard to get anyone that can fill her place. But so it is we shall drop away one by one. The world will move along just the same in a few years hardly anybody will miss us. Only a few of our nearest friends. Well ma I have thought for some time that we should move but here we are yet. It begins to look like a move. The cavalry moved across the river Saturday night & yesterday (Sunday). There was considerable firing in front of us this morning. I understand that our forces are in Culpepper. They only found a small force to oppose them. I should not wonder if the whole line advanced. But they may not. Some think that Lee is withdrawing his forces out of Va. & some think that he is concentrating his forcer for the purpose of invading Md. & Pa again this fall. It is my opinion that he intends to go north. If he does there will be another terrible battle & I think it will wind him up. I think that the Rebs have given up gaining their independence but they are that mean that they want to do us all the damage that they can. I believe that they would be satisfied if they could destroy the Army of the Potomac. They will have a sweet time of

it I think but then they may destroy a great many of us. Well enough of this. My health is pretty good. I still remain in the company. I understand that the General wishes to leave those that are detailed in the ambulance corp. with their companies until we move. Well for my part I had rather go there at once for it will be easier for me if I can only stay in that place until my time is out. I shall be glad for it is just as good a place as I want. I shall have a horse to ride & take care of & have three ambulances & nine men to see to. I hope that there will be no fail about going there. You see it is a great deal safer for it is hardly ever that we have to go near the fighting. Well I wrote to Ed about sending me a box. If he does I want him to put me in a pair of suspenders. You need not send any dried fruit nor any such. Wait until we get into winter quarters if we do at all. Then I think that I shall want some such. Well you may thing that I am asking a good deal & I think I am too but you must have patience with me & I will try & make it up to you if I live & if I do not live why it will have to go with the rest of my indebtedness. We have had one or two good heavy showers but the sun is very hot. The nights are quite cool. We get daily papers for five cents a piece. We keep pretty well posted in the news of the day. If they call out the militia for state defense I do not want Ed to go for if the rebs get up into Pa again the militia will have something to do they will not fare as well this time as they did in the summer. They will have to fight this time. The old army was mad because the militia did not get there to help them. Well ma I shall have to close. I shall look for a letter tonight. I should not wonder if we got our pay this week that is if we do not move. Give my best respects to all inquiring friends. My love to you all. Yours ever.

September 20, 1863 - Near Culpepper Court House, Va.
Dear son I will try to write you a few lines today. I wrote your ma day before yesterday. It was raining like sudds then, but it cleared off. In the afternoon the sun shown hot. In the evening we had a hard shower & it came off very cool. Today is pleasant & nice. I thought when we came here that we should have a fight before this time but the enemy remains quiet so far as we can see. But I presume they are studying up mischief. They are sharp & I presume our generals are engineering as well as they. We shall have to wait & see who comes out best. I received a letter from Sabra on the night of the 18th. She says that Henry is quite poorly. I hope that he will be careful of himself & get along. I feel much

obliged to my relatives for their kind regards for me & I hope my life will be spared to see them again. My health is very good. I am still with the company but I hope that I shall get that place that I spoke about. I will let you know when I get it. The detail is made & all that is wanting is an order on our Col. & he will send them at once. Well Ed we got our pay after I sent that letter so ma so I will enclose $2 dollars in this letter & you & ma can do as you please with it. This town of Culpepper contains about 4000 inhabitants & I should think it had been quite a place before the war. I have only been in sight of the place. We are now encamped about 2 ½ miles North West of it on the turnpike leading form Sulpher Springs to Culpepper & from thence to Gordensville. I see by the papers that North Carolina wishes to get back into the Union. I wish all the states would come back & save bloodshed. But if they will not they must be made to. I hope that Gov. Curtain will be elected this fall. I think it will have a great influence in putting down this rebellion. I think that the voters do not look to the interest of their country as much as they ought. They should sacrifice party & personal feelings & use every means in their power to crush this rebellion out. After this is done it will be time for them to form their political parties. When this war is over the parties will be different. There will be no abolitionist party. The main questions will be tariff & national banking system etc, etc. Let the people at home consider what the soldiers undergo for their country. Sacrifice life, home & comfort, toil through heat & cold, mud & sleet, sleep on the cold ground & what is it for? It is for our government & how are we to have a government? by maintaining it of course. It is our duty to support the administration although you know as well as anyone that I done all I could against Lincoln's election & that I done with a clear conscience. But when he was elected it was my duty to support him as our chief magistrate. It is the duty of every good citizen to be governed by those that are elected by the voice of the people & they that are elected have a duty to perform. They are governed by the Constitution & so long as they do not violate that what difference does it make to us who administers it. I am satisfied that if Lincoln had gone by the name of Democrat & had done just what he has done a great many that condemn him would have praised him instead. I suppose that the Copperheads will be down on me but I do not fear them. I have faced my country's foes & I have suffered a great deal for my country & I mean to act conscientiously. I always have & always mean to. I may have been wrong a great many times but it was an error of the head & not of the heart. I am as liable to err as the rest of mankind. I shall have to close. Give my best respects to all inquiring friends. Tell Henry that I was in a great hurry when I wrote to him & he must excuse all mistakes. My love to you all. I will send Billy 20 cents from his pa.

September 22, 1863 - Near Culpepper, Va.
Dear wife & children I received a letter from you night before last the same day that I wrote to Ed. So now I will try & answer it. I was glad to hear that you were all well. So far you have been blessed above a great many other families. I still hope that our lives & health will be spared us to meet again but of that we cannot tell. You said in your letter that H. Champion was dead. It will be a heavy blow for his parents. I suppose they thought a great deal of him but when a person's time comes, friends cannot save him. Death is no respecter of persons. The rich as well as the poor, the high as well as low, all must bow to the stern decree of the Almighty. Death is certain. Well ma I think the prospect for a move is good but I do not like the way they serve us. They are a going to make us carry seven days rations. Now we cannot do it, no way & carry the rest of our things. I think it is mean to use soldiers in this way. We must carry our blankets & tents or we shall suffer with cold for it is very cold nights now & if we throw away our rations (which we shall have to) then we shall have to go hungry. Well it is hard any way you can fix it & I shall be very glad when this war is played out I tell you. It is little comfort that we can take at any rate. Last night they called me up a little after midnight in the cold to draw four days rations which with the three days that we had on hand made seven. I expected that we should have marched at daylight this morning but it is now ten o'clock & we have no orders for marching but we may have any moment. Such is a soldier's life. We cannot call a moment our own but must be ready to start at any time. I sent twenty dollars in that letter that I wrote to Edward & will send you two dollars in this so it will make just forty that I have sent on four months wages. You know that you sent me two so I send this to make that up. I suppose that I ought to send more but you know that it is hard to live on just the rations that we draw, but I suppose that I could. When you see the prices that we have to pay you will not wonder that it takes off money to buy a few luxuries. Cheese 40 cts pr lbs., butter 60 cts, raisins 50cts, fine cut tobacco 12, 3 cent papers, for

one dollar & everything else in proportion. You will see by those figures that a person will soon spend his wages. The first thing he knows he is strapped. I suppose I could get along without any of those things except tobacco, but you see there is two others that tent with me & they furnish nicknacks & I do not wish to be stingy & mean & you know it was always my make to keep my end up with the rest. We buy condensed milk to put in our coffee. That cost 75 cts pr can. One can will last three of us about four days. It makes a great addition to our coffee. Well ma I have given you a pretty good history of my money. I have not spent any for liquor but should as like as any way if we could have got any for a half way decent price. Well ma my health is good & I hope it will remain good to the end of the war. Give my best respects to all inquiring friends. My best love to you all. Yours ever.

September 30, 1863 - Near Culpepper Court House
Dear wife & children I received a letter from you last night & tonight I received one from Hannah. I was very glad to hear from you & her too. It does me good to hear that you are all well & have enough to make you comfortable. It would do me good to come home & see the trees loaded down with apples but I guess it would do me more good to eat some of those good apples that you spoke of. Well if we have good luck & live our time out we may have the privilege of doing so. In your letter you spoke about sending me some apples in the box but you had better not for it may be a long time coming through & they would rot. I did have some hopes of getting home this fall but I guess it will fail. I have not got that position that I spoke of. The detail is made & I supposed that before we moved that there would be an order for us to report there but they have not sent any order yet. I should not wonder if I got cheated out of it yet but I hope not. Well it would be just my luck I presume that I shall have to take things as hard as ever. Well only give me health & strength & I can do as much as any of them. We went on picket yesterday & came back to camp this forenoon. I have had so much to do that I could not get time to write until this evening & I guess that it will bother you to read this for I cannot see the lines on this paper. Well ma I am glad that you have apples plenty so that you can spare to those that have not any. It is more pleasant to give than receive. I presume that Edward has told you that I have had some correspondence with Norman & that was what I based my hopes on for getting home to election, but I guess that the time is so short that he cannot

accomplish what he wished to. My health is good as usual. I feel rather lame & stiff those cold mornings but I am like an old horse, when I get limbered up I can keep agoing all day. You of course get the news in the papers a great while before you can get letters from me. We have had a good many times since we have been here. Orders to march & expected a fight long before this. But I am happy to say we have not any more signs of a fight now than when we first came here. Our attention is directed to the Army of the Cumberland. We do hope & pray that Bragg will be whipped soundly. If his army is broken up I think that Lee's army will leave Va. I hope they will. It is rumored here that we are a going to fall back on the defenses of Washington. It is reported that two or three corps has left this army & reinforce Burnsides & Rosecrans & some more are to leave for Charleston SC. But I do not credit all the stories. I should not wonder if we moved toward Richmond but we cannot tell anything about what we shall do. Well ma it is very dry & the days are warm, the nights are cool. Last night I slept in the open air with only one blanket. The folks up there would think this rather tough but this is nothing for us. We have harder things than those to put up with. Well ma I must close hoping that we shall live through it all & meet again. Give my best respects to all inquiring friends. My love to you all. Yours ever.

Well as I had not much to do today I thought that I would name over a few of those things that I wanted you to send if you had not already sent that box. Well one pair Kipp boots size No 8, 1 pair suspenders, one pair mittens, 4 lbs. fine cut chewing tobacco, the butter & honey you may send just as you think best. I should like a great many things but after all I had rather be at home where I could enjoy such things. Well time wears away considerably. Over half of our time has expired. Let us hope that if I have to stay the rest of it that it will soon pass by. Well I cannot think of anything else to write so I will quit for the time. Good day.

October 1863

October 3, 1863 - Near Culpepper Court House, Va.
Dear wife & children I received a letter from you last night stating that you were all well & that money had come through safe. Well I am glad for I had considerable anxiety about it. I was afraid that it might miscarry. Well that is got along with only I wish the amount had been as large again, but small sums are better than none. I was

glad to hear that you were all well & have plenty to make yourselves comfortable. You have more apples than I expected you would have. If Henry makes them into cider there will be enough for both of you. If you only had those apples here you could make quite a little fortune off them. Apples sell here for five cts. apiece & we do not see many at that. Well enough of this. I am glad that our eight days rations are played out. We only have three days on hand. We have had orders to fix up our camps & make ourselves as comfortable as we can. But this is no sign that we shall stay any length of time for often we have done the same & had to move before we had got half fixed & it may be so this time. I wish now that you had sent that right through & it would have been here by this time but then we did not know. It did look like a fight then & I expected long before this that there would have been a hard battle, but I am glad that we have been left so long in peace. I should be very glad if there should not be any more fighting. If they (that is the South) would submit & lay down their arms & I believe they would if it were not for their friends in the North. I hope they will see their folly & stop where they are. This has been the most cruel war ever known in the world. The most desperate & I hope it will do the greatest amount of good. It certainly has cost the most in the sacrifice of human life. Yesterday & last night it rained like fury & was quite cool. This morning it is clear. The sun shines but I think it will not be fair long. Perhaps it will storm before night. You spoke about them mittens such as I had last winter. They are better than any gloves & I guess are cheaper. Those that I had last winter I lost in the Chancellorsville fight. You know I lost all my clothes there save what I had on my back. Well ma you may send that box any time that you have a mind to. I do not know but it would come as safe at one time as another. I am still with the company. There has been no order for us yet. I have been in hopes that I should get that place but cannot tell how it will go. I wish that I might for it would be so much easier for me. Well there is no other way only to take things as they come. My health remains good yet. Edward wrote that he had rented the Blacksmith shop. I hope you will have luck to get the rent. Every little helps you know. I hope that Henry will work in the wood shop so that it will be of some benefit to you. I do not know what you will do for wood this winter, but I suppose that there will be some way provided. But after all I cannot help but feel uneasy about you but there is one good thing. I do not feel uneasy about

257

you as some do about their wives. There is one fellow in our company by the name of Penny that I have wrote his letter for. For some time he has just got news that his wife has left three small children & run away with another married man who has left a wife & four children. They live in Dimack Township. This makes two or three cases of that kind that has happened in that neighborhood in a short time (their husbands in the army). Well it does seem as though the devil was in them. This Penny's wife wrote first rate letters to him & appeared to be a pious woman. He said that he never doubted her fidelity to him before. He feels very bad. He is a first rate soldier but he cannot read nor write. He tents with me so I do his writing & reading letters for him. Well ma I must close for want of room to write more. Give my respects to all inquiring friends. My love to you all. Yours ever. Good day. Write often.

October 7, 1863 - Near Culpepper Court House, Va.
Dear wife & children having a little leisure time I thought that I would write you a few lines although I have no news to write. We have moved our camp a short distance since I wrote you last. We have a very nice place now for a camp & we have our little tents fixed up as comfortable as the circumstances will admit of. But I think that we shall not remain here long. We have all sorts of rumors that the rebels are in our rear. Well if they are we shall find it out when our supplies are cut off. It is time that they were doing something of that kind for that will wake some of our fellows up. It is about time that we had something exciting but for my part I don't care to have such excitement. I have not had a letter from you in five days & that seems rather a long time to wait but may be that I shall get one tonight. Day before yesterday we took an expression of our Regt. in regard to governor of state. The vote stood thus, Gov. Curtin got all the votes but eight. Seven of that eight said that they would not vote at all & one voted for Woodward & this man deserted & went home & stayed seven months & would never have come back had it not got so hot in his neighborhood that he could not stay without being arrested for desertion. So he came back a few days ago under the late order of Gen. Meade. That is if they will come back of their own accord he will not punish them only with taking off their back pay. Such is the character of the only man in our Regt. that voted for Woodward. This would indicate that if the soldiers in the field

could vote, Gov. Curtin would be elected by one of the largest majorities entirely. So much for politics in camp. It is true that it does not do much good but it will give our friends at home some idea how we would like to have them vote. Well ma I should like to be in old Rush just about this time & see how you are getting along & get recruited up some. To be sure our duties are not very hard just now but it is confinement. After all we have company drill every forenoon & then we have Brigade drill three times a week & the worst of all we have to go out every Sunday on review. This takes all the forenoon with all our traps on. It is very tiresome work & I contend it is all together wrong, contrary to the President's orders. He issued an order some time ago that all unnecessary work on the Sabbath should be dispensed with & I think that such shows are unnecessary & do no good, only annoys the soldier & makes them complain the more. (Well if they think that there is no hereafter let them work. There is a time coming when the smoke of our dung will go as high as theirs.) Well enough of this. My health is midling good. I am still with the company. The Col. tells me that I shall have that chance to go into the ambulance corps when the order comes. I have been in hopes that it would come soon. Well I guess that I have wrote enough for this time so I will close. Give my respects to all inquiring friends. My love to you all. Yours ever.

October 21, 1863 - Near Catlet Station, Va.
Dear wife & children I take this opportunity to let you know that I am still alive but I am not in first rate health. I tired out just one week ago yesterday. Since then I have seen pretty hard times. I was two days behind our Regt. on the retreat on the account of being tired out, but I came up with them at Fairfax Station. Since then I have had a pass to ride in the ambulance & have got along very well. I was sorry that I did not get that place before we had to move. I am afraid that I shall not get the chance of going there for they do not make the detail yet. The Col. says if I do not get that place he will get me some other place where it will be easier for me for I cannot stand it to march with my load. Well ma since I wrote to you last I have run some very narrow chances. We broke up camp at Culpepper on Saturday Oct. 11, marched about 12 miles, stopped for the night. Sunday morning we started for the Rappahannock in the course of the day we were drawn up in a line of battle twice & we saw one of the finest cavalry charges that I ever saw. Ours of course drove the enemy. It was a hard march

259

that day & took us until midnight to get across the river & this we had to wade. I took a hard cold & it settled all over me. That is the reason that I gave out Monday. We lay at this ford guarding it. Tuesday at break of day we commenced our march. The enemy on our flank so that we had to keep skirmishers out all the time. About the middle of the afternoon we came upon them at a place called Auburn. There we had quite a sharp fight with them (before we had got there. I tired out so that I could not carry my gun & equipment so I was not in the fight but the bullets flew thick where I was). Our brigade was ahead. Our loss was light & our men soon put them to flight. That night I got lost from our Corps. There was three or four of us together. The next morning we started, did not suppose there was any danger but the first thing we knew the rebs rose up & fired upon us. They were within 2 or 3 rods of us. But as good luck would have it they did not hit us. Penny was with me. He lay down but I tell you I ran like a deer. They all the time firing at me. The 2nd army corps were close to us & they charged upon the rebs & captured 30 or 40 or them before they could get away. Penny came out safe & is with me yet. Well we kept with the 2nd corps that day until we came up to Bristo Station when the rebs pitched on them again in heavy force. I tell you the bullets flew thick for a while. We got out of that safe & started for our wagon train that we could see in the distance. We got in with them & kept along until midnight, then lay down by the side of the road & slept until morning. We then kept on our march with the train until just at night we came up with our corps, found our boys all glad to see us. They expected we had gone to Richmond. Well ma I feel thankful that it is not any worse with me than it is. This was Thursday night. Friday we had to witness the execution of a deserter. He sat on his coffin. 12 men were drawn up in line & all shot at a time. He fell into his coffin pierced with 11 balls. He never stirred after the fire. This was a hard sight. I received a letter from Ed the night of the 12 & I got one from you dated 15 & one dated 12, those I got the $19^{th.}$ I had begun to think you had forgotten me. Before we left Culpepper I had not had a letter from you for ten days. I hope you will not neglect me so long again. I did hope that I should have got home to election but was disappointed. But I see the election has gone right. Well ma I must close & will write to you soon again. This is the first chance that I have had to write since I left Culpepper so you must excuse this poor letter. Give my best respects to all inquiring friends. My love to you all. Yours ever.

PS. I was quite surprised to see that letter that I wrote Norman in the paper but I guess that it did not do any hurt, if it did not do any good. I had rather you would not publish my letters for I do not have a chance to take any pains with them.

1864

The Civil War drags on. Luther is gone. John's hope of ever going home alive is all but gone. John is now part of the invalid corps, as age, illness, injury and battle wounds have all caught up with him. He is a Sergeant, and can't believe that his existence has been reduced to a miserable military existence. Yet he still has hope. Hope that the South will collapse. Hope that the war will end. Hope that one day he will return to be with his wife and children.

1864

February 1864

February,1864 - Depot Camp Cliffburne Barracks, DC.

Dear wife & children having a little leisure I thought that a few lines from me would interest you. Well ma I have no news to write except the weather is fine like spring. My health is good & I enjoy myself very well. The duties that the privates have to do is hard. Every man that is not excused by the doctor has to go on guard every other day. I think it is outrageous but I cannot help them. My duty is not as hard now. I am getting the hang of it better & like it better than I did. I guess that I was a little homesick & since I made a good visit feel better. You may tell Edward to send me the county paper for I may stay here all winter & may stay my time out & then we may move in a short time. We cannot tell what a day may bring forth. There is quite a lot in my company getting their discharges & for my part I hope all the lame & lazy will get away from here. They are a great trouble to me, if I only had a company of able-bodied men I would not care for all the duties they could heap upon us. Well enough of this. Well ma how glad I shall be if I live my time out & once more get home there to stay. I am sick of this military & hope that we shall all of us soon see the end of it. The more we hear from the South the more we are convinced that they cannot hold out much longer. Well God speed the time that we shall see peace restored to our Country. The sufferings that the Southern people have to endure is terrible, but let them remember they have brought it on themselves. There is nobody to blame in their case, but it is strange that people living in the North enjoying the comforts of life & the blessings of peace should be so shortsighted as to counsel their fellow beings to resist the laws & constituted authority. Well dear me there is some fools left yet, but more knows than fools. Well ma I must close. Give my respects to all inquiring friends. My love to you all. Yours ever.

February 12,1864 - Depot Camp Cliffburne Barracks, Va.

Dear wife & children I received a letter from you on the 10th dated 8th. I was glad to hear that you were well but sorry that you feel so down hearted. I hope I shall live to get out of this miserable concern. I have been trying some time to get an examination before the doctor. Well this morning I went before the board and they thought they could not discharge me so my hopes are gone on that point. I think it is mean for I know they have discharged a good many in my company that is not half as bad off as I am but that is just my luck. Well yesterday there was thirteen in my company got their discharge and in a few days more there will be some ten or twelve more. Well I am glad to see them get away. I only wish that I might be as lucky. Well enough of this. If they fill this company up and get some scripts here then kiss my arse for all the duty they got out of me. I have done my share. (Well I have just been called to the Capt. Office & there found the Board had ordered my discharge. hip hip hurrah.) So keep dark. If nothing happens I shall be at home in three weeks on less. Don't say anything about it nor let anyone know one word. I want to take them by surprise. I had felt downhearted all the forenoon and discouraged and when I commenced this letter I did not think I should hear such good news. I am almost afraid to believe it myself for fear there will be some slip about it. I suppose it will take all of this month for my papers to get around. Well I shall wait very patiently for them. I guess you may answer this letter and I will write again & let you know how I get along. Well ma I hope my papers will go through quick so I will not write any more now. Give my respects to all inquiring friends. My love to you all. Good day. Yours ever.

N.S. I have not received that letter from Henry that you spoke of & I am very sorry to hear such news from the River. Well they need not get in a family way because I think myself just as good as they. I little thought they would treat any of us cooly. Oh what I mean when I said you might answer this letter was this that I guess I shall have time to get an answer from this before my discharge comes for you know that just as soon as I can get out of this I shall start for home.

The end.

The Diary of Luther A. Granger

Source of these letters:
Army War College, Carlisle, Pennsylvania
Civil War Miscellaneous collection
Luther Granger, Ca. A, 57th Penna. Inf.
Letters 1861 - 1863

As I was conducting research at Bowdoin College in New Brunswick, Maine, I discovered (with the capable help of the Bowdoin librarian) that the Army War College located in Carlisle, Pennsylvania had a collection of letters that were written by Luther A. Granger. These letters afforded me the opportunity to find out what John's brother was thinking and writing right alongside of John. Here is Luther's story.

January 1862

January 21, 1862 Headquarters Washington, Camp Mercer, Co A 57 Regt.

Dear Father & Mother. This morning seeing that John has been writing a few lines to you I will do the same. For I might as well write as to be setting around. It has rained for the last four or five days as for the mud being deep John has told you in his letter it makes it very disagreeable getting around. So much so that we hardly drill at all. Yesterday we drilled a very little and shot at targets. Some three or four times we shot a piece. We made very good shots. Although they are some very awkward persons in the company. Although there is some very good marksman in the company. The talk is that we shall have to go over the Potomac this week but I hope not till the weather is better than it is now for the mud is deep that we should mire. But when we are called upon we must go for there is no use of complaining or grumbling for we are sworn to obey our officers and they are sworn to obey their superiors and they have to move when they are commanded. Let the case go as it may whether the mud is knee deep or not, but what is the use of talking about for if we come to serve our country we must expect to endure hardship if we would be good soldiers. For my part I expect to suffer as long as I remain in service of my country but still I do not want to suffer unnecessarily for we have to endure enough for any person should endure. At the best this travelling in mud almost up to our waist is more than weak nature can endure and sleeping on the cold ground at night. But still nature will get harder to it in a measure so we can endure more than we really think we could in the first place. I know for one that I never thought I could endure hardships as I have done while here and I presume that we could endure more than we have done since we have been in the service. I guess I will say no more about this matter and will close my preamble for I guess that you will think it is as much as you will wish to read. I hope that the next time I write I shall be able to write some news but now there is no great news to write but what you have heard relative to the war. I hope the matter will close for I think I could get of this scrape with a good stomach for I have no desire to stay here on government expenses for I think that the farmers will have enough taxes to pay if this war should close. I hope you will not be forgetful of us down here but will write as often as you can and mother I would say to her that I have not received that letter that she was a going to write. I hope she will not forget it but will write without fail. I will try to write a longer letter than this next time and I hope a more sensibler one for I am ashamed of it but there is so much noise and confusion that a person cannot think. So I will say good by for this time. Excuse all mistakes and poor writing. This from your son L A Granger

To: Juliett Granger & Mr. Dennis Granger, Rush PA

February 1862

February 14, 1862 - Headquarters, Washington DC
Camp Mercer 57th Reg PV

Dear Wife. I feel in duty bound to find a little fault this morning and for why is because you are so negligent in writing. For over one week has elapsed since I have received any letter from you. I well know how it is with a person when he is surrounded with friends they become forgetful of friends that are far away. Perhaps I might be so to I cannot say. Anyhow I will not find as much fault as I might for I might be the same if I was at home and you were away. Anyhow I will think so and not blame you. I will write less and perhaps it will be as well. Anyhow I will try to content myself that way. I got my likeness taken the other and shall send it by Philo when he goes home. He has not started yet and I do not know how soon he may. His boy is before the board to be examined to see whether he cannot get his discharge. If he does he will start for home on the morrow. I hope he will get his discharge for he is not able to endure the hardship of a soldier. His health is very poor since he had the measles. So much so that he cannot drill. Philo is getting impatient to get home. I do not blame him for this staying around here is enough to kill a person that is not used to it. For my part I have got harden to it so I can stand most anything even to thunder for the cannon roar is full as hard if not harder. I care not soon I am called into the battlefield. This staying here and doing no good to ourself or our fellow man is poor poop. I came here to fight and that I wish to do and if it is my lot to die on the battlefield so well so good. I shall not falter at that for some must die on the battlefield and it is no better for me than many others. So of our company say that they wish that they could get in some secluded spot where there is no danger. Not so with me although I cant say that I hanker to have a fight I would rather this rebellion would cease and that we might return to our home and friends but as they are bound to fight it out I want to have a hand in the muss. For I do not wish to stand neutral by any means. I guess I will say no more about it but try to bring this letter to a close for I guess it is useless for me to write so long a letter as there is nothing very essential transpired since I last wrote for I write on every two or three days but now I have stopped writing so much for I think it useless to worry your patience with so much writing as I have written. I guess I will wait two weeks before I write again unless something more than usual has prevented you from writing perhaps sickness has been the cause of your delay for writing. If such is the case you are excusable if not you are not excusable. I will send you a couple breastpins. You may give them to Lucy and Emma if you are a mind so to do or you may keep them just as you are a mind. I guess I will not ask you to write soon for I know you will but will say write when you get ready. Excuse all mistakes. This from your husband and friend. Luther A. Granger.

March 1862

Sare Brush Near Yorktown

Dear Wife. I once more embrace this opportunity of writing a few lines to you by the way of letter. Although I do not know how long I shall have to write for we are called about every two or three hours. Some of the time we are called up two or three times in a night. This is what a person calls soldering no baby playing. Night before last we were called up at half past nine and marched about one mile and a half and drawn up in a line of battle. One half of us were permitted to lay down while the rest of us kept awake. And so we kept doing till day light then we were relieved and went to camp but we had no more than got into our camp before we were ordered out again. But our stay was of short duration. The skirmish was mostly all over when we got out it was between a majors Reg and the reels. They took twenty rebels prisoners besides killing quite a number of them and heavy pieces of artillery and quite a number of other things with the loss of but four men killed and some few slightly wounded. That was our loss of men. It seems that we are very fortunate in every movement and I hope they may till this war shall close. We have every reason to thank God for our success. As for our Reg we have had but one killed and four wounded that has been lucky for us. That one that was killed was killed by the bursting a shell from the enemies gun. How long we can say that is more than I can say but I hope that we may ever be as fortunate as we have been. But as for that we cannot expect for & would be an utter impossibility for so many men as have in our Reg to escape without some getting killed if we have a great fight. Although we do not expect to have a great deal of fighting to do from the simple reason that our artillery will do the bombarding while we will support them in the rifle pits secure from shot and shell. The general says that he will bombard six weeks before he will lose one hundred men. The men place the utmost confidence in General McClellan. He is most every day along the lines to view the works. He says that he intends to throw 1000 shells in a minute that is saying a great deal. But when a person sees the batteries that he has placed in different places we have no reason to doubt his word in the least. I expect that the day the performance opens there will be a great noise for of course the enemy will respond for a while. But I hope it will be of short duration for I hate to hear the thunder of the cannon. It is hard enough to hear what we are said to under the present circumstances for there is not a day but we hear a hundred and that has been the case for about three weeks. There has been thundering every day and are looking forward to the day when either the north or south shall be the master. I hope the day is not far distant when we shall see the stars and strips are floating over the whole south and the citizens return to their peaceable homes and enjoy the friends of home for I am getting tired of this. Living away from home and friends is not what is cracked up to for I find hard and at this present time to sleep out of doors in rain storms as well as sunshine. There is no getting rid of duty unless you play up sick and that I am bound not to do as long as I can move around for this playing up sick when a person is well is very wrong. I would not dare to try to play up sick unless I was sick for I fear that I should be in earnest. So I would be sorry in the end. My health never was better than it has been through the winter and spring regardless of the weather we have been exposed to since we enlisted many has been the time that we have come to our tents wet to the skin without any way of drying and layed down with wet clothes on to sleep and slept till morning very sound. When they come a fair day we are able to dry them that is our luck but it will soon be warmer weather so we can enjoy our selves better if it should rain. I guess I will write no more about for the present trying to think of something of more importance for there is nothing very nice only that I am in good health ready to take rations as they are dealt out for me from time to time. I will say no more at the present time for I fear that you cannot read it. Give my love to all my friends and keep a good share yourself. Write as soon as you can and often as you can and I will do the same. Excuse all mistakes and poor writing for I am in a hurry. Good by for this time. This from your Husband friend. Luther A. Granger

To Sabra and Clara Granger. Direct your letter as you have done.

May 1862

May 16 1862 - Camp Sickles Near Potomac Creek

Dear Wife. This makes the fourth letter I have written since I came over the river. But enough of this for I must write and not brag for I have been negligent enough about writing before to make it all up for my writing so often at the present. Inver will cut the caper again that I did this time or when we march before for some eight days before we marched that I did not write because I did not receive any letter from you. I had been writing two letters a week before that. I find Sunday morn has come and I have not finished my letter yet. I guess I will try and finish it. I am cooking some fresh beef for the boys so I take my writing utensils with so I can finish this letter. The weather is very warm here at the present so much so that it would be uncomfortable to cook in the tent therefore I have gone to the spring to do my work. I would like to be at home to spend the Sabbath but such is not the case to day so I must content myself for the present but I hope that I may soon spend more than one Sabbath at home for I think I have staid away long enough for once. I saw Philander the other day he is wounded in the arm but I guess not very serious so but that he soon will get along. Wes I guess run right into the rebels lines and was taken prisoner for I have not heard from him. Most of the rest have turned up. Some were wounded if he had been wounded we should found it out for all our wounded are inside of our lines well provided for. I guess he is a prisoner and gone to Richmond. I do not worry about for the last I see him he was making tracks to the rear. He thought but it was toward the Rebel lines for we were surrounded by the rebs on every side. Come very near being captured by them our whole brigade. We got out by the skin of our teeth. But enough I guess I have written most enough for once for my cooking bothers me and I have to just see to it. I will try and write a long one next time if there is any more cooking to be done some must do it besides me. I am well as I can wish excepting the piles. They trouble me a very little. I have not reported myself for duty yet but think I shall on the morrow. Give my love to all my friends and keep as much as you please yourself. This from your husband and best friend. L.A. Granger.

PB. I sent forty eight dollars by express the other day and I hope you have got it before this.

May 29 1862 - Two miles the other side of Bottom Bridge

Dear Wife. Knowing as at least have a relation of your anxiety I have tried although feebly for I am feeble owing to my sickness since one week ago last Sunday evening. I must confess that I have seen the hardest time in my life. I was sent up to a place called the White House Hospital but Care of the doctor I could not get owing to clothing going another way. I had to go about they said about two and a half miles where they would be. It was eight o'clock in the morning and it was sundown when I got through but when I got through I found no conveniences there but there I rested for the night and in the morning thank God I felt like another man. Although very weak the exertion of the day had broken the fever. I took a good cup of tea and hearing that our Regt was but two miles in advance I thought I would try to go where it was but before I had went one mile and a half before it rained. I got into a house and staid all night very comfortable. The next morning I started for the Regt hoping to over take it but I got greatly disappointed for they having left a few minutes before I got there. I tried to follow but did not get far before I had to rest for the night. Then next morning I felt so poorly that I did not try to move but having a chance to send a word to my company where I was the Captain sent a man to take care of me but he was a poor stick. There were other boys there and he had rather play cards than wait on me but still I should not find fault only should say I lived through and that was lucky for me. After two or three days I thought I would go to the Regt hearing that they were but two miles in advance. I started with a good resolution but my heart almost failed before I arrived to their encampment. When I got there I found they had gone on one mile and a half farther but found the sick and the Doctor there so I shall not leave here unless I can get better quarters in some other place. I found Fred sick the whole length and a greater baby I never saw. He was a going to do and that as sure. I could but laugh to hear him groan and so did all the sick for they thought it was a game he has got of playing sick when he gets in front of the enemies works. It is not the first time he has done the same trick and if our troops are successful in taking Richmond he will be well enough right although he took on so the doctor sent him back a few miles to a kind of hospital and I am very thankful to think that was the case he dreadfully wanted. I should go along with him he said perhaps we would get sent to the Philadelphia hospital and then we would play sharp and get home but the poor boy will get greatly for the doctor told what hospital he sent him. I have seen it. It is a forsaken place and everyone must wait on their own person. No one to wait on the sick for there is none sent there but what they think are able to take care of themselves. He cannot call on this and that to wait on him but it will be wait on yourself. He with think that corps does

May the 30 1862 (picking up from the May 29 letter)
not eat. I guess I have said enough about Fred. Perhaps he is sicker than I think for buy still my charity is small for him but not so with Henry Hinds for he has ever been on til now he is sick and I fear very sick indeed. I am afraid he will not recover right away if ever. He received the sympathies of the company while Fred the reproaches. That is quite a contrast but enough of the boys is enough so I will say no more about them.

When I was at Cumberlanding before I was taken sick I wrote you a long letter stating that I had sent you twenty five dollars by Addams Express and I was sorry that I did not send thirty but I am glad that I stuck to as much as I did since I have been sick I could not eat any of the rations that we draw so I purchase all that I eat and that is no great I will assure you. But everything here cost money. Butter is fifty cent a pound and eggs are forty cents a dozen and other things according. So you see it would cost a well man something if he had to buy his rations. I guess I will close my penciling for I have been two days a drying to do what I have done. I heard from John yesterday. He is keen. He gets his rations of liquor and had has drawd it ever since they left Cumberlanding. Wilson Terry has come up with the Regt so they say but I have not seen him as yet. I hope that the next time I write I shall be free of the ague and I am sure I can write a more interesting letter. My resolution never was as good as at the present time nor have I had such faith to believe this thing will be wiped out in a short time that is this rebellion. Write as soon as you get this direct your letters as before only if you are a mind you may put it on Kearney Division instead of Hamilton's for we got a new General at York Town. Our old one was put under arrest and what they done with him I know not, nor is it any of my affair. I thought I would not tell you of the change but still I thought you would find out fast enough. I will close by saying good by write often and don't worry about me for I think I stand anything now. This from your husband and best wisher. To Sabra & the rest of our family.

June 1862

June 8 1862 - Seven Miles from Richmond
Letter Describing the Peninsular Battle
Dear Wife. Knowing that you would worry about me knowing of my sickness but my health is as good as bran new. Although I do not feel quite as strong as I did before I was taken sick my mind is so much stronger than it was when I wrote before that I do not feel like the same person. I know that I did write foolish for my mind was very weak and I think at the best very foolish and laboring under the fever and as the doctor said I broke it by my exertion not by medicine for I had none. My officers gave me great praise for my resolution. I had the best of resolution. I was bound to get well for I never once thought of giving up and I thank God that he gave me such a resolution. I found him good in time of need. I could say with the psalmist he was my refuge and I hope I shall not be forgetful of his mercies in time of health. I wish to live unto him daily as I live upon him. God has said that he is ever ready to remember those that look unto him. John's health is poor. He has the rheumatism some so he cannot move with the Regt as soldiers do in ranks. I hope he will not be so long for I should hate to move and leave him behind. But such is the fate of war. But when I was left behind I was suffering from the fever I well know that he felt bad to leave me. He could follow up the Regt in the rear but he would have to move very slow. He feels quite well at that so much so he can eat his ration as well as myself and I do believe that if it was not laying on the ground he would be as smart as ever in a short time but the ground is bad for the rheumatic pains and a sort

of the age with it. It makes him move very slow. But as for me I feel limber as an eel. Perhaps you may think I am more spiritly than when at home. I know for one thing that I am a great deal heartier than when I was at home for I know that I can stand more than I could when I first left home. If you should doubt it you would not if you should see the fare we have. You would not doubt my story but enough of this. The truth of the army sufferings will never be known by mankind and I hope that it may never be known. Why our army fights at all is more that I can account for. From the simple reason that pride causes us to stand to the rack hay or no hay. God being for us perhaps is the cause and another think is that rebellion is about played out for McClellan thinks that this is the last struggle we shall have with the foe. McClellan praises our Division greatly for what they done on that day Sunday morning. What of the Division was not in the fight Saturday afternoon was in on the morning and they did suffer half as our brigade did on Saturday for they had to fall back on account of vastly superior number. But they did not fall back until they had strewed the ground with the dead and wounded. Our boys did not suffer much till they had to fall back from their covering. Then the enemy had a good chance to pepper them with balls and it was the greatest wonder that they did not all get killed. But still they killed and wounded full more than one third that was in the engagement that I know myself. If they say what they may in the paper the killed and wounded in our company was 14. Our company was cut up more than any company and it was very small. On the day of the fight not numbering more than forty. I guess I will say no more about our company. Our colonel was wounded twice very dangerous. Our major was killed right down and adjunct of the Regt is very sick and our Preacher is sick also. We have a lieutenant colonel is yet with us that is all the line officers that are left. Some of the captains got wounded but one lieutenant. I guess I will not say much more for I guess that I shall weary your patience by writing so long. I would give you the description of the scene but papers may give you a description of the battle in killed and wounded. I will some day give you something of a true detail of the killed and wounded for I believe I know milling well for I have learnt from experience and from officers so I can tell very near the just amount. But the rebels boys we more than two thousand more than ours. God alone knows home may were left unburied. They say that there was one field covered so thick that a person could walk over the field by stepping on their bodies. I could walk over there if had wished but I have seen sights enough. The artillery right close to where we are in camped in the road they layed five to six deep cut down by grape from our cannon. Our men done great work Sunday morning. I will not try to say anything more about that for it makes me feel sick to think of it. Write as often as you can and I will try and do the same. You have a good chance to write and if you don not receive a letter from me you must write often. If you did not receive one from me for I am moving all around from time to time. Give my love to all my friends if any such should be and keep a good share yourself. This from your husband and best friend. L.A. Granger.

July 1862

July 13th 1862 – Camp near Harrisons landing
Dear Wife. Fearing owing to the excitement that was prevalent at the time I wrote before that my letter did not go through I have taken this afternoon hoping that if that letter did not get through this one would for I expect from a natural consequence you would worry about me owing to the great fight we had on our retreat. I told you in the other that on Monday I was not in the fight but was on Friday before. If I had not been detailed on other business I should have been in. For it was not through fear that kept me out nor is they any of the Regt thank God that thinks so either for I never yet have showed the white feather as yet and I hope I may not although there are others that if I am any judge played off. I will not mention their names for there is no use. Wilson I guess got onto the sick boat and got off that way. He had better go and see Miss Low. If you want to know any particulars just inquire of Cornelia she can tell you enough to satisfy anyones mind. I thought I would not say a word about it but they keep up correspondence all the time so I think folks ought to know it. He is not the person I took him to be and should it be generally known in Rush what I know he would not be thought the world of in that place. But I shall not say no more. It will leak out in time for there is nothing mean but what will come in time and I should rather it would come out by some other one than me. Or at least I will wait a while before I expose it to the public. But still I think I should do him and her both justice if I did it. But I hesitate for his friends

275

sake not for his or her feelings for I think them both worse than the brutes and I believe that god will yet visit them both in judgment for their misdemeanor and I care not how soon for I think such conduct should not go unpunished. But enough of this. John is detailed for a quartermaster of the company so that excuses him from all duty that is hard or fighting if he could get his discharge I should be glad for I think this business is too hard for him as well as myself. But I think if now I am careful of my health I shall get along well enough but John is not agoin to be fit for hard labor nor will he have to do any hard work as long as he holds the office he now holds. But that does not seem to answer the contract for he would like to get off nor do I blame him for it is a hard place for so old a person as he is and health so poor as his is. But regardless of his poor health he stands in far better than I should think he could under the present circumstances. We are nicely situated now about three miles from the river and things look quite good here. So much so that we can rest day and night without being molested. That seems nice for the last six weeks we have been molested both day and night. We have just come in from off picket. No enemy was seen in that section and I hope we shall not be troubled with them any more til we get rested for I have soldiered it so long that I am getting wore out and ant rest and rest we must have or we shall go under the sod. What rest we have had has given us new life and vigor and if we can have time the most of us will recruit up. But enough of this. Fred Hines is at home and if it is so you can I wish you would send me two light shirts for here we have to wear wollen. Colored if you could get them and one or two pair of light pants for woolen feels most to heavy and I expect he will be coming back one of these days. How soon I know not. You can get some old or new satchel and send them in it perhaps you could send them by Dallas. You may get two dozen of eggs and boil them slack done and bake me up some cake and do them up for I am in want of them very much. I wrote to Norman to send me some pain killers. If he should send them I would be glad for I think I stand in need of some such medicines. If I do not have some to take the water is so poor that I shall get the fever for the fever rages to quite extent especially the ague. There is a great many causes of the last mentioned diseases. Should you think of it send some dried beef along for that would taste good in this dry country. Write as soon as you receive this without delay and send long that dollar if you have not sent it before. We are to draw two months or should have said 4 months pay the next time they owe me over four months and a half pay due me now from the government. I have received one dollar from you. Write soon. Good by. This from your husband and best friend. To Sabra and Clara Granger.

October 1862

Conrad Ferry, October 5, 1862

Dear Wife. It seams like a great privilege to be blest with the means to write with although the convenience are not as good as might be but still as for the conveniences we can get along with if we only have the material to do with and a little time is sufficient for a soldier. There is no great news to write if there is we do not get hold of them in this region of country. We hear nothing that is going on seldom get the paper and when we do we get no news. Things are kept very secret for some cause. I hope for the best for I think one spill that the news of the movement of the Army was to generally known by both the rebels and our men but now news are suspended by some one order perhaps Halleck. I cannot tell it seams that the old gentleman is Secretary of War while George B. has command of the united forces. All I have to say is bully for that although I have felt like cursing him in days that are gone but that day is passed and I feel as though he was the man to lead us on to victory or death. I trust to victory for I do believe that ours yet shall prove successful. Although we have had a dark place in history for a short time I hope yet it may lighten up and we soon see a bright time in life. I would to God this day that the North & South could settle there difficulties on satisfactory terms to both parties but I fear that quite a spell will elapse before this thing will satisfactorily be settled. But perhaps the thing will be settled before we know it. But still I do not worry fearing that it will be closed nor do I fear or worry much either way. Trust in God for the result hoping for the best. If I am blest with health and strength I shall be thankful and feel to praise him for his goodness. I find there is nothing like good health for it has been so long since I have had good health til the present. I think if cold weather comes on my health will greatly improve. Cool air seams to agree with me first rate. The winters are not so cold here but a person can well stand the weather without grumbling but the warmest weather comes hard on me. Perhaps I am notional if such is the case so let it be. I feel so now. John health is very good but he is homesick some or al least would like to se home first rate and who would not. He must have a heart of stone if home would not come acceptable at the present time after being so long in the service as I have been and many others. If I could but come home and stay for two or three weeks I should feel satisfied to come back and stay with the army for quite a spell. The captain says that we shall have the privilege of going home this fall or winter. All married men shall certainly have the privilege of going home. Let the case go as it may for my part I am bound to go home some way if not by fair means I will by foul. But I guess I shall get home without any doubt. I suppose John will try to get home first and undoubtedly will unless we both come home together for he is the oldest man and the oldest one will get home first. As far as that is concerned I will not complain for I am next to the oldest one in the company. We had older men than either but they have got their discharge or are away at the hospital sick. I guess there is but one older man than myself or John and that man has been under the doctors care all summer and now he is away at the hospital. I think it is doubtful of his return to the Regt. I think he is rather playing out at the best but still I have no right to judge therefore I will say no more about it. He knows and that is enough.

As for Steve I have not seen him since we left Arlington Heights but are in hopes we will soon get orders to move back or else that the rest of the Division will come up with us for I would dreadfully love to see him and all the rest of the boys from Susq & Bradford for they seamed to be a good lot of boys or at least the most of them did. I would like to know where Orlo was for I would write him a line if he never answered it. I believe I wrote last and I have written to all my friends last. Father & Mother White I have wrote some three or four letter to them since I have received any from them. Father & Mother Granger I could not tell but a number they can tell and still if I had time I would not hesitate in writing to them again. It is not because I have in the least forgotten them that I do not write but knowing that you live there they hear from me often from that source therefore that keeps me from writing to them. I must write to the friends at the river for it has been a long time since I have written. I received a letter the day we left Arlington Heights and I have not answered it yet. Shame for me for being so negligent but still I shall try to form some kind of an excuse for you know that I will try to form some kind of an apology for lazyness will get some shield to cover her slothfulness. I think the most of the time I have had a good excuse. John has been blessed with paper but kept it from me or at least I did not know til now he has been lucky for him for he used my postage stamps for he has had none of his own for over one month but those he used of mine and he has been very free with that that did not belong to him when we received our pay he sent all his money home that the left for he owed some twelve dollars in the company and he sent home forty dollars. So all the money that was kept was my money and he had a pocket book so he kept and spent it very freely til I found that he had but three dollars left and nothing to show but a watch a little child would not been more selfish than he was and now if I get tobacco or anything I have to divide for he has no money to get any with nor have I now but I am bound to try to get along someway til I get some from home. Send me two more shirts if you can and tell me what they cost and write often. This from your husband and best friend. L. A. Granger to Sabra & Clara Granger.

December 1862

December. 17 1862 - Near Falmouth VA
Battle of Fredericksburg, VA
Dear Wife. Through the mercies of God I am spared to write to you again although I must confess that the thing of writing has looked rather scaly since I wrote before. I thought it very doubtful case of my hardly living to tell the tale but they say some are spared and so was in our case. But few comparative to the number that was engaged in the fight. John & myself came off without a scratch but still enough others were hurt to make it all up. Why we were spared God above knows. I hope for some good end. Wm. B. Hinds was mortally wounded. Henry Hinds came out safe with a scratch. No one else from our company was hurt that you are acquainted with. There was but thirty-five or six was all that was engaged in the fight from our company. Two was killed dead, four wounded. We know of six missing either killed wounded or prisoners. We hope they are not hurt but will yet turn up as some of our men have since the fight safe and sound. Last Saturday the fight was and Monday evening we returned back across the river. I guess that the generals thought the place was to hot for them or at least I thought so for my part and I hope that I may never see so

hot a place again. I received a letter from you Monday on the battlefield the enemy drawed up in line of battle not more than forty rods just in good shooting distance. I read it in a hurry tore it in pieces thinking that if I was shot no rebel should get the letter. I must confess that I could not tell now much you wrote for my mind was on anything else but letters. I believe there was nothing very secret if they were I have forgot. You stated in your letter that you did not know whether I had received those likenesses. I have certainly wrote about it in three letters before this. I know of a certainty that you do not receive over half the letters I write for I have averaged two letters most of the time a week ever since I have been in this place and when we were on the march I wrote one once a week all but one time and that time you remember when that was and I wrote not having the time over ten days betwixt times but enough of this for I must for this time but will write again this week if live is spared. I am yet fat as a bear eat like hog and can have my whiskey twice a day if I wished but do not drink much. I have drinken one drink that is all as yet. I will send this letter inside of Johns for I do not think it long enough to pay the postage on it. John has wrote midling short letter. Also next time I write I will give you a full detail of things in reality. This from your husband and friend.

N.B. I guess you may send that box of things if you will. I have received two dollars from you since I came hear no more.

Near Falmouth VA December 19,1862
Dear wife. As I told you in my other that I would write you a letter of some length I though I would commence this morning. Although there has nothing of much importance happened since I last wrote but as the other was nothing but a substitute I will fulfil my promise by writing long enough letter this time. Although I may take two days to accomplish it because to day is washing day and last week we were a marching and fighting so I had no time to wash and I have plenty dirty cloths to wash. I wish you were here to help. I guess we would get through sooner but enough of this. I told you in my other letter that I would give you as near a correct account of the battle of Fredericksburg as I could and I will do so although I may differ from the paper correspondent whether I do or not I believe I saw as much of the scene as any one paper correspondent or not. So I will commence my tale. Last week Tuesday evening we received orders to be ready to march with one

hours notice after Wednesday six o'clock. So we held ourselves in readiness for the march but did not start till Thursday morning eight o'clock. That was the commencement of the bombardment of that noted place Fredericksburg. Most of the day was occupied in artillery firing long just at night our troops crossed the river or at least a portion of them. Our division did not cross that night but stayed this side. The next afternoon we received orders to cross the river three miles below but did accomplish it until the next day at noon. Then we were pushed forward to the front where the enemy were in force. The Pennsylvania reserves were drawn up in line of battle. They went into the engagement first. How long they were in is not more than I can say but not long. I assure you our brigade was ordered in double quick to check the enemy before they farther advanced the rest of our division being back in the rear or at least they had not arrived on the spot in time to go in with us. The enemy seeing the weakness of that point concentrate their forces on that point. The scene became terrific. Our brigade determined not to yield but we were overpowered by numbers. We had to fall back a short distance and just at that critical moment one brigade from our division happened to arrive to our assistance. Then we made the rebel fall back to the woods. We held the field the rest part of the day. That night our reg. (what was left) was put out in front to watch the progress of the enemy and were relieved in the morning before light and went back to the rear of the division for guard to prevent any from falling back. We remained there all that day it being Sunday. Monday morning we were again ordered to the front, not a very desirable place I assure you. It looked as the old saying is rather bilious to see the enemy drawed up in the line of battle about forty rods off. It was anything but a pleasant sight to lay on your arms expecting every moment that the battle would open but fortunate for us they did not commence the fray. About three o'clock a flag of truce went in for the purpose of removing the dead and wounded inside of our lines and the rebels inside of theirs. It was the greatest sight I ever saw, two hostile armies meet shake hands in the most friendly terms and then at their work they went they carrying our dead and wounded to a certain fence that being the division line and we carrying theirs. As there was but one hour given for the removal it had to be accomplished under a run. It was the greatest sight I ever saw when the hour was up. Each one had to return to his own lines whether their work was done or not. I guess ours were mostly removed but not so with the rebels. They had many left yet but that night we fell back over the river so they had a chance the next morning to get their men. Why we fell back is best known to the one who ordered us over the river. I have my opinion but will not express it because I cannot turn one hair white or black. Therefore I will keep my mouth shut thinking that a silent tongue makes no enemies if not any friends. But enough of this for the present which will be the next move I know not nor do I much care for. I am contented with my lot let come what will or at least I try to be and am willing to endure most any hardships to crush this rebellion. Could peace be once more restored this once happy republic. I think for once I could enjoy peace and freedom once more if it could be obtained and I hope that may soon be the case. We are now in our old camp trying to enjoy our lives if we had a few luxuries from home. I think we could make camp life sweet. I guess you will think I am an old beggar. I must confess that I have a great liking for luxuries home or abroad it makes but little difference where it comes from. I could eat it if it came from you. I guess I will say no more about for I have begged enough and I do not fear but what the friends from old Rush will send us something if they have a chance. I want to come home this winter if there is half a site for me but cannot tell you now how that will be till we get settled down. Some say we are going back to Washington this winter. I hope we may if we do I will be pretty sure to come home.

I have seen Steve since the fight. He came out all safe. Their Regt was not in the fight. They came out safe and sound. His health is good so is Johns & mine. I have no reason to complain but to thank God for his goodness and guess I will close for I think I have kept my promise good on length if not very sensible excuse all mistakes and write soon. This from your husband and friend. Luther Granger.

(Portion of a letter not dated) You said in your letter that you freely forgive me for all the wrongs that I have committed to you and you asked me to forgive you. All that I can say is this. All that is past I do forgive and may you long and happy live and peace and plenty be your lot. I do not want you to suffer because I do but perhaps I do not have as much ask ought to for I have done a great many wrongs and all the way that a person can atone for the past by living well in the future that is all the atonement we can make. I guess I will say no more about that for we both have done wrong and need much reformation. All that I care for now is your touch for I suffer more for that than anything else that I can think of now. So much so that I cannot hardly sleep nights. If you could see me now you would hardly know me for my face is all covered with hair. You must pay mother that two dollars that I borrowed of her and the interest and the rest of it you may keep till you receive another letter from me for I may want some of and if I do I will let you know next time. As for Cornelia you need not worry for when John pays me then I can talk about paying that but John says that he is willing to turn it to me. Write as soon as you receive this.

April 1863

April 1, 1863 - Camp Bell Near Potomac
Dear Wife. It is with joy I seat myself for the purpose of writing a few lines to one that is not forgotten although many months has elapsed since I last say you. I hope that so long a time will elapse again before I am permitted to see my friends in old Rush. I thought one spell that I should have to be sent to the hospital but I feel somewhat better to day. I am in hopes to get along without any trouble. I was in hopes one spell that I might get sent back to the hospital but I got to thinking it all over. I think the best thing I can do is to stay with the Regt as long as I can and when I can stand it no long try and get my discharge for here in the world no one can tell what he will meet with. My officers are first rate kind & obliging. Seem to do everything they can for my comfort. I must always respect them for the kindness they have shown me through my sickness. As for Steve I guess he has got smart or at least if I could eat as much to a meal as he could I should think I was well enough as for my part I do not eat much as yet but think I shall come to my appetite a few days for I feel quite good at hears. John A. Wilson seems to enjoy first rate health which seems good. If my health is poor I believe I know what good health is. If I do not now enjoy it at the present but enough of this for I guess you will think me old granny. Enough for once writing about my sickness and various other thing. I feel very anxious to hear from home often as long as the small pox rages in that place. I hope the worst cases are over and that place will soon be free from that disease for it is a fearful disease in an neighborhood not because it is so fatal as many with proper care but because you can get no care taken of you whilst you are sick. It is a very catching disease

and those that are not afraid of it themselves do not wish to go where it is for fear of exposing others for my part I have no fear of the disease on my part but still if I was there I should avoid going around where it was. Not for my sake but for others. I guess I have said enough about it therefore I will drop that part of my subject and I guess all others for there is no great news to write only we are ordered to be ready to march with but short notice but I guess we shall not move far as long as the mud is as thick as it now is. I must soon close for it is getting time for one to write short letters when they write as often as I do. As for furlough I guess I can get one for a longer time than ten days. If I can I shall surely be at home one of these days. I want you should feel encouraged for I think this thing rebellion is on its last legs and if so it must soon be brought to a close. Everything look promising and encouraging may no dark cloud over shadow us again. I must close my preamble by saying you must write often and I will do the same. Excuse all mistakes. This from your husband & best friend. Luther A. Granger, To Sabra J. Granger

April 1863

April 6, 1863 – Camp Bell, VA.
Mrs. Sabra J. Granger, Orphans House, Wilkes Barre, Leuzerne County, Pennsylvania
Dear Wife. You may think strange in my writing so often but such is my nature. I must busy myself some way as I have nothing to do only lay around camp as I am off form duty these days. I have not done any for quite a while nor shall I till I feel sound and able for duty again. I have often done duty when I was not able but that thing has played out with me. I am willing for one to do as far as I can consistently but going any further I am not willing for I have seen to much soldiering to be carried away by every little emulation that may arise. I have seen as poor a spell of health this spring as I ever have seen since I have been in the service. Although I have wisely kept it from you for I know you would worry which would be a natural consequence for I should do the same by you if you were sick. I have put the best side of the picture out as long as I remained so poorly as I was but as my health is fastly mending again and there is no probability of fever setting in as there has been I am not afraid to write. When John came home I was prostrate almost as you may say for I did not set

up half the time. But I charged him very particular not to mention it to any of my friends and I guess he done the fair thing for I never heard as he told it to anyone while home. I have seen some pretty tough days since that time to you had better believe but thank God I feel encouraged for it seems as though those poor days were passed and I am in hopes if I am very careful that I shall enjoy good health as brand new. I think I am a going to get home for some reason I cannot say but I feel as though I should and all creation cannot get it out of my mind but I shall till I am convinced otherwise. From what I now see the thing the colonel is home on a visit now and when he gets back I shall try my hand for a chance and I think my chance stands good although I may be mistaken. But I cannot see it so now for the colonel is a great friend of mine and I think will do the fair thing and if there is a chance I will have it I never have asked him for anything yet but what he was willing to grant it nor do I think he will refuse of doing all he can to get me home I have great faith as far as that is concerned but enough of this you need not be surprised when I come if I am discharged for that may be the case. Strange things as that has happened and no one hurt at that. If I am discharged it shall be honorably not trying by going off and playing sick as some few did I could mention and did not succeed their undertakings whilst others did. You know who I mean therefore I will not mention their names. I guess I have wrote enough of this trash so I will think about closing my letter as I write very often you cannot expect I will write much at that time. The boys are out on picket I did not go out for fear the exposure might be too much for me they enjoy good health. I might say the best of health is bestowed upon them. John looks as tough as a bear and so does Wilson. I heard form Warren White this morning. He enjoys good health. I intend going down this week and seeing them. As for Orlo I wrote a long time ago to him but received no answer but as I have his address I shall write again. I wrote to Norman to get me a gold pen and told him you would let him have the money for what I cost. Do it and I will send you as much. No more at present. This from your husband & friend L.A.Grager

NB. I received a letter from you at Saturday eve.

May 1863

May 7 1863. Camp near Potomac Creek VA

Dear Wife. Knowing your anxiety I have taken this morning to drop a few lines to you. We arrived in camp last night after nine days hard marching & fighting. Also never did an army march with greater rapidity or fight with greater desperation than did the Army of the Potomac. We fought them hard driving them some of the time we were driven by them. Such is the fate of war. What we accomplished God knows. As for me I cannot tell only I have my mind relative to it. Although it may differ from the paper correspondence for they will make it out to suit the times. Therefore I will give as near a account or detail of the matter as I can for I was an eyewitness of the scene too much for my own good. For I saw or heard more balls fly than I wish to hear. Our brigade was the first to engage them Sunday morning the day of the hard fighting. Such a fight I never before witnessed as was on that morn. The air was full of bullets and shells. Mans life was in jeopardy in any place whether up to the front or in the rear. Many were wounded running back to the rear. The army was regularly panic stricken at first but with rigid and strict guards was at last quieted and drove the enemy back. Or in others words held them in check. Some of our army run back and crossed the river bother officers & men. All I can say is such officers as those should be tried by court marshal and shot down for cowardice. If officers are allowed to run what confidence has the men to fight. If their officers will run of course the men will. For my part I think justice should be done. Should it commence at home for without order all are confusion. But enough of this. Such things as panic are frequent and when it happens perhaps men and officers are too much blamed for it. Our big officers get out. Generals rush a large force against some weak point in the line causing the line to be broken at that point confusing the men which are stationed to strength or hold that point causing panic amongst others and so it goes. I guess I will not weary your patience by going on with a lengthy detail of matters and things. Suffice it to say we had a hard fight losing a great many men and I think the rebels lost more for they rush on with furious impetuosity right up as it were to the mouth of the cannon. They acted more like animals than men but thank God they did not accomplish what they undertook. Although they wounded and killed many of our men but they did not annihilate the whole Potomac Army. They will find they are a few left to fight them yet. I am not quite discouraged yet nor do I mean to get although it seams fate is against us at times. Perhaps all things will work together for good for those that love and serve God. I must acknowledge that we are trusting too much to man. I will make a long matter short. I will say Steve came out all safe and sound. John the same. Philand got wounded in the arm & as we were obliged to fall back from that point I think he was taken prisoner by the enemy. He has been taken one before. As for Wesley Devine, I could not say but think perhaps he will turn up in a few days for he is very timid and I think he may turn up in the rear for he ran back toward the rear. He might got wounded or killed for that though for I mind the balls flew over my head like hail stones. Wilson Terry got wounded slightly but not seriously unless some disease sets in. Lieutenant H. H. Hinds was wounded slightly. Captain Lyons was also wounded and quite a number others in our company but none you know. I expect we will soon leave this place for I think we will be marching out of this place in a few days. But enough of this I guess I will close my preamble by saying you must not get discouraged because you do not hear from me oftener for we may be marching for a while before we get settled again. I expect to see some hardships for a time. Don't get afraid for if God be for us who can be against us. He has protected my life so far and I am willing to trust in him yet. I lost those likenesses you send me last Sunday in the fight but I worry the most about my bible of anything I lost. Let it go I should feel thankful I come off with my life if I did get a slight wound on my arm. It keeps me from carrying a gun. You must write often and I will do the same when I can if we lay around here we can write often. I wish we might lay around for a few days and get rested but as for the rest god knows what and when we march. I cannot tell nor do I wish to know. They say old Abe Lincoln is down on a visit to the Army. How true it is I cannot say. So good bye for this time. This from your husband & friend.

Undated letter

Dear Wife. You may think strange of my not writing before but the truth of the matter is this I have been trotted about so much and no place to write that I have neglected writing until the present. I now seat my self upon the ground take my knapsack on my knees and try to write with a pencil for our ink bottles got broke a moving around from place to place. You must not think hard if I write a short letter this time for the place of writing is very hard. Too much so for a free born person like myself. It is warm weather down here. Only in the morning then it feels cold from the ocean breezes. We are lying about three miles from fort Monroe. A very pleasant place indeed. I think it is the nicest country I ever saw. So much so that I have in love with it if my friends were with me. We expect a little fight every day for we are within about three miles of the enemies works but we have been nearer than that and did not have any fight for the enemy evacuated their works and fled and they may so do with this for it is not very strongly fortified nor are any of their places hen our army moves upon them for that body of the Army that we belong to are almost one hundred thousand strong and but little opposition is made for the army is well drilled and a good competent officers who understand their business. Our generals are tip top men. Our men like them first rate and would fight for them to the last. But enough of fighting if all things work for good I trust this war will close within two months if we have no pull backs for every movement counts the enemy fly before us. They burnt the city of Hamton and now it is nothing but desolate ruins. It looks hard you had better believe. What good it could do them is more than I could say. I expect that they did not want us to get them in our hands. They have burnt up a number of millions of dollars. What good it is to them they know not as there is a great many false rumors afloat so that you cannot believe one half what you hear. As for that report of Bull Run there was nothing in it although our friends was afraid that there was some trap set for them at that place so that they moved with the utmost caution into the place. But we lost no lives when we went into that place so that report was made out of whole cloth. There was nothing in it. Should you hear any report do not think I am hurt till you hear from some of company for we shall not get into a fight but what some one will live through and then you will hear from them. I will try and write. Let me be in what place I may for I find I can scribble even let me be where I will if I have money enough to pay the postage and that I have not had money to send letters until to day. I made out to get a little money enough to buy tobacco and pay postage I would be glad if I had one or two dollars for we have to do without our pay till some time in May and I am afraid that it will be longer for the government is quite in debt and I am afraid it was hard.

I received four letters yesterday it being the first mail that we had received for over one week but now our mail will follow us where ever we go through thick and thin. I received a letter from George Mitchel about ten days ago. I hope that I shall see him before three weeks roll around. We expect to be in Richmond before one week rolls over our heads if the bridges get completed so we can. We should have been there before this if the rebels had not burnt the bridges. No more at present. Write soon. Give my love to father & mother and all my friends and keep the most yourself.

The End

Luther Granger Died on July 2, 1863 during the afternoon of the second day of the Battle of Gettysburg. He was shot in the head by advancing Confederate troops near the Sherfy Farmhouse.

Luther Granger's Pension Papers

These papers identify Sabra as Luther's widow and her filing date as October 22, 1863.

Appendix A
United States Civil War Timeline

1861 – THE START OF THE CIVIL WAR

January 1861

The South Secedes.

Newly-elected but not yet inaugurated, President Abraham Lincoln was opposed to slavery. South Carolina, whose economy heavily depended on slave labor, perceived a threat to their residents' livelihood and convened their delegates for a vote to secede from the United States of America. Six more states quickly followed South Carolina's lead and also voted for secession: Mississippi, Florida, Alabama, Georgia, Louisiana, and Texas. Four additional states threatened secession and soon joined with the Confederate States of America—Virginia, Arkansas, Tennessee, and North Carolina.

February 1861

The South Creates a Government.

Montgomery, Alabama provided the site for the initial seven seceding states' convention. Here the secessionists framed the Confederate Constitution, similar in tone and format to the United States' but with greater autonomy awarded to each individual state. Prior to holding official elections, Jefferson Davis was appointed provisional president of the Confederacy.

The South Seizes Federal Forts.

Lincoln's immediate predecessor, James Buchanan, refused to surrender Federal forts in the South to the seceding states, so the southern states' troops seized them. South Carolina troops successfully intervened when a Federal ship attempted to deliver supplies to its own fort. The ship was effectively repulsed and forced to return to New York with its contents intact.

March 1861

Lincoln's Inauguration.

President Lincoln's inaugural speech was designed to appease both the North and the South—both pro- and anti-slavery constituencies. On March 4th, he had no plans to abolish slavery in those states where it existed, but he voiced his opposition to secession. Aware of the factions, he hoped to resolve the differences without warfare.

April 1861

Attack on Fort Sumter.

Lincoln gave fair warning to South Carolinians that he planned to send supplies to Fort Sumter, so that any hostilities could be avoided. Robert Anderson, Commander of Fort Sumter, was asked by the South Carolina troops to surrender immediately, because they were afraid that a trick was afoot. Anderson offered to surrender, but only after he had exhausted his supplies. This delay was unacceptable to the South, who fired shots on April 12th, and the Civil War began. Eventually, Fort Sumter fell to South Carolina.

Four More States Join the Confederacy.

Virginia, Arkansas, Tennessee, and North Carolina quickly realigned themselves following the Fort Sumter attack, and Virginia's Richmond became the Confederate capitol.

June 1861

West Virginia is Born.

Sentiment in the vast State of Virginia was divided, and counties in the western region chose not to secede along with the remainder of the State. The newly formed State of West Virginia was admitted to the Union on June 20, 1863.

Four Slave States Remain in the Union.

Delaware, Kentucky, Maryland, and Missouri were four states who, though they upheld slavery, did not join the Confederacy. Their divided loyalties required substantial political maneuvering combined with Union military coercion to keep them in the Union fold.

July 1861

First Battle of Bull Run.

Union General–in–Chief Winfield Scott ordered General Irvin McDowell to advance against Confederate troops stationed in Manassas Junction, Virginia. McDowell's troops were not yet proficient in war tactics, being greenhorn volunteers. Initial success enjoyed by McDowell soon was blighted by the introduction of Confederate reinforcements, and the Southern victory resulted in his chaotic retreat toward Washington, D.C. with his Federal troops.

General McDowell is Replaced.

President Lincoln, upon his Union troops' defeat, immediately replaced McDowell with General George B. McClellan, who would organize and train the Army. The threat of a protracted war loomed large on the horizon.

A Blockade of the South.

The Union Navy, having been much improved, initially implemented an effective blockade of the Confederate coastline. However, in response, the South constructed smaller, faster ships that could out-run and out-maneuver the Union vessels.

November 1861

Port Royal, South Carolina.

On November 7, 1861, Union Captain Samuel F. DuPont's warships silenced Confederate guns in Fort Walker and Fort Beauregard. These victories enabled Union General Thomas W. Sherman and his troops to occupy, first, Port Royal and subsequently, all of the now-famous Sea Islands of South Carolina.

1862 – SHILOH, NEW ORLEANS, FREDERICKSBURG, ANTIETAM

January 1862

Abraham Lincoln Takes Action.

President Lincoln, on January 27th, issued a war order that authorized the Union to launch a unified and aggressive attack against the Confederacy. General McClellan chose to ignore the order and soon would face consequences.

March 1862

McClellan Loses Supreme Command.

On March 8th Lincoln, who had grown impatient with McClellan's lack of response, issued an order that would reorganize the Army of Virginia and relieve McClellan of his Supreme Command. Lincoln, however, did recognize McClellan's leadership abilities, and so the President awarded him command of the Army of the

Potomac. The first order for this group would be to attach Richmond; this move began the Peninsular Campaign.

Battle of the "Monitor" and the "Merrimac."

The North's Navy consisted of several large vessels that, in sheer size and number, overwhelmed the South. Creative Confederate engineers capitalized on an opportunity to compete more effectively with the North, and they converted a scuttled Union frigate—the U.S.S. Merrimac—into an iron-sided vessel which they re-christened the C.S.S. Virginia. March 9th brought with it the very first naval engagement between ironclad ships, and the Monitor fought the Virginia to a draw, but not before the Virginia had sunk two wooden Union warships off Norfolk, Virginia.

April 1862

The Battle of Shiloh, Tennesee.

Union General Ulysses S. Grant's forces had assembled at Shiloh, Tennessee, only to be attacked by the Confederates on April 6th. At the end of the day, the Federal troops were nearly defeated, as fighting was suspended at sundown. Grant was the grateful recipient of reinforments who arrived during the night, and by morning, the Union commandeered the field. The exhausted and depleted Federal forces did not follow the retreating Confederate troops, as losses on both sides were tremendous. Casualties among Union troops numbered 13,000, out of 63,000; Confederate troops had 11,000 dead, out of 40,000 men.

Fort Pulaski, Georgia.

Union General Quincy A. Gilmore only required two days' worth of fighting—April 10th and 11th-- to overcome Fort Pulaski, an imposing masonry structure near the mouth of the Savannah River in Georgia. The Southern stronghold was rapidly pummeled into submission and surrender.

New Orleans, Louisiana.

Union Flag Officer David Farragut led a successful assault from the Mississippi Delta up the River, finally commanding New Orleans by April 25th.

The Peninsular Campaign.

Union General McClellan's direction, his troops evacuated Northern Virginia to being the Peninsular Campaign. They encamped in Yorktown by May 4th. At Williamsburg, sufficient numbers of Confederate troops forced McClellan to halt. At the ready behind the fighting front were the majority of the Confederate Army, so the Union Army was forced to await reinforcements. Begun in April, this Campaign lasted through July.

May 1862
"Stonewall" Jackson Defeats Union Forces.

General Thomas J. "Stonewall" Jackson commanded the Confederate troops in the Shenandoah Valley, where they attacked the Union Army and forced them to retreat across the Potomac. The Union troops, fearing subsequent encroachment on Northern territory, hastily repositioned themselves to defend their Capitol.

June 1862
The Battle of Seven Pines—Fair Oaks.

The fighting begun on May 31st, when the Confederate Army launched an initiative against the Federal forces at Seven Pines. Last-minute reinforcements saved the Union from a serious defeat. Confederate Commander of the Army of Northern Virginia, Joseph E. Johnston, sustained a severe wound and had to be replaced by Robert E. Lee.

July 1862
The Seven Days' Battles.

The Peninsular Campaign was waged between June 26th and July 2nd, with a new battle being fought nearly every day. Union and Confederate forces clashed at Mechanicsville (June 26-27); Gaines's Mill (June 27); Savage's Station (June 29); Frayser's Farm (June 30); and Malvern Hill (July 1). Finally, on July 2nd the Confederates withdrew to Richmond, and the Campaign ended.

A New Commander of the Union Army.

Appointed General-in-Chief of the Union Army on July 11th was Major-General Henry Halleck.

August 1862
Pope's Campaign.

The Union's defeat at the Second Battle of Bull Run, on August 29-30, eventually led to General Fitz-John Porter's exit from the

Union Army by 1863. The latter's dismissal from the Army was effective by 1863, due to his failure to commit his troops to battle quickly enough to support Pope.

September 1862

Harper's Ferry.

Union victories were notched at South Mountain and Crampton's Gap; General McClellan had successfully overcome General Lee. However, McClellan couldn't reposition his troops rapidly enough to save Harper's Ferry, where General Jackson, on September 15th, defeated McClellan. Losses included both a great number of men and a large quantity of supplies.

Antietam.

General McClellan rallied on September 17th to overcome General Lee near Sharpsburg, Maryland. This day became known as the bloodiest one of the war—2,108 Union soldiers were killed, with 9,549 wounded; and 2,700 Confederates were killed, with 9,029 wounded. There was no clear and decisive winner, but Lee was awarded the defeat because he had his troops withdraw to Virginia. Meanwhile, both the British and French were closely observing the War's progress, carefully weighing their decision to recognize the Confederacy; following this battle, they opted to delay their decision. President Lincoln seized this opportunity to issue his Preliminary Emancipation Proclamation on September 22nd. This decree freed all slaves in areas rebelling against the United States, to be effective January 1, 1863.

December 1862

The Battle of Fredericksburg.

Union General McClellan's slow movements, coupled with both General Lee's escape and continued raiding by Confederate cavalry, led to consternation and dismay among several Northerners. Lincoln, in response, appointed Major-General Ambrose E. Burnside to replace McClellan. Burnside's tenure was short-lived when, following a series of repelled attacks against entrenched Confederate forces at Fredericksburg, Virginia, Lincoln didn't hesitate to install General Joseph Hooker as Burnside's successor.

1863—EMANCIPATION, CHANCELLORSVILLE, VICKSBURG, GETTYSBURG

January 1863

Emancipation Proclamation.

President Lincoln agonized over the issues of slavery and the division of the Union. The delicate balance between the slave-holding border states and the radical Union Republicans who advocated total abolition, was extremely difficult to maintain. Lincoln carefully weighed the salient points from the different viewpoints. Already, Congress had been moving toward abolition. In 1861 an Act stating that all slaves employed against the Union were to be considered free; in 1862, another Act was passed freeing all those slaves of men who chose to support the Confederacy. Some Union generals, General B. F. Butler in particular, declared slaves who escaped to their lines "contraband of war," not to be returned to their masters. Others declared that slaves of men rebelling against the Union were to be considered free. Lincoln, in the midst of this dilemma, listened to his constituents' growing support of abolition and issued the Emancipation Proclamation on January 1, 1863. All slaves in areas still in rebellion were now free, according to the Federal Government.

March 1863

The First Conscription Act.

Congress was alerted to the diminished numbers of troops in the Army and Navy, and concluded that voluntary enlistments were insufficient if the Union were to garner a final victory in this war. The Conscription Act made eligible for military service any man between the ages of 20 and 45. However, Congress enacted two different methods for deferral: first, a man could send in a substitute, should he be called; second, he could pay a fee in lieu of serving. Discrimination was keenly felt among the poor in New York City, and riots of protest soon broke out among the working-class neighborhoods. When the Confederacy attempted a similar conscription, similar reactions were provoked.

May 1863

The Battle of Chancellorsville.

Union General Hooker began an offensive on April 27th, whereby he crossed the Rappahannock River to attack General Lee's forces. Brilliantly, Lee divided his men into three groups and surprised the Union Army by attacking them on three fronts and almost completely defeating them. Acknowledging Lee's victory, Hooker back-tracked across the Rappahannock. The Confederates' extremely high number of casualties, however, made this victory a hollow one.

The Vicksburg Campaign.

General Grant had as his assignment the eventual capture of Vicksburg, Mississippi—a fortified city considered essential to the Union's plans to regain control of the Mississippi River. Grant had managed several smaller victories around the city, then actually laid siege to the city on May 22nd. Following six weeks of fighting, Confederate General John Pemberton surrendered both the city and 30,000 men. Grant's next conquest was Port Hudson, Louisiana, placing the entire Mississippi River under Union control. The Union's victories had effectively divided the Confederacy, in terms of geography and fighting forces.

June 1863

The Gettysburg Campaign.

General Lee, being a superb strategist, mapped an attack on Union forces on June 13th in Winchester, Virginia. Once he had claimed victory there, he moved his men north to Pennsylvania. Union General Hooker's attention was diverted from his original course of action to attack Richmond, to that of pursuing Lee on the northern trek. Respect for his commander, General Halleck, never truly blossomed, so Hooker tendered his resignation on June 28th. Lincoln next named General George Meade as Commander of the Army of the Potomac.

July 1863

Gettysburg, Continued.

Meade's first assignment was to continue the pursuit of Lee's troops as they made their way North. On July 1st, an accidental encounter between the two forces began the Battle of Gettysburg. Meade's Army had greater numbers and held more promising defensive positions and so won the battle. Lee's retreat into Virginia went unanswered this time. Militarily speaking, the Battle of Gettysburg was the so-called high-water mark of the Confederacy, because it ended Confederate hopes of gaining formal recognition by foreign governments. President Lincoln was later to designate and dedicate a portion of the Gettysburg battlefield as a National Cemetery, and it was here that he delivered his memorable "Gettysburg Address" on November 19th.

September 1863

The Battle of Chickamauga.

Union and Confederate forces clashed at Chickamauga Creek in Tennessee on September 19th. After a brief skirmish, Union forces led by General Rosecrans retreated to Chattanooga, and the Confederates regained control of the battlefield.

November 1863

The Battle of Chattanooga.

Union troops successfully defended Chattanooga against the Confederates on November 23-25, which victory set the stage for General Sherman's Atlanta Campaign. After Rosecrans's debacle at Chickamauga in September, Confederate troops under the direction of General Braxton Bragg moved into position among the ring of mountains surrounding the vital railroad center of Chattanooga. General Grant was summoned to step in and rescue the Union; he steadily buttressed the offensive strength and burst the blockade in a series of brilliantly executed attacks.

December 1863

The Siege of Knoxville.

Strategically, the Union forces were somewhat compromised following September's loss at Chickamauga. Bragg dispatched forces under Longstreet's command, to drive Burnside out of Eastern Tennessee. Burnside sought refuge in Knoxville, which he successfully defended against Confederate assaults. Longstreet withdrew on December 3rd.

1864 – WILDERNESS, PETERSBURG, ATLANTA, AND PRESIDENT LINCOLN'S RE-ELECTION

May 1864

Grant's Wilderness Campaign.

General Grant, having been promoted to Commander of the Union Armies, planned to engage Lee's forces in Virginia, persevering until Lee's troops were destroyed. An inconclusive three-day battle in the Wilderness ensued as North met South. Grant emerged victorious, even though his side sustained more casualties, only because Lee had no reinforcements.

The Battle of Spotsylvania.

Grant relentlessly continued to attack Lee, fighting for five days at the Spotsylvania Court House. Grant vowed to fight all summer, if need be.

June 1864

The Battle of Cold Harbor.

Cold Harbor saw Grant again attacking Lee, but Grant lost 7,000 men here in twenty minutes. Lee suffered fewer casualties, but his army never truly recovered from Grant's incessant attacks, and this was Lee's last clear victory of the War.

The Siege of Petersburg.

General Grant's plans were to seize Petersburg, situated south of Richmond, and then approach the Confederate Capitol from the south. His plan failed to materialize, and what resulted was a ten-month siege, with the concomitant loss of thousands of lives on both sides.

July 1864

Confederate Troops Approach Washington, D.C.

General Lee's call for reinforcements led Confederate General Jubal Early to march into Maryland in support of Lee. Union troops repelled Early's men when they came within five miles of Washington, D.C., and on July 13th, Early was driven back into Virginia.

August 1864

General William T. Sherman's Atlanta Campaign.

Union General Sherman left Chattanooga and was soon confronted by Confederate General Joseph Johnston, who held off Sherman's forces, even though Sherman out-numbered him two-to-one. Johnston's foolhardy tactics, however, led his superiors to replace him with General John Bell Hood, who was soon to be defeated. Hood ultimately surrendered Atlanta, Georgia, on September 1st. Sherman occupied the city the following day. After nearly four months of constant maneuvering and extensive hard fighting, Sherman forced Hood to abandon Atlanta altogether. Gone for the Confederacy was its principal munitions center. Sherman remained there for nearly three months, giving his war-worn men well-deserved rest and accumulating much-needed supplies. Morale among the men began to improve measurably.

November 1864

General William T. Sherman's March to the Sea.

General Sherman, along with his rested men and rejuvenated supplies, continued his march through Georgia to the sea. In the course of the march, he cut himself off from his supply routes, planning for his men to live off the land. They cut a swath 300 miles in length and 60 miles wide, leveling anything in their way. Factories, bridges, railroads, and public buildings all met destruction at Union hands.

Abraham Lincoln is Re-Elected.

Incumbent President Abraham Lincoln was again nominated by the Republican Party, with Andrew Johnson for Vice-President; the Democratic Party's nominees were General George B. McClellan, President, and George Pendleton for Vice-President. Two things made Lincoln's re-election not so certain: first, the voters in the North were war-weary; and second, Lincoln had vetoed the Wade-Davis Bill, which required the majority of the electorate in each Confederate state to swear past and future loyalty to the Union before the state could officially be restored to the Union. Radical Republicans deemed Lincoln too lenient. However, Sherman's victory in Atlanta boosted Lincoln's popularity, and he won re-election by a wide margin.

December 1864
Fort McAllister.

Sherman, having already led his troops for a month's march through Georgia, stormed Fort McAllister for a victory on December 13th. Eight days later, Savannah itself fell into Union hands. The Fort was ordered dismantled on December 24th, in preparation for Sherman's further movement northward. General William B. Hazen, 2nd Division, 15th Corps, along with Major Thomas W. Osborn, Chief of Artillery, completed this task by December 29th, storing the guns at Fort Pulaski.

1865 – THE END OF THE WAR AND THE ASSASSINATION OF PRESIDENT LINCOLN

January 1865
The Fall of the Confederacy.

Successful Union troops had, by this time, blockaded Confederate supply routes and severe shortages of food and munitions wreaked havoc among the C.S.A. men. While starving soldiers deserted Lee's armies, even the stop-gap measure approved by Jefferson Davis to arm slaves as a means of augmenting the ranks was neither sufficient nor timely enough to boost the ranks. This measure was never fully effected.

February1865
Sherman Marches through North and South Carolina.

General Sherman moved his Army north from Georgia through South Carolina and toward North Carolina, leaving wanton destruction in his path.

A Chance for Reconciliation is Lost.

President Lincoln, still intensely aware of the widely disparate opinions held by Union members and Confederate secessionists, agreed to have Jefferson Davis send his delegates to meet with the President and his Secretary of State, William Seward. However, when Davis insisted on Lincoln's recognition of the South's independence as a prerequisite for this meeting, Lincoln flatly refused, and so the conference never occurred.

April 1865

Richmond Falls.

General Lee, albeit with drastically reduced numbers, attacked Grant's forces near Petersburg on March 25th. Having suffered this defeat, Lee was determined to conquer again, and he lost again on April 1st. Finally, on April 2nd, Lee evacuated Richmond, the Confederate Capitol, and proceeded west to link up with the other forces. As part of this evacuation, Lee's troops ignited a fire, which raged along the waterfront but, fortunately, was extinguished just short of Thomas Jefferson's Capitol.

The Defense of Washington.

President Lincoln and his Administration were determined to make the Capitol safe from enemy incursions, and so ringed the City with a chain of forts manned by substantial garrisons of artillerists and other troops.

Surrender at Appomattox Courthouse.

General Grant surrounded Lee's forces by April 7th and demanded Lee's surrender. The two commanders met at Appomattox Courthouse on April 9th and there and then agreed on the terms of surrender. All of Lee's men were sent home on parole—soldiers with their horses, officers with their weapons. Lee forfeited the remainder of the equipment.

The Assassination of President Lincoln.

President and Mrs. Lincoln enjoyed outings to the theater. On April 14th they attended a performance of "Our American Cousin" at Ford's Theater in Washington, D.C. Mid-way through the presentation, John Wilkes Booth stole into the President's box and shot Lincoln at point-blank range. Booth was an actor from Maryland who was obsessed with avenging the Confederate defeat. Lincoln's wounds were gravely serious, and he died the next morning. Booth, after firing his gun, leaped from the Presidential box to the stage and sustained a broken leg. He managed to escape to Virginia. Union soldiers pursued Booth and eleven days later, they cornered Booth in a burning barn. One of soldiers fatally shot him. Nine other people were involved in the assassination: four were hanged; four, imprisoned; and one, acquitted.

May 1865

Final Surrenders among Remaining Confederate Troops.

The Confederate troops who had managed to survive this long were defeated between the end of April and the end of May. Jefferson Davis was finally captured in Georgia on May 10th.

The Grand Review of the Army.

The Army of the Potomac paraded before the reviewing stands in Washington, D.C. on May 23rd.

The Execution of Captain Henry Wirz.

Captain Henry Wirz, notorious Superintendent of the Confederate Prison at Andersonville, Georgia, faced trial by a military commission. General Lew Wallace presided over the trial, which lasted from August 23rd to October 24th. Found guilty, Wirz was hanged in the yard of the Old Capitol Prison on November 10th.

Appendix B
Timeline of the 57th Pennsylvania Veteran Volunteers

1861	
1861	
November 1	Muster in Camp Curtin, PA
December 14	Departure for Washington, D.C.
1862	
January, - February	Service in defense of Washington, D.C.
March 16-18	Moved to Virginia Peninsula
April 5 – May 4	Siege of Yorktown
May 5	Battle of Williamsburg
May 31 – June 1	Battle of Fair Oaks, Seven Pines
June 25 – July 1	Seven Days before Richmond
June 25	Oak Grove
June 29	Peach Orchard and Savage Station
June 30	Charles City Crossroads and Glendale
July 1	Malvern Hill
July 2 – August 16	Duty at Harrison's Landing
August 16-26	Centerville
August 20	Skirmish at Bull Run
August 28	Pope's Campaign in Northern Virginia
August 29	Groveton
August 30	Bull Run

September 1	Chantilly
September 2 – October 10	Guard Fords at Monocacy River to Conrads Ferry
October 11 – November 19	March up the Potomac to Leesburg, then to Falmouth, Virginia
November – December 15	Battle of Fredericksburg, Virginia

1863

January 20 – 24	Burnside's Second Campaign Mud March
February, March, April	Falmouth, Virginia through April 27, 1863
April 27 – May 6	Chancellorsville Campaign
May 1-5	Battle of Chancellorsville
June 11 – July 24	Gettysburg Campaign
July 1-3	Battle of Gettysburg
July 4-5	Pursuit of Lee into Virginia
July 23	Wapping Heights
July 25 – October 9	Duty on the Line of the Rappahannock River
October 9-22	Bristoe Campaign
October 13-14	Auburn and Bristoe
November 7-8	Kelly's Ford, then to the Line of the Rappahannock
November 26 - December 2	Mile Run Campaign
November 27	Paynes' Farm

1864	
January 1 – April 30	57th PA Veteran Vols on Furlough
May 4-6	Rapidan Campaign
May 7	Battle of Wilderness
May 8	Laurel Hill
May 8-12	Spottsylvania Court House
May 12	Assault on the Salient
May 19	Harris' Farm
May 23-26	North Anna River
May 26-28	Line of the Pamunkey
May 28-31	Totopotomoy
June 1-12	Cold Harbor
June 16-18	Before Petersburg
June 18, 1864 – April 2	Siege of Petersburg
June 22-23	Weldon Railroad
July 27-29	Demonstration north of the James River at Deep Bottom
August 13-20	Demonstration north of the James River at Deep Bottom
August 14-18	Strawberry Plains, Deep Bottom
August 25	Ream's Station
September 29 – October 2	Poplar Springs Church
October 27-28	Boydton Plan Road, Hatcher's Run
December 7-12	Expedition to Weldon Railroad

1865	
February 5-7	Dabney's Mills, Hatcher's Run
March 28 – April 9	Appomattox Campaign
March 30-31	Boydton Road
April 2	Fall of Petersburg
April 6	Sailor's Creek
April 7	High Bridge, Farmville
April 9	Appomattox Courthouse; the Surrender of General Lee and the Army of Northern Virginia
April 9 – May 2	Burkesville
May 2-12	March to Washington, D.C.
May 23	Grand Review of the Army of the Potomac
May 25 – June 29	Alexandria, Virginia
June 29	57th PA Veteran Volunteered Mustered out of the Army

Appendix C
Fox's Regimental Losses

57th Pennsylvania Infantry

Graham's Brigade: Birney's Division; 3rd Corps

Total Casualty Count

Colonel William Maxwell, Colonel Charles T. Campbell, Colonel Peter Sides, Colonel George Zinn

Key:
- **K**.........Killed outright or died of battle wounds
- **D**.........Died of disease, accidents, in prison, &c.
- **O**.........Officers
- **M**.........Men
- **T**.........Total Casualties
- **E**.........Total Enrollment

	K	K	K		D	D	D	
Companies	O	M	T		O	M	T	E
Field - Staff	2	3	5		0	0	0	18
Company A	1	17	18		0	20	20	210
Company B	0	16	16		0	26	26	172
Company C	0	20	20		0	24	24	166
Company D	1	13	14		0	25	25	166
Company E	3	14	17		0	17	17	142
Company F	0	15	15		0	19	19	145
Company G	0	14	14		0	19	19	124
Company H	1	13	14		0	16	16	134
Company I	3	11	14		0	26	26	152
Company K	1	15	16		0	25	25	162
Totals	**12**	**149**	**163**		**0**	**217**	**217**	**1591**

163 Killed, out of 1591 = 10.1% of Total Enrollment

12 Officers + 149 Men Killed/Mortally Wounded + 217 Men Lost to Disease = 378 Total Casualties. Losses by Battle (Total = 163)

Killed or Mortally Wounded

Yorktown, VA	1	
Wilderness, VA	38	
Fair Oaks, VA	16	
Spotsylvania, VA	8	
Glendale, VA	13	
North Anna, VA	2	
Malvern Hill, VA	2	
Cold Harbor, VA	1	
Manassas, VA	1	
Siege of Petersburg, VA	8	
Fredericksburg, VA	28	
Peeble's Farm, VA	1	
Chancellorsville, VA	20	
Boydton Road, VA	2	
Gettysburg, PA	18	
Hatcher's Run, VA	1	
Mine Run, VA	1	(March 25, 1865)

Appendix D
A Compendium of the War of the Rebellion

by

Frederick H. Dyer

Volume III

REGIMENTAL HISTORIES (Page 593 – 594)

57th REGIMENT INFANTRY, PENNSYLVANIA
VOLUNTEERS

Organized at Harrisburg December 14, 1861. Left State for
Washington, D. C., December 14. Attached to Jameson's Brigade,
Heintzelman's Division, Army Potomac, to March, 1862. 1st
Brigade, 3rd Division, 3rd Army Corps, Army Potomac, to
August, 1862. 2nd Brigade, 1st Division, 3rd Army Corps, Army
Potomac, to March, 1863. 1st Brigade, 1st Division, 3rd Army
Corps, to March, 1864. 2nd Brigade, 3rd Division, 2nd Army
Corps, to June, 1865.

SERVICE.-Duty In the Defences of Washington, D. C., till March,
1862. Moved to the Virginia Peninsula March 16-18. Siege of
Yorktown April 5-May 4. Skirmish Yorktown April 11. Battle of
Williamsburg May 5. Battle of Fair Oaks, Seven Pines, May 31-
June 1. Seven Days before Richmond June 25-July 1. Oak Grove
June 25. Peach Orchard and Savage Station June 29. Charles City
Cross Roads and Glendale June 30. Malvern Hill July 1. Duty at
Harrison's Landing till August 16. Movement to Centreville
August 16-26. Skirmish at Bull Run August 20. Pope's Campaign
in Northern Virginia. Battles of Gainesville August 28; Groveton
August 29; Bull Run August 30; Chantilly September 1. Guard
fords from Monocacy River to Conrad's Ferry till October. March
up the Potomac to Leesburg, thence to Falmouth, Va., October 11-
November 19; Battle of Fredericksburg, Va., December 1215.
Burnside's 2nd Campaign, "Mud March," January 20-24, 1863. At
Falmouth, Va., till April 27. Chancellorsville Campaign April 27-
May 6. Battle of Chancelloreville May 1-5. Gettysburg (Pa.)
Campaign June 11 - July 24. Battle of Gettysburg, Pa., July 1-3.

Pursuit of Lee July 5-24. Wapping Heights, Va., July 23. Duty on line of the Rappahannock til October. Bristoe Campaign October 9-22. Auburn and Bristoe October 13-14. Advance to line of the Rappahannock November 7-8. Kelly's Ford November 7. Mine Run Campaign November 26-December 2. Payne's Farm November 27. Veterans on furlough January to March, 1864. Rapidan Campaign May 4-June 12. Battles of the Wilderness May 5-7; Laurel Hill May 8; Spottsylvania May 8-12; Po River May 10; Spottsylvania C. H. May 12-21. Assault on the Salient May 12. Harris' Farm May 19. North Anna River May 23-26. Line of the Pamunkey May 26-28. Totopotomoy May 28-31. Cold Harbor June 1-12. Before Petersburg June 16-18. Siege of Petersburg June 16, 1864, to April 2, 1865. Weldon Railroad June 22-23, 1864. Demonstration north of the James at Deep Bottom July 27-29, and August 12-20. Strawberry Plains, Deep Bottom, August 14-18. Ream's Station August 25. Poplar Springs Church September 29-October 2. Boydton Plank Road, Hatcher's Run, October 27-28. Expedition to Weldon Railroad December 7-12. Consolidated to five Companies January 11, 1865. Dabney's Mills, Hatcher's Run, February 5-7. Appomattox Campaign March 28-April 9. Boydton Road March 30-31. Fall of Petersburg April 2. Sailor's Creek April 6. High Bridge, Farmville, April 7. Appomattox C. H. April 9. Surrender of Lee and his army. At Burkesville till May. March to Washington D. C., May 2-12. Grand Review May 23. Duty at Alexandria till June. Mustered out June 29, 1865.

Regiment lost during service 12 Officers and 149 Enlisted men killed and mortally wounded and 217 Enlisted men by disease. Total 378.

Appendix E
General Orders No. 48.

O.R.--SERIES I--VOLUME LI/1 [S# 107]

HDQRS. FIRST DIVISION, THIRD CORPS, May 16, 1863.

The brigadier-general commanding division congratulates it on its achievements of the 2d and 3d of May. The division pierced the center of the enemy's column, captured over 700 prisoners, then returning, breaking through the enemy, who closed in its rear, executed successfully the order of the major-general commanding the army to attack the enemy at midnight; then, receiving the enemy's attack at daylight, held their hordes in check and at bay until ordered to withdraw and hold a position of honor given to it in front of the new lines. The division has added to the reputation gained at Williamsburg, Fair Oaks, Glendale, Malvern, Manassas, Chantilly, Fredericksburg, and can now add to those names The Cedars and Chancellorsville. With unabated confidence in the gallant generals commanding the corps and the army, this division awaits with impatience the order to again meet the enemy of our country. Our rejoicing is mingled with regret for the slain and wounded, but the recollection of their bravery and martyrdom will be fresh with us evermore and incite us to still greater efforts. The brigadier-general commanding division announces the following names of meritorious and distinguished non-commissioned officers and privates selected as the recipients of the Kearny cross, the division decoration. Many deserving soldiers may have escaped the notice of their commanding officers, but in the selection after next battle they will doubtless receive this honorable distinction. This cross is in honor of our old leader and the wearers of it will always remember his high standard of a true and brave soldier and will never disgrace it.

57th Pennsylvania Volunteers.

Name and rank.	Company
Sergt. Charles P. Post	A
Private Amos Miller	H
Corpl. J. W. Granger	A*

Sergt. Franklin Shaw	H
Corpl. Sumner E. Lines	A
Sergt. John Burnsides	H
Sergt. Ira E. McKnight	B
Corpl. Henry Forbes	H
Private James Ramsey	B
Sergt. Samuel Shields	I
Private Simeon Hahn	B
Private Levi Christ	I
Sergt. Ieovia Allen	C
Private Charles Maxum	I
Sergt. Michael Maloy	C
Private Horace Sweet	K
Private David Monihan	C
Private Jonas Snow	K
Sergt. Walter Rice	E
Private William Murray	K
Private Henry Kreuninger	E
Corpl. M. A. Irwin	F
Corpl. J. K. Hamilton	F
Sergt. H. R. Douglas	F
Sergt. John C. Taylor	F

While many regiments were recognized under General Order No. 48, I have listed only those recipients of the Kearney Cross that are from the 57th Pennsylvania Veteran Volunteers.

*Note that John W. Granger is listed as a Corporal.

Appendix F
No. 133. -- Reports of Maj. Gen. David B. Birney, U. S. Army, commanding First Division of, and Third Army Corps.

O.R.--SERIES I--VOLUME XXVII/1 [S# 43] -- Gettysburg Campaign

HDQRS. BIRNEY'S DIVISION, *THIRD CORPS, August 7,* 1863.

COLONEL: I have the honor to submit the following report of the movements and actions of this division from June 28 to July 3, during which time it was under my command:

On the morning of June 28, the Third Corps, under my command, marched from Middletown, Md., to Frederick, at which place Major-General Sickles reported for duty and relieved me from the command of the corps. I resumed command of this division, and marched to Walkersville, on the road to Taneytown, and bivouacked beyond the town.

On June 30, it remained in bivouac until 3 p.m., and I then received orders to proceed immediately to Emmitsburg. Under orders from Major-General Sickles, the command bivouacked within 1½ miles of the town.

On the morning of July 1, the division took position beyond Emmitsburg, toward Gettysburg, covering the road from Fairfield and Gettysburg.

During the afternoon of the same day, at 2 o'clock, I was ordered by Major-General Sickles to proceed immediately to Gettysburg with my First and Second Brigades and three batteries, reporting to Major-General Howard, then engaged with the enemy. The Third Brigade, Colonel De Trobriand, was left in position at Emmitsburg, covering the road referred to and as a protection to the corps trains.

My command reached Gettysburg at 5.30 p.m., marching with enthusiasm and alacrity over the road, rendered almost impassable by mud and the passage over it of the First and Eleventh Corps through the rain.

On the morning of July 2, about 9 o'clock, the Third Brigade, Colonel De Trobriand, relieved by orders of the commanding general, rejoined the division.

At 7 a.m., under orders from Major-General Sickles, I relieved Geary's division, and formed a line, resting its left on the Sugar Loaf Mountain and the right thrown in a direct line toward the cemetery, connecting on the right with the Second Division of this corps. My picket line was in the Emmitsburg road, with sharpshooters some 300 yards in advance.

At 12 m., believing from the constant fire of the enemy that a movement was being made toward the left, I received permission from Major-General Sickles to send 100 of Berdan's Sharpshooters, with the Third Maine Regiment as a support, and feel the enemy's right. I sent Capt. J. C. Briscoe, of my staff, with the reconnaissance, which was under Colonel Berdan's command. They advanced from the peach orchard out the Millerstown road, and entered the woods in order to flank the enemy. The skirmishers of the enemy were driven in, but three columns of their forces were found marching to our left. The force sent by me was driven back by overwhelming numbers, with the loss of about 60, killed and wounded.

Communicating this important information to Major-General Sickles, I was ordered by that officer to change my front to meet the attack. I did this by advancing my left 500 yards, and swinging around the right so as to rest on the Emmitsburg road at the peach <ar43_483> orchard. He also informed me that a division from the Second and one from the Fifth Corps had been ordered to be in readiness to support me.

My line was formed with Ward on the left, resting on the mountain, De Trobriand in the center, and Graham on my right in the peach orchard, with his right on the Emmitsburg road. Smith's battery of rifled guns was placed so as to command the gorge at the base of the Sugar Loaf Mountain; Winslow's battery on the right of Ward's brigade, and a battery from the Artillery Reserve; also Clark's and Ames' batteries to the right, in rear of the peach orchard, supported by Graham's brigade, and the Third Michigan, from the Third Brigade, and the Third Maine, from the Second

315

Brigade. Randolph's, Seeley's, and Turnbull's batteries were placed near the Emmitsburg road, on the front, parallel with it. I immediately sent an aide to Major-General Sykes asking for the division promised to support my left. I now opened (say at 3.30 p.m.) with Clark's and Smith's batteries upon the columns of the enemy moving toward our left, parallel with the Emmitsburg road.

At 4 o'clock the enemy returned the artillery fire on my entire front, and advanced their infantry *en masse,* covered by a cloud of skirmishers. Major-General Sykes reached my left opportunely, and protected that flank. A portion of his command, under General Barnes, had been placed in rear of the right of De Trobriand's brigade, but during the fight he withdrew his force, and formed some 300 yards farther in the rear.

As the fight was now furious, and my thin line reached from Sugar Loaf Hill to the Emmitsburg road, fully a mile in length, I was obliged to send for more re-enforcements to Major-General Sickles, and Major Tremain, aide-de-camp to the commanding general, soon appeared with a brigade of the Second Corps, which behaved most handsomely, and, leading them forward, it soon restored the center of my line, and we drove the enemy from that point, to fall with re-doubled force on Ward's brigade. My thin lines swayed to and fro during the fight, and my regiments were moved constantly on the double-quick from one part of the line to the other, to re-enforce assailed points.

I cannot estimate too highly the services of the regiments from Burling's brigade, Second Division (the Fifth, Sixth, and Seventh New Jersey volunteers and Second New Hampshire). These regiments were sent to me during the contest, and most gallantly did they sustain the glorious reputation won by them in former battles.

Graham's brigade was subjected at the point of the angle of the line on the Emmitsburg road to a fearful artillery fire, enfilading his line, but this brigade, with the assistance of the Third Maine, from the Second Brigade, and the Third Michigan, from the Third Brigade of this division, held the peach orchard until nearly dusk, when, finding the right unsupported, it fell back to the next ridge.

At 6 o'clock I found Major-General Sickles seriously wounded, and, at his request, took command of the troops. I immediately visited Humphreys' division, and, finding that the enemy, advancing through a gap in the line of my division, would take it in reverse, I ordered a change of front. General Humphreys accomplished this promptly under a most effective artillery and musketry fire, and, advancing his division rapidly, recaptured several batteries that the enemy had temporary possession of.

Major-General Hancock reached me about 7.30 o'clock with a brigade <ar43_484> of fresh troops, and, at his request, I assigned them a position. My division was relieved from the front line by the Second and Fifth Corps toward dusk.

The annexed tables of casualties show the nature of the engagement and its terrific character.(*) Several of my regiments lost more than 50 per cent. of their number and almost every officer engaged. One regiment, the One hundred and forty-first Pennsylvania Volunteers, Colonel Madill, lost, out of 200 taken into the fight, 149 men and officers killed and wounded.

Accompanying this report I send those of the brigade and regimental commanders, which give in detail the movements of their commands. Every regiment of my command did its whole duty, and officers vied with each other in honorable emulation to repel the masses that were hurled on my small division for three hours.

The batteries were well handled, and I have no report of any guns being lost, as, in retiring, we hauled the disabled pieces from the field.

The First Brigade, composed of Pennsylvania regiments, commanded by Brig. Gen. C. K. Graham, tried with its skeleton ranks to even outdo Chancellorsville. General Graham was wounded and fell into the hands of the enemy, with Lieutenant-Colonel Cavada, of the One hundred and fourteenth Pennsylvania Volunteers, and Major Neeper, of the Fifty-seventh Pennsylvania Volunteers. The Fifty-seventh Pennsylvania Volunteers, Colonel Sides; Sixty-third Pennsylvania Volunteers, Major Danks; Sixty-eighth Pennsylvania Volunteers, Colonel Tippin; One hundred and fifth Pennsylvania Volunteers, Colonel Craig; One hundred and fourteenth Pennsylvania Volunteers, Lieutenant-Colonel Cavada, and the One hundred and forty-first Pennsylvania Volunteers, Colonel Madill, composed this brigade, and have made its reputation equal to any in this army. General Graham showed the same coolness, daring, and endurance under the terrible fire that distinguished him at Chancellorsville.

The Second Brigade, Brigadier-General Ward, held also a post of great honor and importance, and fully sustained its old reputation. The First U.S. Sharpshooters, Colonel Berdan, and Second U.S. Sharpshooters, Major Stoughton; Third Maine, Colonel Lakeman; Fourth Maine, Colonel Walker; Twentieth Indiana, Colonel Wheeler; Ninety-ninth Pennsylvania, Major Moore; One hundred and twenty-fourth New York, Colonel Ellis, and Eighty-sixth New York, Lieutenant-Colonel Higgins, composed this brigade.

Colonel Walker, who had so distinguished himself on the Peninsula and at Manassas, Chantilly, Fredericksburg, and Chancellorsville, was seriously wounded; and those gallant officers, Colonels Ellis and Wheeler, fell, dead, with their crowns to the foe, at the head of their regiments. I am indebted to Brigadier-General Ward for his cordial co-operation.

The Third Brigade, Colonel De Trobriand commanding, held the center of my line. The Fortieth New York, Col. T. W. Egan; Third Michigan, Colonel Pierce; Fifth Michigan, Lieutenant-Colonel Pulford; Seventeenth Maine, Lieutenant-Colonel Merrill; and One hundred and tenth Pennsylvania, Lieut. Col. D. M. Jones, composed this brigade.

Colonel De Trobriand deserves my heartiest thanks for his skillful disposition of his command by gallantly holding his advanced position until relieved by other troops. This officer is one of the oldest <ar43_485> in commission as colonel in the volunteer service; has been distinguished in nearly every engagement of the Army of the Potomac, and certainly deserves the rank of brigadier-general of volunteers, to which he has been recommended.

The Fortieth Regiment New York Volunteers, Colonel Egan, was sent by me, under charge of Captain Briscoe, aide-de-camp, to strengthen General Ward's line, and, led by its gallant, dashing colonel, charged the enemy and drove him back from his advanced point, and poured the most terrific fire into his ranks. This regiment is composed of the old Fortieth, and gallant men from the Eighty-seventh, One hundred and first, Thirty-eighth, and Fifty-fifth New York consolidated with it, making a glorious unit.

The Seventeenth Maine Regiment, Lieutenant-Colonel Merrill, was driven back from its position by overwhelming force, but, responding to my personal appeal, again charged the enemy across the small wheat-field, and retook their position. This regiment behaved most gallantly, and evinced a high state of discipline. Their enthusiasm was cheering, and the assistance rendered by its charge most important.

I have already mentioned the valuable aid rendered to me by the command of Colonel Burling, commanding the Third Brigade of the Second Division. This officer and his gallant old regiments never did better service at a better time.

I annex a map, showing the position of my troops and the batteries supported by us.(*)

In a special report to be made under paragraph 743, Revised Regulations, I will mention those officers and soldiers deserving special mention.

Colonel Berdan, of the Sharpshooters, and Captain Briscoe, of my staff, deserve mention for their services in leading the reconnaissance before the battle, and for the valuable information derived from it.

The two regiments of sharpshooters, under Colonel Berdan and Major Stoughton, were of the most essential service in covering my front with a cloud of sharpshooters, and pouring a constant and galling fire into the enemy's line of skirmishers.

All of the members of my staff were efficient and ready with their services in the field.

During July 3, this division, under command of General Ward, was held in reserve, and during the heavy artillery fire of that day was brought up under it to support General Newton's line. The enemy were, however, repulsed without its assistance.

Annexed is a list of casualties(+) and map alluded to in my report.

I am, your obedient servant,

D. B. Birney, *Major-General, U.S. Vols., Comdg. Division.*

Lieut. Col. O. H. HART, *A. A. G., Third Corps.*

HEADQUARTERS THIRD ARMY CORPS, *In the Field*

July 4, 1863.

GENERAL: In compliance with a circular from headquarters Army of Potomac, of this date, I have the honor to report as follows:

A portion of the First Division, with Colonel Eustis' brigade, of the Sixth Corps, is on the front line, on the left of the Second Corps.

SKETCH SHOWING POSITION HELD BY BIRNEY'S DIVISION

during action near Gettysburg, on the 2d of July, 1863.

Prepared, by direction of Maj. Gen. D. B. BIRNEY,

by Capt. J. C. BRISCOE, A.D. C.

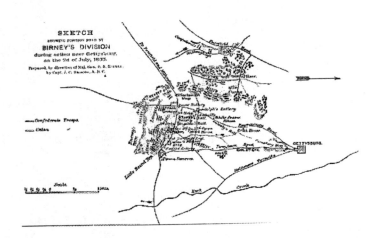

SKETCH SHOWING POSITION OF THE 3D CORPS,

July 4, 1863.

Prepared, by order of Maj. Gen. D. B. BIRNEY,

by Capt. J. C. Briscoe, A.D. C.

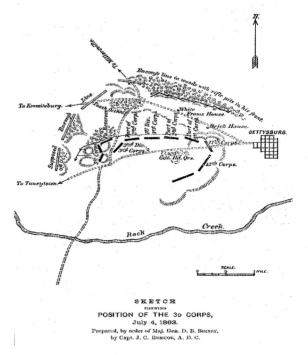

SKETCH
SHOWING
POSITION OF THE 3D CORPS,
July 4, 1863.
Prepared, by order of Maj. Gen. D. B. Birney,
by Capt. J. C. Briscoe, A. D. C.

Four regiments from this division have been detached with the Second Corps since yesterday. I respectfully request that they be relieved and returned to my command.

The Second Division is held in reserve, supporting the right of General Sykes' line and the left of the Second Corps.

Inclosed I have the honor to forward a sketch showing the actual position of my troops.(*)

Yours, respectfully,

D. B. Birney, *Major-General, Commanding.*

Brig. Gen. S. WILLIAMS, *Assistant Adjutant-General.*

Appendix G
Headquarters Second Army Corps

November 8, 1864

Major-General MEADE:

The following is the result of the election in the artillery brigade of this corps: Battery F, First Pennsylvania, Lincoln, 69; McClellan, 46. Battery L, Fourth New York. Lincoln, 50; McClellan, 29. Twelfth New York Independent Battery, Lincoln, 42; McClellan, 16. Eleventh New York Independent Battery, Lincoln, 75; McClellan, 25. Sixth Maine Battery, Lincoln, 58; McClellan, 3. First New Hampshire Battery, Lincoln, 51; McClellan, 2. Battery B, First Rhode Island, Lincoln, 12; McClellan, 0. Battery C, Fourth New York, Lincoln, 15; McClellan, 18; Lincoln's majority, 233. These are all the batteries that vote except G, First New York, whose votes were sent home sealed. The following is the result in the Third Division, Major-General Mott's: Seventeenth Maine Volunteers, Lincoln, 198; McClellan, 47. First Maine Heavy Artillery, Lincoln, 60; McClellan, 0 (greater part of this regiment are at Cedar Level--their votes not yet received). Second U.S. Sharpshooters, Lincoln, 87; McClellan, 20. Ninety-ninth Pennsylvania Volunteers, Lincoln, 147; McClellan, 81. One hundred and tenth Pennsylvania Volunteers, Lincoln, 91; McClellan, 72. **Fifty-seventh Pennsylvania Volunteers, Lincoln, 95; McClellan, 33**. One hundred and forty-first Pennsylvania Volunteers, Lincoln, 195; McClellan, 5. Eighty-fourth Pennsylvania Volunteers, Lincoln, 115; McClellan, 46. One hundred and fifth Pennsylvania Volunteers, Lincoln, 136; McClellan, 73. Fifth Michigan, Lincoln, 157; McClellan, 65. First U.S. Sharpshooters, Lincoln, 22; McClellan, 0. Lincoln's Majority in Third Division, 861. The returns from First and Second Divisions not yet received.

Winf'd S. Hancock, *Major-General.*

Appendix H
Widow's Claim for Pension

Cornelia Granger seeks a pension following John's death

WIDOW'S CLAIM FOR PENSION.

State of _Pennsylvania_ }
County of _Susquehanna_ } ss.

ON THIS _29th_ day of _August_ .... 187_7_ personally appeared before me, a _for Prothy_ of a Court of Record in and for the County and State aforesaid. _Cornelia Granger_ a resident of _Jessup_ .... in the County of _Susquehanna_ and State of _Pennsylvania_ aged _57_ years, who being duly sworn, makes the following declaration, in order to obtain the Pension provided by the Act of Congress approved **July 14, 1862.** That she is the widow of _John W. Granger_ who was a _Pvt._ in Company _"K"_ commanded by _Capt. Peter Sides_ in the _57th_ Regiment of _Pa. Vol._ in the War of 1861 ; that her maiden name was _Cornelia Granger_ and that she was married to said _John W. Granger_ on or about the _20_ day of _February_ 18 _46_, at _Brush_ in the County of _Susquehanna_ and State of _Pennsylvania_ by _Robert Winfield Esq._ and that she knows of no record evidence of said marriage.

SHE FURTHER DECLARES that said _John W. Granger_ her husband, died in the service of the United States aforesaid at _Jessup, Fairdale, PO_ in the State of _Pennsylvania_ on or about the _7th_ day of _April_ 187_7_ of _Rheumatism and Militated_ _Organic diseases_ acquired while in the service of the _U.S._ She also declares that she has remained a widow ever since the death of said _John Granger_ and that she has not in any manner been engaged in, or aided or abetted, the rebellion in the United States; and she hereby appoints _Gilmore &_ _Co Washington DC_ as her lawful Attorney, with power of substitution, and authorizes _that_ to present and prosecute this claim, and to receive her pension certificates. The following .... the names .... date .... of birth and place .... of residence of all the children of her deceased husband who were under sixteen years of age at the time of his death.

My Post Office address is _Fairdale Pa_

If mark is made, two citizens who sott sign here.

Y. M. Harrison M.D.   _Cornelia Granger_
Eva Harrison   (Signature of Claimant).

ALSO PERSONALLY APPEARED before me _G. M. Harrison M.D._ and _Eva Harrison_ residents of _Fairdale Susq_ County, and State of _Pennsylvania_ to me well known as credible persons, who being duly sworn, declare, that they were present and saw said _Cornelia Granger_ sign her name to the foregoing declaration, and that they have every reason to believe, from the appearance of said applicant, and their acquaintance with her, that she is the identical person who represents herself to be, and know that said deceased recognized said applicant as his lawful wife, and that she was so recognized by the community in which they resided; and that they have no interest, direct or indirect, in the prosecution of this claim.

Y. M. Harrison M.D.
(Signatures of Witnesses)
Eva M. Harrison

323

John W Granger and Cornelia Munger
were married Feb 20. 1840

State of Pennsylvania
Susquehanna County ss.

I, W W Simrell Prothonotary of
the Court of Common Pleas in and for Susquehanna
County do hereby certify that a bible was presented
before me at my office in Montrose (by E Granger
son of John W Granger dec'd purporting to be
the family bible of Cornelia Munger) with the
above marriage recorded in it. The date of said
bible was, A.D. 1814. W W Simrell
                                    Prothonotary

JAN 28 1878

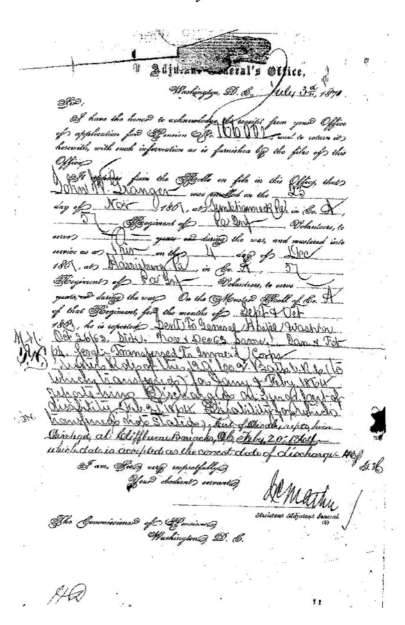

ORIGINAL INVALID PENSION.

Claimant, *John W. Granger. (deceased)*

P. O. *Rush*   Rank, *Pri.*

County, *Susquehanna,*   Company, *A.*

State, *Pa.*   Regiment, *57; Pa. Vol.*

Attorney.

Fee,

Rate,   *per month, commencing*

Disabled by

Submitted for *Rej.* *May 8* , 1878 by *J. H. Patrish* , Examiner.

Approved for *Rejection*   Approved for

*No accrued pension – Soldier
made more than 5 years after discharge
and claim not completed before death*

May 18. 1878 . Reviewer.   ,187 . , Med. Referee.

Enlisted *Mar 25* , 1861.   service from

Mustered *Dec 4* , 1861. 18 , to   ,18 , in

Discharged *Feb 20* , 1864.

Declaration filed *May 25* , 1871. Not in military or naval service since

Last material evidence filed , 18 *Feb 20*, 1864, when discharged.

BASIS OF CLAIM.

*Alleges that in Oct. 1863 while on the retreat from Culpepper
to Fairfax Station. Va. he became lame and sore and
was ruptured.*

326

ARMY OF THE UNITED STATES.

CERTIFICATE

OF DISABILITY

FOR DISCHARGE.

1st Sergeant John W. Granger, of Captain *C. P. Davis* Company, *12/C* of the *1st Battalion* Regiment of United States *Invalid Corps*, was enlisted by *Captain W. G. D.* at *West Chester Penna*, on the *twenty-fifth* day of *October* 1861, to serve *three* years; he was born in *Rutland* in the State of *Pennsylvania*, is *forty-three* years of age, *five* feet *eleven* inches high, *light* complexion, *gray* eyes, *brown* hair, and by occupation when enlisted a *Wagon Maker*. During the last two months the said soldier has been unfit for duty *eighty* days.*

Transferred to the Invalid Corps pursuant to Special Orders No. 315 dated Adjutant Generals Office July 18, 1863 from Company A Fifty seventh Regt Penna Vols

STATION: *Depot Camp Cliffburne Bks D.C.*

DATE: *February 12th 1864*

                                                                    W. Garris Capt
                                                                    L. Watt

                                                        Commanding Company

I certify that I have carefully examined the said *Sgt John W. Granger* of Captain *C. P. Davis* Company, and find him incapable of performing the duties of a soldier because of *Chronic Rheumatism & Debility. Contracted since enlistment. Incapacitation.* *He desired to be unfit for duty in D.C. and is discharged at his own request.*

                                                                    A. Williams
                                                                    Surgeon
                                                                    in charge First Hosp

DISCHARGED, this *20th* day of *February* 1864, at *Depot Camp Bks*
Cliffburne Barracks D.C.

                                                        Geo A Woodward
                                                        Col 22d Reg't R. C.
                                                        Commanding the Reg't

The Soldier desires to be addressed at

Town...................

County........................ State...................

*See Note 1 on the back of this † See Note 2 on the back of this.

(A. G. O. No. 100 & 101—First.)   [DUPLICATES.]

John's First Letter From Camp
November 19, 1861

the Surgon thinks camp life will do me good I could get along first rate if it was not for sleeping cold at night please send me a good old Comforter and two towels by Armstrong I may stay here all winter and may not we may start for Washington in three of four weeks we do not know any thing about it the Company seem to like me first rate they were determined that I should not come Back it may turn out for the best yet time will tell it may make a Steady man of me yet here our orders are verry strict and I for one shall obey orders if ever I do come back you nor the Children shall not have it to say that I made a ass of my self I should like to see you and the Boys and hope I shall as soon as Spring I am a writing on a board sitting on the floor holding it in my lap nerves not verry steady and am afraid they will not be when I think of wife and Children do not greive nor give way to bad feelings take care of your health

I intend this by A W Being
he intends to start for home this
afternoon I shall write to you
again as soon as we can get our
tent arranged and my feelings settled
a little, you may think my feeling
would not be worked up to this
pitch but I have feelings yet
but enough of this our camp is
large and a good many thousands of
Soldiers here I must close for all
is ready to start so good by
god bless you from your ever
loving Husband J McGranger
To Cornelia
and Edward
M B Granger
Direct Camp Curtain
in care of Cap Thurston

John's Letter Describing the Death of Luther
July 5, 1863

Near Gettysburgh Pa

July 5 1863 Sunday 12 Oclock
Dear wife & children it is by the
mercy of God that I am alive to
write you a few lines to let you know
how I am another big battle has been
fought & my life & health is spared &
So far I am not hoart but their a great
many have gone to their long homes only
eight left in our company how Shall
I tell the Sad news Brother Luther
is among the Slain he was Shot
through the head & killed instantly
he never knew what hurt him
he was killed on the 2nd of July &
we found his body this morning
the Rebels held the part of the field
that we fought in until last night
they had took all of his money
Some six or eight dollars it is
reported that they have left last

night large details are out
on the Battle field Buiring
the dead you the field is covered
with dead for 4 days we have
had hard fighting here & some
the hardest I ever saw nearly 3/4 of
our Regt is gone oh how sad &
lonely I feel I shall have to close
for now I hear the cannons roar
& we shall have to fall in I
suppose I shall be glad if I live
until this is over & then I will
try & give you some account of
this great field I guess that the
enemy have not gone far for our
men are after them to tell you
I must bid you good day hoping
our life will be spaired to see you
again give my love to all
My best love to you & children yours ever
to Camelia Edward   J M Granger
& Billy Granger

1864

Depot Camp Cliffbourne Barracks Co No.

Dear Wife & children I received a letter from you on the 10th dated 6th & one to day dated 8th I was glad to here that you were well but sorry that you feel so down hearted I hope I shall live to get out of this miserable consern I have been trying sometime to get an examination before the doctors well this morning I went before the board and they thought they would not discharge me so my hopes are gone on that point I think it is mean for I know they have discharged a good many in my company that is not half as bad off as I am but that is just my luck well yesterday there was thirteen in my company got their discharge and in a few days more there will be some ten or twelve more well I am glad to see them get away I only wish that I might be as lucky well enough of this if they fill this conserns up and get some ____ here they will not care for all the duty they get out of me I have done my share (well I have just been called to the captains office & there found the board had ordered my discharge (see his letter)

to keep dark & if nothing happens I shall
be at home in three weeks or less don't say
anything about it nor let anyone know one
word I want to tell them by surprise
I had felt downhearted all the summer
and discouraged and when I commenced this
letter I did not think I should have such
good news I am almost afraid to believe
it myself for fear there will be some slip
about it I suppose it will take all of
this month for my papers to get around
well I shall wait very patiently for
them I guess you may answer this letter
and I will write again to let you know
how I get along well and if my papers
will go through quick So I will not write
any more now give my respects to all
enquiring friends my love to you all good day
                        Yours ever B. W. Granger

to Cornelia Edward
to Billy Granger

PS I have not received that letter from [illegible]
that you spoke of & I am very sorry to hear
such news from there well they may not get
me a forty's war because I think myself just as
good as they I little thought by writing that any of
us could

I intend this By A W Being,
he intends to Start for home this
afternoon I Shall write to you
again as soon as we can get our
tent arrainged and my feelings Settled
a little, you may think my feeling
would not be recollect up to this
pitch But I have feelings yet
but enough of this our camp is
large and a good many thousands of
Soldiers here I must Close for all
is ready to Start So good by
god bless you from your ever
loving Husband J McGranger
To Cornelia
and Edward
W B Granger

Derect Camp Burton
in care of Cap Hewett

Rick Muzzey

Louis J. D'Angelo

Lou grew up in Glassport, Pennsylvania, 15 miles southeast of Pittsburgh, Pennsylvania. Graduated from the Indiana University of Pennsylvania in 1983, and the University of Maryland School of Law in 1991. It was during the mid-1990's that his interest in the history of the US Civil War turned into this project.

The original concept called for this to be a printed collection of the letters. This would allow for reading the letters without excessive handling of them. The project seemed to grow from there. You can reach Lou via e-mail at LouDAngelo@aol.com.